Mexican American Biographies

Mexican American Biographies

A HISTORICAL DICTIONARY, 1836–1987

Matt S. Meier

Greenwood Press

NEW YORK • WESTPORT, CONNECTICUT • LONDON

Library of Congress Cataloging-in-Publication Data

Meier, Matt S.
  Mexican American biographies.

  Includes index.
  1. Mexican Americans—Biography—Dictionaries.
I. Title.
E184.M5M454   1988   920′.00926872073   87-12025
ISBN 0-313-24521-5 (lib. bdg. : alk. paper)

British Library Cataloguing in Publication Data is available.

Library of Congress Catalog Card Number: 87-12025
ISBN: 0-313-24521-5

First published in 1988

Greenwood Press, Inc.
88 Post Road West, Westport, Connecticut   06881

Printed in the United States of America

The paper used in this book complies with the
Permanent Paper Standard issued by the National
Information Standards Organization (Z39.48-1984).

10   9   8   7   6   5   4   3   2   1

Contents

Preface

This historical dictionary of Mexican American biography is the outcome of an idea and research going back to the early 1970s. If one looks at biographical reference tools available in libraries, one will find works with titles like *Dictionary of American Negro Biography*, *Who's Who in American Jewry*, and *Ukrainians in North America*; but no extensive biographic work on Mexican Americans has previously been available. There has for some time been a need for a comprehensive biographical dictionary of Mexican Americans.

Until now the only Mexican American biographical collections have been general Latino works like *Rising Voices: Profiles of Hispano-American Lives* (1974) by Al Martínez and the fifty-six short biographies appended to *The Proud Peoples: The Heritage and Culture of Spanish-Speaking Peoples in the United States* (1972) by Harold J. Alford. Or they have been regional biographical collections like *Los Patrones: Profiles of Hispanic Political Leaders in New Mexico History* (1980) by Maurilio E. Vigil, *Hispanos: Historic Leaders in New Mexico* (1985) by Lynn I. Perrigo, and *Mexican American Movements and Leaders* (1976) by Carlos Larralde. Lastly, there have been the more or less biographical treatments of various limited groups like *Chicano Scholars and Writers: A Bio-Bibliographical Directory* (1979) by Julio A. Martínez, *Chicano Authors: Inquiry by Interview* (1980) by Juan Bruce-Novoa, *Chicano Literature: A Reference Guide* (1985) by Julio A. Martínez and Francisco A. Lomelí, *The National Directory of Chicano Faculty and Research* (1974) edited by Reynaldo Flores Macías and Juan Gómez-Quiñones, *Who's Who: Chicano Officeholders, 1983–84* (1983) by Arthur D. Martínez, and *Mexican American Artists* (1973) by Jacinto Quirarte. All these and other general biographical sources have been consulted for this work.

It is hoped that this attempt to identify *prominentes* in the Mexican American experience will fill a void and provide both students and scholars with a useful reference tool for basic information on Mexican American figures from the period of the Texas revolution in the mid–1830s to the present time. It is a comprehensive dictionary of some 270 biographies, nearly 200 of them contemporary Mexican

Americans. A special effort has been made to include women and men representing virtually all important fields of endeavor.

The determining criteria for inclusion in the dictionary presented some problems. The standards I set were, I suggest, realistic yet flexible: a significant level of achievement in professional life as recognized by the subject's peers (scholars, writers, artists, athletes, musicians, singers, actors, businessmen/businesswomen); a position of considerable civic responsibility (ambassadors, congressmen, government officials, governors, large-city mayors). These criteria vary somewhat from the nineteenth to the twentieth century and are admittedly subjective; what might be considered achievement in the middle and late nineteenth century may seem less important today as we approach the end of the twentieth century. A primary concern was the role of the biographee in the Chicano experience; most historical figures appearing in surveys of Mexican American history are included. Generally the persons selected have, or had, recognition beyond their states or local areas and influence on their areas of expertise. By the very nature of the criteria some areas of the Mexican American experience may have a larger representation than others. Within the Chicano community there are various points of view, and certainly there will be no unanimity on who should be included in this dictionary. While I thank all those who helped me make the selections, ultimately the final responsibility for this work rests on my shoulders. I hope it will be accepted as my small contribution to Chicano studies. I also hope that it will save users expenditure of time and energy.

The biographies are not regarded as complete; there are inevitable and intentional omissions of detail within each. The length of individual biographies varies somewhat with the importance of the biographees; however, because information is spotty or incomplete on some of the nineteenth-century figures the length of their biographies may not necessarily reflect my judgment of their importance in the Mexican American experience. They focus basically on public and professional life. I have included, where available, information on the biographees' social and intellectual formation, particularly their academic training. I have not included family information (e.g., marriage, children) except where that seemed to contribute to their public service or development in their chosen fields, that is, their artistic or literary production or their achievements in business, sports, government, community, and academia. The evidence of signal achievement as shown by appointments, awards, and prizes has been specially noted. In almost all cases the biographies are followed by suggestions for further reading; in a very few cases of contemporaries no printed material was found to be available. In the area of contemporary Chicano *prominentes* a special problem arose in some cases. Letters sent to many of them requesting biographical information went unanswered. As a result, in some instances deserving Chicano figures had to be reluctantly dropped from the original list; in other cases recent biographical information is limited or absent.

The arrangement of this dictionary is largely self-explanatory. The *prominentes* are listed alphabetically. Names like Lorenzo de Zavala I have listed under the surname (Zavala) rather than under *de*. The user is cautioned that names like Chávez and González are spelled by some possessors Chaves and Gonzales. These latter appear first, of course. I have used accents where required by Spanish orthography, although in some cases the bearer of the name may not consistently use them. When the name of a person mentioned within a biography is followed by an asterisk, that person is also a biographee. Following the dictionary there are appendixes listing the biographees by fields of professional activity and by state. In the first case a biographee may appear under more than one listing; in the second, where a biographee's career developed in more than one state, he or she is listed under the one that seemed most appropriate. Finally there is a general subject index.

In the matter of terms of identification, I use Mexican American and Chicano interchangeably, especially after the beginning of the twentieth century. This does not preclude the use of Chicano at times to connote a proud ethnicity. To avoid overuse of one or two words, the terms Latino, Hispano, Hispanic, Spanish-speaking, Tejano, Nuevo Mexicano, and Californio are also used. Although these last three are Spanish terms, I have capitalized them in accordance with English practice and not italicized them; they are also used to distinguish between the people (in these states) of Mexican culture or descendence and the Anglo (American) inhabitants.

Finally, any reader who might have the temerity to read this work from beginning to end will find, as I did in preparing it, that there are identifiable commonalities in these life stories. He or she will also encounter a fairly complete history of the Mexican American experience. In predominantly Anglo America, Mexican Americans have been outsiders for the most part. Their life stories illustrate the diversity and complexity of their struggles to enter the mainstream, to be accepted, and to have their contributions to American life recognized. Clearly, that struggle for full acceptance—social, economic, and political—is far from ended.

Acknowledgments ———

It is, of course, obvious that a work of this nature is possible only because of the active cooperation and help of many persons. To begin, I wish to acknowledge with gratitude the support of my chairman, my dean, and the academic vice president of Santa Clara University—which included two small summer presidential grants and one quarter's sabbatical leave. For their willingness to help me in identifying prominent Mexican Americans in their geographical areas I want to thank Christine Marín, Félix D. Almaraz, Jr., Carlos Cortés, and Evelyn López (widow of my old friend Lino López), who took a personal interest in the *Dictionary*.

I owe a great deal to Charlie Ericksen who kindly allowed me to use the biographic files of Hispanic Link in Washington, D.C. Lee Sachs, who lent invaluable help in the early stages of collecting biographical materials, also deserves special recognition and a warm note of thanks. I also wish to thank the many reference librarians in the Southwest who helped me in the accumulation and verification of data, and especially reference librarians at Santa Clara University, Stanford University, and the Chicano Studies Library, University of California, Berkeley. I am also indebted to my colleagues in various disciplines here at Santa Clara University who answered questions in their fields of expertise; I owe a special debt to Professor Francisco Jiménez on whom I leaned for help and advice so often.

For their help in preparing the manuscript I wish to thank my wife Bettie, who typed the first draft and who always seemed to know what I meant to write rather than what I wrote; Linda Campbell, who shaped up the final copy; Kendall Stratford, who helped proofread the manuscript; and Cherie Rieger, who helped clarify some of the strange mysteries of the word processor and typed part of the manuscript as well as the extensive correspondence involved with the project. I hope that the *Dictionary* will justify their interest and concern.

Mexican American Biographies

A _____

ABELARDO. See DELGADO, ABELARDO BARRIENTOS.

ACOSTA, MANUEL GREGORIO (1921–), painter, muralist, sculptor. Manuel Acosta was born 9 May 1921 in the small village of Villa Aldama just off Highway 140 west of Jalapa in the Mexican state of Veracruz. He studied art at the University of Texas at El Paso, at the Chouinard Art Institute in Los Angeles, and with private tutors.

In the mid-1950s Acosta painted a number of murals for banks and other semipublic buildings in Texas and New Mexico. In 1958 he had his first exhibition, and four years later had his first one-man show at Chase Gallery in New York. In 1969 he did a portrait of César Chávez* for a *Time* magazine cover. His works are held in a number of private and public collections throughout the United States including the National Portrait Gallery in Washington, D.C. He also has acted as advisor to the Texas Commission on the Arts and Humanities.

FURTHER READING: *Who's Who in American Art,* 16th ed., 1984.

ACOSTA, OSCAR ZETA (1936–), writer, lawyer, activist. Oscar Acosta was born 8 April 1936 in the border town of El Paso, Texas, of Mexican immigrant parentage. The family moved to California's great central valley while Oscar was a youth. Here he attended high school and upon graduation entered the U.S. Air Force during the Korean conflict. He mustered out of the service in 1956 after four years and enrolled in college where he studied creative writing. At the beginning of the 1960s he graduated and took a job on a San Francisco newspaper while he attended law school in the evening. In 1966, having passed his state bar examination, he went to work for the East Oakland Legal Aid Society.

Persistent doubts about his self-identity and a dormant interest in writing led him to quit his legal job, and in the late 1960s he became a political activist and began writing. In 1972, taking the middle name Zeta, he published *The Autobiography of a Brown Buffalo* and in the following year its sequel, *The*

Revolt of the Cockroach People. These two semiautobiographical novels describe, in part, Acosta's stereotypical search for self-identity in the midst of a hypocritical Anglo society at a time of great turmoil for Chicanos. Since 1974 Oscar Acosta has been inactive. Along with José Antonio Villarreal* Acosta was on the cutting edge of the Chicano literary renaissance. The republication by Bantam in 1974 of *The Revolt of the Cockroach People* makes him one of a handful of Chicano novelists published by commercial publishers.

FURTHER READING: Julio A. Martínez and Francisco A. Lomelí, *Chicano Literature: A Reference Guide*, Westport, Conn.: Greenwood Press, 1985; Charles M. Tatum, *Chicano Literature*, Boston: Twayne Publishers, 1982.

ACOSTA, ROBERT J. (1939–), educator. Robert Acosta was born blind 24 April 1939 in Los Angeles, to an old Californio landowning family. Despite his blindness he was encouraged by his family to lead a normal, active life. After graduating from John Marshall High School in 1957, he entered California State College (today University) at Los Angeles and four years later received his B.A. in social studies. In 1967 he earned a second B.A. at California State, in English.

After college Acosta went to work as a teacher of the blind in high school. Animated by family support, he founded The Blind College Students of Southern California and cofounded the Northern California Blind Student Organization. He also organized The Blind Teachers of California. For his leadership role in helping the blind in 1968 he was named one of America's Ten Outstanding young men by the National Junior Chamber of Commerce.

FURTHER READING: Harold J. Alford, *The Proud Peoples: The Heritage and Culture of Spanish-Speaking Peoples in the United States*, New York: David McKay Co., 1972.

ACUÑA, RODOLFO (1932–), author, professor, activist. Born in the middle of the Great Depression, 18 May 1932, in Los Angeles, Rudy Acuña grew up and received his early education there. After graduating from Loyola High School in 1951, his further education was interrupted by service in the U.S. Army from 1953 to 1955. Two years later he completed his B.A. degree at Los Angeles State College (today University) and in 1962 earned his M.A. Meanwhile he had also begun to teach at local high schools and colleges. He was perhaps the first person to teach a course in the history of the Mexican American—at Mount St. Mary's College in 1966. Two years later he received his Ph.D. in (Latin American) history at the University of Southern California. After teaching briefly at California State College, Dominguez Hills, Acuña moved to San Fernando Valley State College (today California State University, Northridge) where he still teaches. Seeing the need for an activist academic approach, he founded the department of Chicano Studies at Northridge.

Rodolfo Acuña has authored four books and numerous articles on Mexican Americans. He is perhaps best known for his text, *Occupied America: The Chicano's Struggle Toward Liberation* (1972), in which he explained the Mexican American experience within a framework of internal colonialism. A revised edition titled *Occupied America: A History of Chicanos* (1981) abandoned the internal colonial model. A revised third edition is scheduled to come out in late 1987. In addition to his teaching and writing Acuña has also been deeply involved in community organization and the Chicano Movement.

FURTHER READING: Julio A. Martínez, *Chicano Scholars and Writers: A Bio-Bibliographical Dictionary,* Metuchen, N.J.: The Scarecrow Press, 1979; Arturo Palacios, *Mexican-American Directory,* 1969–70 ed., Washington, D.C.: Executive Systems Corp., 1969.

ALEMANY, JOSE SADOC (1814–1888), missionary, bishop. José Alemany was born at Vich in the Catalan province of Barcelona, Spain. Entering the Dominican order at age fifteen, he studied six years in Spain and then completed his religious education in Italy. A few years after his ordination to the priesthood he was sent to the then western frontier of the United States where he became a citizen in 1845. When California was made a part of the United States at the end of the Mexican–U.S. War he was appointed first bishop of the Diocese of Monterey, which then included part of Utah and Nevada as well as all of Alta and Baja California. Three years later he was appointed head of the newly created Archdiocese of San Francisco.

During his thirty years as archbishop of San Francisco Alemany was successful in coping with the rapid growth within the area of his jurisdiction, now limited to the entire state of California and part of neighboring Nevada and Utah. In those years he fought against Know-Nothingism and anti-Catholicism, imposed tithing on Californios, and supported Spanish-language schooling. He also succeeded in getting back church title to some California mission lands and in collecting from Mexico the unpaid interest on the Pious Fund. As archbishop of San Francisco he took an active role in U.S. episcopal affairs and in 1884 at Baltimore chaired a bishops' commission which led to the publication of a uniform national catechism—the famous Baltimore Catechism (1885).

In December 1884 he resigned as archbishop and returned to Catalonia spending his final years as a parish priest in Valencia.

FURTHER READING: John B. McGloin, *California's First Archbishop: The Life of Joseph Alemany, O.P., 1814–1888,* New York: Herder and Herder, 1966.

ALONZO, JUAN A. (1936–   ), cinematographer. Juan Alonzo was born in Dallas, Texas, and grew up in Mexico when his parents returned to their native country during the Great Depression. As a teenager Juan came back to Dallas, where he completed his high school education. In school he was greatly interested in the arts and excelled in courses in speech, debate, and theater. After high school he worked at various Dallas theaters and television stations, usually in sets and lighting. Meanwhile he developed a puppet show, which soon became a local television success and took him to Hollywood.

In Hollywood, on the basis of a homemade movie, Alonzo was hired to shoot a short, which subsequently was nominated for an Academy Award. A second successful short got him a job in 1962 as cinematographer for major documentary producer David L. Wolper. Eight years later he began to work on feature films, and in the 1970s he averaged three films a year. Among his best known films are *Chinatown*, which earned him an Oscar nomination, *Farewell, My Lovely, Harold and Maude, Sounder,* and *The Bad News Bears*.

FURTHER READING: Ray Herbeck, Jr., "The Hard Eye of John Alonzo," *Nuestro* 2:6 (June 1978).

ALURISTA (ALBERTO URISTA HEREDIA) (1947–   ), poet, activist, teacher. Born in Mexico City 8 August 1947, Alberto Urista spent the first dozen years of his life in Mexico—in Cuernavaca and Acapulco. He moved in his early teens to California where he graduated from San Diego High School, attended Chapman College, and completed his B.A. in psychology at San Diego State University in 1971. He later earned his M.A. and in 1982 his doctorate in Spanish literature at the University of California, San Diego. Meanwhile he taught creative writing and Chicano literature at San Diego State University; in 1974 he was visiting lecturer at the University of Texas, Austin.

Considered the leading Chicano poet of the 1960s, Alurista actively participated in the Chicano Movement by helping to formulate the "Plan of Aztlán" and by using his poetry to awaken the public conscience. As a student and community activist he helped found various student and community organizations. In 1967 he was a cofounder of the Movimiento Estudiantil Chicano de Aztlán (MECHA) at San Diego State University. In the early 1970s he helped organize Toltecas en Aztlán, Centro Cultural de La Raza, and the Concilio por la Justicia in the community; while at the university he helped develop the Chicano studies program (1968) and the Centro de Estudios Chicanos (1969).

Alurista's early poetry, published in the collection *Floricanto en Aztlán*, became the point of departure for other Chicano poets. It reflected the political and social convulsions of the late 1960s and was seminal in both content and form. Thematically Alurista originated and explored the Amerindian ideology of Aztlán—an ideology that defined the Chicano in terms of his indigenous Mexican heritage and his experience living in the United States. Stylistically, by using Spanish and English in one poem, he popularized the writing of poetry in bilingual form. He was one of the first Chicano poets to create poetry by using the language spoken by many Chicanos in everyday conversation. In addition to *Floricanto en Aztlán* he published five other poetry anthologies: *Nationchild Plumaroja* (1972), *Timespace Huracán* (1976), *A'nque* (1979), *Spick in Glyph* (1981), and *Return: Poems Collected and New* (1982). He edited two anthologies: *Festival Floricanto I: An Anthology of Chicano Literature* (1974) and *Festival Floricanto II* (1976), and with his wife edited the literary journal *Maize*. He has written numerous essays on Chicano culture, literature, and the Movement, and is also the author of television scripts, an allegorical play, *Dawn*, and a children's book, *Tula y Tonán*. Currently he is teaching in the Spanish department at California Polytechnic State University, San Luis Obispo.

FURTHER READING: Juan Bruce-Novoa, *Chicano Authors: Inquiry by Interview*, Austin: University of Texas Press, 1980; Julio A. Martínez and Francisco A. Lomelí, *Chicano Literature: A Reference Guide,* Westport, Conn.: Greenwood Press, 1985; Charles Tatum, *Chicano Literature*, Boston: Twayne Publishers, 1982.

ALVARADO, JUAN BAUTISTA (1809–1882), political leader, governor. Born in Monterey of an important Californio family, Alvarado obtained an excellent education with the personal tutorship of the last Spanish governor of Alta California, Pablo Vicente de Solá. His education and family influence helped make him at a young age an important northern Californio leader, a position that he used to obtain for himself and his supporters both political power (in competition with southern Californio leaders) and former mission lands. In 1836 he was instrumental in ousting the Mexican officials sent by President Antonio López de Santa Anna and in establishing California as a sovereign state until Mexico should return to its earlier federalist system of government.

Alvarado became provisional governor and his uncle, Mariano Vallejo,* was appointed military commander. In 1839 Alvarado was officially appointed to the governorship. A falling-out between Vallejo and Alvarado and the latter's poor health led him to turn over his authority to the newly appointed Mexican governor, Manuel Micheltorena, in 1842. Three years later, in 1845, he helped oust Micheltorena. During this time he served as customs collector at Monterey, where he owned a store, and in 1845 he was named representative to the National Congress in Mexico City. He did not assume the duties of his office, however, as a result of the U.S.–Mexican war.

During the U.S. invasion of California in 1846 Alvarado took no part in the Californios' resistance to the Americans and withdrew from politicial life under parole. In the following year, without ever having occupied it, he was pressured to sell his "floating" Mariposa land grant, received from Governor Micheltorena, to John Charles Fremont for $3,000 in order to pay creditors. Two years later he left Monterey, retiring to San Pablo on the east shore of San Francisco bay where his wife Martina Castro de Alvarado owned a large rancho. He spent the rest of his life there as a private citizen, much respected by all Californians, struggling against squatters and writing his extensive memoirs.

FURTHER READING: Juan Bautista Alvarado, *Vignettes of Early California: Childhood Reminiscences of Juan Bautista Alvarado*, San Francisco: Book Club of California, 1982; Rockwell D. Hunt, *California's Stately Hall of Fame*, Stockton, Calif.: College of the Pacific, 1950.

ALVAREZ, EVERETT, JR. (1937–   ), naval aviator, attorney, public official. Alvarez was born in Salinas, California, of farm worker parents from Mexico and grew up there. At home his parents emphasized hard work and education as the way to succeed; he worked after school hours from his early youth. After high school he entered Hartnell College and then continued his education at Santa Clara University, where he graduated in 1960 with a B.S. in electrical engineering. A naval pilot in the Vietnam conflict, his Skyhawk fighter was shot down over the Gulf of Tonkin on 5 August 1964 while he was attacking a PT-boat base. He was held prisoner by the North Vietnamese for over eight and a half years—the longest captivity of the war. After his release in February 1973 and his return to the United States he attended the Naval Post-Graduate School at Monterey, California, where he earned an M.S. in systems analysis in 1976. He was then appointed assistant program manager for the Navy's Air Systems Command in Washington, D.C., a position he held until his retirement four year later. Upon retirement Alvarez began studies toward completing a J.D. degree at George Washington University and went to work for a firm of patent attorneys. In mid-1981 he was appointed deputy director of the Peace Corps by President Ronald Reagan and a little more than a year later was named deputy administrator of the Veterans Administration, a position he still holds and which places him in charge of nearly 700 V.A. facilities, mostly medical.

Alvarez received an honorary doctorate in public service from Santa Clara University in 1982; he holds numerous military awards, including two Purple Hearts, a Distinguished Flying Cross, and two Legions of Merit. He also has a city park, a municipal housing development, and a naval housing project named in his honor.

FURTHER READING: Ignacio García, "America Says, 'Welcome Home,' " *Nuestro* 6:9 (November 1982); John Hubbell, *P.O.W.*, New York: Reader's Digest Press, 1976; Al Martínez, *Rising Voices: Profiles of Hispano-American Lives*, New York: New American Library, 1974; Verónica Salazar, "Alvarez Survived to Help Others," San Antonio *Sunday Express News* (2 October 1983).

ALVAREZ, FRANCISCO SANCHEZ (1928–1980), chemist. Frank Alvarez was born at Jalapa in Veracruz state, Mexico, and grew up there. After graduating from Colegio Cristoforo Colón, he studied in the Faculty of Chemistry at the Universidad Nacional Autónoma de México in the capital. In 1953 he completed his undergraduate studies and joined Syntex (Mexico) as a research assistant. Two years later he began graduate studies in organic chemistry at Harvard University with the well-known Professor Louis Fieser. In 1957 he returned to Syntex in Mexico as a development research scientist. In 1964 he came to Syntex, Palo Alto, California, as a department head in development research, and in 1973 he was appointed Principal Scientist. He played an important role in Syntex's development.

Dr. Alvarez's most notable achievement in the field of organic chemistry was his work on the processes for the production of Norethindrone, a principal component of many birth control pills, and Synalar, an important topical anti–inflammatory drug. He also made major contributions to the basic methodology for the synthesis of prostaglandins and novel polyflourinated corticoids. In addition to being the author of over fifteen scientific publications, Dr. Alvarez is listed as the inventor in over eighty U.S. and foreign patents.

ALVAREZ, MANUEL (1794–1856), fur trapper, merchant, political leader. Alvarez was born in Spain, moved to Mexico, and came to the United States in his late twenties, first settling in Missouri. Here he became a participant in the recently developed trade with Santa Fe. He soon moved from Missouri to Santa Fe, where he opened a general store. In addition to his involvement in the Santa Fe trade he developed into an important figure in the fur trade in the Northwest Territory, active especially in the Continental Divide area of the Green, Yellowstone, and Snake rivers. With the waning of the fur trade, Alvarez returned to Santa Fe in 1834 to join a partner in managing the store that he operated successfully until his death.

In 1839 Alvarez was appointed United States consul in Santa Fe by the Van Buren administration and filled that post until the American takeover seven years later. During this time he became a U.S. citizen. Because of his long stint as consul he had a considerable circle of Nuevo Mexicano friends. This fact enabled him to help Colonel Stephen W. Kearny and his Missouri volunteers achieve the initially peaceful occupation of New Mexico. In the aftermath of annexation by the United States, Alvarez took an active political role in the effort to establish immediate civil government. He became one of the principal organizers of the statehood party, served in the elected legislature, and in 1850 functioned briefly as acting civil governor. After the statehood movement was devastated by the Compromise of 1850, which assigned territorial status to New Mexico, he remained in the new government as a minor appointed official until his death in Santa Fe in 1856.

FURTHER READING: Thomas E. Chávez, "Don Manuel Alvarez (de las Abelgas): Multi-Talented Merchant of New Mexico," *Journal of the West* 18:1 (January 1979); Thomas E. Chávez, "The Life and Times of Manuel Alvarez, 1794–1856," Ph.D. diss., University of New Mexico, 1980; LeRoy Hafen, *The Mountain Men and Fur Trade of the Far West*, Vol. 1, Glendale, Calif.: A. H. Clark, 1965–1972; David Weber, *The Toas Trappers*, Norman: University of Oklahoma Press, 1971.

AMADOR, LUIS VALENTINE (1920–   ), medical doctor, teacher. Luis Amador was born at Las Cruces in south central New Mexico and grew up and was educated there. After completing his B.S. at New Mexico State University (Las Cruces), he was accepted as a medical student by Northwestern University in Evanston, Illinois. In 1944 he was awarded his M.D. After a year's residency in neurology and neurosurgery, he entered the Medical Corps, U.S. Army, and served at Letterman Hospital in San Francisco from 1946 to 1948, reaching the rank of captain. After his army service he was senior resident neurosurgeon for the Illinois Research and Educational Hospitals and for the Illinois Neuropsychiatric Institute. In 1950 he was appointed research associate of the Rockefeller Institute for Research in Europe and two years later lectured to the Scandinavian Neurological Society. In 1954 he was named a Guggenheim fellow. During the remainder of the 1950s he lectured at the University of Freiberg in Germany, at the New England Neurological Society, at the Academy of

Neurological Surgeons, at New York University, and at the Second International Congress of Neurological Surgeons.

From 1966 to 1978 Dr. Luis Amador was clinical professor of neurological surgery at the University of Chicago; since 1978 he has been professor of neurological surgery at Northwestern University. He is a member of and has been an officer in a number of professional societies including the International Society of Pediatric Neurosurgery and the American Society of Stereotaxic Neurosurgery. Dr. Amador is the author of articles in his field of specialization in various professional journals and books.

FURTHER READING: *Who's Who in America, 1984–85*, 43rd ed., 1984.

ANAYA, RUDOLFO A. (1937–   ), novelist. The son of Nuevo Mexicanos Martín and Rafaelita (Mares) Anaya, Rudolfo was born 30 October 1937 in Pastura, a small village of the bleak Llano Estacado area of New Mexico. Shortly after his birth the family moved to the county seat, Santa Rosa, on the Pecos River, where he grew up and began his education. In 1956 he graduated from Albuquerque High School and attended Browning Business School for two years. He then entered the University of New Mexico, from which he received his A.B. in literature in 1963 and his M.A. in the same field five years later. From 1963 to 1970 he taught English in Albuquerque public schools and then spent two years as director of the Counseling Center, University of Albuquerque. In 1974 he became a professor at the University of New Mexico where he teaches creative writing and English.

Rudolfo Anaya started writing as a child and began to write seriously as an undergraduate student. After some efforts in the areas of poetry and painting, in the early 1960s he decided on the novel as his métier and began writing what eventually evolved into *Bless Me, Ultima*. This became his first and perhaps most famous novel and in 1971 received the Premio Quinto Sol literary award. It was published in the following year by Quinto Sol Publications and was soon followed by the other two novels of the trilogy, *Heart of Aztlán* (1976) and *Tortuga* (1979). During this period he also coedited *Voices from the Rio Grande* (1976), *Cuentos Chicanos* (1980), and *Ceremony of Brotherhood (1980)* and wrote a screenplay, *Bilingualism: Promise for Tomorrow* (1976). In the early 1980s he published *Cuentos: Tales from the Hispanic Southwest* (1980), a collection of short stories, *The Silence of the Llano* (1982), and most recently a cultural reminiscence titled *A Chicano in China*. Anaya has also had short stories published in a variety of journals and magazines and is the author of two plays, *The Season of la Llorona* (1979) and *Rosa Linda* (1982).

One of the leading Chicano novelists, Rudolfo Anaya has been the recipient of numerous awards and honors. In addition to the Premio Quinto Sol (1971) he received the University of New Mexico's Mesa Chicano Literary Award (1977), the Governor of New Mexico's Public Service Award (1978), National Endowment for the Arts Creative Writing Fellowship (1980), the Before Columbus Foundation's American Book Award for *Tortuga* (1980), an invitation to read at the White House in a Salute to American Poets and Writers (1980), governor's Award for Excellence and Achievement in Literature (1980), honorary doctorate of humane letters, University of Albuquerque (1981), a three-year W. K. Kellogg Foundation Fellowship (1982), and many others. In March 1987 he was one of six distinguished Hispanic writers who participated in a Rutgers University lecture series. He has been invited to lecture and read his works at numerous universities and colleges, and has served as a judge on various panels in literary contests.

FURTHER READING: Juan Bruce-Novoa, *Chicano Authors: Inquiry by Interview*, Austin: University of Texas Press, 1980; Julio A. Martínez and Francisco A. Lomelí, *Chicano Literature: A Reference Guide*, Westport, Conn.: Greenwood Press, 1985; Charles Tatum, *Chicano Literature*, Boston: Twayne Publishers, 1982.

ANAYA, TONEY (1941–), politician. Toney Anaya, the seventh of ten children of a Nuevo Mexicano cowboy and laborer, was born 29 April 1941 in the small town of Moriarty, New Mexico, thirty-five miles east of Albuquerque. He grew up in a three-room adobe house with a dirt floor and no electricity or plumbing. Although both his parents had only a couple of years of schooling, they constantly urged their children to get a good education. Toney attended the tiny school in Moriarty and by the second grade was also working both before and after school at his older brother's grocery and at family chores. After high school he attended New Mexico Highlands University in Las Vegas on a Sears Foundation scholarship; he then went to Washington, D.C., where he worked for Senator Dennis Chávez* while he completed his B.A. in political science and economics at Georgetown University. Four years later, in 1967, he obtained his law degree at the Washington College of Law, American University.

After working for Senator Chávez, Toney Anaya took a position in the U.S. Labor Department, and in 1966 went to work as legislative counsel to New Mexico's senator Joseph Montoya.* Two years later he was admitted to the practice of law in the District of Columbia, in New Mexico, and before the Supreme Court. Returning to New Mexico in 1970, he entered private law practice, but within a year accepted an offer from Governor Bruce King to become his administrative assistant. After two years with King he again returned to private practice, but with an eye to a political future. In 1974 he ran for election as New Mexico's attorney general and won, serving until 1978. Unable by law to succeed himself, he campaigned for the U.S. Senate that same year but lost to Republican Pete Domenici in a close race. Continuing to practice law as a senior partner in the firm of Strumor, Gonzales & Fruman, he also began to prepare for the governorship race.

In November 1982 Anaya was elected governor of New Mexico. As governor one of his early acts was to host a number of outstanding Latino leaders and with them to form "Hispanic Force 84" to enhance the political clout of Hispanics in the presidential election year. During his governorship as in his years as attorney general, he piloted his course aggressively against conventional political winds. He increased state income taxes, raised taxes on oil, and put through a tough affirmative action program. Late in March 1986 he proclaimed New Mexico a sanctuary state for Central American refugees. All of these things have led to bitter power struggles that have antagonized some New Mexican voters.

Since 1984 Toney Anaya has been spoken of as a potential vice-presidential candidate. He is generally considered to have ambitions for national political office. In mid-January 1987 he was appointed president of the Mexican American Legal Defense and Education Fund (MALDEF).

FURTHER READING: "Looking Out for No. 1," *Time* (31 October 1983); "Toney Anaya," *PSA Magazine* 20:3 (March 1985); Maurilio Vigil, "The Election of Toney Anaya . . . ," *Journal of Ethnic Studies* 12:2 (Summer 1984).

ANGEL, FRANK, JR. (1914–   ), educator, administrator. Frank Angel was born 26 February 1914 in the New Mexican university town of Las Vegas, east of Santa Fe. He grew up and was educated here, and on completing high school in 1932, began his career as an educator by teaching elementary grades in one- and two-room rural schools of San Miguel County. After five years he went to Santa Fe to teach in Nambe Experimental Community School. During World War II his career was interrupted by service as a bomber pilot in the Pacific Theater, but upon his release he returned to education. In 1949 he earned his B.S. in elementary education at the University of New Mexico and two years later an M.S. in education at the University of Wisconsin. With the help of a John Hay Whitney Foundation fellowship he received his Ph.D. in education administration in 1955 at the University of California in Berkeley.

From 1955 to 1971 Frank Angel was professor of educational administration at the University of New Mexico. During this time he also served as chairman of a committee of the New Mexico Educational Association and as an executive secretary to the New Mexico School Boards Association. In 1972 he was inaugurated president of New Mexico Highlands University—the first Spanish-speaking president of a four-year liberal arts school in the United States. As president from 1972 to 1976 he established a number of policies and projects to meet the needs of New Mexico's minority student population, black, Indian, and Chicano. Frank Angel is also the author of a number of articles and papers on the education of Mexican Americans.

FURTHER READING: "First Hispano College President in U.S.: New Mexico Highlands University," *La Luz* 3:3 (June 1974); Julio A. Martínez, *Chicano Scholars and Writers: A Bio-Bibliographical Dictionary*, Metuchen, N.J.: The Scarecrow Press, 1979; Theodore E. B. Wood, *Chicanos y Chicanas Prominentes*, Menlo Park, Calif.: Educational Consortium of America, 1974.

APODACA, JERRY (1934–   ), politician, businessman. Jerry Apodaca was born 3 October 1934 and grew up in the south-central New Mexican town of Las Cruces in which his family had lived for over a century. He graduated with a Bachelor of Science degree in education from the University of New Mexico where he was also an active sports enthusiast and star football halfback. After graduation in 1957 and a three-year stint at teaching history and coaching, he returned to Las Cruces and opened a successful insurance agency, followed later by a real estate agency and retail shoe stores. Turning to politics, Apodaca was elected to the state senate in 1966 on the Democratic ticket. Three years later he was elected head of the state Democratic party. After eight years in the state legislature he decided to run for governor of New Mexico. Supported by liberals, labor, and Chicano activists, he won the Democratic nomination for the governorship in June 1974 by beating five opponents. In the general elections that followed, his dynamic and aggressive campaigning won him the governor's chair.

On 1 January 1975 Jerry Apodaca, age forty, became the twenty-second governor of New Mexico and the first Hispanic governor since Octaviano Larrazolo* over fifty years earlier. Apodaca proved to be a strong and resourceful governor. In April 1975 he began the reorganization of state government by creating a cabinet system in which 117 agencies were subsumed under twelve departments. During his term the education budget got its largest increase ever. Soon after his inauguration his interest in the energy issue got him elected cochairman of the Four Corner Regional Commission, and later he was named the first chairman of the western governors' regional energy policy agency. In 1977 he was recipient of the Award for Distinguished Service to Higher Education as well as honorary degrees from Our Lady of the Lake University in San Antonio, Texas, and from Eastern New Mexico University. Late in 1978 he was named chairman of the President's Council on Physical Fitness and Sports by Jimmy Carter.

Prevented from running for a second term by the state constitution, Jerry Apodaca devoted himself to business interests upon leaving the governorship. He became involved in the development of several racquetball clubs and serves as chairman of both the New Mexico and Texas racquetball associations. He also serves on the board of directors of the Philip Morris company and of ENREC, an energy and recreation company. In the political area he became chairman of the National Issues Council, an agency for putting forward business interests in national programs and legislation. Apodaca has kept his political options open. In 1979 he was among the top contenders for the position of U.S. ambassador to Mexico, and two years later he ran unsuccessfully for the United States Senate.

FURTHER READING: José Z. García, ''Jerry Apodaca: Running Unscared,'' *Nuestro* 2:11 (November 1978); ''Roger Langley's Hispanic Beat,'' *Hispanic Business* 1:3:9 (July 1979); *Who's Who in America, 1978–1979*, 40th ed., 1978.

ARAGON, JOHN A. (1930–), educator, administrator. Born in a Mexican barrio of Albuquerque, New Mexico, on 3 May 1930 in the depths of the Great Depression, John Aragón grew up and received his elementary schooling there. After his high school education at Northern New Mexico Normal School in Rito, Rio Arriba County, he entered New Mexico Highlands University. In college he was active in student government and sports and graduated in 1952 with an A.B. in English. Out of college he began his educator's career by teaching high school in Española and Los Alamos. For three years (1956–1959) he worked for the New Mexico Education Association as director of professional services and during this time earned an M.A. in education at the University of New Mexico (UNM), awarded in 1959. At the end of the 1950s he began studies at UNM for his doctorate in education, at the same time working as executive secretary to the New Mexico School Boards Association from 1959 to 1965.

In 1965, having completed his doctoral degree, John Aragón began teaching in the Department of Education at the University of New Mexico. After a period representing the university in Ecuador, he returned in 1969 to direct the university's Minority Groups Cultural Awareness Center and to teach in the Education Department. During the 1970s he was several times a top contender for high-level administrative positions in the university system and in 1975 was appointed president of New Mexico Highlands University, replacing his friend Frank Angel* the following year. He served as president until 1984.

Dr. John Aragón has received numerous citations and awards from professional and civic organizations as well as foreign governments. Perhaps the most prestigious was the George I. Sánchez* Award, which was presented to him by the National Education Association in 1973 for innovative practices in bilingual education and for improving cultural understanding. He has also been a consultant to numerous educational and governmental agencies including the Department of Health, Education and Welfare, the Agency for International Development, and the Ford Foundation.

FURTHER READING: Tomás O. Martínez, "Dr. John Aragón: Leading New Mexico Educator," *La Luz* 3:2 (May 1974); *Who's Who in America, 1984–1985*, 43rd ed., 1984.

ARCHULETA, DIEGO (1814–1884), political and military leader. Born of a prominent and well-to-do local family in the Rio Arriba country of New Mexico during the uncertainties of the Mexican war for independence, Diego Archuleta received his early education in the town of his birth, Alcalde. Later he became a student of Fr. Antonio José Martínez's* school at Taos and from there went to the seminary at Durango, Mexico, to study for the priesthood. After completing eight years of preliminary study toward ordination, he decided that his vocation lay elsewhere and left the seminary.

Returning to New Mexico in 1840, Archuleta joined the New Mexico militia as a captain and took part in meeting the threat of the Texas Santa Fe Expedition the following year. From 1843 to 1845 he served as New Mexican representative to the national congress in Mexico City. Upon his return to New Mexico from the capital, he was promoted to colonel in the departmental militia, second in command to the governor, General Manuel Armijo.* When American forces invaded New Mexico in 1846, Archuleta followed the governor's example of giving no resistance to General Stephen W. Kearny. Apparently disappointed at not being given a prominent role in the American government which was quickly set up, he took a leading role in the two abortive Taos rebellions of late 1846 and early 1847. When the second revolt was suppressed, Archuleta fled southward into Chihuahua where he remained until the passions aroused by it had cooled.

Upon his return to New Mexico, Archuleta took the oath of allegiance to the new American government and, like Fr. Martínez, took the lead in seeking the most advantageous use of U.S. institutions. During the 1850s he was repeatedly elected to the New Mexico legislative assembly where he spoke out for Nuevo Mexicano interests. In 1857 he was made U.S. Indian Agent to the Utes and Apaches, an appointment he held until the Civil War broke out. With the coming of the war he joined the New Mexico militia with the rank of lieutenant colonel and was soon raised to the rank of brigadier general. He was also reappointed as Indian agent by President Abraham Lincoln. During the Civil War and the postwar period he was elected to the upper house Legislative Council for seven terms and twice served as the president of the Council. In 1884 he died of heart failure while serving in the legislature and was buried with great honors as befitted a native Nuevo Mexicano of great dedication and patriotism. Diego Archuleta was a leading New Mexican in politics and in military matters under the Mexican and United States governments. Always he was a patriotic Nuevo Mexicano first, looking out after the good of his people and the territory of New Mexico.

FURTHER READING: Ralph E. Twitchell, *The History of the Military Occupation of the Territory of New Mexico from 1846 to 1851*, Chicago: Rio Grande Press, 1963; Maurilio Vigil, *Los Patrones: Profiles of Hispanic Political Leaders in New Mexico History*, Washington, D.C.: University Press of America, 1980.

ARCINIEGA, TOMAS A. (1937–), educator, administrator. Born in El Paso, Texas, on 5 August 1937, Tomás Arciniega grew up and received his early education there. He entered New Mexico State University at Las Cruces, earned his B.S. in teacher education in 1960, and then transferred to the University of New Mexico where he obtained his M.A. (1966) and his Ph.D. in educational administration (1970). After filling teaching and administrative posts in the University of Texas at El Paso during the late 1960s and early 1970s, in 1973 he moved to California to become dean of the School of Education at San Diego State University for seven years. In 1980 he transferred to Fresno State University as academic vice-president. Three years later he was selected from 120 candidates by California State University trustees to be the president of Bakersfield State College in the southern San Joaquin Valley. He is the first Hispanic to be appointed a president in the California state system.

Tomás Arciniega is an acknowledged expert on educational topics, particularly educational programs and bicultural education, and has authored two books and numerous articles on a wide variety of education topics. He has also given numerous conference talks, especially on education as it affects the Mexican American. He has been honored as one of the top 100 academic leaders in higher education in the United States. Currently he is a member of the Board of Trustees of the Tomás Rivera Center at the Claremont Graduate School in southern California as well as president of Bakersfield State College.

FURTHER READING: Shirley Armbruster, "Hispanic FSU Official Sets Precedent," Fresno *Bee* (20 July 1983); Julio A. Martínez, *Chicano Scholars and Writers; A Bio-Bibliographical Directory*, Metuchen, N.J.: The Scarecrow Press, 1979.

ARIAS, RONALD F. (1941–   ), journalist, author, teacher. Born in Los Angeles on 30 November 1941, Ron Arias spent his early years in that city and in El Paso with his grandmother. His primary education took place principally in these two large Mexican American centers, but his secondary education was spread over a much wider area where his military stepfather was stationed. In the various high schools he attended he was active on the school paper—an involvement he continued later in college.

Awarded an Inter-American Press Association scholarship to Buenos Aires, Argentina, Arias worked there on the English-language *Buenos Aires Herald* in 1962 and also had a number of articles published in U.S. papers. This stint of journalism was followed by brief service in the Peace Corps in Peru, where he headed a community development program near Cuzco. Returning to the United States, he resumed his studies, leading to a B.A. degree in Spanish in 1966 and an M.A. degree in journalism the following year from the University of California at Los Angeles. During this time he continued his involvement in journalism, writing for a number of journals and news agencies, including the Copley syndicate, the Associated Press, *Atlanta Weekly*, and *Christian Science Monitor*.

After completing his university studies Arias worked in South America for the *Caracas Daily Journal* in 1968 and was editor for the Inter-American Development Bank from 1969 to 1971. In the latter year he began teaching journalism and literature at San Bernardino Valley College in California. During the 1970s and early 1980s he continued to combine the professional careers of teaching and freelance commercial writing, which has included television scripts. He has also been a contributing editor to *Revista Chicano-Riqueña* and *American Book Review*.

Arias, a journalist by predilection, has written a wide variety of articles, interviews, human interest stories, travelogues, scripts, and short stories with some emphasis on fantasy. He is best known for his novel, *The Road to Tamazunchale* (1975), which has been judged an outstanding work of Chicano fiction and which won him a National Book Award nomination. Like many of his short stories it combines subtle social commentary and fantasy; much of the novel's action takes place in the imagination and dreams of its leading character.

FURTHER READING: Juan Bruce-Novoa, *Chicano Authors: Inquiry by Interview*, Austin: University of Texas Press, 1980; Julio A. Martínez, *Chicano Scholars and Writers: A Bio-Biblilographical Directory*, Metuchen, N.J.: The Scarecrow Press, 1979.

ARMIJO, MANUEL (1792–1853), governor, businessman. Son of Lt. Vicente Ferrer Armijo, Manuel was raised on the family's Hacienda San Antonio near Alameda, just north of Albuquerque. He appears to have had an education befitting a son of a *rico*, although we know little about it. By his late twenties he had become an influential and well-to-do landowner, and as soon as trade between Santa Fe and the Missouri frontier was opened, he became one of a handful of Nuevo Mexicanos deeply involved in it and in its extension into Chihuahua.

From 1827 to 1829 Armijo served as a capable territorial governor of Nuevo México; in 1837 he led a counterrevolution to put down the Santa Cruz rebellion, part of the Nuevo Mexicano reaction to President Santa Anna's centralist government, and served a second time as governor till 1844. During this time he was also appointed *comandante general* for Nuevo México in the continual war against the depredations of Apaches, Comanches, and Navajos. However, he had fewer than 100 presidial troops, and he believed peace with the Indians might be more readily achieved through a combination of persuasion, trade, agriculture, and military readiness. His second governorship was dominated by concern about Anglo encroachment and highlighted by his successfully putting an end to the Texas Santa Fe expedition of 1841, which earned him a cross of honor from the president of Mexico, a ceremonial sword from the people of Chihuahua, and an undying hatred from Texans. As governor he increased his business importance by authorizing numerous large land grants, some to friends; in some he held an interest. Many of these grants were awarded because of his concern to protect Nuevo México against Indians, Texans, and the United States. He also continued to be active in the Santa Fe trade, where his use of the governor's power to modify Mexican tariff regulations earned him an undeserved unsavory reputation among many Anglos.

In 1845 after three short-term interim governors, Armijo was returned to the governorship and continued his earlier frontier policies. In all, between 1837 and 1846 he gave out over one half of the total of 31 million acres granted in Nuevo México between the sixteenth century and 1846. When invasion by the Americans under Colonel Stephen W. Kearny began in the latter year, Governor Armijo prepared a force to resist. Then, apparently swayed by his evaluation of the situation and by the counsel of friends and advisors, he decided against vain resistance and fled south across the Rio Grande into Chihuahua without engaging the enemy. His actions led some to suspect that he had sold out to the Americans. In fact, he was later imprisoned briefly for treason by the Mexican government, but the indictment was dropped for lack of evidence. After the Treaty of Guadalupe Hidalgo ended the war, Armijo returned to New Mexico, settling quietly on a ranch he owned near the small town of Lemitar on the west side of the Rio Grande just north of Socorro. He resumed his cattle raising and trading and in 1850 even ran for election to a local office, but lost. When he died three years later on December 9, his will included a bequest of $1,000 to establish a public school.

Much of nineteenth-century opinion and modern evaluation of Armijo is greatly distorted by ethnocentric anti-Mexican bias of mid-nineteenth century Anglos.

FURTHER READING: Paul Horgan, *The Centuries of Santa Fe*, New York: E. P. Dutton & Co., 1965. For a more positive view see Janet Lecompte, "Manuel Armijo and the Americans," *Journal of the West* 19:3 (July 1980); Ward Alan Minge, "Frontier Problems in New Mexico Preceding the Mexican War, 1840–1846," Ph.D. diss., University of New Mexico, 1965; David J. Weber, *The Mexican Frontier, 1821–1846: The American Southwest under Mexico*, Albuquerque: University of New Mexico Press, 1982.

ARMIJO, SALVADOR (1823–1879), merchant, politico. Born in Albuquerque, the fifth of six children, Salvador Armijo was the youngest son of politically important Ambrosio Armijo and nephew of the outstanding New Mexican governor, Manuel Armijo.* We know little of his youth, but he evidently received some education, since he was literate in Spanish and English. He also acquired a practical education in ranching, farming, and the mercantile business. By his mid-twenties he began to acquire land near Albuquerque and immediately began developing it. He also had a large home and a store in the city. Salvador readily accepted American control in 1846 and quickly found supplying the food and fodder needs of the U.S. Army quite profitable. By the end of the 1850s his mercantile business and his model ranch and farm operations had made him one of the wealthiest and most important citizens of Albuquerque.

The coming of the Civil War found Armijo staunch in his loyalty to the North, and in late 1861 he enlisted in the local militia. The Confederate invasion of New Mexico led to heavy confiscation of his stock of staples, and as soon as the Southern forces were driven back to Texas, he concentrated on restoring his business to its earlier success. In 1864 he organized a freighting and mercantile partnership called Salvador Armijo e Hijo and soon opened branch stores in a number of nearby small towns. The one at Peralta, twenty miles downriver from Albuquerque, was most successful, and in 1875 he made it his headquarters and opened a hotel there. In addition to his mercantile operations he was also an important cattle and sheep raiser, and by 1870 had 300 acres planted in wheat, corn, and beans.

Armijo's economic and family position almost inevitably involved him in politics. His first public office was as alcalde of Albuquerque in 1851–1852, and a decade later he was elected clerk of the probate court. In 1863 he was president of the Albuquerque Board of Aldermen, and four years later became Bernalillo County treasurer. By the latter 1860s he was the chief leader of the local Republicans and was active in promoting plans for a variety of civic improvements, including railroad construction.

In 1878 Armijo returned to Albuquerque where he built a large home, established a store on the plaza, and returned to sheep raising on shares. In the spring of 1879, while in Arizona looking after his 10,000 ewes, he fell ill and died. He was important in easing somewhat the transition from the old to the new way of life in the Southwest.

FURTHER READING: John O. Baxter, "Salvador Armijo, Citizen of Albuquerque, 1823–1879," *New Mexico Historical Review* 53:3 (July 1978).

ARREGUIN, ALFREDO MENDOZA (1935–   ), painter. Alfredo Arreguín was born in Morelia, capital of the Mexican state of Michoacán, son of Félix Arreguín-Vélez and María (Mendoza Martínez) Arreguín. At a very early age his artistic talents became evident, and when he was eight his grandfather bought him paint and brushes and enrolled him in the local fine arts school. Five years later his father's move to Mexico City interrupted his artistic development, and his father persuaded him to enroll in engineering studies there. He later switched to architecture. In 1958 his study of English led to a friendship with a Seattle, Washington, couple named Dam who were touring Mexico. At the invitation of the Dams Arreguín subsequently came to the United States and lived with them in Seattle. Soon he began the study of architecture at the University of Washington but lost interest and switched to interior design and finally decided seriously on art. In 1969 he completed his B.A. and two years later earned his Master in Fine Arts, both from the University of Washington.

Disconcerted by the academic trend toward abstract expressionism and self-doubtful, Arreguín abandoned painting for three years and turned to drawing. This turn to drawing led Arreguín to develop his own meticulous personal calligraphy and developed his skill at breaking down larger compositions into groups of interrelated segments. By 1974 he merged this drawing technique with his painting skills leading to his unique calligraphically patterned paintings. Most of these are vistas developed by multiple patterned layers and filled with exotic tropical flora and fauna. Toward the end of the 1970s he began a period that centered on pre-Columbian sculptural motifs, retained his intricate surface patterns, but sometimes opened paintings up from his earlier dense compositions. Beginning about 1980 he added the new dimension of luminosity, ultimately merging light and pattern. Arreguín's works all derive from his Mexican heritage, especially his recollections of the varied folk arts of his native Michoacán and his interest in pre-Columbian art. In recent years he has included human figures in some paintings and has experimented in clay.

Arreguín has had a long history of successful solo and group exhibitions beginning in 1971 and continuing to the present. Along the way he has received numerous honors, awards, and prizes. In 1974 and 1975 he won second prize and honorable mention at the Grand Galleria National Exhibition; in 1978 and 1979 his paintings won second and third prize at the Pacific Northwest Arts and Crafts Fair. In the latter year Arreguín won the prestigious Palm of the People Award at the Eleventh International Festival of Painting at Cagnes-Sur-Mer, France. Since then he has been awarded two National Endowment for the Arts grants (1980 and 1985) and has been appointed to the Seattle Arts Commission and to the Board of Artistic Directors, Pacific Arts Center, in Seattle. In 1985 one of Arreguín's paintings titled "Birds of Paradise" was chosen by UNICEF for the cover of its Christmas card and in June 1986 he was chosen to receive a Governor's Arts Award by the Washington State Arts Commission "in recognition of artistic excellence and outstanding contributions." In 1986 he participated in three traveling exhibitions and was invited by the School of Art of the University of Washington to lecture on his paintings. His works are listed in museums, galleries, and collections all over the United States and abroad. He is currently scheduled for one-man shows in Seattle, Washington, D.C., and Scottsdale, Arizona (1987).

FURTHER READING: David Arteaga, "Alfredo Arreguín: An Artist and his Work," *La Voz* (March 1985); Charlene B. Cox, "Arreguín's Artistic Designs," *Américas* 37:1 (January–February 1985); David Schaff, *Alfredo Arreguín* (exhibition catalogue, 1981); Jerry Szymanski, "Alfredo Arreguín," *Southwest Art* (October 1985); Yvonne Yarbro-Bejarano, "The Form of Dreams: The Art and Thought of Alfredo Arreguín," *Metamorfosis* 3:2; 4:1 (1980, 1981).

ARRIOLA, GUSTAVO MONTAÑO (1917–   ), cartoonist. Gustavo Arriola, son of Mexican immigrants, was born in Florence, Arizona, fifty miles southeast of Phoenix. When he was eight, the family moved to Los Angeles where he grew up and received his early education. He graduated from Manual Arts High School where he specialized in visual arts courses and after graduation went to work for Screen Gems, assigned to "Krazy Kat" cartoons. Work in movie animation for Columbia and Metro-Goldwyn-Mayer eventually led to his developing a comic strip classic—Gordo, which began in 1946 as a syndicated strip for United Features. Gordo was, of course, a stereotype, and Arriola was aware of that; in the 1950s he changed Gordo in advance of the rising feeling about ethnic stereotypes.

In 1960 Gus Arriola and his wife made the first of many trips to Mexico, and as a result Gordo became a tour bus driver, and Arriola began to fill his comic strip with ancient Mexican art and bits of modern Mexican culture. In 1979 the San Diego Museum of Art did a "Gordo's World" exhibit, placing blow-ups of Arriola's strips side by side with corresponding folk art sculptures. From 1961 to 1964 the Arriolas ran a Mexican folk art shop in Carmel, California, where they had moved. In 1985, after forty years of Gordo, Gus Arriola retired—and Gordo finally got married. Arriola was recipient of the Best Humor Strip awards from the National Cartoonists Society in 1957 and 1965.

FURTHER READING: Al Morch, "Mexican art through a cartoonist's eyes," *San Francisco Examiner* (24 September 1979); Michael Robertson, "Gordo's Last Day As a Bachelor," *San Francisco Chronicle* (1 March 1985); *Who's Who in America, 1982–1983*, 42nd ed., 1982.

ATENCIO, ALONSO CRISTOBAL (1929–   ), biochemist, educator. Alonso Atencio was born 24 June 1929 in Ortiz, a tiny town in south central Colorado on the border with New Mexico. He grew up there attending local schools and helping his father with the cattle on their ranch. After high school he enlisted in the U.S. Navy and later served as a medical corpsman with the First Marine Division in Korea. Mustered out of the Navy after the Korean truce, he spent two years breaking and training quarter horses and then enrolled in the University of Colorado at Boulder. In 1958 he earned his B.S. in chemistry there, followed by an M.S. in biochemistry at the University of Colorado, Denver in 1964 and a Ph.D. in medicine three years later. While still an M.S. candidate, he was invited to present a paper at an international medical symposium in Scotland in 1963. After receiving his doctorate he received a postdoctoral fellowship in biochemistry at Northwestern University in Illinois.

In 1970 he accepted a dual position at the New Mexico University School of Medicine as professor in biochemistry and assistant dean for student affairs. The second half of his job was the result of his concern about the needs and opportunities of Mexican American students. To discharge his double responsibilities, he immediately inaugurated and directed a basic science enrichment program and a summer science program. To help Latino graduate students, he founded and presides over a Foundation for Promotion of Advanced Studies.

Alonzo Atencio served on several national boards concerned with health issues in the 1970s. He has written articles for various professional journals and is active in professional societies. His area of interest and research is the hormonal control of biosynthesis in mammals.

FURTHER READING: Harold J. Alford, *The Proud Peoples: The Heritage and Culture of Spanish-Speaking Peoples in the United States*, New York: David McKay Co., 1972; *American Men and Women of Science*, 16th ed., 1986; *Who's Who in America, 1976–77*, 39th ed., 1976.

AVILA, JOAQUIN G. (1948–   ), attorney. Joaquín Avila was born of immigrant Mexican parents in Compton, California, a suburb of Los Angeles. His father was a foundry worker and his mother, who had a college preparatory education, worked in a sweatshop. Joaquín developed a strong academic curiosity during his high school years, became interested in science, and graduated as valedictorian and top student in his senior class at Centennial High School. He entered Yale University with the intention of becoming an astrophysicist but changed his major to government. From Yale he went on to Harvard Law School where he received his degree in 1973. For a year he clerked in the Alaska Supreme Court and then in 1974 came to the Mexican American Legal Defense and Education Fund (MALDEF) in San Francisco as a staff attorney. Two years later he was promoted to associate counsel of MALDEF's Texas operation. In 1982 he was elected president of MALDEF, replacing Vilma Martínez.*

As president of MALDEF Avila directed his attention to getting results—to improving the political, economic, and social position of Latinos. In a time of strong challenges to civil rights gains he had earlier won notable victories overturning discriminatory at-large election systems in Texas and invalidating a 1980 Texas reapportionment plan, which violated Mexican American voting rights. He was also a powerful force behind the extension of the Voting Rights Act of 1982 by Congress. In August 1985 he stepped down as MALDEF president.

FURTHER READING: Francis J. Flaherty, "The Struggle Continues," *The National Law Journal* 5:27 (14 March 1983); *Maldef* (June 1985).

B

BACA, ELFEGO (1865–1945), sheriff, lawyer detective, folk hero. One of the most fascinating Mexican American folk heroes to emerge at the end of the nineteenth century, Baca was born in Socorro County, New Mexico, of humble parentage. Not long after his birth the family moved to Topeka; here Elfego grew up in the turmoil of the post–Civil War Kansas frontier. When he was fifteen, his father moved the family back to New Mexico where the latter became the town marshall of Socorro. The family's return to New Mexico coincided with a heavy influx of Anglo settlers and especially of Texas cattlemen.

In 1884, while still a teenager, Baca had his most famous experience. On an electioneering trip, self-appointed special deputy Baca rode into the town of Frisco where a group of Texas cowboys, in their boozy high jinks, were using animals and their Mexican owners for target practice. Baca's taking one of the cowboys prisoner led to an escalating conflict in which about eighty of them cornered him the following day. He took refuge in the house of a friend, and after a siege of thirty-six hours and over 4,000 shots he had killed four cowboys, wounding eight more. Finally surrendering to a deputy sheriff he knew and trusted on promise of a fair hearing, he ultimately was tried in Albuquerque and was acquitted.

As a result of the case Baca became an instant folk hero among Nuevo Mexicanos, and his fame helped him in his subsequent long political career. He ran for some public office in virtually every election after reaching voting age. He was successively deputy sheriff, county clerk, mayor, district attorney, sheriff, and Socorro County superintendent of schools. After reading for the law with the local judge during this period, Baca was admitted to the bar in 1894 and began private practice in Socorro.

In 1910 Baca moved to Albuquerque and in the following year became a Republican candidate for the lower house in New Mexico's first state elections. He lost. During this time he also was busy as a mine promoter, worked as a glorified bouncer in a Ciudad Juárez gambling house, and represented the Victoriano Huerta government of Mexico. After Huerta's ouster from the presidency of Mexico, Baca continued to represent him in his U.S. exile at Fort Bliss, Texas. Huerta's death in 1916 ended Baca's lingering hope of becoming an important figure in the Mexican political scene. Two years later Baca was elected sheriff of Socorro County, a position he continued to hold intermittently during the 1920s.

Elfego Baca was sufficiently well known throughout the state at this time to be mentioned occasionally as a possible gubernatorial candidate. His broad experience in campaigning and his vote-getting potential came to the attention of the leading New Mexican liberal politico, Bronson Cutting. The result was a wary political alliance that lasted until Cutting's death in 1935. During this time Baca published a Spanish-language weekly, *La Opinión Pública*, in Cutting's support and also did some political detective work for him. After Cutting died, Baca, now in his early seventies, continued to work as a private detective and lawyer. He was licensed to practice before the U.S. Supreme Court, but never did. After several years of ill health he died at age eighty in August 1945, a year after an unsuccessful bid for the Democratic nomination for district attorney. He was survived by his wife of sixty years, one son, and five daughters.

FURTHER READING: V. B. Beckett, *Baca's Battle*, Houston: Stagecoach Press, 1962; Kyle S. Crichton, *Law and Order Limited: The Life of Elfego Baca*, Santa Fe, N.M.: New Mexican Publishing Co., 1928; William A. Keleher, *Memoirs: 1892–1969; A New Mexico Item*, Santa Fe, N.M.: Rydal Press, 1969.

BACA-BARRAGAN, POLLY (1941–   ), politician. Polly Baca-Barragán, a fourth-generation Coloradan, was born in La Salle, a small town near Greeley. After attending the Greeley high school, where she became involved in the Adlai Stevenson Young Democrats Club, she entered Colorado State University at Fort Collins, where she studied political science and in 1960 became the campus coordinator for the Viva Kennedy campaign. Upon graduation from college in 1963 she worked in Washington, D.C., as editor for two large union publications and pursued some graduate studies at American University. During the last years of the Lyndon Johnson administration she served as public information officer for the Cabinet Committee on Opportunities for the Spanish Speaking. When Robert Kennedy began his campaign for the Democratic presidential nomination in 1968, she joined his team as deputy director of the Hispanic division.

Traumatized by Kennedy's assassination, Polly left politics temporarily, taking an extended recuperative trip through Latin America. Upon her return she worked as director of Research Services for the Southwest Council of La Raza for two years. From 1971 to 1972 she served as director of Spanish Speaking Affairs for the Democratic National Committee.

In 1974 the Colorado state representative seat in her district fell vacant, and she decided to campaign for the nomination. She won it and was easily elected to the House of Representatives. Four years later she was also successful in her bid for a Colorado senate seat, the first Chicana to be elected to that office. In 1982 she was easily reelected to the state senate.

Polly Baca has been the recipient of numerous political and other honors and awards. Since 1981 she has been vice chair of the Democratic National Committee and currently also chairs the Colorado Senate Democratic caucus. Previously she was appointed to the executive committee of the Democratic Committee and to the board of directors of the Mexican American Legal Defense and Education Fund (MALDEF) as well as many other national and Colorado state boards. In 1968 she was selected as Outstanding Young Woman of America. During the 1970s she was named woman of the future by two national magazines. In 1980 she was one of eight state legislators picked by the American Council of Young Political Leaders to take part in a study tour of the Soviet Union, and a year later she was one of fifteen Americans chosen by the German Marshall Fund to participate in a "Successor Generation" seminar held outside Brussels, Belgium.

FURTHER READING: "Baca, Chávez Announce Plans," *Nuestro* 10:2 (March 1986); Lucy Chávez, "Colorado's Polly Baca-Barragán," *Nuestro* 4:2 (April 1980); "Hispanas Conocidas," *La Luz* 6:11 (November 1977); "Polly Baca Barragán: A Woman on the Move," *La Luz* 9:6 (August–September 1981); *Who's Who in the West, 1984–1985*, 19th ed., 1984.

BACA ZINN, MAXINE (1942–   ), sociologist, professor. Maxine Baca was born in Santa Fe, New Mexico, on 11 June 1942. After completing high school she entered California State College (now University) at Long Beach, from which she graduated in 1966 with a B.A. in sociology. Two years later she began graduate studies at the University of New Mexico and received her master's degree in sociology there in 1970, at the same time acting as instructor in the department. She then entered the doctoral program in sociology at the University of Oregon where she held a graduate teaching fellowship (1971–1973) and a Ford Foundation dissertation fellowship (1973–1975) and received her Ph.D. in 1978. Meanwhile in 1975 she began teaching at the University of Michigan at Flint, where she is currently professor in the sociology department. In 1984 she was visiting scholar in the Center for Research on Women at Memphis State University, and two years later was appointed visiting professor of sociology at the University of California, Berkeley.

Dr. Baca Zinn's areas of specialization are sex and gender roles, sociology of the family, and race and ethnic relations. She has published a dozen articles in scholarly journals and has read numerous papers and made invited presentations at various association meetings, conferences, and colloquia. Currently advisory editor to *Gender and Society*, from 1980 to 1983 she served as associate editor of *The Social Science Journal* and edited volume 19, no. 2, a symposium on social science research about Chicanos. She is the author of chapters in two sociological works and has coauthored two books with Dr. Stanley Eitzen:

Diversity in American Families, to be published by Harper and Row in 1987, and *The Reshaping of America*, forthcoming from Prentice-Hall.

Active in professional organizations, Maxine Baca Zinn was elected to a three-year term on the executive council of the American Sociological Association in 1985 and in that same year was president of the Western Social Science Association. Currently she serves on the Committee on Women's Employment and Related Social Issues, National Academy of Sciences.

FURTHER READING: Julio A. Martínez, *Chicano Scholars and Writers: A Bio-Bibliographical Directory*, Metuchen, N.J.: The Scarecrow Press, 1979.

BAEZ, JOAN (1941–   ), folksinger, political activist, songwriter. One of three daughters of Dr. Albert V. Báez, Mexico-born U.S. physicist and Professor Joan Bridge Báez, a drama teacher, Joan Báez was born 9 January 1941 in Staten Island, New York. She grew up in a number of college towns, showing great musical talent, learning to play the guitar at twelve, and later singing in the Palo Alto (California) High School choir. As a Mexican American who did not speak Spanish, she also grew up suffering an identity confusion. When the family moved from Stanford University to Harvard in the late 1950s, her interest in folk music was aroused by folk musicians in the Boston coffee shops, and her musical education expanded. Because of the social content of many folk songs, her Quaker upbringing, and her own experiences with racial prejudice, she quickly developed a social awareness and soon began her own career as a folksinger.

Joan Báez made her professional debut at the 1959 Newport Folk Festival where the stunning impact of her beautiful, clear voice awed the audience. Within a few years her simple style and pure soprano voice brought her a nationwide following. In the 1960s and early 1970s she frequently participated in antiwar rallies and demonstrations for equal rights for blacks and farm workers. In 1962 her political activities landed her on the cover of *Time*. She marched with Martin Luther King, Jr., held benefits for César Chávez's farm workers, confronted denials of civil rights, challenged the draft, and refused to pay taxes to be used in the Vietnam War. Her interest in world peace led to her founding the Institute for the Study of Nonviolence in 1965 and Humanitas International in 1979, and to her participation in and support of the work of Amnesty International.

Meanwhile, Joan Báez has made over thirty record albums, eight of which were gold albums (over 500,000 copies sold), and numerous singles. During the 1980s she has moved from pure folk into the broader field of balladry, but her political interests remain the same. In 1981 and 1983 she did a European concert tour which led to two new albums, "European Tour" and "Live Europe '83." In the summer of 1985 she opened the American half of the Live Aid concerts in Philadelphia, and in 1986 she participated in a six-city Amnesty International tour. On 22 June 1987 her first studio album in eight years, "Recently," was released by Gold Castle Records. Her best known single records are "There But For Fortune" and "The Night They Drove Old Dixie Down"; among her most successful albums were "Diamonds and Rust" (1975) and "Lovesong Album" (1976). Her second autobiography, *And A Voice to Sing With: A Memoir*, appeared late in 1986. (She published an earlier autobiographical reminiscence, titled *Daybreak*, in 1968.)

FURTHER READING: Joan Báez, *Daybreak*, Garden City, N.Y.: The Dial Press, 1968; *And A Voice to Sing With: A Memoir*, New York, N.Y.: Summit Books, 1986; Tim Goodman, "The Voice of Social Conscience," Palo Alto, Calif.: *Peninsular Times Tribune Calendar* (1 June 1986); Colman McCarthy, "Baez Comeback," *Washington Post Magazine* (1 December 1985).

BAÑUELOS, ROMANA ACOSTA (1925–), businesswoman, U.S. treasurer. Romana Acosta was born 20 March 1925 in the small Arizona copper-mining town of Miami of undocumented Mexican parents. During the Great Depression at age six she was forced to accompany her repatriating parents to Mexico. With her family resettled on a small ranch in the north Mexican state of Sonora, she grew up and was educated there. Toward the end of World War II at age nineteen she moved back to the United States, settling in Los Angeles, where she worked in a laundry and a clothing factory. In 1949 she began a small tortilla factory with $400 savings and subsequently developed and expanded it to a $12 million a year business, Ramona's Mexican Food Products, Inc., employing 400 workers and producing two dozen food items. In 1964 she diversified her business interests by helping to establish in East Los Angeles the Pan American National Bank in which she was a director and chairman of the board.

In 1969 Romana Bañuelos was named Outstanding Businesswoman of the Year in Los Angeles and less than two years later President Richard M. Nixon appointed her treasurer of the United States. The first Mexican American and the sixth woman to hold that post, she served from 17 December 1971 to 14 February 1974. While retaining some interest in politics, she has since devoted herself principally to her business activities.

FURTHER READING: Diana Martínez, " 'The Strength is in Money,' Says Romana Bañuelos," *Nuestro* 3:5 (June/July 1979); *Who's Who in America, 1976–1977*, 39th ed., 1976.

BARCELO, MARIA GERTRUDIS ("LA TULES") (1800–1852), businesswoman. Gertrudis Barceló was born in the Mexican state of Sonora of an upper-class family and had the rare privilege for a woman of the day—an education. Sometime before 1823 the family moved to Nuevo México and in that year was living in the small village of Valencia on the east bank of the Rio Grande just south of Albuquerque. Also in that same year Gertrudis married, retaining her maiden name, her property, and her right to make contracts. In 1825 she was operating a game of chance in a mining camp in the Ortiz Mountains south of Santa Fe. A decade later she and her husband were living in Santa Fe, and apparently she was already well established in society there.

By the end of the 1830s La Tules was a person of considerable importance and was reputed to be an advisor to her close friend, Governor Armijo.* In addition to operating an elegant gambling hall she reportedly was a heavy investor in the Santa Fe trade and had acquired several houses in Santa Fe. Her tastefully decorated home was the frequent rendezvous of fashionable and influential Santa Fe male society. For the first half of the 1840s she reigned as the arbiter of society and fashion in that city; but Anglos, whom she welcomed, saw her through narrow-lensed, puritanical glasses as an infamous and dissipated woman. Although her salon declined as a social center after the American occupation, she apparently continued her gambling activity until mid-century. Anglo leaders considered her too disreputable to associate with, but they were willing to accept her financial, and possibly political, support. Gertrudis Barceló died in the early spring of 1852 and was buried with great pomp and ceremony—to the extent of $1,600 in expenditures.

FURTHER READING: Janet Lecompte, "La Tules and the Americans," *Arizona and the West* 20:3 (Autumn 1978).

BARELA, CASIMIRO (1847–1920), senator, businessman. Casimiro Barela was born 4 March 1847 at Embudo, New Mexico, and grew up there and at Mora where he began his education. At Mora he came to the attention of the pastor (later archbishop) Jean B. Salpointe, who undertook the lad's education. For four years he lived and studied with Fr. Salpointe and then returned home to start the Barela Mercantile Store with his father and brothers. In 1867 the family moved to Las Animas County in southern Colorado, where the father and sons engaged in stockraising and later in merchandising. In 1869 Casimiro began his public life with election as justice of the peace. Two years later he was appointed county assessor and was elected to the territorial legislature. At the end of his legislative term he won reelection and in 1874 was elected sheriff of Las Animas County.

In 1875 Casimiro Barela was elected as a delegate to the state constitutional convention in which he took a leadership role. He secured provision in the Colorado constitution for protection of the civil rights of the Spanish-speaking as well as for publication of all laws in Spanish and English for twenty-five years. He was elected to the first state senate in 1876 and was regularly reelected thereafter. A strong Democratic leader in southern Colorado, he was twice elected president of the senate by his fellow legislators. He was also elected and appointed to various national, state, and local offices of importance and was even appointed consul at Denver for Mexico and Costa Rica. Not even his switch from the Democratic to the Republican party in 1900 prevented his reelection, but it did reduce his subsequent majorities, and in 1916 at age sixty-nine he was defeated for the state senate.

Barela retired to devote more time to his extensive properties in Colorado, New Mexico, and old Mexico and to his large cattle-raising operation (third largest in the state). He remained highly respected for his long record of public service and his political integrity and was widely known as "The Perpetual Senator" and "El Padre del Senado del Estado de Colorado." His long and successful career came to an end with his death in December 1920.

FURTHER READING: José Fernández, *Cuarenta años de legislador: biografía del Senador Casimiro Barela*, reprint, New York: Arno Press, 1976; Leroy Hafen, *Colorado and Its People*, 4 vols., New York: Lewis Historical Publishing Co. 1948.

BARELA, PATROCINIO (1902–1964), *santero*, artist. Born in the mining town of Bisbee, Arizona, Patrocinio Barela was the son of a Mexican folk healer and itinerant worker father. His mother and only sister died before he was five, and he and his brother Nicolás grew up in a succession of farms and labor camps where his father worked. When his father settled in Cañón near Taos, New Mexico and remarried, Patrocinio sporadically attended school, where he was encouraged to draw, carve, and mold clay figures but never learned to read and write. At age eleven he ran away from home. As a result he was boarded for a while with a black family in Denver, Colorado, by juvenile authorities. Here he learned English and Anglo culture.

As soon as he was old enough, Patrocinio became an itinerant laborer, traveling around the West for years and earning a bare living. In 1930 he returned to New Mexico and settled in Cañón. He soon married a woman with three children and, to support his new family, did odd jobs. Sometime in the very early 1930s he discovered in himself an extraordinary ability to carve and began to make religious figures.

When Franklin D. Roosevelt's New Deal came to New Mexico in 1933, Barela was one of many Nuevo Mexicanos who found employment in its programs. His carving skills were brought to the attention of the Federal Art Project (FAP) director, and in 1936 Barela went to work for FAP in Taos. In that same year an exhibit of art work done under the auspices of the FAP at the Museum of Modern Art included his work. Barela evolved his style and expanded his subject matter to include *bultos*, figures expressing the universal themes of birth, suffering, and death. He also carved doors and massive Spanish colonial-style furniture. His work soon achieved wide recognition, and in 1939 a collection of his carvings was exhibited at the New York World's Fair.

When the FAP was terminated in 1943, Barela set up a workshop near his house, where he continued to carve *bultos* when he was not working as field hand to support his family. Despite his growing fame, he continued to act as his own salesman during the post–World War II era, in emergencies sometimes selling his work for a trifle. In late October 1964 Barela died as the result of a fire that broke out in his workshop during the night.

An excellent collection of Barela's carvings is on display in the Harwood Foundation of the University of New Mexico at Taos. In addition, examples of his work over the years have been purchased by various museums including the Museum of Modern Art in New York, the New Mexico Museum of Fine Arts, the San Francisco Museum, the Dallas Museum, and the Baltimore Museum.

His works are also extensively represented in many private collections throughout the country. Articles about him and his work have been published in *Time*, *Life*, *New Mexico Quarterly*, *Américas*, and other journals.

FURTHER READING: Mildred Crews, "Saint-Maker from Taos," *Américas* 21:3 (March 1969); Mildred Crews et al., "Patrocinio Barela, Taos Wood Carver," *La Luz* 3:8 (November 1974); Vernon Hunter, "Concerning Patrocinio Barela," in *Art for the Millions*, ed. Francis V. O'Connor, Greenwich, Conn.: New York Graphic Society, 1973; Lenore G. Marshall, "Patrocinio Barela," *Art* 30:11 (August 1956).

BARRIO, RAYMOND (1921–   ), writer, teacher, artist. Born 27 August 1921 in West Orange, New Jersey, Raymond Barrio grew up there, but has spent most of his life since high school in California. During World War II he served in Europe in the U.S. Army from 1943 to 1946. He studied at City College of New York, the University of Southern California, and Yale University, and earned his B.A. in humanities from the University of California, Berkeley (1947) and a bachelor of fine arts degree from Art Center College, Los Angeles (1952). During most of the 1950s his primary interest was in painting rather than writing, and he made a living from the sale of his paintings, which were shown in more than eighty exhibitions across the United States. Marriage and a family turned him to teaching in the early 1960s as a more secure livelihood. He taught at a number of two-year colleges in the San Francisco Bay area, at San Jose State University, at Sonoma State University (California), and at the University of California at Santa Barbara. While he specialized in teaching art history and etching, he has taught a wide variety of courses from anthropology to writing. He has now retired from teaching and devotes his full time to writing.

Although Barrio first looked on writing as an avocation, as early as 1966 he created his Ventura Press in order to publish his works. Since then he has written a large number of articles and books, often illustrated with his own etchings and mostly self-published. He is best known as the author of *The Plum Plum Pickers* (1969), which has sold over 30,000 copies and is considered to be one of the leading novels of the contemporary Chicano literary renaissance. In *The Plum Plum Pickers* Barrio presents a fictional portrayal of Mexican American migrant experiences that elaborates in a historical way the group's struggle for a better way of life. He has also authored *Experiments in Modern Art* (1968), *Mexico's Art and Chicano Artists* (1975), *The Devil's Apple Corps* (1976), and a number of other works. Since 1980 he has authored a weekly newspaper column titled "Barrio's Estuary," and in 1985 he published *A Political Portfolio*, a collection of these columns. Selections from his writings, especially *The Plum Plum Pickers*, have been widely reprinted in anthologies. He also has written articles published in art magazines and short fiction for literary journals.

FURTHER READING: *Contemporary Authors*, New Revision Series, vol. 11, 1984; Nasario García, "Nasario García Interviews Raymond Barrio," *Revista Chicano-Riqueña* 13:1 (Spring 1985); Julio A. Martínez and Francisco A. Lomelí, *Chicano Literature: A Reference Guide*, Westport, Conn.: Greenwood Press, 1985; *Who's Who in America, 1984–1985*, 43rd ed., 1984.

BEAUBIEN, CARLOS (1800–1864), landowner, merchant, judge, fur trapper. Charles H. Trotier, Sieur de Beaubien, a naturalized Mexican, was born in the province of Quebec, Canada, of a noble family but moved to St. Louis, where he worked in the fur trade as a teenager. In 1823 he traveled to New Mexico with fellow fur trapper and trader Antoine Robidoux just after that area was opened up by the Missouri–Santa Fe trade. Beaubien developed a lucrative business in Taos, owned a rancho, married a Nuevo Mexicana of prominent family, took Mexican citizenship in 1829, and became a local justice of the peace. Early in 1841, in partnership with Guadalupe Miranda, this shrewd man was awarded by Governor Manuel Armijo* a large land grant later widely known as the Maxwell grant after his son-in-law.

When the United States invaded and took over New Mexico, Beaubien, as one of the "American Party," strongly supported the new government of Colonel Stephen Kearny, who named him a judge of the new high court. He presided over the trial of those charged in the Taos rebellion of January 1847. Despite his death sentence for the leaders, some of whom were responsible for the murder of his son Narciso, he continued to be highly respected. In 1848 he was a member of the convention that met at Santa Fe to petition for statehood and of the 1849 convention, which favored territorial status. During the last decade of his life Beaubien, pursuing a vision of a great landed "empire," concerned himself primarily with his land grants. He remained a leading New Mexico figure of great influence and popularity among both Anglos and Nuevo Mexicanos.

FURTHER READING: Howard R. Lamar, *The Far Southwest, 1846–1912*, New York: W. W. Norton & Co., 1977; Ralph E. Twitchell, *The History of the Military Occupation of the Territory of New Mexico . . .* , reprint, New York: Arno Press, 1976.

BENAVIDES, PLACIDO (1836–1919), rancher, Raza leader. Plácido Benavides was born in Louisiana, to which his Tejano parents, who supported the Texas revolt against Mexico, nevertheless were forced to flee to avoid violence from Anglos after the Alamo and Goliad battles. After two years in Louisiana the family was able to return to its Texas ranch near Lavaca Bay. We know little about Plácido's early years, but in the mid-1850s he and his mother moved southwest to the Corpus Christi area in order to live on an uncle's ranch. Soon Benavides began acquiring land, which became the basis of his own ranch. During the Civil War he fought for the Confederacy and by the end of that conflict was a successful stockraiser. A decade later his worth had increased greatly; he owned 1,120 acres of land and a herd of 345 horses worth $10.00 apiece.

In 1875 a Corpus Christi–Laredo railroad was begun, and the route ran through Plácido's property. When the railroad was completed, he acceded to a request to locate a depot on his lands and later donated eighty acres around the depot for what was to become the town of Benavides, Duval County, Texas—named after him. During the 1880s he continued his horse raising, experimented with cotton as a crop, and took an interest in local politics. For the rest of his life

Benavides remained a prominent figure in Duval County, one of the very few Mexican Americans to have a town named after him.

FURTHER READING: Arnoldo de León, *Benavides: The Town and Its Founder*, Benavides, Tex.: Benavides Centennial Committee, 1980.

BENAVIDES, SANTOS (1823–1891), politician, merchant, soldier. Santos Benavides was born in Laredo, Texas, son of the Mexican captian in command of the troops stationed there and of a granddaughter of Tomás Sánchez, founder of Laredo. He grew up in Laredo attending school there and abroad, obtaining an excellent education for the times. He also learned the many aspects of cattle raising and acquired a basic knowledge of merchandising by clerking in a Laredo general store. At the end of the 1830s he actively participated in the Mexican border separatist movement and early in the American period became active in local Texas politics, where he supported the plantation aristocracy.

At the outset of the Civil War the company of troops he had helped raise to protect settlers against Indian raids became a part of the Confederate forces, and Benavides was named a major in the 33rd Texas Cavalry. During the war years he was aggressively active in the Texas-Mexican border region, recruiting Mexican Americans for the South and, most important, securing the vital cotton trade with Mexico from the attacks of border bandits, the followers of Juan "Cheno" Cortina,* and raiding Indians. He was quickly promoted to colonel, the highest military rank of any Mexican American in the Civil War, and was recommended for promotion to general toward the end of the fighting.

After the war Benavides organized a mercantile business at Laredo in partnership with his younger brother Cristóbal. In time S. Benavides and Brother developed an extensive wholesale and retail business on both sides of the border. Several years later the partnership was terminated, and Santos operated the firm by himself until his death more than two decades later. During the 1870s his Mexican business interests involved him in opposing General Porfirio Díaz's attempts to unseat President Sebastián Lerdo de Tejada's government.

In the post–Civil War period Benevides quickly accepted the verdict of the war and returned to active political life. In 1856 he had been elected mayor of Laredo and two years later, chief justice of Webb County. Now he was twice elected alderman in Laredo and from 1879 to 1885 was elected to the sixteenth, seventeenth, and eighteenth state legislatures, in which he played an important role on several committees. As might be expected of a Mexican border separatist and ex-Confederate, he was always a staunch supporter of states' rights. In 1884 he was named a Texas commissioner to the World's Cotton Exposition in New Orleans, partly because of his political position and partly because of his prominence as a Texas cotton grower. He died on 9 November 1891, highly esteemed as an eminent soldier, citizen, and gentleman.

FURTHER READING: Carlos Larralde, *Mexican American Movements and Leaders*, Los Alamitos, Calif.: Hwong Publishing Co., 1976; John D. Riley, "Santos Benavides:

His Influence on the Lower Rio Grande, 1823–1891," Ph.D. diss., Texas Christian University, 1976.

BRAVO, FRANCISCO (1910–   ), physician, civic leader, businessman. Born 2 April 1910 in the small southern California agricultural center of Santa Paula of Mexican immigrant parents, Francisco Bravo grew up and was educated there. In Santa Paula High School he was an able student despite extensive after-school work at home and around town to help support the family. During summers the family followed the agricultural harvests. After high school he entered the University of Southern California school of pharmacy and continued to support himself by working at various jobs and following the crops in summer.

After graduation in the mid–1930s, Francisco Bravo took a position as a pharmacist. While working, he continued his education at the University of Southern California, earning a master's degree in sociology. By this time the young pharmacist-/sociologist decided to study medicine. After six years at Stanford University he received his M.D., and later did four years of postgraduate work in surgery. Dr. Bravo returned to Los Angeles and began to set up a private practice. He also opened a free medical clinic for Mexican Americans in 1941. However, his work was interrupted by World War II, when he joined the U.S. Medical Corps, serving for more than three years in the South Pacific. At the war's end he returned to his civilian practice and his clinic. He also set up scholarships for students of Mexican descent, enabling them to study pharmacy, medicine, nursing, dentistry, and teaching.

An extremely energetic man, Dr. Francisco Bravo also extended his horizons beyond medicine. In 1964 he was one of the founders, president, and chairman of the board of the Pan American Bank in East Los Angeles. He is a prominent southern California agriculturist, operating a 1,500-acre, $5 million farming project in La Puente, California, where he raises citrus, grain, hogs, and cattle. He is also a real estate developer. With these varied interests he has been selected to serve on numerous medical, civic, and governmental committees and boards—a service he performs gladly. Among his more rewarding appointments have been as advisory board member of the University of California, Riverside, and Los Angeles State University and as a member of the board of directors of the National Conference of Christians and Jews. Believing strongly in participation in community affairs, Dr. Bravo has taken an active role in politics and in 1967 was appointed by the mayor of Los Angeles as one of six persons to serve on the committee to revise the city charter.

FURTHER READING: Al Martínez, *Rising Voices: Profiles of Hispano-American Lives*, New York: New American Library, 1974; Arturo Palacios, ed., *Mexican American Directory*, 1969–1970 ed., Washington, D.C.: Executive Systems Corp., 1969.

BUONO, ANTONIO DEL (1900–1975), labor organizer, community leader. Born in El Paso of a Mexican mother and a Sicilian immigrant father, Antonio was forced to leave school at age ten when his father died and he had to help support the family. In his mid-teen years he lived in northern Mexico, where he worked for Mormon farmers who had emigrated from the United States. Moving to California in the early 1920s, he continued to work in the fields until 1927 when he moved into landscape work in the Los Angeles area. During the depression years of the 1930s he drew upon his reading about social movements and began organizing landscape gardeners and farmworkers. From this beginning he expanded to organize other workers in Los Angeles, Orange, and San Diego counties and to occupy various labor union positions. In 1938 Governor Culbert Olson named del Buono to the state Labor Commission, but he turned the offer down, concentrating on his horticulture education instead. In 1947 he received his certificate in Ornamental Horticulture from California State Polytechnic College. About this time del Buono moved to Camarillo, California, where he worked in horticulture.

Del Buono continued to be interested in problems of the poor and was influenced by Sol Alinsky, César Chávez,* and Fred Ross, Sr. In the early 1950s he became president of the Oxnard (California) Community Service Organization and took an active role in local politics, arranging voter registration drives and working in political campaigns. A decade later he moved to Gilroy, California, where he helped establish a local office of the California Rural Legal Assistance (CRLA). In 1965 he began a ten-year career as field representative for the CRLA, meanwhile also teaching in the School of Social Work at San Jose State University and giving lectures at other educational institutions. When state regulations forced his retirement at age seventy-two, he began working with a Gilroy senior citizen group, Las Rositas. This last activity was cut short by his death in 1975. An omnivorous reader, Antonio del Buono was largely self-taught and throughout his long life preached the importance of education—"the magic key."

BURCIAGA, CECILIA PRECIADO DE (1945–   ), administrator, educator. Cecilia Preciado was born 17 May 1945 in Pomona, California, and grew up and received her early education in nearby Chino. When she graduated from high school, she persuaded her father to let her enter California State University, Fullerton, where she received her B.A. in 1968. During the following years she taught in high school and adult education and completed her M.A. in the field of sociology policy studies at the University of California in Riverside. In 1970 she took a position with the U.S. Commission on Civil Rights in Washington, D.C., and two years later became a research analyst for the commission.

Cecilia Preciado de Burciaga returned to California in 1974 as assistant to both the president and provost of Stanford University for Chicano affairs. Three years later she was promoted to the job of assistant provost for faculty affairs and was named one of the California representatives to the National Conference for the Observance of International Women's Year at Houston, Texas. This return to the national scene led to her being selected by President Jimmy Carter as one of forty women on his National Advisory Committee for Women in the following year. In 1985 she was promoted to associate dean of graduate studies

at Stanford, making her one of the highest-ranking Hispanic women in higher
education and extending her influence beyond Stanford University.

As a result of her minority and feminist interests and her academic role
Burciaga is a member of numerous boards and commissions in California and
nationally and has been especially involved in activities for the advancement of
women. She is currently a member of the Board of Trustees of the Educational
Testing Service in Princeton, N.J., serving on the Committee on Minority
Graduate Education. Among her honors is the Eleanor D. Roosevelt
Humanitarian Award from the San Francisco United Nations Association.

FURTHER READING: "Cecilia Preciado de Burciaga," *La Luz* 6:11 (November
1977); Lois Coit, "Remembering the 'Ones Not There,' " *The Christian Science Monitor*
(31 July 1984); Lynn Johnson, "Cecilia Burciaga Encourages Political Involvement,"
Aurora (March 1979).

BURCIAGA, JOSE ANTONIO (1940–   ), artist, poet, journalist, writer. Born
of Mexican immigrant parents in the Texas border town of El Paso, José Antonio
Burciaga grew up and received his early education there. His mother, who had
been a schoolteacher in Mexico, early inculcated in him a love of reading, and
he showed a talent for drawing from kindergarten on. Growing up, he took no
art courses but read voraciously, especially biographies and the novels of J. D.
Salinger and Ernest Hemingway. In 1960 he joined the U.S. Air Force and spent
one year in Iceland and three in Spain, where he discovered the poetry of Federico
García Lorca. In the Air Force writing was an important part of his job. Released
from the service, he entered the University of Texas at El Paso, took his first
art lessons, and graduated in 1968 with an A.B. in fine arts. He has since taken
graduate coursework at several institutions. Out of school, he got a job as a
graphic artist working for the Civil Service and later for the Central Intelligence
Agency in Washington, D.C.

In 1974 Burciaga had the first exhibit of his art—about thirty paintings—at
L'Enfant Plaza Theatre in Washington, D.C., and also moved to California.
Here he began to take part in the Bay Area Chicano art movement and to expand
greatly his writing activities. In 1976 he self-published a volume of poetry with
poet Bernice Zamora under the title *Restless Serpents*, the best known of his
literary works. In the following year he received considerable publicity over a
protest that he and a fellow muralist made at the dedication of their mural, titled
"Danzas Mexicanas," in Redwood City, California. During this time he also
was doing a good deal of cover art and illustration for a wide variety of
publications including first and second grade bilingual readers of the Macmillan
Publishing Company. In addition, he was working as an artist-illustrator for the
Stanford Research Institute and was project director of the Multicultural Task
Force, San Mateo County Arts Council. Between 1969 and 1976 he had more
than a dozen one-man shows.

Beginning about 1977 Burciaga greatly enlarged his literary output. In addition
to short stories and expository articles published in journals and anthologies, he

wrote articles for newspapers all over the United States. He also began writing essays for Hispanic Link, a Washington-based news service which spread his literary reputation even wider. In the past three or four years most of his artistic output has been concentrated in the field of journalism, but he continues to be widely known as a muralist and illustrator.

Burciaga's art has been exhibited in Washington, Atlantic City, San Francisco, El Paso, Ciudad Juárez (Mexico), and in many California cities. In addition to all this he has found time to initiate a well-received career as a comedic actor. He is currently putting together a collection of his essays for publication.

FURTHER READING: Nasario García, "Interview with José Antonio Burciaga," *Hispania* 68:4 (December 1985); Julio A. Martínez, *Chicano Scholars and Writers: A Bio-Bibliographical Directory*, Metuchen, N.J.: The Scarecrow Press, 1979.

C

CABEZA DE BACA, EZEQUIEL (1864–1917), political leader, newspaperman. Born into the important and large Cabeza de Baca clan during the waning days of the Civil War on the family ranch near Las Vegas, New Mexico, Ezequiel was destined to surpass his father, Tomás, who was a judge and member of the territorial legislature. He received his elementary school education in Las Vegas where he later also attended the Jesuits' Las Vegas College from 1878 to 1882 as a day student. After completing his formal education, he first worked as a mercantile clerk, then taught for several years in rural schools of New Mexico, worked as a railroad postal clerk, and also served as deputy clerk of the probate court.

At the beginning of the 1890s Ezequiel went to work for Félix Martínez,* a leading southwestern politician and businessman. In 1891 he took the job of associate editor of Martínez's weekly newspaper, *La Voz del Pueblo*, and two years later began working as deputy clerk for Martínez when the latter was elected to a four-year term as secretary to the Fourth District Court in San Miguel County. Both activities gave him direction and experience in what was to become his life's work. Along with Martínez he was also active at this time in founding and organizing El Partido del Pueblo Unido, a populist third-party movement in northeastern New Mexico that challenged the dominant Republican party. After some limited success, the elections of 1894 saw Ezequiel running for the clerkship of the probate court; however, he was defeated. In 1900 he became a quarter owner of *La Voz del Pueblo*, which had developed into a powerful political voice attracting readers even outside the state.

In the ensuing decade Ezequiel Cabeza de Baca became a leading political figure in the northeastern part of the state as the result of his newspaper editorship and his increasing involvement in the Democratic party, in which he rose to county chairmanship. Both in the newspaper and in politics he was a strong advocate of La Raza rights, especially in education and land issues. Although he had opposed ratification of the 1910 New Mexico constitution as too weak in protecting Hispanic American rights, he was nominated and elected as the state's first lieutenant governor in the following year, and in 1913 was number two in the legislature's vote for U.S. senator. As lieutenant governor he used his influence to support education bills in a Republican-controlled legislature. At the end of his term as lieutenant governor, despite his ill health, he was unanimously nominated and then elected to the governorship. A month and a half after his inauguration he died of pernicious anemia in Santa Fe on 18 February 1917 and was buried in Las Vegas. In addition to the positions already mentioned, Cabeza de Baca also served as deputy assessor, business manager of *La Voz*, treasurer of the Martínez Publishing Company, and delegate to the Democratic National Convention as well as various local Democratic conventions.

FURTHER READING: Anselmo Arellano, "Don Ezequiel C de Baca and the Politics of San Miguel County," M.A. thesis, New Mexico Highlands University, 1974; Maurilio Vigil, *Los Patrones: Profiles of Hispanic Political Leaders in New Mexico History*, Washington, D.C.: University Press of America, 1980.

CABEZA DE BACA, FERNANDO E. (1937–   ), businessman, governmental leader. A direct descendant of the famous Spanish explorer, Alvar Núñez Cabeza de Vaca, Fernando was born in Albuquerque, New Mexico, one of five children of Hispanic schoolteacher parents. After spending part of his early childhood in El Paso, Texas, he was reared and educated in New Mexico. At the end of the 1950s he received his degree in public administration from the University of New Mexico in Albuquerque and later studied law at the University of New Mexico school of law. During the Vietnam conflict he served in the U.S. Army Intelligence Airborne Corps, coming out of the war disabled and decorated.

In the late 1960s and early 1970s Fernando served as commissioner of the New Mexico department of transportation, as special assistant to the chairman of the U.S. Civil Service Commission, and as western regional director in the Department of Health, Education and Welfare as well as chairman of the Federal Regional Council for the Western United States. In September 1974 Gerald Ford appointed him special assistant to the president. In this role he became, at thirty-seven, both the youngest and the highest ranking federal executive of Hispanic descent.

Fernando Cabeza de Baca has had a long history of involvement in veterans' service organizations and civil rights groups such as the American Legion, DAV, LULAC, and IMAGE. He has been equally prominent in the leadership of business organizations including the Latin American Manufacturers Association, Hispanic Coalition for Economic Recovery, and Center for International Private Enterprise. He is past chairman of the Advisory Committee on Minority Business of the U.S. Department of Commerce. He is president of the Del Bac Company and an associate of the Vanir Group, Inc., a national real estate development firm. He has also been extremely active in Republican party politics, largely at the national level.

An authority on minority businesses, Cabeza de Baca has lectured widely on the free enterprise system; he was a visiting lecturer at Harvard University. He has been awarded honorary doctorates by Whittier College (California) and the University of Windsor (Canada).

FURTHER READING: "Presidential Assistant Fernando C. de Baca," *La Luz* 4:5 (September–October 1975).

CAMARILLO, ALBERT M. (1948–   ), historian, professor. Albert Camarillo was born 9 February 1948 in the southern California town of Compton, the last of six children born to Rose (López) and Benjamín Camarillo. He grew up and received his early education in Compton and in 1966, with a scholarship from the Mexican American Political Association, followed an older brother to the nearby University of California at Los Angeles (UCLA). Greatly influenced by the Chicano Movement of the late 1960s, he changed majors from biology to history and received his A.B. four years later. With the help of a UCLA graduate fellowship and later Ford Foundation fellowships, he entered the doctoral program in history, centering on the Mexican American, and earned his Ph.D. in 1975. He then accepted a position as assistant professor of history at Stanford University, having previously been a lecturer in urban studies at Yale University in the summer of 1971 and having taught the academic year 1971–1972 at the University of California at Santa Barbara. He is currently associate professor of history at Stanford and director of the Inter-University Program for Latino Research.

Albert Camarillo's principal scholarly work is *Chicanos in a Changing Society* (1979). He is also the author of *Chicanos in California* (1984), a popular history, and currently is under contract with Oxford University Press for a book titled *Mexicans in American Cities*. He has edited or coedited *The State of Chicano Research in Family, Labor, and Migration Roles* (1983), *Work, Family, Sex Roles, and Language* (1980), *The American Southwest: Myth and Reality* (1979), and *Furia y Muerte: Los Bandidos Chicanos* (1973). Active in bibliographic studies, he is the compiler of *Latinos in the United States* (1986), *Mexican Americans in Urban Society: A Selected Bibliography* (1986), and *Selected Bibliography for Chicano Studies* (1975). He is the author of a dozen published articles and five times as many papers or presentations on a variety of Mexican American topics. Deeply interested in research and the educational problems of Mexican Americans, Camarillo was actively involved in the founding of the National Association for Chicano Studies. From 1980 to 1985 he was the founding director of the Stanford University's Center for Chicano Research. He was also a cofounder of the Inter-University Program for Latino Research and since 1985 has served as its executive director.

FURTHER READING: Kay Mills, "Beyond the Barrio, History and Hope," *Los Angeles Times* (22 December 1985); Karen J. Winkler, "A Grant-seeking Scholar is Told: Sorry, Look Elsewhere," *The Chronicle of Higher Education* (3 September 1986).

CAMPA, ARTHUR LEON (1905–1978), folklorist, professor. Arturo Campa was born 20 February 1905 in the Mexican west coast town of Guaymas, Sonora, to Methodist missionary parents. When his father was killed by Villistas nine years later, the family moved to Texas, where Arthur grew up on a ranch near El Paso. He received his early education in El Paso and also worked as a delivery boy to help with family finances. After high school Campa attended the University of New Mexico at Albuquerque, graduating in 1928 and teaching for one year at Albuquerque High School. He then returned to the university for graduate studies and received his M.A. in 1930. During the ensuing decade he taught in the modern language department at the university while he worked in the summers on his doctorate at Columbia University. His formal education culminated with his Ph.D. from Columbia in 1940. Six years later he left the University of New Mexico to accept a position as chairman of the modern languages department of the University of Denver. He continued as chairman of the Department of Modern Languages and Literature and taught there until he retired in 1972.

During World War II Professor Campa saw service in Italy and North Africa as a combat intelligence officer in the Air Force and subsequently served in various capacities for the U.S. Department of State. As the result of State Department sponsorship as a lecturer in Spain, he was named a corresponding member of the Real Academia Hispano-Americana at Cádiz. Between 1955 and 1957 he served as cultural attache to the U.S. embassy at Lima, Peru.

Campa's particular area of interest was folklore, especially of the Southwest, and he wrote on the legends of that area and on cultural differences between Anglo and Mexican Americans. He was active in a number of folklore societies of the U.S. and Latin America. Among his important publications are *A Bibliography of Spanish Folklore in New Mexico* (1930); *Spanish Religious Folktheatre in the Southwest* (1934); *Treasures of the Sangre de Cristos* (1962); and his posthumously published *Hispanic Culture in the Southwest* (1979).

FURTHER READING: *Contemporary Authors: A Bio-Bibliographical Guide to Current Authors and Their Works*, vols. 17–18, Detroit: Gale Research Co., 1967; Philip Sonnichsen, ''Arthur León Campa,'' *La Luz* 7:12 (December 1978).

CANALES, ANTONIO (1800–1852), soldier, politician. Born in the important northeastern Mexican center of Monterrey into a large border clan, Canales studied for the law and became a young liberal lawyer supporting the 1824 Mexican federalist constitution. Like most Mexican leaders in the northeast he strongly opposed President Antonio López de Santa Anna's converting the Mexican republic into a centralist state in the mid–1830s. As *comandante* in the state of Tamaulipas, he supported the Texans in their protest against Santa Anna's government until their intent to establish complete independence of Mexico became evident. After Texas independence he favored the creation of a northeastern Republic of the Rio Grande, encompassing the Nueces Triangle as well as the south side of the river and in 1839 organized a revolt from his headquarters north of the Rio Grande.

In January 1840 Canales and other federalist leaders from Tamaulipas, Nuevo León, and Coahuila met at Laredo, where they organized a provisional government with Canales as commander in chief of the ''army.'' They proclaimed Laredo their capital. Defeated by central government forces in March, they withdrew into Texas where they regrouped and recruited volunteers. With unofficial Texas government aid and a group of Anglo Texan auxiliaries they recrossed the Rio Grande in June and were defeated a second time. Canales now deserted his allies and made his peace with Mexican centralism. He was rewarded with a commission as general in the army and now fought against his former federalist friends. Later during the United States invasion of Mexico by General Zachary Taylor's army he led a guerrilla action against the Americans. After the war he became governor of Tamaulipas in 1851, a position he still held when he died the next year.

FURTHER READING: Paul Horgan, *Great River: The Rio Grande in North American History*, vol. 2, New York: Rinehart, 1954.

CANDELARIA, NASH (1928–   ), novelist, marketing expert. Nash Candelaria was born 7 May 1928 in Los Angeles, California, where his father was a postal clerk but is a Nuevo Mexicano by feeling and background. His ancestry goes back to the seventeenth century in New Mexico as do his cultural memories, and he considers himself a Nuevo Mexicano accidentally born in California. As he grew up, mostly in Los Angeles in Anglo neighborhoods, and excelled in high school where he was a student body officer, he also spent summers in Los Candelarias near Albuquerque in an Hispanic environment. Urged by his father to get a good education, he entered the University of California at Los Angeles and graduated in 1948 with a B.S. in chemistry.

After college he first went to work for a local pharmaceutical firm, Don Baxter, Inc., and also began to read extensively and write seriously, taking evening courses in writing and scripting. When the Korean conflict erupted in 1950, he enlisted as a lieutenant in the Air Force, and while in the service wrote his first novel. After Korea he considered going back to college, but instead in 1953 he took a job as a technical writer with Atomics International, followed by several positions in communications and marketing. In 1967 he went to work as advertising manager for Varian Associates, Inc., a scientific instrument firm of Palo Alto, California. During this period he also wrote six more (unpublished) novels; in 1977 he self-published *Memories of the Alhambra*. Five years later, after an unclear illness, he resigned from Varian to devote himself full time to his writing. However, in 1985 the economics of novel writing forced him to take a job as a marketing writer.

As a writer Nash Candelaria is best known for his somewhat autobiographical *Memories of the Alhambra*. While working for Varian he continued to write his trilogy, begun with *Memories* and now expanded to a quartet. He found a publisher for his sequel, *Not by the Sword*, which came out in 1982, and three years later published the third novel of the quartet, *Inheritance of Strangers*. In the first half of the 1980s he also published nearly a dozen short stories. *Not by the Sword* received the Before Columbus Foundation's American Book Award and was a finalist for the Western Writers of America's Best Western Historical

Novel award. Currently he has a collection of short stories in press with the Bilingual Press under the title *The Day the Cisco Kid Shot John Wayne*. Candelaria is considered by many to be one of the top ten Chicano novelists. His novels have been excerpted and his short stories reprinted in many anthologies. In March 1987 he lectured at Rutgers University as part of a series featuring six distinguished Hispanic writers.

FURTHER READING: Jane Bowden, ed. *Contemporary Authors*, vols. 69–72, Detroit: Gale Research Co., 1978; [Juan] Bruce-Novoa, "Nash Candelaria: An Interview," *De Colores* 5:1, 2 (1980); Julio A. Martínez and Francisco A. Lomelí, *Chicano Literature: A Reference Guide*, Westport, Conn.: Greenwood Press, 1985.

CARBAJAL, JOSE M. J. (also CARVAJAL) (c. 1810–1874), political leader. Carbajal was born in San Antonio, Texas, at a time of great confusion and uncertainty resulting from the Mexican revolution for independence from Spain. His father died while he was quite young, and as a lad entering his teens, he became a friend of Stephen Austin who was closely associated with his cousin, José Antonio Navarro.* In 1823 he accompanied a friend of Austin's to Kentucky, where he went to school and later apprenticed at the tanning and saddle-making trades. While in Kentucky, he came under the influence of the religious reformer Alexander Campbell and became a convert to his Disciples of Christ protestantism. In 1830 he returned to Texas where Austin secured for him an appointment as a surveyor. As result he became one of the founding settlers of Martín de León's Texas colony at Victoria. During the difficulties between the Texans and Mexican president Santa Anna's centralist government he acted as secretary to the San Antonio *cabildo*. Early in 1835 he was elected to represent San Antonio in the Coahuila-Texas legislature and in the following year was chosen as a delegate to the Texas constitutional convention but was unable to attend.

During the Texas revolt against Mexican centralism Carbajal fought with the rebels, was captured by Mexican forces, was imprisoned at Matamoros, and later escaped. Forced into a long exile at New Orleans along with the de León family after the battle of San Jacinto and having been stripped of his lands, he ceased considering himself a Texan. After Texas independence he returned to Texas seeking help in his fight for an independent republic of the border region, a Republic of the Sierra Madre. In 1839–1841 he was a leader along with Antonio Canales* in the so called "War of the Federation" against Mexico, and in 1846–1847 he fought against the U.S. in the United States–Mexican War.

Between 1851 and 1855 José Carbajal led a number of filibustering attacks on local Mexican forces, always in the name of federalism. He settled first in Coahuila and then in Tamaulipas, where he had become *comandante* of the state troops by 1861. In the next year he joined the Mexican liberals and was appointed governor of Tamaulipas by Benito Juárez. After fighting against the French invaders with the rank of general of division, he was sent in 1865 as President Benito Juárez's confidential agent to the United States to secure financial aid and military supplies. He later moved across the Rio Grande into Hidalgo County, Texas, on the border and in 1872 recrossed the river, settling in Soto La Marina, Tamaulipas, away from the border. Here he died two years later.

FURTHER READING: Harbert Davenport, "General José María Jesús Carabajal," *Southwestern Historical Quarterly* 55 (April 1952); Ernest C. Shearer, "The Carvajal Disturbances," *Southwestern Historical Quarterly* 55 (October 1951).

CARDENAS, ROBERTO L. (1920–   ), army officer. Roberto Cárdenas was born 10 March 1920 in Mérida, the capital of Yucatán, Mexico. The family immigrated to the United States, and he grew up in San Diego where he attended school. At nineteen he joined the California National Guard and earned his pilot wings and second lieutenant's commission a few months before Pearl Harbor. Between 1941 and January 1944 he served in various capacities as an instructor and flight test officer and then went overseas as a B–24 pilot. After being wounded in a bombing mission over Germany, he was returned to the United States where, after further training, he became an experimental test pilot. He was deeply involved in pioneering the new jet aircraft development in the Air Force. From 1949 onward he attended a number of service schools and served in various administrative positions. In 1955 he graduated from the University of New Mexico with a B.S. in mechanical engineering.

From 1955 to 1957 Cárdenas served as commander of three Air Force units in Okinawa and on his return to the United States was sent to the Air War College. In August 1958 he was assigned to USAF headquarters for a four-year period in which he served as deputy chief and chief. At the end of this term he returned to a field command at MacDill Air Force Base in Florida and then went back to Okinawa from 1964 to 1966 as commander of the Eighteenth Tactical Wing. After three years of command in the United States and promotion to brigadier general, in July 1969 he was assigned as vice-commander of the Sixteenth Air Force headquartered in Spain. Two years later he assumed duties on the Joint Strategic Target Planning Staff.

General Cárdenas has been the recipient of numerous medals and decorations; among them are the Air Medal, Air Force Commendation Medal, Legion of Merit, and Distinguished Flying Cross.

FURTHER READING: José Andrés Chacón, "Brigadier General Roberto L. Cárdenas," *La Luz* 1:9 (January 1973).

CARR, VIKKI, (FLORENCIA BICENTA DE CASILLAS MARTÍNEZ CARDONA) (1940–   ), singer. Born in El Paso, Texas, on 19 July 1940, the eldest of seven children born to Carlos Cardona, construction engineer, and his wife and raised in southern California, Vikki Carr grew up singing. Her father played the guitar at home, and at age four Florencia made her singing debut in a Christmas play. The family had moved to California while she was still an infant and she grew up in Rosemead, an eastern suburb of Los Angeles, attending parochial school and then Rosemead High where she took all of the music courses she could and participated in all of the musical productions. On weekends she sang with local bands, and on graduation in 1958 she accepted a job as soloist with Pepe Callahan's Mexican-Irish Band. From then on it was a steady rise in the night club circuit: Palm Springs, Reno, Las Vegas, Lake Tahoe, Hawaii; by the early 1960s she had become one of the top female vocalists in the country. In the process she shortened her rather long name to Vikki Carr; she remained (and remains) proud of her Mexican heritage, always making a point of it to her audiences. She has continued a deep involvement in Mexican American concerns, especially education.

Back in southern California Vikki was signed up to a long contract by Liberty Records, became a guest star on virtually every major television variety show in the U.S., and did six specials in London for English television. In 1966 she recorded ''It Must be Him,'' which skyrocketed her to fame in England and later became a big hit in the U.S. There followed successful tours to England, Australia, Mexico, Venezuela, El Salvador, and Panama. Her status as an international star was confirmed in 1967 by a command performance for Queen Elizabeth, followed in 1970 by a White House concert at a dinner in honor of Venezuelan president Rafael Caldera, a performance at the inaugural of the Kennedy Music Center, and another White House concert for President Gerald Ford. Vikki Carr also turned to musical comedy, receiving high critical acclaim for her lead roles in ''The Unsinkable Molly Brown'' and ''South Pacific'' in 1968 and 1969. In 1983 she had a starring role in a Broadway musical. She has made over thirty record albums.

In 1968, hearing of the financial difficulties of Holy Cross High School in the San Antonio barrio, Vikki Carr initiated the first of a series of annual benefits that have netted about a quarter of a million dollars for the school. Two years later she established the Vikki Carr Scholarship Foundation to encourage Chicano students to go on to college; by the early 1980s the foundation had awarded over 100 scholarships to students who went to Yale, Harvard, Radcliffe, Stanford, and other universities. Vikki Carr personally participates in the final screening and selection process. She has also done benefit performances for a wide range of organizations: March of Dimes, Vista, Tuberculosis Association, American Cancer Society, St. Jude Children's Research Hospital, and others.

In addition to her command performances for royalty and presidents, Vikki Carr has received numerous honors. For her contributions to Chicano education, the young lady who never went to college was awarded an honorary doctorate in law by the University of San Diego, and in 1970 the *Los Angeles Times* named her Woman of the Year. That same year Mexico gave her the award Visiting Entertainer of the Year, and two years later she was given the Singer of the Year award by the American Guild of Variety Artists. In 1976 for her work and interest in Chicano education she received the For God and Youth award, and at the end of the 1970s she was named Woman of the World by the International Orphans Fund. In 1981 she received the Humanitarian award from the Hispanic magazine *Nosotros*. She was named Woman of the Year by the

League of United Latin American Citizens (LULAC) in 1983 and in the following year received the Hispanic Woman of the Year Award from the Hispanic Women's Council.

FURTHER READING: Army Archerd, "Vikki Carr: From Saloon Singer to Concert Performer," *Saturday Evening Post* (September 1975); Vikki Carr, "Building Higher Horizons," *The News-San Antonio* (14 September 1981); David García, Jr., "Florencia Bisenta de Casillas Martínez Cardona: It Must be Her," *Nuestro* 3:7 (Fall Special 1979); Al Martínez, *Rising Voices: Profiles of Hispano-American Lives*, New York: New American Library, 1974; *Who's Who in America, 1984–1985*, 43rd ed., 1984.

CARRILLO, EDUARDO (1937–   ), artist, muralist, teacher. Born in the southern California town of Santa Monica in 1937, Eduardo Carrillo grew up in Los Angeles where he attended Catholic grade and high schools. Upon graduation from high school, in 1955 he enrolled in Los Angeles City College and a year later transferred to the University of California at Los Angeles (UCLA). After three years of study at UCLA he went to Spain where he studied drawing at the Círculo de Bellas Artes in Madrid from 1960 to 1961. He then returned to his studies at UCLA, earning his B.A. in the following year and his M.A. in 1964.

With experience as a teaching assistant during his last year at UCLA Carrillo began teaching art in San Diego for the University of California from 1964 to 1966. For the next three years he was in La Paz, Baja California Sur, where he established and operated a Centro de Arte Regional for local youths. Here he and his wife taught a variety of art skills; Carrillo devoted most of his time in this period to ceramics. In 1969 he returned to California to teach art at California State University, Northridge. Inevitably he also became deeply involved in the Chicano Movement, which was developing rapidly at that time. After a year at Northridge he accepted a position in the art department at California State University, Sacramento, where he continues to teach.

Since his college days Eduardo Carrillo has exhibited his paintings widely, first in Los Angeles and elsewhere in southern California and later in the north. As early as 1963 he was included in a Houston, Texas, group exhibit of Painters of the Southwest. Five years later he was represented in a juried show at Bellas Artes in Mexico City. Carrillo is also a muralist of some note. In 1970 he and three other Chicano artists painted a mural in the Chicano library at UCLA, and later he also did a mural in Sacramento's Mexican barrio. Since the early 1970s, disillusioned with aspects of the Chicano Movement, he has turned from murals and political themes in his art to meticulously detailed imaginary landscapes painted in oils on wood.

FURTHER READING: Jacinto Quirarte, *Mexican American Artists*, Austin: University of Texas Press, 1973.

CARRILLO, LEO(POLDO) A. (1881–1961), actor, comedian. Leo Carrillo was born 6 August 1881 in the central plaza area of Los Angeles to Juan José Carrillo, scion of an old California family. While he was still a child, the family moved to nearby Santa Monica, and he grew up and received his education there. In school he showed great interest and skill in drawing and was a champion swimmer. Out of school at age sixteen he first worked clearing railroad right of way and then used his savings to study art in San Francisco. This study led to a job in the *San Francisco Examiner* art department, and that in turn led to a career in vaudeville. A serious student of his fellow man, Carrillo had a speaking knowledge of Chinese, Italian, and Japanese, as well as a complete command of English and Spanish. He used this knowledge in his vaudeville act, which consisted of dialect stories.

About 1915 Leo Carrillo began the transition from vaudeville to the legitimate theater. He played a variety of romantic stage roles during the 1920s, one of his plays, *Lombardi, Ltd.*, running on Broadway for two years. With the advent of talkies at the end of the 1920s he moved naturally into films, first at Warner Brothers and then at Metro-Goldwyn-Mayer. He also moved back to California from New York. In Hollywood he played both romantic leads and, especially later, an exuberant, talkative sidekick to the hero. He played in more than fifty films between 1930 and 1950 and is best remembered as the witty, fractured-English-speaking partner of the Cisco Kid.

Known worldwide because of his many films, he was appointed "Goodwill Ambassador to the World" by the governor of California—a role that he enjoyed immensely and that gave him access to the great of the world. In later life he was a frequently seen figure on his beautiful palomino in California fiestas, rodeos, and parades. He was also genuinely interested in California's past, read much of its early history, and transmitted the Californio oral tradition that he had heard from his elders. In the 1940s California governor Earl Warren appointed him a Beaches and Parks Commissioner, a position he took quite seriously for fourteen years.

FURTHER READING: Leo Carrillo, *The California I Love*, Englewood Cliffs, N.J.: Prentice-Hall, 1961.

CARTER, LYNDA CORDOBA (?–   ), actress. The youngest of three children, Lynda Carter was born in Phoenix, Arizona, of a Mexican mother and an English father. After her early education in Phoenix she studied at Arizona State University in Tempe. She has been active as a performer in the field of entertainment since age fifteen both as an actress and as a singer. For four years she toured the U.S. with The Garfin Gathering.

Lynda Carter has been in several television movies and appeared in television variety specials; she is best known for her performance in the television serial "Wonder Woman" from 1976 to 1979. In the early 1970s she was chosen Miss World-USA, and in 1983 the Hispanic Women's Council named her Hispanic Woman of the Year. She heads Lynda Carter Productions and is associated with Maybelline Cosmetics.

FURTHER READING: Marie Martínez, "Lynda Córdoba Carter," *Latina* 1:3 (1983); *Who's Who in America, 1984–1985*, 43rd ed., 1984.

CASAS, MELESIO (1929–   ), artist, teacher. Melesio Casas was born in El Paso, Texas, on 24 November 1929 and grew up there. He attended what is today the University of Texas at El Paso, graduating in 1956, and then went to Mexico City to study at the University of the Americas. After receiving his master of fine arts degree in 1958, he returned to Texas. In the following year and during the first half of the 1960s his paintings won several local (Texas) awards. During this time he also began his art teaching career; he taught at El Paso and, beginning in 1961, at San Antonio College in the areas of design and painting. Increasingly concerned with minority economic and social problems, in the early 1970s he was one of the founders of an outspoken and militant group of young artists, the Con Safo Painters.

Melesio Casas has exhibited his paintings in numerous galleries in Texas and New York and has had one-man shows in San Antonio, El Paso, and Mexico City. He is perhaps best known for a series of paintings he calls Humanscapes which show some influence of movies and television. He has been cited by critics for his success in combining form and social commentary.

FURTHER READING: Jacinto Quirarte, *Mexican American Artists*, Austin: University of Texas Press, 1973; *Who's Who in American Art*, 16th ed., 1984.

CASTAÑEDA, CARLOS E. (1896–1958), historian, educator. Born 11 November 1896 in the Mexican border town of Ciudad Camargo, Carlos Castañeda was the seventh child of a Mexican teacher of Yucatecan birth and San Antonio, Texas, education. Because of the imminence of Mexico's Great Revolution, in 1908 the family moved across the Rio Grande to Brownsville where Carlos began his American education. Although his parents died while he was in the eighth grade, he managed to graduate in 1916 from the Brownsville High School. He was class valedictorian and the only Mexican American.

Castañeda's work and excellent grades earned him an academic scholarship, and in 1917 he entered the University of Texas. Early the next year he enlisted in the U.S. Army, serving as a machine-gun instructor for the duration of World War I. After the war he returned to the university, only to be forced to drop out later for lack of funds. Spending a year working in the oil fields, he returned to his studies in 1920 and in 1921 earned his B.A. in history and membership in Phi Beta Kappa. After two years of high school teaching and graduate studies he received his M.A. in 1923 and was appointed associate professor in the Spanish Department at William and Mary College in Virginia.

Castañeda returned to the University of Texas as a librarian in 1927 and the next year published his *The Mexican Side of the Texas Revolution* based on Mexican documents. His critical editing of Fray Juan Morfi's "lost" *History of Texas* completed his Ph.D. requirements in 1932, and its publication brought him considerable fame. As a result in 1933 he was commissioned by the Knights of Columbus to write a history of the Catholic church in Texas for the upcoming Texas centennial. This became his monumental *Our Catholic Heritage in Texas*, a six-volume work completed between 1936 and 1950 and much more than a church history. While working on this project, he also continued teaching at the University of Texas. In 1939 he finally became a member of the History Department and in that same year was elected president of the American Catholic Historical Association. He was also appointed to editorships on the *Hispanic American Historical Review*, *The Americas*, and *The Handbook of Latin American Studies*.

Throughout his life Castañeda wrote articles and books on Mexican history and culture and on the American Southwest. Few American historians have received more honors than Dr. Castañeda. He was appointed honorary member of various Latin American historical associations, and from Spain received the Order of Isabel La Católica, to mention only some of his foreign recognition. A life devoted to historical scholarship produced twelve outstanding books and over eighty-five articles. He died 4 April 1958.

FURTHER READING: Félix D. Almaraz, Jr., "The Making of a Boltonian: Carlos E. Castañeda of Texas—the Early Years," *Red River Valley Historical Review* 1 (Winter 1974); "Carlos Castañeda," *La Luz* 3:10–11 (January–February 1975); *Directory of American Scholars*, 3d ed., 1957; J. Lloyd Mecham, "Carlos E. Castañeda, 1896–1958," *Hispanic American Review* 38:3 (August 1958).

CASTILLO, LEONEL J. (1939–   ), politician. Leonel Castillo, son of a Tejano shipyard foreman, was born 9 June 1939 in Victoria, seat of Victoria County, seventy-five miles northeast of Corpus Christi. He grew up and attended school in Victoria and Galveston, where he graduated in 1957 from Kirwin High School. He entered St. Mary's University in San Antonio, majored in English, became an activist, and graduated in 1961. After college he joined the Peace Corps and served in the Philippines from 1961 to 1965. Upon his return to the United States he began graduate studies in the University of Pittsburgh's social work program and in 1967 he earned his M.S.W. in the field of community organizing.

From Pittsburgh Castillo moved to Houston as superintendent of the Neighborhood Centers Association and also began to take an active role in local political organizations. Three years later he won a surprise victory in the 1970 race for city controller over a twenty-five-year incumbent. Four years later he set his sights on the chairmanship of the Texas Democratic party, didn't make it, reorganized his plan, and in 1976 made a deal by which he became party treasurer. In 1977 President Jimmy Carter appointed Leonel Castillo to head the Immigration and Naturalization Service (INS). After thirty months of trying to modernize the INS, to reduce violence on the border, and to emphasize service rather than enforcement, he resigned in August 1979. Despite his resignation he continued to express his views on immigration topics and returned to Houston to head Castillo Enterprises there.

FURTHER READING: Jack Anderson, "A Shepherd-Policeman for New Americans," *Washington Post Parade* (5 November 1978); René Castilla, " 'Lone' Takes the Reins at INS," *Nuestro* 1:9 (September 1977).

CASTRO, RAUL H. (1916–), lawyer, diplomat, governor, politician. Castro was born in the Sonora copper-mining town of Cananea of poor parents, who took their family across the border to find greater opportunity in the United States. His early years were spent in Pirtleville, Arizona, on the border near Douglas where he received his early education. After the death of his father in 1929, he went to work as a miner, agricultural worker, and ranch hand, in this way later financing his education at Northern Arizona University at Flagstaff. While at Flagstaff, he also began a boxing career, which ultimately led to a regional middleweight championship. In 1939 he was naturalized. After graduation in that year he turned professional boxer briefly, worked for the State Department for five years, and taught Spanish at the University of Arizona in order to be able to continue his study of law there. With a law degree in hand he went into private practice at Tucson and also began his political career.

Between 1951 and 1964 Castro served in various elective and appointive positions including county attorney and superior court judge. In 1964 he was appointed U.S. ambassador to El Salvador by the Lyndon Johnson administration and remained in that position until 1968, when he was named ambassador to Bolivia. In the following year, after Republican Richard Nixon's inauguration, he returned to the United States to campaign for the governorship of Arizona. After losing his bid for governor in 1970 by a narrow margin, he practiced international law in Tucson, operated a ranch, and took an active civic leadership role. Four years later he was successful in his gubernatorial race and on November 5 became the fourteenth governor of Arizona—and the first Mexican American. In 1977 he resigned the governorship to accept an appointment as ambassador to Argentina from President Jimmy Carter and remained in that position until 1980. Since then he has been practicing international law in Phoenix, Arizona.

Raúl Castro has been the recipient of numerous awards and medals including honorary doctorates from Northern Arizona University, Arizona State University, and the University of Guadalajara (Mexico); he received the University of Arizona's Distinguished Citizens Award, the Daughters of the American Revolution's Americanism Medal, Outstanding Naturalized Citizen Award, and various others.

FURTHER READING: "La Luz Interview: Governor of Arizona," *La Luz* 4:5 (October 1975); Geoffrey P. Mawn, "Raúl Héctor Castro: Poverty to Prominence," in Manuel P. Servín, *An Awakened Minority: The Mexican-Americans*, 2d ed., Beverly Hills, Calif.: Glencoe Press, 1974; *Who's Who in American Politics, 1981–1982*, 8th ed., 1981.

CASTRO, SALVADOR B. (1933–), teacher, activist. Born in Los Angeles on 25 October 1933 of Mexican immigrant parents, Sal Castro as a small child accompanied his parents in their repatriation to Mexico during the years of the Great Depression. He began his schooling in Mexico, but it was interrupted when he was eight by his family's return to the United States. In Los Angeles he attended parochial schools, graduating from Cathedral High School in 1952. After serving two years in the armed forces during the Korean conflict, he enrolled in Los Angeles City College. Here he became so deeply involved in political activism that his scholastic career faltered, but he received his A.A. degree in 1957 and his B.A. from Los Angeles State College (today University) five years later. During this time he was active in the Democratic party as well as the Mexican American Political Association (MAPA).

After college Sal Castro began teaching history and government in the Pasadena and then the Los Angeles city schools. In March 1968 the walkouts of Chicano students—about 5,000 mostly from Garfield, Lincoln, Wilson, and Roosevelt high schools—brought Sal Castro to the spotlight. After two weeks of speeches, demands, picketing, sit-ins, sympathy demonstrations, and mass arrests, Sal Castro, who became the symbolic leader, and twelve others were indicted on charges of felonious conspiracy for allegedly organizing the demonstrations. Although the California Appeals Court later cleared the thirteen, Sal Castro continued to be barred from teaching. Not until five years later, in 1973, was he given a teaching assignment—at Belmont High School where the students were 70 percent Mexican American.

FURTHER READING: Arturo Palacios, ed., *Mexican-American Directory*, Washington, D.C.: Executive Systems Corp., 1969.

CAVAZOS, LAURO F., JR. (1927–   ), professor, administrator, university president. Lauro Cavazos was born 4 January 1927 on the King Ranch in Texas where his father Lauro, Sr., was employed. After high school he entered Texas Technological University at Lubbock and received his B.A. in zoology in 1949. Two years later he completed his M.A. in zoology at the same institution with a concentration on cell formation and function, and then went on to Iowa State University where he received his Ph.D. in physiology in 1954.

From 1954 to 1964 Lauro Cavazos taught anatomy in the Medical College of Virginia at Charlottesville, advancing from instructor to associate professor. In 1964 he moved to Tufts University School of Medicine in Medford, Massachusetts, and eight years later became the associate dean, then acting dean, and in 1975 the dean of the Tufts School of Medicine. Five years later he was selected as president of Texas Technological University with a professorship in anatomy and in the biological sciences. Since 1980 he has been president of Texas Tech and of the university's Health Sciences Center.

Dr. Lauro Cavazos's basic research interest is the physiology of the reproductive tract and he is the author or co-author of some seventy articles and abstracts dealing with the subject. He is also the author of articles in several edited texts and has authored and coauthored two guides to dissection in human anatomy. He has been appointed to many boards and organizations as a consultant and advisor, including the Pan American Health Organization, and has served as editor for several medical journals. He received a distinguished alumnus award both from Texas Technological University (1977) and Iowa State University (1979). In 1983 he was named Hispanic Educator of the year by the Texas chapter of the League of United Latin American Citizens (LULAC). In the following year he received the Outstanding Leadership Award in the Field of Education from President Ronald Reagan and in 1985 was awarded a Distinguished Service Medal from the Uniformed Services University for the Health Sciences. Dr. Cavazos has also been active in community affairs.

FURTHER READING: *Who's Who in America, 1982–1983*, 42nd ed., 1982.

CERVANTES, LORNA DEE (1954–   ), poet. Lorna Dee Cervantes was born 6 August 1954 in San Francisco of an old Californio family that had settled originally in Santa Barbara. When she was five, her parents separated and she and her brother moved to San Jose with their mother. Here she grew up and received her early education. The family experienced great poverty, and Lorna developed a very negative reaction to the San Jose public schools. Becoming acquainted with poetry through her musically inclined brother's songbooks, she began writing poems when she was eight. By the time she was fifteen she had put together a small "book" of her poems.

During the next few years, at the end of the 1960s, Lorna Dee Cervantes became politicized as a result of the Chicano Movement. She was active in the American Indian Movement and the Chicano Movement, working at the Centro Cultural in San Jose; and at eighteen she became involved with a *teatro* group. As a result of reading her poetry at a *teatro* festival in Mexico City in 1974, a number of her poems were published in the *Revista Chicano-Riqueña* in the following year. In the early 1970s she enrolled at San Jose State University but then dropped out to start a literary magazine, *Mango*. In 1976 she began sitting in on some university classes and after a few years resumed her degree studies. In 1984 she earned her B.A. in creative arts from San Jose State. She is currently a graduate student at the University of California at Santa Cruz.

At the end of the 1970s Lorna Dee Cervantes submitted a collection of her poems to the University of Pittsburgh Press, which published them in 1980 under the title of *Enplumada*. This makes her one of the very few Mexican American poets published by a mainstream press. She has also had her poetry published in journals in Mexico and England. Cervantes sees her poetry as being personal and often autobiographical, but also at times feminist and political. Critics have praised her poems as carefully worked, reworked, and polished and as being outstanding in Chicano poetry.

FURTHER READING: Wolfgang Binder, ed., "Partial Autobiographies: Interviews with Twenty Chicano Poets," *Erlanger Studien*, Band 65/I (1985), Erlangen, Germany: Verlag Palm & Enke Erlangen; Julio A. Martínez, *Chicano Scholars and Writers: A Bio-Bibliographical Directory*, Metuchen, N.J.: The Scarecrow Press, 1979; "People on the Move," *Caminos* 1:7 (November 1980).

CERVANTEZ, PEDRO (1915–   ), artist. Born in the small town of Wilcox in extreme southeastern Arizona of Mexican parents who had emigrated the year before from Durango state, Pedro Cervántez grew up and went to school in the tiny settlement of Texico in New Mexico, on the border with Texas just east of

Clovis. During the depression years of the mid–1930s he, along with other New Mexican artists, was employed in the Federal Art Project (FAP) of the Works Progress Administration. The 1936 FAP exhibit in New York City of work done under its auspices, held at the Museum of Modern Art, included one of his easel paintings and thereby gave him his first national exposure. Two years later he was one of ten Americans included in the museum's publication, *Masters of Popular Painting: Modern Primitives of Europe and America.*

From 1938 to 1940 he studied art at Eastern New Mexico University in Portales, about twenty-five miles south of Clovis. During World War II he spent nearly five years in Europe in the armed services, which gave him the opportunity to see and carefully study works of the great European masters. After the war he returned to New Mexico, studying painting at the Hill and Canyon School of the Arts in Santa Fe from 1949 to 1952.

Since World War II Cervántez, who operated a commercial art business in Clovis, has had numerous exhibitions which have brought him considerable renown. In addition to the Museum of Modern Art, his works have been exhibited at the Whitney Museum of American Art in New York, at the Dallas Museum of Fine Arts, at the Colorado Springs Fine Arts Center, and elsewhere including Miami, San Antonio, and Albuquerque.

FURTHER READING: Holger Cahill et al., *Masters of Popular Painting: Modern Primitives of Europe and America*, New York: Museum of Modern Art, 1938; Jacinto Quirarte, *Mexican American Artists*, Austin: University of Texas Press, 1973.

CHACON, FELIPE MAXIMILIANO (1873–?), publisher, writer. Felipe Chacón was born 6 December 1873 in Sante Fe, New Mexico, the son of an important early New Mexico newspaper publisher, Urbano Chacón. From the late 1860s to the mid–1880s his father published *El Explorador* in Trinidad, Colorado, *El Espejo* in Taos, and *La Aurora* in Sante Fe, and Felipe was exposed to the life of journalism.

Although he was orphaned at age thirteen, Felipe had the advantage of a good education at Santa Fe, first in the public schools and then in the Colegio de San Miguel. As an adult he was engaged in various business enterprises and, like his father, edited a number of local Spanish-language newspapers. Among them were: *La Voz del Pueblo* in Las Vegas, *El Faro del Rio Grande* in Bernalillo on the Rio Grande north of Albuquerque, *El Independiente* in Las Vegas, and *El Eco del Norte* in Mora, just north of Las Vegas.

From his teen years onward Felipe Chacón showed a dedication to the Spanish language and literature and began writing poems while still a teenager. Later he wrote poetry and essays of great literary quality in both Spanish and English. In 1924, while publishing and editing *La Bandera Americana* in Albuquerque, he wrote and published an excellent example of his literary skills under the title *Obras de Felipe Maximiliano Chacón, El Cantor Nuevomexicano: Poesía y Prosa.*

CHACON, JOSE ANDRES (1925–   ), engineer, administrator. José Chacón, the eldest of six sons in a Nuevo Mexicano family, was born 16 August 1925 in the tiny town of Peñasco, just south of Taos. He grew up in this mountainous region during the depression years, receiving his early education in Catholic schools. While a senior in high school, he became interested in aviation. In the latter years of World War II he was an aerial gunner in the U.S. Navy and fought in the Pacific theater. After the war he received an appointment to West Point where he completed his B.S. degree in engineering in time to receive his commission as a second lieutenant and serve in the Korean conflict as a navigator-bombadier. He was awarded the Distinguished Flying Cross and a dozen other decorations as a result of his Korean service.

Out of the army, in 1954 Chacón joined the Sandia Corporation, an Albuquerque contractor to the Atomic Energy Commission. In Albuquerque he continued his studies, receiving his M.A. from the University of New Mexico in 1959; at the same time he volunteered on several civic and governmental organizations. Five years later he took a leave of absence from Sandia to go to Peru as director of a Peace Corps project, the Cooperative League of U.S.A. In 1968 he ended his connection with the Sandia Corporation to serve on the President's Committee on Mexican American Affairs. The following year he was appointed executive director of the committee, and then was named technical assistance officer in the Equal Employment Opportunity Commission. Shortly thereafter he began studies at George Washington University toward a Ph.D. in business administration. Chacón has also found time to write a syndicated column, "The Minority No One Knows."

FURTHER READING: Harold J. Alford, *The Proud Peoples: The Heritage and Culture of Spanish-Speaking Peoples in the United States*, New York: David McKay Co., 1972; Theodore E. B. Wood, *Chicanos y Chicanas Prominentes*, Menlo Park, Calif.: Educational Consortium of America, 1974.

CHACON, ROBERT (1952–   ), fighter. Bobby Chacón was born and grew up in the San Fernando Valley just north of Los Angeles. At fourteen he began to run with a Latino street gang which called itself The Group and quickly developed a reputation as a tough street fighter. Soon he dropped out of high school and, encouraged by his girlfriend, began boxing. After a brief period as an amateur fighter, at twenty he turned professional and in his first year won fifteen consecutive fights, fourteen by knockouts. In September 1974 he became the world featherweight champion by defeating the veteran Venezuelan fighter, Alfredo Marcano. Success led to high living and to added pounds, and in June 1975 a badly out-of-shape Chacón lost his title to Rubén Olivares in a match that lasted only two rounds. Quarrels between his wife, who wanted him to give up boxing, and Chacón ultimately led to her suicide and to his serious rededication to the ring.

In December 1982 Chacón regained the world title by defeating Mexico's Rafael Limón, but the boxing commission later stripped him of his title as the result of a nonapproved fight. After two bouts in the first half of 1984 Chacón found it harder to line up fights. A divorce suit filed by his second wife later that year, after a severe beating and felony assault charges, seemed to indicate his big fight is to control his own anger.

FURTHER READING: K. Patrick Conner, "Bobby Chacón: Fighting Is All He Has Ever Known," *This World* (6 January 1985).

CHAVES, JOSE FRANCISCO (1833–1904), political leader, lawyer, soldier, rancher. Chaves was born in what is today Bernalillo County, near Albuquerque, of an extensive pioneer Nuevo Mexicano family. His father, Mariano Chaves, was an important political figure in the Mexican territorial government, occupying several high positions under Governor Manuel Armijo* at the end of the 1830s. After his early education in Nuevo México and Chihuahua, José Francisco was sent to school in St. Louis by his father, so he might be able to cope with the westward floodtide of American frontiersmen. There followed a brief return to Nuevo México because of the U.S. war with Mexico, after which he went to New York to complete his education, including some study of medicine. When he was nineteen or twenty he returned to take over operation of the family ranch, his father having died in the meantime. In the 1850s these ranching activities led to his participation in various Indian campaigns. This military experience served him well during the Civil War, and he was commissioned major and later lieutenant colonel in the First New Mexico Infantry militia regiment.

After the war Chaves studied law and actively entered the New Mexico political arena while continuing his ranching and farming activities. He was elected New Mexican territorial delegate to the U.S. Congress in several bitter, brawling campaigns and served three terms between 1865 and 1871. Four years later he was elected to the New Mexico territorial Legislative Council and reelected until his death thirty years later. During this time he was chosen president of the council eight times and also served as district attorney, state superintendent of schools, and delegate to the 1889 state constitutional convention. In the late 1800s he provided dynamic Nuevo Mexicano political leadership, fighting the Santa Fe Ring and strongly supporting territorial Governor Miguel Otero, Jr.* In 1903 he was appointed state historian but was killed before his term began. On the night of 26 November 1904 he was assassinated by an unknown assailant at Pinos Wells, New Mexico. The murder was rumored to be politically motivated and connected with his opposition to the infamous Santa Fe Ring. Despite a $2,500 reward offer by the legislature, his murderer was never identified.

FURTHER READING: William A. Keleher, *Turmoil in New Mexico, 1846–1868*, Santa Fe: Rydall Press, 1952; Lynn Perrigo, *Hispanos: Historic Leaders in New Mexico*, Santa Fe: Sunstone Press, 1985; Maurilio Vigil, *Los Patrones: Profiles of Hispanic Political Leaders in New Mexico History*, Washington, D.C.: University Press of America, 1980.

CHAVES, MANUEL ANTONIO (1818–1889), trader, rancher, soldier. Born during the latter years of the Mexican revolution for independence at Atrisco, across the Rio Grande from Albuquerque, Manuel Chaves was descended from an old, large, and important Nuevo Mexicano family that arrived in the 1590s with Juan de Oñate, the founder of the colony. As a lad he labored at the usual tasks of Nuevo México frontier children—tending sheep, collecting firewood, and helping in the many arduous tasks of wresting a living from the arid soil. Although a nephew of Governor Manuel Armijo,* he was forced to flee to St. Louis, Missouri, in late 1839 because of a bitter quarrel with the governor that ended in threats against Chaves's life. Two years later he returned to Santa Fe just in time to take part in meeting the threat of the Texas Santa Fe expedition. He quickly settled down to trading and raising sheep and cattle, and in 1844 he married and established himself in Santa Fe.

When U.S. forces under Colonel Stephen Kearny invaded and took over Nuevo México, Chaves became involved early in the plotting of the first Taos rebellion against the Americans. As a result he was arrested and charged with treason, but acquitted in January 1847 and released. When the second Taos revolt broke out a week later, he was one of the Nuevo Mexicanos who helped suppress it. After the Treaty of Guadalupe Hidalgo he went back to ranching and trading with Chihuahua merchants and local Indian groups. During the early 1850s he took part in a number of military expeditions against hostile Navajos, Utes, and Apaches, quickly acquiring considerable acclaim as a scout. In 1857 he was appointed chief of scouts in the Gila expedition against the southern Apaches and after continued display of leadership qualities, four years later was given command of Fort Fontleroy on the edge of Navajo territory in northwestern New Mexico.

Meanwhile the Civil War had broken out, and a large Texas force under General Henry H. Silbey was pushing up the Rio Grande valley threatening Albuquerque and Santa Fe. In March 1862 the Confederates captured Albuquerque and then Sante Fe, despite valiant resistance. In the most brilliant action of the New Mexican fight against the invaders Chaves, as chief scout, led a volunteer force of Coloradans under Major John Chivington through Glorieta Pass, southeast of Santa Fe, thereby flanking the Confederate army. As a result the entire enemy supply train was seized and destroyed; this loss forced Silbey to retreat down the Rio Grande and marked the beginning of the end of Confederate efforts to take first New Mexico and then California with its gold mines. With the end of the Civil War in New Mexico Chaves was discharged from the service and returned home to take up civilian life again. He found his rancho herds and flocks almost completely wiped out by Indian raiding during the war years. In the decade following the war his stock raising again became highly profitable as the nomadic Indian tribes were increasingly pacified and placed on reservations.

In 1876 Chaves, his wife, and eight children moved to a new frontier in western New Mexico where his half-brother Román Baca had settled about a decade earlier. Here in his early sixties Chaves undertook the immense task of creating a new home for himself and his family. Despite considerable pain from old wounds that had never properly healed he worked unceasingly with his wife and children to build an extensive rancho, to which he added by buying land from neighbors. Until his death at seventy-one, El Leoncito, the Little Lion, as he was known, remained the commander of Company F of the San Mateo territorial militia.

FURTHER READING: Marc Simmons, *The Little Lion of the Southwest*, Chicago: The Swallow Press, 1973; Ralph E. Twitchell, *The History of the Military Occupation of the Territory of New Mexico . . .*, reprint, New York: Arno Press, 1976.

CHAVEZ, (FRAY) ANGELICO (1910–   ), clergyman, author, historian, poet. Angélico Chávez was born at Wagon Mound, Mora County, in northeastern New Mexico, eldest of ten children of Fabian and Nicolasa Chávez, and was baptized with the name Manuel Ezequiel. As a child Chávez experienced the hardships of poverty. At age seven he entered the Mora public school, staffed at that time by Sisters of Loretto, and seven years later he began his seminary studies at the Franciscan order's preparatory school, St. Francis Seminary in Cincinnati, Ohio. After completing his studies at this institution, where he also began to write, he entered the novitiate with the name Fra Angélico and in 1933 graduated from Duns Scottus College in Detroit. Following further studies at the Franciscan House of Studies at Oldenburg, Indiana, he was ordained a priest in the Order of Friars Minor (Franciscans) in Santa Fe on 6 May 1937.

Fray Angélico immediately began a missionary career devoted to Indians and fellow Nuevo Mexicanos, living at Peñablanca, New Mexico, on a Pueblo reservation, where he was also postmaster. In 1943 in response to the U.S. Army's need for Spanish-speaking chaplains he volunteered and served in the South Pacific until the end of World War II. Throughout all this time—from high school on—he continued his writing, especially poetry.

For the next quarter century Fray Angélico returned to his busy missionary life among the Rio Grande Pueblo Indians and greatly expanded his activity as an author. Celebrating mass, hearing confessions, baptizing and officiating at weddings and funerals for his poor Indian and Nuevo Méxicano parishioners, he also found time to write poetry, fiction, history, documentaries, essays, book reviews, and a newspaper column. He also restored some old New Mexican chapels and churches, some of which he adorned with his murals. In 1951–1952 he was recalled by the War Department for service in the Korean war—time he spent in Germany. In 1959 he was named pastor of the church at Cerrillos, a small town southwest of Santa Fe, and after five years there was transferred to Albuquerque because of his poor health. At the beginning of the 1970s he left the priesthood and the Franciscans in order to devote himself to historical writing. Because of his extensive archival research experience he was appointed archivist of the Santa Fe archdiocese in the early 1970s by Bishop Robert F. Sánchez.* Since his "retirement" he has continued his scholarly historical work and writing.

Fray Angélico Chávez has written numerous articles, essays, and poems, and is the author of over twenty books. The best known of his published works are *Origins of New Mexico Families in the Spanish Colonial Period* (1954); *Our Lady of the Conquest* (1948); *When the Santos Talked* (1977), reprint of 1957 edition; *Coronado's Friars: The Franciscans in the Coronado Expedition* (1968); *My Penitente Land* (1974); *The Domínguez-Escalante Journal* (translator) (1976); and his most recent and perhaps most important work, *But Time and Chance: The Story of Padre Martínez of Taos, 1793–1867* (1981).

FURTHER READING: Walter Briggs, "Biographical Sketch of Fray Angélico Chávez," *New Mexico Magazine* 51:1–2 (January–February 1973); Robert Huber, "Fray Angélico Chávez, 20th Century Renaissance Man," *New Mexico Magazine* 48:3–4 (March–April 1970).

CHAVEZ, CESAR ESTRADA (1927–   ), labor organizer. César Chávez was born on a family farm near Yuma, Arizona, on 31 March 1927 to a poor Mexican American family barely eking a living out of marginal land. During the depression days of the 1930s the Chávez family, like many other southwestern farm families, lost its land through a tax sale and was forced to join the migrant stream that flowed from harvest to harvest. Young César grew up in the shacks of farm labor camps, attended about thirty different schools, and eventually reached the seventh grade. As a youngster he worked in the fields with his parents, helping to harvest the many commercial crops of fruits and vegetables.

Toward the end of World War II Chávez served two years in the U.S. Navy in the Pacific theater. Upon being discharged from the service he returned briefly to migrant farm work, joining the National Agricultural Workers Union, and then in 1950 settled down with his wife in San Jose, California. Here through a local priest he met Fred Ross of Saul Alinsky's Industrial Areas Foundation, who was organizing Community Service Organizations (CSO) locally. On the lookout for leadership potential, Ross persuaded the skeptical young worker to become a volunteer organizer for the CSO. From Ross Chávez quickly learned organizing and leadership skills and in his spare time began filling in some of the gaping holes in his formal education. After years of establishing CSO chapters, organizing voter registration drives, and helping workers with their many problems, in 1954 he became a paid CSO organizer and four years later was named CSO director for California and Arizona. At this time he became deeply interested in the problems of organizing farm workers. The CSO leadership was not sympathetic to his ideas, and when his proposal to develop a farm labor union was again rejected at the 1962 CSO conference, Chávez resigned.

Chávez, then thirty-five, moved to Delano and in the heart of California's great central valley began to develop his first farm workers' organization. With the help of Fred Ross, Dolores Huerta,* Gilbert Padilla, and others and by dint of an eighteen-hour day the National Farm Workers Association (today the United Farm Workers of America, AFL-CIO) was slowly created. Based on hard, unremitting work, personal contact, and deep-felt concern, the organization was as much a cooperative as a union. And above all, it was César Chávez.

In September 1965 Chávez took his fledgling union of about 1,700 members into a grape strike in the Delano area. Viewing the strike as a part of a national movement for greater social justice rather than a simple labor dispute, Chávez skillfully appealed to America's feeling of fairness. He presented the strike as *la causa*, the cause, based on two principles: nonviolence and national liberal support. The long five-year struggle was punctuated by a series of dramatic events: the March–April 1966 march to Sacramento, the intrusion of the Teamsters Union later that year, Chávez's 1967 twenty-five-day fast, the national boycott of all table grapes in the spring of the following year, and the spread of the grape boycott to Europe in 1969. Finally, after five years, the grape strike ended in July 1970 with three-year contracts for the workers, and Chávez turned his attention to the Salinas, California, lettuce fields where another long struggle began to shape up.

In 1973 César Chávez suffered a severe setback when many valley grape growers failed to renew their contracts, complaining of UFW inexperience and shortcomings in administration. This reverse seemed offset two years later by the passage of the 1975 California Agricultural Labor Relations Act, which provided secret-ballot union elections that Chávez had strongly supported and growers had opposed equally vehemently. Chávez has since come to feel that dependence on the 1975 act to solve the union's problems was an error. Although he has continued in the early 1980s to campaign for or against election issues, there has also been a partial return to the earlier consumer boycott idea, but with up-to-date techniques. Using a printing press, computers, direct mailings, and television advertisements in an operation run out of La Paz (Keene, California), the union's headquarters since 1971, Chávez hopes to turn around the trend against his union and unionism in general. The likelihood of this reversal was reduced by Chávez's introduction of Synanon ideas into the union and the firing in 1977 of many old-time central staff members.

In this continuing struggle the UFW's great strength and greatest weakness is César Chávez's personal and absolute leadership; César's great strength and greatest weakness is his view that the union is a community (*la causa*) rather than a labor organization. To his agribusiness opponents he appears a stubborn, relentless labor organizer; his supporters see him as a dedicated, ascetic twentieth-century saint.

FURTHER READING: Tony Castro, *Chicano Power: The Emergence of Mexican America*, New York: Saturday Review Press, 1974; Jeff Coplon, "César Chávez' Fall From Grace," *This World, San Francisco Examiner & Chronicle* (21 October 1984); Lynn Faivre, *Chávez: One New Answer*, New York: Praeger, 1970; Judith Gaines, "César Chávez and the United Farm Workers," *Nuestro* 9:9 (November 1985); John Hubner, "The God of the Movement," *West, San Jose Mercury News* (19 August 1984); Jacques E. Levy, *César Chávez: Autobiography of La Causa*, New York: W. W. Norton & Co., 1974; Peter Matthiessen, *Sal Si Puedes: César Chávez and the New American Revolution*, New York: Random House, 1969; Jean M. Pitrone, *Chávez: Man of the Migrants*, New

York: Pyramid Communications, 1972; Ronald Taylor, *Chávez and the Farmworker*, Boston: Beacon Press, 1975.

CHAVEZ, DENNIS (1888–1962), senator, New Mexican leader. Born 8 April 1888 in a small community west of Albuquerque and christened Dionisio, Chávez was the third of eight children of a poor Nuevo Mexicano family. A family move to Albuquerque seven years later enabled him to attend school, but family poverty caused him to drop out at the eighth grade to go to work delivering groceries for the next five years. He did not, however, abandon his education. An interest in history and biography led to many evenings in the public library and to a deep interest in politics, long before he could vote. From 1906 to 1915 he worked for the Albuquerque city engineering department. In 1912 he took an active interest in New Mexico's statehood and four years later worked as Spanish interpreter for the successful Democratic candidate for the U.S. Senate, Andrieus Jones. Jones obtained a clerkship in the Senate for the ambitious young man, who also managed to enter the law school at Georgetown University.

In 1920 Dennis Chávez was awarded his Bachelor of Laws degree and then returned to Albuquerque where he initiated a successful law practice and ran for public office in the classic pattern of American political advancement. As he rose in Democratic party ranks he campaigned for and was elected to a seat in the state legislature and in 1930 he easily defeated the incumbent Republican New Mexican congressman to the U.S. House of Representatives. After one reelection to the House, in the 1934 elections he ran for the U.S. Senate seat held by the outstanding and politically powerful Republican leader, Bronson Cutting. After a bitter campaign Chávez was narrowly defeated. Chávez and others challenged the validity of Cutting's reelection, charging vote fraud and carrying the issue all the way to the floor of the Senate. While the challenge was still pending, Senator Cutting was killed in an airplane crash, and Chávez was appointed by the governor to fill the seat until the next election two years hence. Despite some Democratic opposition, Chávez was overwhelmingly nominated and elected in 1936, defeating the very popular Republican contender, Miguel Otero.

As the Democratic senator from New Mexico Chávez was a staunch New Dealer, warmly supporting President Franklin D. Roosevelt's social legislation, but showing independence of thought. In his position as chairman of the Senate Public Works Committee he successfully obtained extensive federal funds for New Mexico in the areas of reclamation, irrigation, and flood control or at least got credit for doing so. Only in one area was his support for Roosevelt less than wholehearted. As a western isolationist at the end of the 1930s, he initially opposed the president's Lend-Lease program to help the beleaguered Allies in World War II, arguing the country should follow a policy of strict neutrality. In national politics he was often a controversial figure because of independent stands he took. During the war years some of his votes in the Senate were less than pleasing to sectors of his constituency, especially his votes supporting liberal social legislation, including an equal rights amendment, which he cosponsored. However, throughout the war and postwar years the loyalty of his Nuevo Mexicano supporters sustained him politically. In the elections of 1946 and 1952 he was able to turn back serious attempts to unseat him. In all, he was reelected to the Senate five times.

During the years after the war Dennis Chávez did some of his best work in the Senate. Perhaps his greatest contribution to his Nuevo Mexicano constituency and to the country as a whole was his support of education and civil rights, especially his strong leadership in writing a bill to create a permanent federal Fair Employment Practices Commission and fighting for its passage. Despite his defeat in this matter in 1946, as a member of a number of important committees he continued to fight for greater economic and social equality, to argue for the inclusion of farm workers in the Wagner-Connery National Labor Relations Act, and to work quietly in the Senate to help the cause of the American Indian. He also was deeply interested in improving U.S.–Latin American relations.

Early in 1960 Senator Chávez became chairman of the Senate Appropriations Subcommittee for Defense. In this key position, despite a second cancer episode, he worked vigorously to support a billion dollar increase in President Dwight Eisenhower's 1960 defense budget and obtained for New Mexico important defense technology installations. At the time of the Bay of Pigs invasion in Cuba he suggested the consideration of a U.S. invasion force. A champion of civil rights and full equality for all Americans to the last, the long and distinguished national career of this son of New Mexico was ended by a heart attack in mid-November 1962.

FURTHER READING: *Current Biography, 1946*, New York: H. W. Wilson Co., 1947. William A. Keleher, *Memoirs: 1892–1969: A New Mexico Item*, Santa Fe: Rydal Press, 1969; Tom Popejoy, "Dennis Chávez," *Hall of Fame Essays*, Albuquerque: Historical Society of New Mexico, 1963; Maurilio Vigil and Roy Luján, "Parallels in the Career [sic] of Two Hispanic U.S. Senators," *Journal of Ethnic Studies* 13:4 (Winter 1986).

CHAVEZ, EDWARD A. (1917–   ), painter, muralist, sculptor. Edward Chávez was born 14 March 1917 in the small New Mexican town of Wagon Mound, northeast of Sante Fe. He became interested in art in high school and attended the Colorado Springs Fine Arts Center for a short time in his early twenties. In 1948, after World War II, he received a Tiffany Foundation painting grant and three years later was awarded a Fulbright grant. Between 1954 and 1958 he taught painting at the Art Students League in New York and then taught at Colorado College in Colorado Springs, at Syracuse University, and at other institutions of higher education. A three-month trip to Mexico in 1954 brought him into contact with Mexican themes, which he follows, and with Mexican artistic expression, which he does not. He has also traveled extensively in Europe.

Edward Chávez's career has been long and varied. Although primarily an easel painter, he has painted a number of murals, mostly in post offices, and is also a sculptor. He has had a large number of one-man shows; his first was in

Denver at age twenty (in 1937). Subsequently he had one-man exhibits in Santa Fe, San Francisco, New York, Rome, and elsewhere. His paintings and sculptures have been singled out for high praise from art critics and have won many awards. They are represented in important museum collections across the United States, including the Museum of Modern Art in New York and the Library of Congress Print Collection. Although influenced by the Mexican muralists, Chávez has been affected far more by the European art and artists and is considered a "mainstream" American artist.

FURTHER READING: Jacinto Quirarte, *Mexican American Artists*, Austin: University of Texas Press, 1973; *Who's Who in American Art*, 16th ed., 1984.

CHAVEZ, FELIPE (1835–1905), merchant, rancher, politician, philanthropist. Born in Las Padillas on the west side of the Rio Grande a few miles south of Albuquerque, Chávez was descended from an important branch of the extensive Chávez clan. Both his father and grandfather had served as governor of Nuevo México. Felipe apparently received the typical education of young *rico* of the day, probably in Missouri or New York, since he spoke English well and later had connections there. At the beginning of the 1860s he was flooded out of Las Padillas and moved, with his bride, twenty miles south to Belen where he started a general store. Following the earlier footsteps of his father and an uncle, he quickly entered the Santa Fe trade and also engaged in cattle and sheep raising on shares. After the Civil War Felipe expanded his financial activities to New York where his agent bought and sold real estate and stocks in his name. Later he also extended his investments to silver-mining properties in Chihuahua. His reputed wealth soon gave him the sobriquet El Millonario and also gave him a voice in politics—usually in the background. At the end of the century his large holdings in Atchison, Topeka and Santa Fe stock were an important factor in persuading the Santa Fe Railroad to run a cut-off from Texas through Belen, which was completed in 1905, the year of Felipe's death. Chávez believed strongly in the importance of education and in his will left $20,000 in a trust fund to support the Felipe Chávez School, which he had founded earlier.

FURTHER READING: Gilberto Espinosa and Tibo Chávez, *El Rio Abajo*, n.p., n.d.; Lee Taylor, *Rio Abajo Heritage*, Valencia County Historical Society, c.1981.

CHAVEZ, JOSEPH A. (1938–   ), sculptor, teacher. Chávez was born and grew up in the Rio Grande river town of Belen, New Mexico. He obtained his art education at the University of New Mexico: B.S. in art education, 1963, M.A. in art education, 1967, and M.A. in art, 1971. He also did postgraduate study at the University of Cincinnati in 1974. Since 1963 he has taught art to high school students in Albuquerque and has also taught and supervised art teachers at the University of Albuquerque and the University of Cincinnati. His sculptures have been exhibited in various fairs and art shows in the Southwest, and he has won numerous awards.

Chávez sculpts in stone, clay, wood, and steel, and his work is described as abstract and often massive, usually with an anthropomorphic feeling.
FURTHER READING: Jacinto Quirarte, *Mexican American Artists*, Austin: University of Texas Press, 1973.

CHAVEZ, LINDA (1947–   ), public official, educator. Born in Albuquerque, New Mexico, on 17 June 1947 of a working-class family of pioneer Nuevo Mexicano descent, Linda Chávez spent her early years there and at age ten moved with the family to Denver, Colorado. After a parochial grade school education, she completed her undergraduate studies in English literature at the University of Colorado, Boulder, in 1970. Subsequently she has done extensive graduate work at the University of California at Los Angeles and at the University of Maryland. An honors student, she also taught at the University of California and the University of Colorado while studying there.

In the early 1970s Linda Chávez worked as a lobbyist for the National Education Association and later for the American Federation of Teachers (AFT), AFL-CIO, where she became assistant to the president, Albert Shanker. Her first political job, in the mid–1970s, was as a staffer for liberal Republican Don Edwards on the House Civil and Constitutional Rights subcommittee. After a stint for the House Committee on the Judiciary, in February 1977 she moved to the Department of Health, Education and Welfare as a presidential appointee to the Office of Education. In midyear she became a consultant to President Jimmy Carter's Office of Management and Budget Reorganization Project and also accepted the editorship of the influential AFT quarterly, *American Educator*. In 1981 she was appointed by the Reagan administration as a consultant to the Action agency and three years later began serving a three-year term on the government's Council of the Administrative Conference.

Linda Chávez's work as editor of *American Education* led to White House attention and her appointment in August 1983 as the first woman on the Civil Rights Commission. Two months later she was appointed by President Ronald Reagan to serve an indefinite term as staff director of the commission. In April 1985 she left that position to accept an appointment as the director of the White House Office of Public Liaison and as deputy assistant to the president, the highest-ranking woman in the White House. Early in February 1986 she stepped down from this prestigious position to campaign for Republican nomination to the U.S. Senate from Maryland. In September she was nominated but lost in the general elections two months later to her Democratic opponent.
FURTHER READING: Pilar Saavedra-Vela, "Linda Chávez: Commentary by a Political Professional," *Agenda* (September–October 1977).

CISNEROS, HENRY G. (1948–   ), mayor, political leader. Henry Cisneros was born in a west-side Mexican barrio of San Antonio in the immediate post–World War II years, the son of a retired civil servant. After his early education in the city's parochial school system he attended Texas Agricultural and

Mechanical University and stayed on after his A.B. to get a master's degree in urban planning. While completing his M.A. he also worked as assistant to the city manager of nearby Bryan, the county seat of Brazos County. In 1970 he returned to San Antonio as assistant director of its Model Cities Program and after a year went to Washington, D.C., where he worked for the National League of Cities and began full-time graduate studies in public administration at George Washington University. During 1971 Cisneros became the youngest White House Fellow in U.S. history, serving as an assistant to the secretary of Health, Education and Welfare. After his White House year he went to Boston and earned a second M.A. in public administration at Harvard University. Having completed his Ph.D. at George Washington University, he returned to San Antonio where he began to teach government at the University of Texas.

In San Antonio Cisneros ran for the city council in 1975 on the Good Government League ticket; he won easily. Quickly gaining a reputation as the city's brightest young politico and as a peacemaker, he was reelected in a landslide two years later. In 1981 Cisneros ran for mayor of the nation's ninth largest city and won with 62 percent of the votes cast. In 1983 he was reelected mayor with 94 percent of the votes and two years later won with 72 percent. Since 1984 as mayor he has pushed a long-term project called "Target '90—Goals for San Antonio," which emphasizes education and economic development. With a $50 per week mayor's salary the Cisneros make ends meet by his teaching at Trinity University and his wife's working. On 4 April 1987 he won a fourth term as mayor with more than twice as many votes as his closest opponent.

Henry Cisneros has been awarded honorary degrees by several universities and in 1982 received the Jefferson Award from the American Institute of Public Service. Despite his Democratic affiliation the Reagan administration appointed him to the Kissinger Commission on Central America in the fall of 1983, and he wrote a partially dissenting opinion to the commission's report, published in the following year. Early in fall 1984 he was elected president of the Texas Municipal League and a couple of months later was chosen second vice-president of the National League of Cities. During the following year he was frequently mentioned as a possible candidate for the U.S. Senate in 1988 or the governorship of Texas in 1990, both possible stepping stones to the White House. Clearly Henry Cisneros is a political leader with considerable potential.

FURTHER READING: Richard Chavira and Charlie Ericksen, "An American Political Phenomenon Called Cisneros," *La Luz* 19:6 (August–September 1981); Katherine Díaz, "Henry Cisneros: Our Hope for Today & Tomorrow," *Caminos* 4:3 (March 1983); Kemper Diehl and Jan Jarboe, *Cisneros: Portrait of a New American*, San Antonio: Corona Publishing Co., 1985; Russ Hoyle, "Now Is the Time, Compadres," *Time* (13 April 1981).

CISNEROS, JOSE (1910–   ), artist, illustrator. José Cisneros was born in the small town of Ocampo in the west Mexican state of Durango. The family was driven northward by Mexico's Great Revolution, and he grew up in the settlement of Dorado in the northern border state of Chihuahua. When he was fifteen, the family moved to the border city of Juárez and he studied art across the river in El Paso at the Lydia Patterson Institute. In the mid–1930s he moved to El Paso and has since lived there. By 1934 he was a largely self-taught artist of sufficient ability to get some of his illustrative work published in Mexico. Three years later he was introduced to Texas publisher Carl Herzog by painter Tom Lea and began to illustrate the former's books on the Southwest. By the early 1970s he had done dozens of books for Herzog and over forty for other publishers as well. In addition he designed decorated maps, greeting cards, and other illustrated materials.

Cisneros's specialty is the many different horsemen of the Mexican border region since the late sixteenth century. He owns a large personal library, which contains data on their outfits, clothing, trappings, and weapons. He has had many exhibits of his horsemen in museums throughout the Southwest and in 1969 received a fellowship to develop this series. Ultimately about 100 of his horsemen drawings will form a collection—and a valuable reference tool.

FURTHER READING: Peggy and Harold Samuels, *Illustrated Biographical Encyclopedia of Artists of the American West*, Garden City, N.Y.: Doubleday & Co. 1976.

CORONA, BERT N. (1918–   ), political activist, union organizer, professor. Bert Corona was born 29 May 1918 in El Paso, Texas, where his family had recently moved from Mexico. He grew up and received his early education there and in 1936 moved to Los Angeles, where he attended the University of Southern California and the University of California, majoring in commercial law. During his college years he supported himself by working as a stevedore, joined Harry Bridges international longshoreman's union, and between 1936 and 1942 participated widely in union organizing for the Congress of Industrial Organizations (CIO) and its affiliate, the United Cannery, Agricultural, Packing and Allied Workers of America.

During these years Corona was also active in politics, campaigning in 1938 to elect Eduardo Quevedo to the Los Angeles city council and later working for Edward Roybal's* election. At the beginning of the 1950s he was a regional organizer for the National Association of Mexican Americans and was also deeply involved in opposing passage of the McCarran-Walter Immigration Act. He continued to work actively in state politics; between 1952 and 1954 he was a member of the Northern California Democratic Campaign Committee. In 1959 he, Quevedo, and others met in Fresno, California, and organized the seminal Mexican American Political Association (MAPA). During the 1960 election he served on the California and national "Viva Kennedy" campaign committees. Two years later he worked on the "Viva 'Pat' Brown" (for governor) campaign and then in 1964 he was cochairman of the Viva Johnson national campaign. In 1967 he was appointed to the U.S. Civil Rights Commission and in the following year was the national coordinator of the Viva (Bobby) Kennedy campaign and a delegate to the Democratic national convention, where he fought for liberal reform candidates. Long a supporter of Tom Bradley, he worked for his election to the mayoralty of Los Angeles and in 1973 finally saw him take office.

During the mid–1960s Bert Corona was deeply involved in the immigration issue as a consultant to the Labor Department. In 1972 he opposed the Kennedy-Rodino Act revision of U.S. immigration legislation. During the 1970s he continued to fight for and speak out for the rights of undocumented workers, and when the Simpson-Mazzoli immigration bill was introduced in 1981, he found himself again in opposition. Throughout the first half of the 1980s he has been deeply involved in the immigration question and the issue of media bias. In May 1982 Corona made headlines in the *Los Angeles Times* as the result of a bitter conflict with some colleagues at California State University, Los Angeles.

Bert Corona's record attests to his preeminence in leadership. In addition to the groups already mentioned, he has organized or helped to organize the Hermandad General de Trabajadores in the Los Angeles area, the National Congress of Spanish-speaking People, the Community Service Organization, and the Mexican Youth Conference. Furthermore, within these organizations he has served in varied and numerous positions of authority and leadership. For example, in MAPA he has held the offices of California state secretary, vice-president, and president. As a teacher he has lectured at Stanford University and taught at San Diego State University, California State University at Northridge, and California State University, Los Angeles. Until March 1978 Corona also served as president of the Association of California School Administrators.

FURTHER READING: Bert Corona, *Bert Corona Speaks*, New York: Pathfinder Press, 1972; John Hammerback, "An Interview with Bert Corona," *Western Journal of Speech Communication* 44 (Summer 1980); Carlos Larralde, *Mexican American: Movements and Leaders*, Los Alamitos, Calif.: Hwong Publishing Co., 1976.

CORONA, JUAN V. (1934–), labor contractor. Juan Corona was born in 1934 at the small town of Autlán about 100 miles southwest of Guadalajara, Mexico, in a large farming family. At age 15 he immigrated to the United States where he worked as an itinerant farm laborer in California. In January 1956 he was committed for three months to DeWitt State Hospital for psychiatric treatment. He obtained a labor contractor's license in 1963 and supplied workers to orchardists in the Sacramento Valley.

In late May 1971 Corona was arrested on the charge of having murdered twenty-five migrant farm workers whose bodies were found buried near Yuba City, California. During his trial charges of racial prejudice were made by individuals and by some Mexican American groups, and national attention was focused on difficulties often faced by Mexican Americans in obtaining equal treatment before the law. After a dramatic and controversy-filled trial he was found guilty on twenty-five counts of first-degree murder on 18 January 1973 and sentenced to twenty-five consecutive life terms in prison.

In May 1978 a court of appeals overturned Corona's convictions and ordered a new trial, principally on the basis that evidence was erroneously suppressed, but also that he was inadequately represented in court. Between 1978 and the second trial in the spring of 1982 intensive investigation of the case led to a new witness, a former Mexican consular official, who testified that Corona had confessed the twenty-five murders to him in 1978. Corona was again convicted. In February 1985 some doubt about this key witness's integrity were raised in the aftermath of a drug-related arrest in Mexico. Corona's lawyers argued that as a result he should have a new trial. In June 1984 Corona, divorced by his wife, blinded in one eye from a prison knife attack, and suffering from three earlier heart attacks, was denied parole.

FURTHER READING: "Evidence Suppressed in Corona Murder Trial...," *The Peninsular Times Tribune* (California) (25 December 1980); "Juan Corona's Attorney Plans Appeal," *San Francisco Chronicle* (27 February 1985).

CORONEL, ANTONIO FRANCO (1817–1894), civic leader, landowner, educator. Antonio Coronel was born in Mexico City on 21 October 1817 in the midst of the Mexican movement for independence. When he was seventeen, the family moved to the northwestern frontier town of Los Angeles in Alta California as members of the Padrés-Híjar colony. Here he grew to manhood and began a career of service to society. Under the independent Mexican government he served as a schoolteacher like his father, territorial deputy, street commissioner, and member of an electoral commission and of the Los Angeles irrigation board. In the waning years of Mexican rule he was made justice of the peace and inspector of the recently secularized missions as well. When the American forces invaded California, he fought against them, but after the Treaty of Guadalupe Hidalgo in 1848 he became a loyal and active American citizen. In April 1848 he was elected to the Los Angeles city council and later that year was appointed to the irrigation board.

At the beginning of the gold rush, Coronel was one of the few fortunate ones who made a modest fortune in the mines in 1848 and in early 1849. Encountering a rising tide of anti-Mexicanism in the gold fields, in the summer of 1849 he returned to Los Angeles where he owned considerable land, resumed his teaching, and soon was elected again to the city council. He was also appointed superintendent of schools. In the 1850s he served in many positions in city and county government including that of county assessor and mayor of Los Angeles. As mayor he spearheaded a movement to initiate a public school, despite some Anglo opposition, and in 1855 Los Angeles's first public school was built. In the late 1850s he took an active role in the efforts to suppress local banditry and other criminal conduct.

During the Civil War Coronel was a city councilman and member of the new Board of Health. In the post–Civil War period he continued to play a broad and active role in southern California Democratic politics, becoming something of a local Mexican American elder statesman. Unlike many Californios he adapted well to the new Anglo environment and remained financially solvent with considerable income from money-lending, grape growing, and his real estate activities. Though he never sought public office, he was sought out by Anglo leaders and in 1867 was elected to state treasurer, a position with great patronage power. He held this office until the mid–1870s when he was elected to the state senate, where he acted as a principal Californio spokesman.

During the 1870s and 1880s Antonio Coronel managed his extensive properties and continued his activities in civic affairs and in state politics. In 1873 he became a part owner of the Los Angeles weekly, *La Crónica*, and remained active in its direction for several years. Suffering poor health from 1893 on, he died on 17 April 1894, ending a long and unusually distinguished career of public service.

FURTHER READING: H. H. Bancroft, *History of California*, vol. 2, San Francisco: History Co., 1884–1890; H. D. Barrows, "Antonio F. Coronel," *Historical Society of Southern California Quarterly* 5:1 (1900); Antonio F. Coronel, "Cosas de California," unpublished manuscript, Bancroft Library, University of California, Berkeley; Marco Newmark, "Antonio Franco Coronel," *Historical Society of Southern California Quarterly* 36:2 (June 1954).

CORTES, CARLOS E. (1934–   ), historian, professor. Born in Oakland, California, on 6 April 1934 of Mexican American parents who had met at the University of California in nearby Berkeley, Carlos Cortés grew up in Kansas City, Missouri, and received his early education there. After completing high school in 1952, he came west to study and four years later received his B.A. in communications and public policy at the University of California at Berkeley. From the University of California he went to New York where he earned his M.S. in journalism at Columbia University in 1957. There followed a two-year stint in the U.S. Army as an information specialist. Out of the service, he worked as executive editor of the Phoenix Sunpapers, a suburban chain of weeklies, from 1959 to 1961. In the latter year he also became a reporter for the Associated Press and entered the U.S. Institute for Foreign Trade to prepare himself for a position as foreign correspondent. Instead, he decided that Latin American history was his real interest and earned his M.A. in Portuguese and Spanish at the University of New Mexico in 1965 and his Ph.D. in history there four years later. In 1968 he came to the History Department of the University of California at Riverside where he has taught since. From 1969 to 1971 he was chair of Latin American Studies; from 1972 to 1979 he chaired the Chicano Studies Program; and between 1982 and 1986 he was chair of the History Department. From 1970 to 1972 he was also assistant to the vice chancellor for academic affairs.

Carlos Cortés has been a scholar of extraordinary industry in several fields: Latin American history, ethnic history, and education, particularly multicultural. He has authored, coauthored, edited, and coedited numerous monographs, books, and articles; he is especially notable as editor of three major reprint series: the Mexican American (twenty-one volumes), the Chicano Heritage (fifty-five volumes), and Hispanics in the United States (thirty-one volumes). He is the author of *Gaucho Politics in Brazil* (1974), which won the Hubert Herring Memorial Award that year, *Three Perspectives on Ethnicity* (1976), *A Filmic Approach to the Study of Historical Dilemmas* (1976), and *Our California* (1983), among others. He also authored "Mexicans" in the *Harvard Encyclopedia of American Ethnic Groups* (1980), which won the 1981 Waldo G. Leland Prize of the American Historical Association, and "Latinos" in the *World Book Encyclopedia* (1981). He has been an editor of *Aztlán*, *Crítica*, and *Social Education* and is a columnist for *Media & Values*. He has served as consultant to well over 200 federal, state, local, governmental, and educational agencies and businesses. In addition he has given numerous invited lectures in South America, Mexico, Europe, and the United States. For the past decade he has been especially interested in researching the treatment of ethnicity and foreigners by the American cinema industry, and many of his recent lectures and papers have been on this topic.

Carlos Cortés is a member of various historical and educational associations; he has served on many governmental, educational, and private boards, councils, committees, projects, and panels. A Phi Beta Kappa student, he was the recipient of various fellowships in graduate school. In 1976 he received the Distinguished Teaching Award from the University of California at Riverside and four years later was awarded the Distinguished California Humanist award of the California Council for the Humanities. He was named 1983 Bildner Fellow of the Association of American Schools in South America and currently holds a Japan Foundation and a Rockefeller Foundation research fellowship.

FURTHER READING: Julio A. Martínez, *Chicano Scholars and Writers: A Bio-Bibliographical Directory*, Metuchen, N.J.: The Scarecrow Press, 1979; "People on the Move," *Caminos* 1:7 (November 1980).

CORTEZ LIRA, GREGORIO (1875–1916), folk hero. Cortez was born on the Mexican side of the U.S.–Mexican border in the state of Tamaulipas, but moved into Texas with the family when he was about twelve years old. He soon joined an older brother, Romaldo, in the migrant life of cowboy and farmworker, meanwhile also marrying and beginning a family. At the turn of the nineteenth century Gregorio and his brother, with their families, settled down on adjacent rented farms in Karnes County, Texas.

Here, on his farm in 1901, Cortez shot and killed Sheriff W. T. Morris in an act of self-defense when the sheriff tried to arrest him for horse stealing. After sending his family to safety in town and later taking his wounded brother for medical care, Gregorio took flight. On foot and horseback, after first walking north for one hundred miles, he headed for the Rio Grande border, pursued by various posses, totaling perhaps 300 men. By evasive tactics Cortez managed to elude his numerous pursuers from 12 June until 22 June, in the process killing another sheriff. On 22 June he was betrayed by an acquaintance and taken prisoner; his entire family, including his four young children, had meanwhile been jailed. In the court cases that followed Gregorio's defense was financed by donations from Mexican Americans, Mexicans, and even Anglo Americans. He was tried for three murders, found not guilty of killing Sheriff Morris, but initially convicted of the other two charges. Later one conviction was reversed on appeal, but in January 1905 he began to serve a life sentence in Huntsville Penitentiary for the third killing. In 1913, after long years of effort on his behalf, Gregorio Cortez was pardoned by the governor of Texas. Virtually everyone who came into extended contact with his straightforward, pleasant personality was won over, and most became convinced of his innocence. However, popular reaction to his release was quite mixed.

Less than three months after his discharge from jail, Gregorio Cortez was south of the Texas border fighting in Victoriano Huerta's army. Subsequently he was wounded in revolutionary fighting and returned to Texas to convalesce. Three years later while celebrating his latest wedding at Austin, Texas, in 1916 he died quite suddenly, probably of a heart attack or stroke.

By his remarkable eleven-day flight and his numerous trials, Gregorio Cortez came to symbolize the conflict between Mexican Americans and Anglo Americans in Texas. His resistance to injustice was seen as a to-be-expected reaction to a double standard of justice in Texas for Anglos and Mexicans. For his resistance to Texas racism he became enshrined as a border folk hero in the ballad, "El Corrido de Gregorio Cortez."

FURTHER READING: José E. Limón, "Healing the Wounds: Folk Symbols and Historical Crisis," *Texas Humanist* (March–April 1984); Américo Paredes, *With a Pistol in His Hand*, Austin: University of Texas Press, 1958.

CORTINA, JUAN NEPOMUCENO (1824–1892), bandit-revolutionary, politician, Mexican governor, rancher. "Cheno" Cortina was born 16 May 1824 on the south side of the Rio Grande at Camargo, Tamaulipas, where his father was town *alcalde* and an important landowner. When his father died in the early 1840s, the family moved to his mother's property, part of the Espíritu Santo grant, near Brownsville, Texas. Little is known of his early life and education, but he seems to have had a rebellious nature and preferred to associate with the *vaqueros* who nicknamed him "Cheno." A bit too young to become involved in the early federalist secessionist movements of Mexico's northeastern frontier, he did fight against the invading forces of General Zachary Taylor during the early stages of the United States–Mexican war. After the Treaty of Guadalupe Hidalgo and a brief stint in the U.S. Quartermaster Corps he settled on a part of his mother's land, developing it into a ranch raising longhorn cattle. Urged on by his mother, Cortina also became active in local politics during the second half of the 1850s and seems to have wielded a good deal of power as a Democratic leader of the Mexican American vote. In this heavily Mexican lower Rio Grande area he soon became aware of the inferior economic and social position that most Mexican Americans were being forced into.

In the summer of 1859 Cortina prevented a Texas marshall from the use of excessive violence in arresting a former employee of his family, wounding the officer in the process. This exploit made him a local hero among the poorer classes, but also forced him to flee across the Rio Grande into Mexico to avoid almost certain imprisonment with the unlikelihood of a fair trial and the possibility of being lynched. Cortina's action aroused the ill-treated Mexican border people, and he soon found himself with a sizable volunteer force, eager to right the wrongs suffered by La Raza. Late in September he led his followers across the river to avenge the killing of some Mexicans and rode into Brownsville in order to seize those responsible. Two days later from his mother's ranch he issued a declaration of grievances that justified his action as a response to Anglo mistreatment. Subsequently he defeated the local Texas militia, Mexican forces from Matamoros, and a Texas ranger group; however at the end of the year U.S. Army troops under Robert E. Lee were brought in and Cortina fled into Mexico. Meanwhile he reiterated his commitment to social justice for Mexicans and his continuing resistance to oppression and the failure of the law.

Cortina's effort to help La Raza proved counterproductive; instead of bringing better treatment, his actions led to greater hatred of Mexicans and more persecution. His actions were viewed by some Anglos as part of an attempt to reconquer Texas for Mexico. In the early 1860s Cortina joined the Mexican forces of Benito Juárez in their struggle against the French intervention and fought under General Ignacio Zaragoza (a Tejano) in many battles including the famous Cinco de Mayo defeat of the French at Puebla. Back on the border in 1863, he was soon promoted to the rank of general and later served the Juárez government as military commandant and acting governor of the border state of Tamaulipas. His anti-Confederate stance during the Civil War led to conflict with Southern forces and to a postwar effort to obtain a pardon for Cortina from the Reconstruction government in Texas. That effort failed.

In 1872 a U.S. congressional committee investigating border banditry concluded that Cortina was largely responsible for the unrest; however, a Mexican commission came to the conclusion that much of the evidence against Cortina was from his enemies. He was arrested in 1875 by the Mexican government for cattle rustling but apparently was never brought to trial. In the following year he supported the revolt of General Porfirio Díaz and was able to return to the border area, only to be rearrested and sentenced to the firing squad. Instead, he was sent to Mexico City where he lived out his life under local arrest. Only once did he return to the border; in 1890 he was allowed to return briefly to visit relatives and friends in Matamoros. When he died in 1892, he was buried with full military honors from the Mexican government.

A center of controversy during his life and today, Cortina seems to have been neither total rogue nor saint, but a product of his time and place. To some he was a bandit and cattle thief; to others he was a valiant defender of the rights and interests of the the poor and powerless.

FURTHER READING: *Juan N. Cortina: Two Interpretations*, New York: Arno Press, 1974; reprint of C. W. Goldfinch's and José T. Canales's works; Lyman Woodman, *Cortina, Rogue of the Rio Grande*, San Antonio: Naylor Co., 1950.

D

DE HOYOS, ANGELA. See HOYOS, ANGELA DE.

DE LA GARZA, ELIGIO. See GARZA, ELIGIO DE LA.

DEL BUONO, ANTONIO. See BUONO, ANTONIO DEL.

DE LEON, NAPHTALI. See LEON, NAPHTALI DE.

DELGADO, ABELARDO BARRIENTOS (1931–). Poet, writer, community organizer. Abelardo, the single name by which he is commonly known, was born in the tiny settlement of Boquilla de Conchos in central west Chihuahua. When he was eleven, he and his mother moved to El Paso, Texas, where he attended public schools and later graduated from the University of Texas with a B.S. degree. After college, marriage, and ten years working in a Catholic youth center in El Paso, he had developed considerable skill as a social worker, community organizer, and lecturer. At the end of the 1960s he moved to Denver, Colorado, where he worked for several years as executive director of the Colorado Migrant Council and also founded a Chicano publishing house, Barrio Publications.

During the 1970s Abelardo traveled throughout the United States, reading his poetry and lecturing at various universities. A prolific writer, he began his first literary efforts while still in elementary school. In all, he has published nine collections of poetry; because of their quality his works have frequently been included in anthologies of Chicano writing. Among his best-known publications are *Chicano: 25 Pieces of a Chicano Mind* (1969), *The Chicano Movement: Some Not Too Objective Observations* (1971), *Bajo el Sol de Aztlán: 25 Soles de Abelardo* (1973), and *It's Cold: 52 Cold Thought-Poems of Abelardo* (1974). In 1977 his short novel, *Letters to Louise*, won the Tonatiuh-Quinto Sol award for literature. Besides writing more than 1,000 poems, Abelardo has found time to teach at the University of Utah, the University of Texas at El Paso, and the

University of Colorado. He is an authority on Caló, a dialect of the barrio. Widely recognized among Mexican Americans for his leadership of the Chicano Movement, he is particularly admired as founder of social service organizations including Maya, Machos, and the Guadalupe Employment Agency. In his poetry Abelardo often expresses his concern for improving conditions for the poorer members of La Raza.

FURTHER READING: Juan Bruce-Novoa, *Chicano Authors: Inquiry by Interview*, Austin: University of Texas Press, 1980.

DE ZAVALA, ADINA. See ZAVALA, ADINA EMILIA DE.

DE ZAVALO, LORENZO. See ZAVALA, LORENZO DE.

E

ELIZONDO, SERGIO D. (1930–   ), professor, poet, educator. Sergio Elizondo was born in the town of El Fuerte in northern Sinaloa, the sixth of seven children in a schoolteacher family. He attended school, first in the town of Sinaloa and then in Culiacán, the capital of the state of Sinaloa. After one year in the Escuela Normal, in 1950 he crossed into the United States. Two years later he entered Findlay College in Ohio, and with time out for service in the U.S. Army in Germany, graduated in 1958 with a B.S. in sociology. He then pursued graduate studies in Romance languages at the University of North Carolina, being awarded his M.A. in 1961 and his Ph.D. three years later. Meanwhile he began teaching, first at North Carolina, then in the University of Texas at Austin (1963–1968), California State University at San Bernardino, Western Washington State College, and New Mexico State University (Las Cruces). At the same time he rose from instructor to full professor and filled the role of department chairman and later dean. He has also served on numerous regional and national educational committees.

Elizondo has been an active participant in the Chicano Movement since the mid–1960s. At the end of that decade he participated in developing the Plan de Santa Barbara, a Chicano plan for higher education. During the 1970s he was an articulate and frequent spokesman on a number of issues affecting Chicanos. Elizondo's best-known work is *Perros y Antiperros* (1972). This Chicano epic is a long poem of social protest, of bitter rejection of the melting-pot concept, a denunciation of Anglo values, and an elevating of Chicano values. Elizondo sees his writing as a part of his efforts to help improve life for La Raza.

FURTHER READING: Juan Bruce-Novoa, *Chicano Authors: Inquiry by Interview*, Austin: University of Texas Press, 1980; Julio A. Martínez, *Chicano Scholars and Writers: A Bio-Bibliographical Directory*, Metuchen, N.J.: The Scarecrow Press, 1979.

ELIZONDO, VIRGIL P. (1935–   ), priest, theologian, social activist. Virgil Elizondo was born 25 August 1935 during the Great Depression in San Antonio, Texas, and grew up there in the Mexican barrio. He attended Catholic grade and high schools and in 1957 graduated from St. Mary's University with a B.S. in chemistry. He then entered the seminary. Six years later, after his religious formation at Assumption Seminary in San Antonio, he was ordained to the priesthood.

In 1968 Father Elizondo attended the second meeting of CELAM, the Latin American Bishops' Council, at Medellín, Colombia, as expert advisor to Archbishop Robert Lucey of San Antonio on Latino matters. After Medellín he went to Ateneo University in Manila where he earned an M.A. in pastoral studies by the end of the following year. Upon his return to San Antonio he was appointed dean of students at Assumption Seminary.

In 1972 Virgil Elizondo founded the subsequently very important Mexican American Cultural Center (MACC), located on the campus of Assumption Seminary. MACC's purpose was to sensitize, educate, and train religious social activists for service among U.S. Latinos and in Latin America. He was also active in the early development of Padres Asociados Para Derechos Religiosos, Educativos, y Sociales (PADRES), an association mostly of Chicano priests concerned about the socioeconomic role and position of Latinos in U.S. society and in the Catholic church. In the late 1970s he took a year off to initiate doctoral studies in religious sciences at the Institute Catholique in Paris. He has since completed his doctorate. During the first half of the 1980s he served as editor for *Concilium*, a series of books on contemporary theological topics by outstanding theologians. A member of the Ecumenical Association of Third World Theologians, he is recognized as the major Mexican American theologian. He also is rector of San Fernando Cathedral in San Antonio and continues to direct MACC, to write, and to lecture.

The Reverend Virgil Elizondo is the author of numerous books on theological topics as they relate to the Mexican American; he has also published many articles on theology and catechetics in both English and Spanish. Some have been translated into French and Italian. A frequent lecturer and keynoter, he has delivered papers at conferences throughout the United States and in Manila and Rome.

FURTHER READING: Julio A. Martínez, *Chicano Scholars and Writers: A Bio-Bibliographical Directory*, Metuchen, N.J.: The Scarecrow Press, 1979; *National Catholic Reporter*, 20 (27 January 1984).

ESCOVEDO, PETER (1935–   ), musician, painter. Pete Escovedo was born of Mexican immigrant parents on 13 July 1935 near Pittsburg, California, at the junction of the Sacramento and San Joaquin rivers. Having a father who sang with local Mexican bands, he was inevitably exposed to Latino music as he grew up in the delta region. With his older brother Coke, he began to play the drums in San Francisco Bay area musical groups, first achieving national recognition in the late 1960s with Carlos Santana's band.

In 1970 Pete Escovedo and Coke with four other musicians formed their own ensemble, which they called AZTECA. A representative of Columbia Records, impressed with the band, took it to London two years later to do a showcase performance and also signed Escovedo to a recording contract. Out of this contract came two albums: "AZTECA" and "Pyramid of the Moon." During the latter part of 1972 and in 1973 Escovedo's band toured the United States with Stevie Wonder and the Temptations. By this time the band had grown to twenty-four members, and it became increasingly difficult to support financially. Ultimately AZTECA dwindled and disbanded. In the second half of the 1970s Escovedo continued to play Bay-area clubs and with his daughter Sheila made two successful albums for Fantasy Records: "Solo Two" and "Happy Together." Late in 1977 he again became percussionist with Carlos Santana's band, doing a world tour, a U.S. tour, and some records. A stalwart supporter of Latin music on the West Coast for two decades, he currently continues to perform in the San Francisco area, often with his daughter as well as other musicians.

In addition to his great skills as a percussionist, Pete Escovedo is a local artist of considerable note. An abstract expressionist showing some influence of pre-Columbian art, he has had a number of local exhibits, and his paintings have been purchased by private collectors.

FURTHER READING: Pedro S. Romero, "Pete Escovedo: A Study in Versatility," *Nuestro* 6:10 (December 1982).

ESPINOSA, AURELIO M. (1880–1958), professor, author. Aurelio Espinosa was born in southern Colorado at Carnero in September 1880 and attended public school in Del Norte on the Rio Grande. One of thirteen children, from youth on he was encouraged to follow his studious bent. In 1902 he received his B.A. in Spanish at the University of Colorado, where he also completed his M.A. two years later. Meanwhile he taught Spanish at the University of New Mexico and at the University of Chicago. At Chicago he studied under Professor Karl Pietsch, an outstanding philologist, and received his Ph.D. *cum laude* in 1909. His doctoral thesis led directly to his appointment as assistant professor at Stanford University in 1909 and was published in three parts between 1909 and 1914. He taught at Stanford the rest of his career, occupying the chair of the Department of Romance Languages and Literature from 1932 to 1953.

At Stanford Espinosa directed over fifty master's theses and twelve doctoral dissertations. He was active in founding the American Association of Teachers of Spanish and in 1918 became the first editor of its journal *Hispania*, a position he held until 1926. Two years later he was elected president of the association. In 1929 he was named president of the Pacific Coast branch of the American Philological Association. From 1914 to 1946 he also served as an editor of the *Journal of American Folklore*, and in the mid–1920s was elected president of the American Folklore Society. During the first half of the 1930s he served as an editor of *The New Mexico Quarterly*, and from 1947 to 1953 he was an associate editor of *Western Folklore*.

A linguistic and folklore scholar of prodigious ability, research, and output, Espinosa authored over thirty textbooks and a dozen scholarly monographs; he published some 175 articles in top journals, and he also translated a number of works, both from English to Spanish and from Spanish to English. He was especially notable for his comparative study of the "tar baby" folk stories, tracing their origins to India. For his scholarship and leadership in Spanish and folklore studies he was honored in 1922 by the Spanish government with knighthood in the Order of Isabel la Católica. In 1950 he was awarded the Grand Cross of the Order of Alfonso el Sabio by Spain. In addition to these and other honors he was made a member of the Royal Spanish Academy, the Instituto de Cultura Hispánica, and other prestigious societies. Among his best-known works are *Studies in New Mexican Spanish* (1909), *Elementary Spanish Reader* (1916), *Cuentos populares españoles* (1946–1947), and *Romancero de Nuevo Méjico* (1953).

FURTHER READING: J. Manuel Espinosa, "Espinosa's New Mexican Background and Professional Career," *The Folklore of Spain in the American Southwest*, Norman: University of Oklahoma Press, 1985; "Spanish Folklore in the Southwest: The Pioneer Work of Aurelio M. Espinosa," *The Americas* 35:2 (October 1978); George McSpadden, "Aurelio M. Espinosa (1880–1958)" *Hispania* 42:1 (March 1959).

F

FERNANDEZ, BENJAMIN (1925–), businessman, politician. Born 24 February 1925 in a converted boxcar in Kansas City, Kansas, Ben Fernández was one of eight children of immigrant Mexican parents. He grew up in urban poverty and during summers worked in the tomato and sugar beet fields of the Midwest with the family. During World War II he served four years in the U.S. Air Force as an enlisted man and at the end of his service enrolled in the University of Redlands in southern California. With the help of the G.I. Bill and his own hard work he was able to complete his undergraduate education in two years, graduating with a B.A. in economics. Out of college, he was recruited by the General Electric Company for its financial management training program. Fernández continued his studies in the evening program of the Graduate School of Business, New York University, earning a master's degree in business administration. He continued work toward a doctorate. Returning to California in 1960, he became a consulting economist in Los Angeles where he specialized in savings and loan associations.

During the 1960s Ben Fernández served on Claremont University Center's board of trustees and also began to take an active role in Republican politics. In 1972 he was national cochairman of the Finance Committee to reelect President Richard M. Nixon and in the following year was sent as special ambassador to the fifth inaugural of President Alfredo Stroessner of Paraguay. He served as national chairman of the Republican National Hispanic Assembly in 1975 and as a member of the Republican National Committee's executive committee in the following year. In November 1978 he announced his candidacy for the Republican nominee to the presidency but lost out to Ronald Reagan, for whom he then campaigned in the 1980 general election.

FURTHER READING: "Benjamin Fernandez, Mr. Hispanic Republican," *La Luz* 6:8 (August 1977).

FLORES, PATRICIO FERNANDEZ (1929–), archbishop. Patrick Flores was born 20 July 1929 in Ganado, Texas, eighth of nine children in a migrant farm-working family. As a boy growing up around Houston he followed the cotton crop northward with his brothers and sisters and dropped out of high school in his sophomore year, at age seventeen, partly as the result of his fragmented educational history. However, he soon returned not only to complete high school but also to go on to studies for the priesthood at St. Mary's Seminary in Houston. After his ordination in 1956 he served fourteen years as a parish priest in various churches of the Houston diocese. Early in 1970 he was appointed titular bishop of Itolica; then with the strong backing of Archbishop Francis Furey he was appointed auxiliary bishop of San Antonio on Cinco de Mayo 1970. Seven years later he was consecrated bishop of El Paso, and in August 1979, after Furey's death, he was elevated to archbishop of San Antonio with César Chávez,* José Angel Gutiérrez,* and 10,000 Mexican Americans in attendance.

Archbishop Flores is basically a moderate who has been extremely active in supporting the civil rights of Mexican Americans. He was chairman of the Texas Advisory Committee of the U.S. Civil Rights Commission and has directly involved himself in the legal defense of Mexican Americans accused of crime, on one occasion donating his episcopal ring to raise defense funds. He has visited migrant farm worker camps in Idaho, Wisconsin, South Dakota, and other midwestern states, living with the workers. For a time in the early 1970s he was national chairman of PADRES, an organization of Mexican American priests. A member of the board of Saul Alinsky's Industrial Areas Foundation, in 1972 he inaugurated a pet project, the Mexican American Cultural Center headed by Father Virgil Elizondo,* to train barrio residents in problem-solving and leadership skills. He helped in the founding of COPS (Communities Organized for Public Service) in 1974 and has strongly supported it since then. As a prelate with great concern for the "Hispanic Church" and chairman of the U.S. Catholic Bishops Committee on the Church in Latin America, Archbishop Flores was one of a group of American bishops who visited Cuba in January 1985 and came away hopeful for the future of the Church there.

FURTHER READING: *American Catholic Who's Who, 1980–1981*, vol. 23, 1980; Rick Casey, "Patricio Flores," *S.A. The Magazine of San Antonio* (December 1979); Al Martínez, *Rising Voices: Profiles of Hispano-American Lives*, New York: New American Library, 1974; "Patrick Flores: The Barrio Bishop," *La Luz* 1:4 (August 1972).

FLORES, TOM (1937–   ), coach, football player. Tom Flores was born 21 March 1937 in Fresno, California, one of two children of a Mexican immigrant father who fled to the United States as a twelve-year-old to escape Mexico's Great Revolution. He grew up in nearby Sanger, attending school there, and working as a youngster in the fields of the San Joaquin Valley alongside his parents and older brother. After graduating in 1954 from Sanger High School, where he starred in baseball, basketball, and football, he went to Fresno City College, where he made Honorable Mention Junior College All-American in football. After his A.A. degree he entered the College (today University) of the Pacific in Stockton (California) from which he graduated in 1958 with a B.A.

degree in education and a football record that included selection for several All-American teams. His efforts to turn professional in 1958 and 1959 were frustrated by an old shoulder injury problem, so he temporarily accepted a coaching job at Fresno High School.

In 1960 Flores joined the original Oakland Raiders football team, and in his six years as quarterback with the Raiders he completed 810 passes for 11,635 yards and 92 touchdowns. In 1967 he was traded to the Buffalo (N.Y.) Bills and after two seasons there completed his playing career at Kansas City with the Chiefs in 1969 and 1970. Almost resigned to entering a business career in plastics, he welcomed an invitation from Raiders head coach John Madden in 1972 to become receivers coach. During his seven years as an assistant coach the Raiders enjoyed great success, reaching the playoffs six times and winning the Super Bowl once. In 1979 Flores replaced Madden as head coach and in the following year piloted the team to another Super Bowl victory. The move of the Raiders to Los Angeles seemed to pose only a temporary setback to Flores. In 1982 he was named Coach of the Year and in the following year again brought the Raiders to a Super Bowl win. In May 1984 the Los Angeles Board of Supervisors awarded Tom Flores a plaque for his contribution to the city's image, especially the 1984 Super Bowl victory.

FURTHER READING: Frank del Olmo, "The Ice Man," *Nuestro* 3:9 (October 1979); "Sports: Tom Flores: Not Settling for Second Best," *Caminos* 4:1–2 (January–February 1983).

G

GALARZA, ERNESTO (1905–1984), labor expert, sociologist, author, educator, labor organizer. Galarza was born in the tiny mountain village of Jalcocotán near Tepic, capital of the western Mexican state of Nayarit. Because of unstable conditions caused by the Mexican Revolution his family moved regularly in search of greater security when he was a lad, living for a while in Tepic, Mazatlán, Nogales, Tucson, and finally settling in Sacramento, California. Here young Ernesto continued the education begun in Mexico and began his adaptation to American culture. When he was suddenly left without an immediate family by the death of his mother and uncle, he remained in high school, supporting himself by working at odd jobs. On completing high school, he was awarded a scholarship for Occidental College in Los Angeles, where he majored in history. From Occidental he went on to graduate studies at Stanford University, receiving his M.A. in history there in 1929, and later capped his education with a Ph.D. with Honors from Columbia University in 1946. He was also awarded the coveted accolade of academia—Phi Beta Kappa.

After college during the 1930s and 1940s, Galarza worked in a variety of occupations centered around three interests: education, labor, and Latin America. In the early 1930s he taught at and acted as codirector of a New York progressive elementary school; between 1936 and 1940 he worked as a research specialist in Latin American affairs for the Foreign Policy Association and as a research assistant in education for the Pan American Union. By accepting promotion in the Pan American Union to chief of the Division of Labor and Social Information, Galarza turned to the interest that was to be central to him for the rest of his life—labor. He left the Pan American Union in 1947 to become more actively involved in labor issues by accepting the position of research director and field organizer for the newly formed National Agricultural Workers Union, A.F. of L. and moved to San Jose, California. He remained with the NAWU for twleve years of its efforts to organize agricultural labor and rose to vice-president and secretary-treasurer. During these years he became intimately acquainted with the problems of farm labor, especially the use and abuse of Mexican workers.

In the decade of the 1960s Galarza was busy in a variety of jobs: editor of *Inter-American Reports*; consultant to the U.S. Civil Rights Commission, the Ford Foundation, and the government of Bolivia (which awarded him the Order of the Condor); and in 1963 and 1964 labor counselor to the Committee on Education and Labor, U.S. House of Representatives. In this last capacity he gave testimony on various facets of the bracero program before numerous government committees. He also became deeply involved in various Mexican American organizations. During the 1970s he continued to be an active spokesman for the rights of farm workers at numerous conferences and was a frequent university lecturer. He was an associate research professor in sociology at the University of Notre Dame and a distinguished visiting professor in the Department of Education at San Jose State University, where he also taught in the Mexican American Graduate Studies program and directed a Laboratory for Spanish Teaching Materials. After several years of poor health he died in San Jose on 22 June 1984.

Out of Dr. Galarza's life experiences has come a variety of publications, a number of them important milestones in the study of farmworker history. The best known are *Strangers in Our Fields* (1956), *Merchants of Labor: The Mexican Bracero Story* (1964), *Spiders in the House and Workers in the Field* (1970), and *Farm Workers and Agri-Business in California, 1947–1960* (1977). He was also the author of the *Louisiana Sugar Cane Plantation Workers*, the *Chualar Accident of September 17, 1963*, and other reports on aspects of agricultural labor in Latin America, Puerto Rico, and Hawaii.

In the early 1970s Galarza became active in developing bilingual education programs and Spanish language teaching materials. Among his publications in this area are a number of mini-books: *Zoorisa*, *La mula no nació arisca*, *Rimas tontas*, *Poemas párvulos*, and *Más poemas párvulos*. He was also the author of an autobiography of his early years, titled *Barrio Boy* (1971).

FURTHER READING: Ernesto Galarza, *Barrio Boy*, Notre Dame, Ind.: University of Notre Dame Press, 1971; *Spiders in the House and Workers in the Field* and *Farm Workers and Agri-Business in California, 1947–1960* are both partly autobiographical; Julio A. Martínez and Francisco A. Lomelí, *Chicano Literature: A Reference Guide*, Westport, Conn.: Greenwood Press, 1985; Gabrielle Morris and Timothy Beard, "Ernesto Galarza: Early Organizing Efforts and the Community," *Caminos* 4:7 (July–August 1983).

GALLEGOS, JOSE MANUEL (1815–1875), priest, political leader. Born in northwest New Mexico in present-day Rio Arriba County in the town of Abiquiu, José Manuel as the son of a prominent family attended the school that Father Antonio José Martínez* organized in Taos. He then went to Durango to study for the priesthood at the school of theology there. Upon graduation in 1840 he was ordained a priest and returned to southwestern New Mexico to work among the people of the town of San Juan. He was later transferred successively to Albuquerque and Santa Fe. During this time he also began his political career.

Elected to the Nuevo México provincial legislature on the eve of American conquest, he served from 1843 to 1846 in the Assembly. After New Mexico became a part of the United States by the treaty of Guadalupe Hidalgo, he was elected to the first Territorial Council in 1851.

When Jean Baptiste Lamy was appointed head of the Catholic church in New Mexico at the beginning of the 1850s, Gallegos was excommunicated by him for practicing concubinage. Separated from the church, he devoted himself even more intensely to his political career, which was opposed by Lamy. With strong support of the Penitentes, a New Mexican lay religious brotherhood, Gallegos was elected territorial delegate to the U.S. Congress in 1853, and two years later his reelection was contested by Miguel Otero, Sr.,* with the help of Bishop Lamy. The election was hotly disputed, and Congress awarded Otero the seat. In 1860 he was elected to the lower house of the territorial legislature and was named speaker of the house. At the end of his term he again ran for the position of territorial delegate, but lost.

Meanwhile the Civil War had broken out, and Gallegos, a staunch Unionist, was imprisoned early in 1862 by invading (Texan) Confederate forces. At the end of the war he was appointed territorial treasurer for a two-year term. In 1867 he won election to the territorial House of Representatives and in the following year was appointed superintendent of Indian affairs in New Mexico. After brief service as superintendent he was again elected in 1870 as territorial delegate to the U.S. Congress. Two years later his reelection bid was defeated. After a short illness he died in Santa Fe on 21 April 1875.

FURTHER READING: Fray Angélico Chávez, *But Time and Chance: The Story of Padre Martínez of Taos*, Santa Fe: Sunstone Press, 1981; Paul Horgan, *Lamy of Santa Fe*, New York: Farrar, Straus and Giroux, 1975; Ralph E. Twitchell, *The History of the Military Occupation of New Mexico from 1846 to 1851*, reprint, New York: Arno Press, 1976; Maurilio Vigil, *Los Patrones: Profiles of Hispanic Political Leaders in New Mexico History*, Washington, D.C.: University Press of America, 1980.

GARCIA, ANTONIO (1901–), painter. Antonio García was born in Monterrey, the capital of the Mexican state of Nuevo León, in 1901. A dozen years later as Mexico's Great Revolution heated up, his family crossed the border and settled in the small south Texas town of San Diego, county seat of Duval County, where he attended school. Beginning in 1926 he studied for four years at the Chicago Art Institute and subsequently studied individually with specialists in portrait painting, watercolor, and painting techniques. During the 1930s he painted a mural at the San Diego, Texas, high school under the auspices of the Works Progress Administration and had one of his paintings exhibited at the Texas Centennial Exhibition at Dallas in 1936. Since the early 1950s he has taught art in the Del Mar College (Corpus Christi) adult education program. He also has regularly conducted art workshops during the summers in Saltillo and San Miguel Allende, Mexico.

An artist with a well-established reputation, Antonio García paints landscapes and sometimes a narrative scene, but specializes in portraiture. In addition to illustrating several books, he has painted frescoes at La Bahía Mission in Goliad, Texas, and at Sacred Heart Church in Corpus Christi. He has also worked on several major murals in Texas and elsewhere, including one at Our Lady of Loreto Chapel in Goliad. His paintings show Chicano cultural influence only in the topics selected, as in his paintings *Aztec Advance*, *Virgin de Guadalupe*, and *Immaculate Conception*.

FURTHER READING: Jacinto Quirarte, *Mexican American Artists*, Austin: University of Texas Press, 1973.

GARCIA, ERNEST E. (1946–   ), public official. Born in the small southwestern Kansas town of Garden City on 12 July 1946, Ernie García was the grandson of a Texas migrant worker. His father, a watchmaker and jeweler, died when he was seven. He grew up in Garden City, receiving his early education in the Catholic grade school and at thirteen entered the Brunnerdale Seminary of the Precious Blood fathers, whom he credits for giving him a strong sense of discipline. After a year and a half he left the seminary and returned to Garden City where he entered the public high school. In 1964 he enrolled in nearby Wichita State University, but his college career was interrupted by the Vietnam War and the draft. He avoided the latter by enlisting in the Marines, where he served until 1968. Out of the service he worked in business for a while and then went back to school at Kansas State University in Manhattan. In 1974 he earned his B.A. in sociology, followed by a M.S.W. with emphasis on large systems administration, and in 1977 he received his M.S. in public administration and political science.

Ernie García, meanwhile, did an internship in the governor's office which led to a job in Washington as legislative aide to Kansas senator Robert Dole in 1977. Three years later he returned to Kansas to run the senator's reelection campaign. With the election of Ronald Reagan to the White House García accepted a position as special assistant to the president, and less than a year later became a deputy assistant secretary of defense to Caspar Weinberger with particular responsibility for relations with Congress. García expects to run for elective office sometime in the future.

FURTHER READING: Stephen Goode, "Ernie García: The Pentagon's Sugar Salesman," *Nuestro* 8:5 (June/July 1984).

GARCIA, HECTOR PEREZ (1914–   ), physician, political and community leader, activist. Born in Llera, a small town in south central Tamaulipas, Mexico, on 17 January 1914, Héctor García was still a small child when his family crossed over into Texas, fleeing from the chaos of Mexico's Great Revolution. His entire schooling was in the United States and in 1936 he graduated with a B.A. from the University of Texas. Influenced by parental emphasis on the value of education and by an older brother, he then entered the University of Texas

School of Medicine and received his M.D. in 1940. After two years of general and surgical internship at St. Joseph's Hospital, Creighton University, in Omaha Dr. García entered the U.S. Army, serving as an officer in the Infantry, Engineer Corps, and Medical Corps in the European theater. For his services he was awarded a Bronze Star and six Battle Stars.

Dr. García returned from the war to establish himself in private practice in Corpus Christi. As the result of prejudiced treatment of Mexican American veterans in the local veterans hospital and especially the Félix Longoria* case, in March 1948 he organized the American G.I. Forum. His objective in the G.I. Forum was to defend the civil rights of Mexican Americans, particularly veterans. Elected first national chairman of the Forum, he became active in other Mexican American civil rights groups, especially the League of United Latin American Citizens (LULAC) and helped found the Political Association of Spanish-Speaking Organizations, of which he was elected first president in 1960.

Civil rights involvement inevitably led to political involvement, and in the presidential elections of 1956 and 1960 Dr. García served on the Democratic National Commmittee. In the latter election he also became national coordinator of the Viva Kennedy clubs and was appointed by President John F. Kennedy as a member of the U.S. delegation signing the 1961 Mutual Defense Agreement between the U.S. and the new Federation of the West Indies. After John Kennedy's assassination Héctor García continued to be equally honored by President Lyndon Johnson, who sent him to the inauguration of President Raúl Leoni of Venezuela in 1964 as his representative with ambassadorial rank. Three years later Johnson named him alternate delegate to the United Nations with rank of ambassador and a member of the National Advisory Council on Economic Opportunity. He also appointed him the first Mexican American member of the United States Commission on Civil Rights in 1968. Four years later he was named a member of the Texas Advisory Committee to the U.S. Commission on Civil rights and in 1974 he became a member of the Advisory Council to the Veterans Administration. He also served as vice-president of the Catholic Council for Spanish Speaking People in the Southwest. Early in 1983 he became involved in the Corpus Christi municipal council election as a critic of Anglo domination despite a 50 percent Chicano population. In May 1984 Dr. García was awarded the Medal of Freedom—the highest U.S. civilian honor—by President Ronald Reagan.

As a result of his long involvement in the civil and human rights movement Dr. García has also been the recipient of many other honors from regional and national organizations. Among them are the Outstanding Democracy Forward Award from the Texas Conference of Negro Organizations and awards from the Marine Corps, the American Cancer Society, and the Veterans of Foreign Wars. In 1965 Panamanian President Marco Robles awarded García the Order of Vasco Núñez de Balboa in recognition of his services to humanity.

FURTHER READING: Arturo Palacios, *Mexican-American Directory*, Washington, D.C.: Executive Systems Corp., 1969; "President Honors G.I. Forum Founder," *Nuestro* 8:4 (May 1984).

GARCIA, MARIO T. (1944–   ), historian. One of five children of middle-class Mexican parents, Mario García was born 19 January 1944 in El Paso, Texas, and grew up and received his early education there in parochial schools. Encouraged by his parents, he entered the University of Texas at El Paso (UTEP) in 1962 and majored in history, earning his B.A. four years later and his M.A. in 1968. He then taught history for a year each at UTEP and at San Jose State University in California. In 1970 he moved to San Diego in the dual role of instructor in Chicano studies and history at San Diego State University and Ph.D. candidate in history at the University of California, San Diego. He completed his doctorate in 1975 and began teaching at the University of California, Santa Barbara, in the History Department and Chicano Studies. He is currently a professor there and has been chairman of Chicano Studies since 1984.

Mario García is best known as the author of *Desert Immigrants: The Mexicans of El Paso* (1981), which won the Southwest Book Award in History from the Border Regional Library Association and the Virginia McCormick Scully Literary Award for the best book on Chicanos or Western Indians. He coedited *History, Culture, and Society: Chicano Studies in the 1980s* (1983). He is also the author of numerous journal articles and chapters in edited books on a variety of topics dealing with the Mexican American experience and with border history and immigration. He has authored newspaper columns in the *El Paso Herald-Post*, in *La Opinion* (Los Angeles), and in *The San Diego Union* and has presented papers at numerous conferences.

Professor García has been honored with a number of major awards. From 1978 to 1979 he was a fellow at the Center for Advanced Study in Behavior Sciences in Stanford, California, was the recipient in 1982–1983 of a National Research Council Post-Doctoral Fellowship, and for most of 1984 was a fellow at the Woodrow Wilson International Center for Scholars, Washington, D.C. His current research and writing centers on his forthcoming book, *Americans All: The Mexican American Generation and the Struggle for Civil Rights and Identity, 1930–1960.*

FURTHER READING: Julio A. Martínez, *Chicano Scholars and Writers: A Bio-Bibliographical Directory*, Metuchen, N.J.: The Scarecrow Press, 1979; *The National Directory of Chicano Faculty and Research*, Los Angeles: Chicano Studies Center, UCLA Aztlán Publications, 1974.

GARCIA, RUPERT (1941–   ), painter. Rupert García was born in the small California gold-mining town of French Camp east of Stockton. He grew up and received his early education in a heavily Mexican milieu in Stockton, where his mother worked in a meat-packing plant. His early introduction to art came from his grandmother, who aroused his interest by showing him how everyday objects could be transformed into folk art. As a youth he used the photographs of screen stars in his mother's collection of movie magazines as the basis for his drawings. After completing high school, he studied art at Stockton Junior College and at the beginning of the 1960s went to San Francisco to embark on an art career.

Encountering disappointment in the field of art, he worked at a series of low-paying odd jobs to survive in the city. Dejected, he returned to Stockton where he soon enlisted in the U.S. Air Force. There followed several years of service climaxed by a tour of duty in Thailand, where he experienced firsthand the horrors of war and death, later vividly portrayed in some of his work.

In 1966 Rupert García returned to the United States, worked in a Stockton factory, and then enrolled in an art program at San Francisco State College (today University) with the help of the G.I. Bill. By 1968 he had completed his A.B. in painting and two years later had earned an M.A. in printmaking while at the same time teaching there in the Ethnic Studies Department. At San Francisco State he inevitably became involved in the political activism of the times and from 1968 to 1975 devoted his artistic talents to making protest posters. In 1970 he was one of the founding members of the Galería de la Raza in San Francisco, a place where Latino artists could show their work. He also did some free-lance writing and graphic art in leftist publications and became increasingly sympathetic to civil rights and Third World causes. In 1973 his first trip to Mexico brought him into direct contact with Mexican social realism. All these influences were reflected in the greater politicization evident in his art work. By the mid–1970s he had come to the view that his expectations were romantic and unrealistic.

Rupert García decided in 1975 to stop producing posters, though he continued to design them. He began to turn to experimenting with pastel and poster paint and thus initiated his period of pastel painting in which the style was more personal and less patently idealogical. In 1975 he enrolled in the graduate art history program at the University of California, Berkeley, and after a hiatus received his M.A. degree in art history in 1979. By the mid–1980s he had reached a new plateau in his art career. In the fall of 1986 he was appointed artist-in-residence at the Mexican Museum in San Francisco. His works have been acquired by such important museums as the National Collection of American Art, Smithsonian Institution, and the San Francisco Museum of Modern Art as well as by many private collectors.

FURTHER READING: Thomas Albright, ''Rupert García: Radical Political Portrait-ist,'' *San Francisco Chronicle* (28 April 1983); *The Art of Rupert García: A Survey Exhibition*, text by Ramón Favela, San Francisco: Chronicle Books, 1986.

GARRIGA, MARIANO S. (1886–1965), bishop. Born in the small Texas coastal town of Port Isabel, just northeast of Brownsville, Mariano Garriga grew up and received his early education there. In 1911, having completed his seminary studies, he was ordained a priest and sent to do missionary work in western Texas. During World War I he served as chaplain from 1916 to 1919 and after the war was assigned as pastor to St. Cecelia's church in San Antonio. From 1915 to 1916 and 1920 to 1935 he was on the faculty of St. John's Seminary in San Antonio. In 1936 he became the first Mexican American to be elevated to the bishopric when Pope Gregory XVI appointed him coadjutor bishop of the

Corpus Christi diocese. In 1949 he succeeded to the episcopal see. Ten years later Bishop Garriga was named "Mr. South Texas" in recognition of his influential role as bishop and as a Texas historian. In 1962 he attended the Second Vatican Council and died three years later at Corpus Christi.

FURTHER READING: Joseph B. Code, *Dictionary of the American Hierarchy (1789–1964)*, New York: Joseph F. Wagner, 1964.

GARZA, CATARINO (1859–1902?), journalist, revolutionary, organizer. Born in the Mexican state of Tamaulipas, near the eastern border town of Matamoros, a decade after the U.S.–Mexican War, Catarino, while still a child, moved with the family across the Rio Grande to Brownsville. He seems to have had a limited education, but somehow developed an interest in literary efforts, writing, and especially journalism. His journal covering the years 1877 to 1889 is one example of this interest. As a young man he clerked in the Brownsville grocery of Bloomberg & Rafael and briefly sold sewing machines, but quickly turned his attention to journalism and organizing mutualist societies.

Garza began his publishing career in Brownsville with his newspaper, *El Bien Público*, and later moved to Eagle Pass, Texas, where he founded *El Comercio Mexicano* in 1886 and *El Libre Pensador* in the following year. In 1888 he moved *El Comercio Mexicano* to Corpus Christi; later he established *El Correo* in San Antonio. These ephemeral journals served to broadcast his liberal ideas, and as time went on he became increasingly critical of the repressive Díaz dictatorship in Mexico and of Texas's ill treatment of Mexicans and Mexican Americans. His acerbic newspaper editorials and articles led to his being shot in 1888 but also made him a leader both in the fight for Chicano civil rights and in the anti-Díaz border revolutionary movement.

As early as 1889 Garza began to use his organizing talent and his support from Mexican Americans to create an armed revolutionary force on the border. What is sometimes called the Garza revolution began in November 1890 with an attack on the Mexican garrison at San Ignacio, Tamaulipas. This action brought protests from the Díaz government and conflict with the Texas rangers and U.S. Army. A second invasion plan was frustrated by U.S. troops. In September 1891 with a half-revolutionary, half-bandit force Garza again crossed the Rio Grande, but his ill-armed troops were defeated and dispersed by the Mexican army. Upon recrossing into Texas, Garza and his men were pursued by U.S. Army troops as well as Texas Rangers but successfully eluded their opponents with extensive help from the local Mexican and Tejano population. Clashes between Garza's forces and the Rangers and Army troops continued until 1893 when his guerrilla fighting came to an end.

Abandoning what had become a serious threat to border stability, Garza fled to Cuba with a few followers and later went to the Isthmus of Panama where he was killed in that Colombian province's fight for independence.

FURTHER READING: "Another Sketch of Garza," *San Antonio Daily Express* (6 January 1892); Frank H. Bushick, *Glamorous Days*, San Antonio: The Naylor Co., 1934;

Carlos Larralde, *Mexican American: Movements and Leaders*, Los Alamitos, Calif.: Hwong Publishing Co., 1976.

GARZA, ELIGIO DE LA ("KIKA") (1927–   ), legislator, lawyer. Born 22 September 1927 at Mercedes, Texas, virtually on the Mexican border, Garza comes from a family with roots in the Rio Grande valley that go back to the early 1700s. After graduating from Mission High School, Garza by struggle and perseverance obtained his education at Edinburg Junior College and at St. Mary's University in San Antonio. In 1952 he was awarded his Bachelor of Laws degree by St. Mary's School of Law and later received a doctorate in jurisprudence. At seventeen he volunteered for the Navy toward the end of World War II and spent two years (1950–1952) in the Army during the Korean conflict as an artillery officer. On being mustered out, he began practicing law and also initiated his career in Texas Democratic politics.

With heavily Mexican American Hidalgo County as his political base Kika was elected to the state House of Representatives in 1952 and was regularly reelected in the next five elections. During his six terms in the Texas legislature he gave evidence of a conservative bent, including opposition to a Texas civil rights law. In 1964 he won a seat in the U.S. House of Representatives and has since regularly been reelected by large majorities. His election to Congress was a milestone for south Texas Mexican Americans, but no political revolution since Garza's political stance has favored conservative, Anglo business interests. During the late 1960s and early 1970s he joined fellow Texas representative, Henry González,* in opposing the militant Chicano leadership of José Angel Gutiérrez* and Reies López Tijerina.*

Garza is a conservative southern Democrat, an active member of the League of United Latin American Citizens (LULAC), the Chamber of Commerce, American Legion, International Good Neighbor Council, Border Development Committee, and many other groups. His voting record sometimes upsets liberal Chicanos, and he has been opposed by the Political Association of Spanish Speaking Organizations. He is chairman of the United States–Mexico Inter-Parliamentary Group of which he has been a member since 1965. He is also chairman, since 1981, of the House Committee on Agriculture and a member of various other House committees as well as the Congressional Hispanic Caucus. In 1978 Mexican president José López Portillo awarded to de la Garza Mexico's highest award to a foreigner—the Order of the Aztec Eagle.

FURTHER READING: *The Almanac of American Politics, 1984*, Washington, D.C.: National Journal, 1983; Alan Ehrenhalt, ed., *Politics in America*, Washington, D.C.: Congressional Quarterly, 1983; Ralph Nader Congress Project, *Eligio de la Garza, Democratic Representative from Texas*, Washington, D.C.: Grossman Publishers, 1972.

GAVIN, JOHN (1928–   ), businessman, ambassador, actor. Born John Anthony Golenor on 8 April 1928 in Los Angeles, California, of an American father and a Mexican mother (Delia Pablos of a Sonoran ranching family), John

Gavin grew up in Los Angeles, attending St. John's Military Academy and Beverly Hills High School. He then attended Villanova Preparatory School at Ojai, California, and entered Stanford University from which he graduated in 1951, having majored in political science and economics. After graduation he served four years in the U.S. Navy with a tour of duty in Korean waters and a stint in Panama as Pan American Affairs officer to Admiral Milton E. Miles.

Released from the Navy, Gavin rather easily made his entrance into films, where his good looks got him romantic leads in a number of Hollywood productions during the second half of the 1950s and the early 1960s. In July 1961 he was appointed special advisor to José Mora (of Uruguay), secretary general of the Organization of American States, and later was given the task of developing public support in Latin America for John Kennedy's Alliance for Progress. During this time he also developed business interests in Latin America: a housing project in Mexico, an egg business in Panama, and plantations in South America. When Ronald Reagan ran for the governorship of California in 1966, Gavin worked for his election and was also active in his subsequent campaigns. When Reagan became president in 1981, he named Gavin ambassador to Mexico, replacing Julian Nava.* As ambassador Gavin aroused a good deal of friction with the Mexican government and society by publicly expressing his opinions, by exerting pressure, and by taking action on issues that Mexicans considered purely domestic concerns. He even openly indicated support of PAN (Partido Acción Nacional), the leading government opposition party. In April 1986 Gavin resigned after five years of often heavy-handed and controversial diplomacy.

For his earlier contributions to better U.S.–Pan American relations Gavin was awarded the Order of Balboa by the Panamanian government and the Ecuadorian Order of the Eloy Alfaro Foundation. An active businessman with long-term interests in Latin America, he was a partner in Panama-Boston Industries, and since 1968 he has been president of Gamma Services Corporation.

FURTHER READING: *Current Biography*, 1962; Blanche Petrich, "Gavin's Resignation Draws a Strong Response," *Voices of Mexico* 0 (June/August 1986); *Who's Who in America, 1984–1985*, 43rd ed., 1984.

GILBERT, FABIOLA CABEZA DE BACA (1898–   ), home economist, author. Born in Las Vegas, New Mexico, of an old Nuevo Mexicano family, Fabiola Cabeza de Baca grew up fluent in both Spanish and English and absorbing knowledge of local dietary and other customs. After high school in Las Vegas she began teaching, at the same time working on her college degree. In 1921 she received her B.A. in education at New Mexico Normal School (now Highlands University) at Las Vegas, and then continued teaching. Six years later she returned to college and in 1929 received a B.S. in home economics from New Mexico State University at Las Cruces. She continued her educational work in the rural areas of northern New Mexico for three decades, learning the Tewa and Tiwa languages, recording social customs, and teaching both Hispanic and

Pueblo Indian women and girls scientific nutrition, using regional recipes. Working for the United Nations in 1951, she established a number of nutrition demonstration centers among the Tarascan Indians of the Lake Pátzcuaro region of Mexico and in the 1960s organized a training program for Peace Corps volunteers.

During these years Mrs. Gilbert had a bilingual weekly radio program on food and nutrition and wrote a weekly column in Spanish for *El Nuevo Mexicano*, a Santa Fe newspaper. As a Cooperative Extension Service agent she also wrote bulletins in Spanish on various aspects of nutrition. Her best known work is *We Fed Them Cactus* (1954); she was also the author of *The Good Life* (1949) and a collection of Mexican recipes that sold over 80,000 copies. All three of her publications reflect Nuevo Mexicano customs and folklore, a subject in which she was greatly interested. She was the recipient of a number of awards, including a Superior Service Award by the U.S. Department of Agriculture. She retired from the Extension Service at the end of 1959.

FURTHER READING: Harold J. Alford, *The Proud Peoples*, New York: David McKay Co., 1972; Lynn I. Perrigo, *Hispanos: Historic Leaders in New Mexico*, Santa Fe: Sunstone Press, 1985.

GOMEZ, GLYNN (1945–   ), painter. Glynn Gómez was born in the small town of Cimarron on the east side of the Sangre de Cristo mountain range in northern New Mexico. As an artist he was virtually self-taught, having briefly attended Los Angeles City College in 1964 to study painting. In the latter half of the 1960s he spent four years in Vietnam as a U.S. Marine. This experience provided him with subjects and settings for much of his early art. After his military service he returned to New Mexico where he continued his painting, often using his early New Mexican years as a source of themes.

Gómez has exhibited his works at various museums and galleries in New Mexico, including the Zimmerman Library Gallery of the University of New Mexico in Albuquerque where he had a ''People in Vietnam'' showing in 1971. In the early 1970s he increasingly turned to New Mexican themes as remembered from his childhood. Many of these works are starkly black and white with the human figures sharply compartmented within large black and white areas.

FURTHER READING: Jacinto Quirarte, *Mexican American Artists*, Austin: University of Texas Press, 1973.

GOMEZ-QUIÑONES, JUAN (1940?–   ), historian, poet, activist. Born in Parral, state of Chihuahua and half-orphaned at birth, Juan Gómez-Quiñones grew up in the greater Los Angeles area, an only child brought up by his father and grandmother. He attended local parochial schools, interested both in sports and academics, and began writing in high school. In 1958 he entered the University of California at Los Angeles, graduating four years later with a B.A. in English literature. At the graduate level he changed interests, earning his M.A. in Latin American studies in 1964 and a Ph.D. in history with specialization in

Latin America eight years later. Meanwhile he began his teaching career at San Diego State University in 1968 and in the following year joined the history department at his alma mater, where he still teaches.

Gómez-Quiñones is the author of four historical works, and editor or coeditor of seven other books published in the United States and Mexico. He also coedited the Arno Press Mexican American collection with Carlos Cortés.* He is best known for his pioneering work *Sembradores: Ricardo Flores Magón y El Partido Liberal Mexicano, A Eulogy and Critique*, published both in English in the U.S. (1973) and in Spanish in Mexico (1977). In addition he has written a score of articles published in the U.S. and Mexico, some translated and many reprinted as chapters in various collected works. Throughout the 1970s he presented numerous papers and critiques at professional congresses, symposia, and conferences in the United States and Mexico. He has had his poetry published in a variety of literary journals and in anthologies. A book of his poems, *5th and Grande Vista, Poems 1960–1973* was published by Editorial Mensaje in New York in 1974.

A political activist since his student years when he was a cofounder of United Mexican American Students (UMAS) and cofounder and director of Chicano Legal Defense, Gómez-Quiñones also helped organize a number of community and educational committees and councils on whose board of directors he then served. He has been active on the board of the Los Angeles Urban Coalition, the Mexican American Legal Defense and Education Fund (MALDEF), the California State University and Colleges Trustees, and other important agencies. His most important contribution to Chicano Studies, in addition to his scholarship, has been his decade-long (1975–1985) directorship of the Chicano Studies Research Center at the University of California, Los Angeles.

FURTHER READING: *Directory of American Scholars*, 6th ed., 1974; Mary Helen Ponce, "Juan Gómez Quiñones: Escolar y Poeta," *Caminos* 4:6 (June 1983).

GONZALES, EUGENE (1925–   ), educator. Gonzales was born in 1925 at Anaheim in southern California. After his early education in Anaheim he attended nearby Whittier College, graduating in 1950 with a B.A. in education and receiving his M.A. from the University of Southern California five years later.

Upon graduation from Whittier, Gonzales began teaching junior high school in that city and soon was advanced to vice-principal of the Walter F. Dexter Intermediate School. His experience in this position qualified him for a job as supervisor of child welfare and attendance. He moved to the Santa Barbara (California) County Schools office in this position and then became coordinator of child welfare services and later coordinator of special education. In 1964 he moved to the state level as assistant to the state superintendent of public instruction and four years later was advanced to the position of associate superintendent of public instruction for California.

In mid–1970 President Richard Nixon appointed Gonzales to the Presidential Commission on School Finance. Gonzales's concern has been the quality of education for minorities with special emphasis on programs for the disadvantaged and on the problem of dropouts. He is the author of numerous articles concerning the education of Mexican American students. In 1968 his alma mater awarded him an honorary LL.D. for his distinguished services to education in California.

FURTHER READING: Arturo Palacios, ed., *Mexican American Directory*, Washington, D.C.: Educative Systems Corp., 1969.

GONZALES, RICHARD ALONZO ("PANCHO") (1928–   ), tennis great. The eldest of seven children born to poor Mexican immigrant parents in Los Angeles, Pancho Gonzales was both active and outstanding in high school sports. When he was twelve, his mother gave him a tennis racquet for Christmas, and he quickly became skilled at the sport. Pancho's disinclination toward school discipline caused him to leave school when he was sixteen to devote his time solely to tennis. In the following year he entered the United States Navy and upon his discharge two years later began playing tennis more seriously then ever. His marriage in 1948 seemed to have a further steadying influence on Gonzales. Almost completely self-taught, he developed a highly individualistic style, which won him his first championship before turning twenty. At twenty-one he turned professional and played in the 1949 Davis Cup competition, winning his two singles matches.

Between 1949 and 1955 Gonzales went into a long slump but then came back to dominate professional tennis until the early 1960s and remained a star player until the beginning of the 1970s. In 1966 he won the World Professional Championship at Wembley, England; three years later he defeated Arthur Ashe to win the Tournament of Champions at Las Vegas; and in 1970 he turned back Rod Laver's threat in the first "world series of tennis" at Madison Square Garden. In 1971, after numerous retirements and an equal number of returns to tournament tennis, he won the Pacific Southwest Tournament at age forty-three.

A colossal natural player who never took a tennis lesson, Gonzales was a colorful and at times temperamental star; as he came to be the "grand old man" of tennis he attracted a broad following of enthusiastic supporters. While remaining an active player, he also turned to coaching and to exhibition tennis. A legend in his own time, he operated the Pancho Gonzales Tennis Ranch at Malibu, California. He has also worked as tennis director of Caesar's Palace in Las Vegas, Nevada, has coached the U.S. Davis Cup team, and played on senior tennis tours.

FURTHER READING: Harold Alford, *The Proud Peoples*, New York: David McKay Co., 1972; Trent Frayne, *Famous Tennis Players*, New York: Dodd, Mead & Co., 1977.

GONZALES, RODOLFO ("CORKY") (1929–   ), community organizer, political activist, Chicano leader. Gonzales was born in the Mexican barrio of Denver, Colorado, of poor parents who were seasonal farm workers. His education, formally in Denver public schools and informally in barrio streets, affected deeply the directions of his personal and professional life. At age ten he was working in the Colorado sugar beet fields, and by the time he graduated from high school at sixteen he was working in a Denver slaughter house. Even before he left school, he had become interested in boxing as a way of escaping poverty, and before he was twenty he entered competitive boxing. In his ring career he won sixty-five of his seventy-five fights. A Golden Gloves champion earlier, at the end of his ring experience he was rated as the third-ranking contender for the World Featherweight title.

In 1953 Corky left the ring to operate a neighborhood bar full time and to work as a bail bondsman. Active in Denver Democratic politics, he advanced to district captain in 1959 and in the following year to coordinator of the Colorado Viva Kennedy campaign for the presidency and to chairman of the local anti-poverty program. Early in 1966 he was accused by a Denver newspaper of discrimination in the antipoverty program and immediately· resigned all his political jobs and ended his Democratic affiliation.

Soon thereafter Gonzales began to develop the Crusade for Justice, a program through which Chicano self-definition and self-determination would be promoted. In 1968 he bought an old school and church building, which were converted into a Crusade school, theater, gym, nursery, and cultural center. During that same year he and Reies López Tijerina* led a Chicano contingent in the Poor People's March on Washington, D.C., where he issued his ''Plan of the Barrio,'' calling for improved education, better housing, more barrio-owned businesses, and restitution of Spanish and Mexican pueblo land grants. In the late 1960s and early 1970s Corky Gonzales was very active organizing and supporting school walkouts, demonstrations against police brutality, and legal cases on behalf of arrested Chicanos. He also organized mass demonstrations against the increasingly unpopular Vietnam War.

Perhaps the most important contribution of Gonzales to the Chicano Movement was his instituting Chicano Youth Liberation conferences which focused and defined the goals of Chicano youths. The first of these massive gatherings was held in Denver for five days in March 1969 and in a document titled *El Plan Espiritual de Aztlán* proposed the concept of Aztlán, the Chicano Indian homeland, identified with the Southwest. In further developing his ideas of Chicano self-determination and nationalism, in the following year Gonzales launched the Colorado Raza Unida party (RUP). Two years later, at the first national convention of the RUP in El Paso, in a divisive power struggle he lost out to José Angel Gutiérrez,* who was elected permanent chairman. During the 1970s Corky's Crusade declined in its importance to barrio people, though the Crusade Center in Denver continued its earlier success.

In the changing society of the 1970s Gonzales himself continued his more subdued activities in support of civil rights for Chicanos and Indians and of the organizing efforts of César Chávez.* In the second half of the 1970s, while remaining head of the Crusade for Justice, Gonzales also returned to boxing, first training amateurs for Golden Glove bouts and then in the early 1980s turning to young fighters who were interested in becoming professionals.

In addition to his accomplishments as a civic leader and businessman Gonzales has achieved a unique position as the foremost poet of the Chicano Movement through his poem *Yo Soy Joaquín* (1967). More important perhaps as an inspirational work than as a literary opus, it has played a central role in the development of Chicano self-identity, especially among youths, and has been reprinted, anthologized, performed, recited, quoted, cited, and analyzed almost ad infinitum. In a way, *Yo Soy Joaquín* is the culmination of Corky Gonzales's outstanding contributions to Mexican American society.

FURTHER READING: Tony Castro, *Chicano Power: The Emergence of Mexican America*, New York: Saturday Review Press, 1974; John C. Hammerback et al., *A War of Words: Chicano Protest in the 1960s and 1970s*, Westport, Conn.: Greenwood Press, 1985; Christine Marín, *A Spokesman of the Mexican American Movement: Rodolfo "Corky" Gonzales and the Fight for Chicano Liberation, 1966–1972*, San Francisco: R and E Research Associates, 1977.

GONZALEZ, HENRY BARBOSA (1916–   ), congressman, lawyer. Henry González was born in San Antonio, Texas, on 3 May 1916 to north Mexican political refugees Leónides and Genoveva (Barbosa) González, one of their six children. He grew up in a family that stressed education and intellectual pursuits, went to San Antonio public schools, and attended San Antonio Junior College, the University of Texas at Austin, and St. Mary's University School of Law in San Antonio. Throughout his schooling he worked part time to help the family. He graduated in 1943 from St. Mary's with an LL.B. and was singled out by his alma mater in 1965 with an honorary Doctor of Laws degree. Following his graduation he worked at a variety of jobs: teacher, operator of a translation service, public relations officer, and chief probationary officer of Bexar County.

In 1950 Henry González entered the political arena by running for the San Antonio city council; he lost, but narrowly. Three years later he was elected and introduced and got passed an ordinance ending segregation practices in city facilities. In 1956 he was elected to the Texas senate—the first Mexican American state senator in 110 years—where he continued to be an outspoken champion of equal rights for all minorities and was especially noted for combating racist legislation. Having attracted national attention in the Senate, in November 1961 González was able to win a special election to fill a Texas seat in the United States House of Representatives and has been regularly and overwhelmingly reelected to that position since. The first Texan of Mexican descent in the House, he stuck to his strong minorities rights stance, identifying himself nationally as a liberal Democrat. In Congress he has introduced and pushed bills that aim to protect the civil rights of minorities and to improve their economic and educational opportunities. Among them are bills for better housing, benefits for farm workers, minimum wage, a youth conservation corps, and adult basic education. In 1964 he contributed significantly to the termination of the Mexican bracero program.

A loyal Democrat, González was cochairman of the Viva Kennedy organization during the 1960 election and four years later filled the same role in the Viva Johnson campaign. Since coming to Washington, he has had an assignment on the House Banking, Finance, and Urban Affairs Committee and has served on many subcommittees. Early in 1981 he became chairman of the Housing Subcommittee on Banking, a position of power he has used with little success in the first half of the 1980s to promote federal housing programs in order to help lower-income citizens. A fighter, even a crusader, for what he believes in, González has been somewhat less passionate in recent years. Despite his generally liberal position, during the 1960s and 1970s he opposed and was vocally critical of Chicano activists. As a result he is regarded by many Mexican Americans as conservative; in turn, he has accused the activist leadership of advocating reverse racism. He does not consider himself an ethnic candidate and has never campaigned as one. In March 1986 González celebrated twenty-five years in the U.S. Congress.

FURTHER READING: Alan Ehrenhalt, ed., *Politics in America*, Washington, D.C.: Congressional Quarterly, 1983; "Profile of a Public Man," *Nuestro* 2:13 (March 1983); Ralph Nader Congress Project, *Henry B. González, Democratic Representative from Texas*, Washington, D.C.: Grossman Publishers, 1972; Eugene Rodríguez, *Henry B. González: A Political Profile*, New York: Arno Press, 1976.

GONZALEZ, PEDRO J. (1895–   ), singer, civic leader. Born in northern Mexico, Pedro González was one of thousands of Mexican teenagers who fought in the 1910 Mexican Revolution. In 1913 he became General Francisco Villa's telegraph operator, a position he held to the end of the revolutionary infighting. In the early 1920s he joined the stream of Mexicans migrating to the United States in search of economic opportunity. Working at first as longshoreman on the San Pedro, California, docks, he soon discovered that people enjoyed his singing. In 1924, at a time when American businessmen were becoming interested in the Spanish-language market, he launched himself into a Spanish advertising radio and record career with a musical group called Los Madrugadores. His early-morning show on KMPC, broadcast from the Teatro Hidalgo in Los Angeles, came to be a staple for the area's Spanish-speaking audience, and he became a household name and a popular hero who soon had his own fan club.

During the repatriation movement of the early 1930s González spoke out against discrimination and deportation as unjust. By 1933 he was viewed by some Los Angeles officials as a troublemaker and, after a period of harassment, was arrested on trumped-up charges of raping a minor. In March 1934 he was found guilty after a trial characterized by ethnic bias and was sentenced to fifty years in prison. He spent six years in San Quentin even though his teenage accuser admitted eight months after the trial that her accusation had been false. In 1940 he was paroled and deported to Mexico. He settled in Tijuana, Baja

California, where he resumed his musical career and continued to be a leader in Spanish-language radio development on the border.

After more than thirty years, in 1971 Pedro González was allowed to return to the United States, largely because of his seven children who were American citizens. He and his wife of nearly sixty years settled in the California border town of San Ysidro across from Tijuana. Here he continued to be an active voice in the Mexican American community during the 1970s and into the 1980s, working for justice and equality for Mexican Americans. In 1981 his decision to tell his life's story led to an award-winning television documentary titled "Ballad of an Unsung Hero" and to a movement for pardon. In addition to the documentary, Pedro González's life has been the basis of two *corridos*, an outdoor mural in San Diego, and various literary works. In December 1984 the mayors of Los Angeles and San Diego declared a Pedro J. González Day to honor the ninety-year old San Ysidro, California, resident.

FURTHER READING: Lorena M. Parlee, "Ballad of an Unsung Hero," *Nuestro* 8:10 (December 1984).

GONZALEZ, RAYMOND E. (1924–   ), ambassador, lawyer. Raymond Emmanuel González was born 24 December 1924 in Pasadena, California, of Mexican American parentage and grew up and was educated there. After high school he entered the U.S. Army in 1943 at age nineteen, serving in the 104th Infantry Division in Europe. At the end of the war he attended the University of Paris in 1946 and completed his B.A. at the University of Southern California three years later. In 1950 he earned his M.A. at the Fletcher School of Law and Diplomacy in Medford, Massachusetts.

Entering diplomatic service González filled a variety of U.S. consular and embassy positions in Latin America and Europe. From 1961 to 1966 he was advisor of the U.S. delegation to the Council of the Organization of American States and for the remainder of the 1960s was first secretary in the U.S. embassy in Costa Rica. After a four-year period as counselor at the embassy in Peru (1970–1974) he was appointed deputy chief of mission to the U.S. embassy in Panama. He was named U.S. ambassador to Ecuador by President Jimmy Carter four years later and held that post until January 1982.

FURTHER READING: *The Bibliographic Register*, Washington, D.C.: The Department of State, 1974; *Who's Who in American Politics*, 8th ed., 1981.

GONZALEZ AMEZCUA, CONSUELO (1903–   ), artist, poet. Born in Mexico, "Chelo" González grew up in the Texas border town of Del Rio. At an early age she showed an aptitude for drawing and persisted in this activity despite absence of family support. Completely self-taught, she developed a unique technique of painting using different colored ball-point pens and cardboard or paper. Her style, which she refers to as filigree, is one of sharply defined forms and intricate linear patterns meticulously detailed. Sometimes her paintings are linked to the poetry she writes, but the latter most commonly develops out of the former. At the beginning of the 1970s the Marion Koogler McNay Art Institute in San Antonio mounted a show of her works, and subsequently she has exhibited in Dallas, New York, Springfield (Massachusetts), and Monterrey, Mexico.

FURTHER READING: Jacinto Quirarte, "Chelo González Amézcua," *Quetzal* 1:2 (Winter 1970–1971); *Mexican American Artists*, Austin: University of Texas Press, 1973.

GONZALEZ MIRELES, JOVITA. See MIRELES, JOVITA GONZALEZ.

GONZALEZ PARSONS, LUCIA (c. 1852–1942), labor leader, feminist. Lucía González was born and grew up in north central Texas in a small town in Johnson County, just south of Fort Worth. Her parents were Pedro Díaz and María González. We know little about her early years, but she seems to have lived with an uncle on a ranch southeast of Fort Worth. When she was about nineteen she married a young journalist, Albert Parsons, and soon thereafter the couple moved to Chicago where Parsons quickly became a leading figure in the local labor movement. Both ardent socialists, Lucía and her husband became prominent in the Socialist party and in the Workingmen's party. At the beginning of the 1880s the Parsons directed their major efforts toward support of the eight-hour-day movement. Lucía also joined the Chicago Working Women's Union and led women's marches of this organization to demonstrate for the eight-hour day and for women's rights. After 1884 she helped her husband edit *Alarm*, the weekly voice of the International Working People's Association, and wrote occasional articles for it.

In the famous Haymarket riot of May 1886 Parsons was one of the eight prominent socialists indicted for murder, although he was not present at Haymarket Square when the bomb exploded. He was one of the seven sentenced to death. After the sentence Lucía led a futile year-and-a-half legal battle all the way to the Supreme Court to reverse the jury's verdict. While she worked as a dressmaker to support herself and her two children, she found time to make speaking tours over the country to arouse popular support for the Haymarket seven and to raise funds for appealing their sentences—all in vain.

After her husband's execution she continued her activities in support of the radical labor movement and helped to found the International Labor Defense (ILD). At the 1927 ILD convention she was the guest of honor in a fortieth anniversary commemoration of the Haymarket executions. She was also one of the founders of the Industrial Workers of the World at the beginning of this century and traveled widely in western United States recruiting members.

Throughout her life Lucía continued to be in the forefront of the struggle for women's rights and for labor justice. Although she was often arrested for her activities, she continued to use her keen mind to write articles for radical labor journals, lead marches, and address demonstrations. Even in her eighties she remained a prominent figure in the International Labor Defense. She died at ninety as the result of a fire that razed her home on 7 March 1942.

FURTHER READING: Carolyn Ashbaugh, *Lucy Parsons*, Chicago: Kerr Publishing Co., 1976; Alfredo Mirandé and Evangelina Enríquez, *La Chicana: The Mexican-American Woman*, Chicago: University of Chicago Press, 1979.

GUERRERO, EDUARDO ("LALO") (1917–   ), singer, composer. Born in 1917 in Tucson, Arizona, of immigrant Mexican parents, Lalo Guerrero was one of many children in a family that could ill afford to dispense with his economic help as a youngster. Growing up in Tucsons's rough and squalid Barrio Libre, he gradually overcame a feeling of shyness and inferiority through a consuming interest in music. At an early age he learned to play both the piano and guitar and to sing Mexican songs his mother taught him. In 1933 during the Great Depression Lalo's father decided to return to Mexico, but after three months in Mexico City the Guerreros returned to Tucson.

During the stay in Mexico Lalo learned more Mexican songs and perfected his guitar style. In Tucson he tried high school for a while but soon dropped out to sing and play in local bars for tips to help support the family. He and three other musicians formed Los Carlistas, who soon became a popular Tucson quartet. In 1937 they left for Los Angeles, where they played various clubs, recorded a few songs, and got a small part in a Gene Autry film. Returning to Tucson as heroes, they were sent in 1939 by the Chamber of Commerce to the Major Bowes amateur hour in New York City, where they also entertained at the World's Fair. Los Carlistas broke up, and Lalo returned to Los Angeles and then to Tucson in pursuit of his musical career.

At the entry of the United States into World War II Lalo left Tucson for San Diego (California) to work in a defense plant and to entertain at military camps and hospitals. At the war's end he moved to Los Angeles, where he continued to play guitar, make recordings, and write songs. Among his early successes were "La Pachuquilla," "Vamos a Bailar," and "Los Chucos Suaves," the latter two used in Luis Valdez's* 1978 musical *Zoot Suit*. Between 1956 and 1968 Lalo had his own club on Whittier Boulevard in Los Angeles, and after a brief rest he opened a club in Tucson. In 1973 he began a long-term arrangement with a Mirage, California, restaurant and moved to nearby Palm Springs. Two years later he was honored by being selected to perform at the Festival of American Folklife in Washington, D.C. In recent years he has been collaborating with his son Mark by writing Spanish lyrics for the latter's music.

In his lengthy musical career Lalo Guerrero has recorded more than twenty albums and has written over 200 songs ranging from sentimental ballads to *corridos* to Pachuco songs to parodies like "Tacos for Two." He is important for giving expression to the feelings of sorrow, pain, and humor in the barrio. Among his best-known songs are "Nunca Jamás," "Canción Mexicana," and the humorous "Las Ardillitas."

FURTHER READING: Dan Guerrero, "Lalo & Mark: The Beat Goes On," *Caminos* 5:6 (June 1984); Thomas E. Sheridan, "From Luisa Espinel to Lalo Guerrero," *Journal of Arizona History* 25 (Autumn 1984); Philip Sonnichsen, "Lalo Guerrero, Pioneer in Mexican-American Music," *La Luz* 6:5 (May 1977).

GUTIERREZ, JOSE ANGEL (1944–   ), educator, judge, organizer, activist. Gutiérrez was born in Crystal City, Texas, to an upper-class Mexican immigrant family. His father, a physician who fought in the 1910 Mexican Revolution, died when José Angel was twelve, forcing the family into farm work in and around Crystal City. He attended grade and high school in Crystal City, distinguishing himself in high school as a champion debater and being elected student body president. After high school he went on to obtain a B.S. in political science from Texas Arts and Industries University at Kingsville, near Corpus Christi. Upon graduation he briefly studied law at the University of Houston, but then in 1968 earned a master's degree in political science at St. Mary's University in San Antonio. Eight years later he completed his doctorate in political science at the University of Texas in Austin; his dissertation topic, "Toward a Theory of Community Organization in a Mexican American Community in South Texas," indicated the direction and evolution of his political ideas in respect to minority community organizing.

In 1967 while a student at St. Mary's, Gutiérrez and several companions organized the Mexican American Youth Organization (MAYO) as an agency to bring about social change, and Gutiérrez was elected its first president. Returning to Crystal City, two years later he began to put into effect his ideas about organizing Chicanos to achieve economic and political power. In the spring of 1970, after a Chicano school walkout, he led a group of local Mexican Americans in creating a political organization, La Raza Unida, for the coming city elections. As a result, he and two other Chicano candidates were elected to the city council, and Gutiérrez won a place on the school board, eventually being elected board chairman. The new school board under his leadership drastically modified the city schools, introducing innovative bicultural and bilingual programs.

The local successes of La Raza Unida in southern Texas inevitably led to pressures to go national, despite Gutiérrez's feeling it was too soon to do so. In 1972 a national convention of La Raza Unida was held at El Paso with over 2,000 delegates in attendance. A divisive struggle for leadership developed between Gutiérrez and Colorado's "Corky" Gonzáles* with the former winning. In the ensuing elections, Chicano candidates had limited success, but two years later Gutiérrez was elected judge of Zavala County. There followed a long period of conflict with the Anglo legal establishment in which charges and countercharges were angrily made. A trip to Cuba in 1975 at the invitation of Fidel Castro led to a widening split within La Raza Unida. In 1981, after a prolonged quarrel over his frequent absences from Texas, Gutiérrez resigned his judgeship to continue a teaching position at Colegio César Chávez in Mount Angel, Oregon. A few years later he became associate professor in social sciences at Western Oregon State College in Monmouth.

FURTHER READING: Tony Castro, *Chicano Power: The Emergence of Mexican America*, New York: Saturday Review Press, 1974; John Hammerback et al., *A War of Words: Chicano Protest in the 1960's and 1970's*, Westport, Conn.: Greenwood Press, 1985; John S. Shockley, *Chicano Revolt in a Texas Town*, Notre Dame, Ind.: University of Notre Dame Press, 1974.

GUZMAN, RALPH C. (1924–1985), political scientist. Ralph Guzmán was born in Mexico's Bajío in the city of Moroleón in southern Guanajuato. Just before the Great Depression of the 1930s the family left for the United States and entered the migrant agricultural stream in the Southwest. As a result Ralph's early education took place in numerous schools in Arizona and California. His mother found work in Los Angeles, and he attended Garfield High School but enlisted in the World War II merchant marines before graduation. After two years he was inducted into the U.S. Navy, where he served as a radio operator from 1944 until 1946. In August 1944 he became an American citizen.

On his discharge from the service Guzmán used the G.I. Bill to enter East Los Angeles Junior College and then Los Angeles State College (today University) where he received his A.A. (1949), B.A. (1958), and M.A. (1960), all in political science. After many interruptions he earned his Ph.D. from the University of California, Los Angeles, in 1970. During the immediate postwar years he was extremely active in community affairs. He played a leading role in the fight for civil rights and in the development of community organizations. He was one of the cofounders of the Community Service Organization (CSO) and a leading Chicano journalist in the Los Angeles area.

In 1952 Guzmán began his academic career by teaching bilingual citizenship classes in the Los Angeles area. Later he was appointed a research fellow in the Falk Foundation Center for Political Research at UCLA, and between 1962 and 1965 he served as associate Peace Corps director in Venezuela and Peru. In 1964 he was named assistant director of the UCLA Mexican-American Study Project, which six years later led to publication of the outstanding resource book, *The Mexican-American People: The Nation's Second Largest Minority*.

Guzmán taught political science at California State University, Los Angeles, in 1968–1969, his first full-time teaching job, and subsequently lectured on Mexican American themes at various major California university and college campuses. In 1969 he joined the new University of California, Santa Cruz, where he educated a generation of Chicano and Anglo students in the Department of Politics and Community Studies. At the University of California, Santa Cruz, he helped establish Oakes College and then took leave from 1978 to 1980 to accept an appointment by President Jimmy Carter as deputy assistant secretary of state for inter-American affairs. In 1981 he assumed a new administrative responsibility as provost of Merrill College, University of California, Santa Cruz. Over the years he served as consultant, board member, and committee member of numerous national, state and local agencies, positions to which he brought high levels of professional competence and expertise. He died of a stroke on 10 October 1985.

Among his more important works, in addition to *The Mexican-American People*, were *The Political Socialization of the Mexican American People* (1976), *The Mexican-American Population: An Introspective View* (1966), and "The Function of Anglo-American Racism in the Political Development of Chicanos" in the *California Historical Quarterly* (September 1971). He was also the author of numerous other journal articles and conference papers.

FURTHER READING: Ralph Guzmán, "Proud Immigrant," *San Antonio News* (2 July 1980); "In Memoriam," *U.C. Mexus News* 16 (Winter 1986); "Ralph C. Guzmán," *Political Science* 29:1 (Winter 1986).

H

HERNANDEZ, BENIGNO CARDENAS (1862–1954), political leader, businessman. Born in Taos, New Mexico, during the Civil War, young Hernández was educated there in both public and private schools. In the 1880s he began his business career, working as clerk in a general store in Taos County. By the early 1890s he had added stock raising to his general mercantile businesses in various towns of north central New Mexico. In 1896 he set up a store in the tiny town of Lumberton in Rio Arriba County virtually on the Colorado border; here he now made his headquarters. Five years later he moved to Tierra Amarilla, the county seat.

In 1900, B. C. Hernández, as he soon became known, initiated a career in politics that was to last a third of a century. In the next dozen years he served Rio Arriba County as probate clerk, recorder, sheriff, treasurer, and tax collector. Very active in Republican politics, he acted as delegate to many state conventions and in 1912 and 1916 was selected as a delegate to the Republican National Conventions in Chicago. In 1912 he was appointed receiver in the land office at Santa Fe and during the following year returned to business activities. In the nonpresidential election of 1914, B. C. was elected to the U.S. House of Representatives and was reelected in 1918. He suffered defeat in the interim presidential-year term, probably because of President Woodrow Wilson's popularity.

At the end of his second term of service in 1921, Hernández was appointed collector of Internal Revenue for New Mexico by the new Republican president, Warren G. Harding, and returned to Santa Fe. He held the position of collector until 1933 when Democrat Franklin D. Roosevelt took office. After his resignation he retired from active political life; he was then seventy-one years old. During the World War II years he served seven years on the Selective Service Board in New Mexico. Shortly after moving to Los Angeles in the early 1950s, Hernández died at age ninety-two and was buried there.

FURTHER READING: Maurilio Vigil, *Los Patrones: Profiles of Hispanic Political Leaders in New Mexico History*, Washington, D.C.: University Press of America, 1980.

HERNANDEZ, BENIGNO CARLOS (1917–   ), judge, ambassador. Benigno Carlos, son of Benigno Cárdenas Hernández,* was born in July 1917 at Santa Fe, New Mexico, in a family active in business, politics, and the Presbyterian church. After his early education in Santa Fe he received his B.A. from the University of New Mexico (Albuquerque) in 1941 and seven years later was awarded his J.D. from DePaul University (Chicago). Between the two degrees he served four years in the U.S. Navy during World War II. Admitted to the New Mexico bar in 1949, he set up his legal practice in Albuquerque that same year. From the beginning of his legal career he was active on numerous commissions and boards. From 1951 to 1952 he was special assistant to the U.S. attorney general at Albuquerque, and a decade later he became a partner in the law firm of Hernández, Atkinson & Kelsey.

In 1967 Hernández was appointed by President Lyndon B. Johnson as U.S. ambassador to Paraguay, where he served for two years. Upon his return to New Mexico he won election to the New Mexico Court of Appeals and served from 1972 to 1974. During this same time he was also a member of the New Mexico Judicial Standards Commission. In 1974 he became chairman of the New Mexico Judicial Council and has continued his service on many judicial and educational boards and committees.

Judge Benigno C. Hernández has been the recipient of numerous service and leadership awards. He has been honored by awards from both the University of New Mexico and DePaul University, as well as various civic organizations. His most prestigious honor is the Grand Master of the Order of National Merit Award, given him by Paraguay upon completion of his term as U.S. ambassador to that country.

FURTHER READING: *American Bench: Judges of the Nation*, 3d ed., 1985/86, Sacramento, Calif.: Reginald Bishop Forster & Associates, 1985; Arturo Palacios, *Mexican-American Directory*, Washington, D.C.: Executive Systems Corp., 1969.

HERNANDEZ, MARIA L. (c. 1900–   ), community leader, activist, feminist. María Hernández was born in Mexico at the turn of the century and crossed the border into Texas during Mexico's Great Revolution. A collaborator of Alonso Perales,* during the 1920s she was one of the founders of the Orden Caballeros de América, which ultimately led to establishing the League of United Latin American Citizens at the end of the decade. Encouraged by her husband, she was one of the organizers of the Liga de Defensa Escolar in San Antonio, Texas, in 1934; through this organization she effectively articulated and advocated community school needs. During and after World War II she continued her activities for civil rights and justice for Mexican Americans, making numerous speeches, protests, and marches. In the 1940s she was the author of two books directed primarily at Mexican nationals, but also indicating her hopes and ideals for Mexican Americans.

When the Chicano Movement began in the 1960s, María Hernández, despite her advanced age, took an interested and active role. The Raza Unida Party

(RUP) of José Angel Gutiérrez* became her focus; she took part in its planning and in the 1972 election stumped extensively in support of its candidates. María Hernández has been important historically in giving a direct sense of continuity to the Mexican American struggle for social justice and civil rights in Texas. She formed an admirable link between the movement in the 1920s and in the 1970s.

FURTHER READING: Martha Cotera, *Profile of the Mexican American Woman*, Austin: National Educational Laboratory Publishers, 1976.

HERRERA, EFREN (1951–), football player. Efrén Herrera was born in Guadalajara, Jalisco, where he grew up and received his early education. When he was fourteen, the family emigrated from Mexico to the small California town of La Puente just east of Los Angeles. Here he attended high school and was so successful in adding football to his earlier soccer skills that he received a football scholarship at the University of California, Los Angeles (UCLA) at the beginning of the 1970s. At UCLA he set new school records in football: most consecutive extra points (48), most field goals in three years (24), and most field goals in one game (4). At the end of his UCLA career he was named to the All-American team. When he graduated in 1974 he received offers for both professional football and professional soccer.

Efrén Herrera joined the Detroit Lions in 1974 but early in the season was picked up by the Dallas Cowboys, where he won a place on the All-Rookie team and later the All-Pro team. In 1977, at his request he was traded to the Seattle Seahawks and for half a decade was their field goal kicker. In the mid–1980s he joined other former football stars doing commercials for Miller Lite beer and United Way.

FURTHER READING: Fernando Domínguez, "Getting His Kicks," *Nuestro* 1:8 (November 1972).

HIDALGO (KUNHARDT), EDWARD (1912–), lawyer, secretary of the Navy. Born in Mexico City on 12 October 1912, Edward Hidalgo came to the United States with his parents while still a small child and was naturalized as a young man. He entered Holy Cross College in Massachusetts, from which he graduated in 1933 with a B.A. *magna cum laude*. Three years later he earned a Doctor of Jurisprudence degree from Columbia Law School and in 1959 received a degree in civil law from the Universidad Nacional Autónoma de México.

After serving as a law clerk in the Second Circuit Court of Appeals in 1936 and 1937, Hidalgo began private practice in the law firm of Wright, Gordon, Zachry & Parlin in New York. During World War II he served for two years as air combat intelligence officer aboard the carrier *Enterprise* and was awarded the Bronze Star. After separation from the Navy in 1946 he resumed law practice as partner in a firm that placed him in charge of its Mexico City office. Two years later he founded (and was a senior partner in until 1965) the Mexico City law partnership of Barrera, Siqueiros & Torres Landa.

Having earlier been a member of the Eberstadt Committee and special assistant to Secretary of the Navy James Forrestal, in 1965 Hidalgo was appointed special assistant to Secretary Paul Nitze and in the following year went to Paris as European representative of Cahill, Gordon & Reindel. After four years in Paris he returned to the United States to become a special assistant and later general counsel to the U.S. Information Agency. From the U.S.I.A. he moved to the U.S. Navy Department in 1977 as an assistant secretary and two years later was appointed secretary of the navy by President Jimmy Carter despite the fact that he worked for the election of Republican candidate Richard Nixon in 1972. While at Navy he negotiated a controversial contract settlement with General Dynamics Corporation. When Ronald Reagan assumed the presidency in 1981, Hidalgo left the Navy. Less than a year later he went to work for General Dynamics and in 1985 defended his conduct before a congressional committee as not improper, since his work for General Dynamics had nothing to do with the Navy.

Edward Hidalgo has been recipient of a commendation ribbon from the U.S. Navy for his services on the Eberstadt Committee on Unification of Military Services, of Knighthood of the Royal Order of Vasa from the government of Sweden, and of the Order of the Aztec Eagle from Mexico. He is the author of *Legal Aspects of Foreign Investment*, published in Mexico.

FURTHER READING: "Firm Hired Ex-Secretary of Navy Who Settled Its Dispute with U.S.," *Miami Herald* (6 May 1984); Edward Hidalgo, "Without Leadership There is No Guidance," *All Hands* 756 (January 1980); "Hidalgo, Valdez Nominated to High Positions," IMAGE *Newsletter* (Fall 1974); "United States Navy," *La Luz* 7:9 (September 1978); *Who's Who in America, 1984–1985*, 43rd ed., 1984.

HINOJOSA-SMITH, ROLANDO (1929–   ), novelist, poet, educator. Rolando Hinojosa was born 21 January 1929 at Mercedes, Hidalgo County, Texas, about thirty miles from Brownsville, the youngest of five children in an Anglo-Mexican marriage. His father was a border person who participated actively in the 1910 Mexican Revolution, ending up a lieutenant colonel. Rolando grew up in the Mexican barrio of Mercedes where he attended grade and high school. During the last year of World War II at age seventeen he enlisted in the army for three years and upon his release entered the University of Texas at Austin. Both in school and in the army he read voraciously and widely in both Spanish and English and also began writing. He graduated from the University of Texas in 1953 with a B.A. in Spanish and a deep interest in Mexican, Hispanic American, and Peninsular literature. During the next decade he taught high school in Brownsville, served in the Korean conflict, and worked at varied jobs. A decade after his graduation he obtained his M.A. in Spanish from New Mexico Highlands University in Las Vegas and in 1970 completed his Ph.D. in Spanish with minors in Portuguese and history at the University of Illinois.

Following a tradition in his mother's family, Hinojosa has devoted much of his life to the field of education. He has taught at the University of Illinois, Trinity University, and Texas Arts and Industries University where he was chairman of the Department of Modern Languages. After serving as dean of the College of Arts and Sciences and later as vice-president for academic affairs for Texas A&I University at Kingsville, Hinojosa accepted the chairmanship of the Department of American and Chicano Studies at the University of Minnesota in Minneapolis. He was twice appointed a visiting professor at the University of Texas at Austin, and in 1981 he returned there permanently as a professor in the English Department.

In 1973, Hinojosa's novel *Estampas del valle y otras obras* led to his receiving the third annual Quinto Sol Award, and three years later his *Klail City y sus alrededores* (1976) won the prestigious Premio Casa de las Américas, an international literary prize. A most prolific writer, he has since published *Korean Love Songs* (1978), a book of poetry; *Generaciones, notas y brechas* (1980); *Claros varones de Belken* (1980); *Mi querido Rafa* (1981), awarded a Southwest regional prize; *Rites and Witnesses* (1982); *The Valley* (1983), a reworked English version of *Estampas del valle*; *Partners in Crime* (1985); and *Dear Rafe* (1985), an English version of *Mi querido Rafa*. An English-language version of *Klail City y sus alrededores* was published by Arte Público early in 1987. In addition he has published numerous poems, essays, and short stories in literary journals and in anthologies.

Rolando Hinojosa-Smith is perhaps the most widely known Chicano author, enjoying an international reputation; he is also a renowned educator and scholar and has been in demand as a consultant. He has given numerous readings of his works and made presentations on radio and television as well as at conferences and seminars. In 1971 he was given the Best in the West award for foreign language radio programming. His works provide the reader with a constantly merging kaleidoscope of the collective Chicano experience in south Texas.

FURTHER READING: Juan Bruce-Novoa, *Chicano Authors: Inquiry by Interview*, Austin: University of Texas Press, 1980; Julio A. Martínez and Francisco A. Lomelí, *Chicano Literature: A Reference Guide*, Westport, Conn.: Greenwood Press, 1985.

HOYOS, ANGELA DE (c. 1945–   ), poet. Born in the north Mexican border state of Coahuila at the end of World War II, Angela de Hoyos grew up in San Antonio, where her family moved when she was three. Here she attended grade school and private secondary school, and later received individual instruction because of poor health. As a child she was greatly influenced by her mother, who recited poetry to her; one of her responses was to compose stories in rhyme. While a high school student she had a number of her poems published in the school paper. In the second half of the 1960s, when she was still in her early twenties, she began to win international recognition as a poet. Inevitably influenced by the Chicano Movement, in the late 1960s she wrote poetry on sociopolitical themes and was invited to read her poems at various centers throughout the southwestern United States.

Although Angela de Hoyos is the most prolific of Chicana poets and has appeared widely in literary journals, not until 1975 was any of her poetry published in book form. In that year *Arise, Chicano! And Other Poems, Chicano Poems for the Barrio*, and *Poems/Poemas* (Buenos Aires) appeared; the first two were heavily flavored by the poet's militant concern about Anglo oppression of Chicanos and their culture. In 1976 *Selecciones* was published in Mexico, and nine years later *Woman, Woman* appeared. Her poetry has been published on five continents and won awards in four of them. She is universally considered to be if not the most important, at least one of the most important Chicana poets.

FURTHER READING: Julio A. Martínez, *Chicano Scholars and Writers: A Bio-Bibliographical Directory*, Metuchen, N.J.: The Scarecrow Press, 1979; Julio A. Martínez and Francisco A. Lomelí, *Chicano Literature: A Reference Guide*, Westport, Conn.: Greenwood Press, 1985; Luis A. Ramos, *Angela de Hoyos: A Critical Look*, Albuquerque: Pajaritos Publications, 1979.

HUERTA, DOLORES FERNANDEZ (1930–), labor organizer. Born in Dawson, a mining town in northeastern New Mexico where her family roots go back to the seventeenth century, Dolores was the daughter of a miner and migrant agricultural worker. While she was still a child, the family moved to Stockton, California, in the great central valley, and she grew up there. In the 1950s she met Fred Ross, Sr., who was helping Mexican Americans organize Community Service Organization (CSO) chapters and began working with him. Through Ross she came into contact with César Chávez,* and when the latter left the CSO in 1962 to organize farm workers, she went with him. She has since dedicated herself to serving agricultural workers through the United Farm Workers (UFW).

At various times organizer, lobbyist, and picket captain, Dolores Huerta spent most of the early 1960s helping to organize migrant workers in the Stockton and Modesto areas. She then went to the central headquarters staff at Delano, California, where she had the opportunity to develop further her unionizing and administrative skills. Soon she made herself César Chávez's most trusted and valuable associate. She played an important role in the negotiation of the contracts that brought an end to the five-year Delano Grape Strike in 1970 and in the subsequent decade-long, on again–off again lettuce strike in the Salinas valley. Experienced in all aspects of union organizing, Dolores Huerta has served as vice-president of the UFW (1970–1973) as spokesperson for the union, developer of labor contracts, chief negotiator, boycott strategist, and lobbyist. She is credited with contributing importantly to the UFW policy of nonviolence. Although a person of great talent and ability, she is unassuming in her quiet dedication to *la causa*. At the same time she is an effective and articulate speaker and politician, and has gained an international reputation. Currently she works out of UFW headquarters at La Paz, California.

FURTHER READING: Mark Day, *Forty Acres: César Chávez and the Farm Workers*, New York: Praeger Publishers, 1971; Alfredo Mirandé and Evangelina Enríquez, *La Chicana: The Mexican-American Woman*, Chicago: University of Chicago Press, 1979.

J

JARAMILLO, CLEOFAS MARTINEZ (1878–1956), folklorist. Cleofas Martínez was born in Arroyo Hondo, a small New Mexican village just north of Taos. She received her early education there and then attended the Loretto Sisters' academies at Taos and Santa Fe. She was an excellent student and became a lifelong admirer of the nuns. As a member of the influential and old Nuevo Mexicano Martínez family, she took a great interest in the folkways of Nuevo Mexicanos, particularly those of her class. As a prominent Nuevo Mexicana, she thus is an excellent example of a culture bearer who shows the fusion of Nuevo Mexicano and Anglo ways of life. The details of her marriage at Taos to prominent young politico Colonel Venceslao Jaramillo in 1898 give an excellent example of this blending.

Cleofas Martínez Jaramillo's interest in Nuevo Mexicano folklore centered largely on the romantic and religious aspects. She was the author of four books on these topics, which made her a leading early New Mexican folklorist: *Cuentos del hogar* (1939), *Shadows of the Past* (1941) probably her best-known work, *Potajes sabrosos* (1942), and *Romance of a Little Village Girl* (1955). Jaramillo was also the founder of La Sociedad Folklórica in the mid–1930s.

FURTHER READING: Carol Jensen, ''Cleofas M. Jaramillo on Marriage in Territorial Northern New Mexico,'' *New Mexico Historical Review* 58:2 (April 1983).

JARAMILLO, MARI-LUCI (1928–   ), professor, diplomat. Marí-Luci Jaramillo was born 19 June 1928 in Las Vegas, New Mexico, of parents who had come from Mexico during the turbulent 1920s. She grew up in Las Vegas during the difficult days of the Great Depression and attended local schools. After high school she worked her way through four undergraduate years at New Mexico Highlands University at Las Vegas (*magna cum laude*, 1955), and in the same year began teaching in elementary schools there. At the same time she worked on her M.A. (Highlands University, 1959, with honors) and her Ph.D. (University of New Mexico at Albuquerque, 1970). Between 1965 and 1969 she was assistant director of the Latin American education program at the University of New Mexico; from 1969 to 1972 she was assistant director for instructional services of the Minority Group Center and then was appointed professor in the Education Department. From 1972 to 1973 she also chaired the Department of Elementary Education. During the late 1960s and early 1970s she was active as a consultant and as a conference and workshop keynote speaker in the field of education. In September 1977 she was appointed U.S. ambassador to Honduras by President Jimmy Carter. When she was replaced by the Reagan administration, she returned to her post in the Department of Elementary Education at the University of New Mexico.

Ambassador Jaramillo is the author of numerous articles in professional journals and of chapters in books on education. Considered one of the country's leading experts on English-Spanish language relationships and bilingual and bicultural education, she has made several films used in educational instruction. She belongs to the National Association for Bilingual Education and many other groups. In 1975 she was named "Outstanding Chicana" by the McGraw-Hill Broadcasting Company and two years later was the recipient of the New Mexico Distinguished Public Service Award. In 1985 she was appointed chairwoman of the Board of Trustees of the new Tomás Rivera Center at the Claremont Graduate School in California.

FURTHER READING: *Hispanic Affairs Newsletter*, Washington D.C.: Office of Hispanic Affairs, 1:3 (March-April 1980); "Hispanic Portraits," *La Luz* 6:11 (November 1977); *Who's Who in America, 1980–1981*, 41st ed., 1980.

JARAMILLO, PEDRO (c. 1850–1907), *curandero*. Pedro Jaramillo was born in Mexico near Guadalajara, Jalisco, about the middle of the 1800s. As a young man he developed skills of faith healing and folk medicine, and at the beginning of the 1880s he moved to the Nueces triangle region of southeastern Texas near present-day Falfurrias. Here he continued to practice folk medicine as he had done in Mexico. In an area where doctors were virtually unknown his skills were in great demand, and his fame spread quickly among the poor Mexican and Mexican American population. At first he traveled from ranch to ranch, but as stories of his cures spread and his reputation grew, increasingly people came to his home at Los Olmos from great distances for his treatments and remedies. When he returned from his trips there would be large numbers of patients— sometimes as many as 400 or 500—waiting for him. He had both Mexicano and Anglo followers, many of whom considered him a veritable saint. After a quarter century of unselfish service to the people of southern Texas this charismatic healer died and was buried in a small cemetery near Falfurrias. Half a century after his death his grave was still a shrine visited by people whose parents or relatives had been helped by Don Pedrito's folk remedies. In some homes his picture or a small statue of him copied from a picture occupied a place of honor on the family altar.

FURTHER READING: Ruth Dodson, *Don Pedrito Jaramillo: Curandero*, San Antonio: Casa Editorial Lozano, 1934; Wilson Hudson, ed., *The Healer of Los Olmos and*

Other Mexican Lore, Dallas: Southern Methodist Press, 1951; Octavio Romano, "Don Pedrito Jaramillo: The Emergence of a Mexican-American Folk Saint," Ph.D. diss., University of California, Berkeley, 1964.

JIMENEZ, FRANCISCO (1943–   ), educator, teacher, administrator, writer. Francisco Jiménez was born of a humble family in San Pedro Tlaquepaque, Jalisco, a small town near Guadalajara. When he was four years old, his father took the family to the United States. Basing themselves in Santa María in Santa Barbara County, California, the Jiménezes joined the migrant stream, following the crops each season. From age six Francisco worked in the fields and attended school only when the harvest season was over at the end of November. In 1958, when he was fifteen years old, he was arrested in his high school classroom as an illegal alien and the family was forced to return to Mexico. Two months later the Jiménezes returned to Santa María with permanent-resident visas.

In Santa María High School Francisco studied and worked as school janitor until he graduated in 1961 with three college scholarships. While attending Santa Clara University in California, he also became a U.S. citizen and at the end of four years graduated with honors in Spanish and a Woodrow Wilson fellowship for graduate studies. At Columbia University, New York, he received his M.A. in 1969 and his Ph.D. in Spanish and Latin American literature three years later. In 1973 he returned to Santa Clara as a member of the Modern Language Department faculty. Four years later he was selected by Governor "Jerry" Brown as a member of the state Commission on Teacher Credentialing. Since then he has twice been reappointed to the commission and was twice elected its chairman. In 1981 his administrative skills were further recognized by Santa Clara's appointing him director of the Division of Arts and Humanities. In September 1986 he was awarded the Sanfilippo Chair in recognition of his scholarship and contributions to education, and in November the California legislature passed a special resolution recognizing his ten years of leadership on the credentialing commission. In May 1987 Governor Deukmejian appointed Dr. Jiménez to the California Council for the Humanities, an affiliate of the National Endowment for the Humanities.

As a writer Jiménez is known for his literary criticism and his short stories, especially "Muerte fría" (1972); "The Circuit" (1973); and "Cajas de cartón" (1973). "Cajas de cartón" won the *Arizona Quarterly*'s 1973 annual award and along with others of his short stories has been republished in a number of anthologies. He also has published numerous articles of literary criticism and several books: *Mosaico de la vida* (1981), *The Identification and Analysis of Chicano Literature* (1979), *Viva la lengua* (1975), and *Los Episodios Nacionales de Victoriano Salado Alvarez* (1974). Currently he has edited *Poverty and Social Justice: Critical Perspectives*, published in 1987 by The Bilingual Press. As cofounder and West Coast editor of the *Bilingual Review* and editorial advisor to the *Bilingual Press* he has added to his role as writer in the development of Mexican American literature.

FURTHER READING: "AMAE Honors Dr. Francisco Jiménez," *Semanario Azteca* 7:314 (3 November 1986); Pat Dillon, "A Teacher with a Mission," San Jose *Mercury News* (7 October 1986); Harry Farrell, "How Francisco Jiménez Became the Pick of the Crop," *California Today* (19 October 1980); Julio A. Martínez, *Chicano Scholars and Writers: A Bio-Bibliographical Directory*, Metuchen, N.J.: The Scarecrow Press, 1979.

JIMENEZ, LUIS A. (1940–   ), sculptor, painter. Luis Jiménez was born in El Paso, Texas, where he grew up and received his early education. Here he began his art education by learning his father's trade of sign painting. After high school he studied architecture and later art at the University of Texas at Austin (UTA), graduating with a Bachelor of Fine Arts in 1964. In that same year he received a scholarship from the Universidad Nacional Autónoma de México, which enabled him to study art and travel in that country for several months. Meanwhile he had begun a career as a muralist by painting a large mural in the UTA engineering building while still an undergraduate student. Very much interested in the machine as a symbol of major importance to American culture and deeply concerned about the relevance of his art to society, he developed the "machine man" as his social commentary. These brightly colored, shiny fiberglass and epoxy sculptures blend the human figure and the machine into a single form.

By the beginning of the 1970s Jiménez had moved to New York where he elaborated his sculpture by adding neon lights. He soon had a number of one-man shows at the Graham Gallery and the OK Harris Gallery. His sculptures have also been included in a number of group shows at important galleries like the Whitney Museum, the Stanford Museum, Brandeis University, and the Stuart Galleries in Los Angeles. He is probably best known for his larger-than-life figure, *Man on Fire*, inspired by the Mexican muralist, José Clemente Orozco, whose works he had seen during one of several trips to Mexico.

FURTHER READING: Jacinto Quirarte, *Mexican American Artists*, Austin: University of Texas Press, 1973; "Wild Western Art," *Américas* 32:10 (October 1980).

JOVA, JOSEPH JOHN (1916–   ), diplomat, executive, ambassador. Jova was born in Newburgh on the Hudson River just north of New York City. After his early education there he attended Dartmouth College, graduating with an A.B. in 1938. He then took employment with the United Fruit Company in Guatemala for four years and served in the U.S. Navy from 1942 to 1947. Upon his discharge from the armed services he became a foreign service officer in the State Department and between 1947 and 1954 filled the post of vice-consul or consul at Basra, Iraq; Tangier, Spanish Morocco; and Oporto, Portugal. He then was appointed first secretary to the U.S. embassy at Lisbon for three years.

After ten years abroad, Jova returned to four years' duty in Washington, D.C., during which time he also graduated from the Senior Seminar on Foreign Policy, Foreign Service Institute. In 1961 he was appointed Deputy Chief of Mission in Santiago, Chile, and in 1965 became U.S. Ambassador to Honduras. Having completed his tour of duty in Tegucigalpa, he became ambassador to the Organization of American States and then served as ambassador to Mexico from 1974 to 1977. He then retired from the Foreign Service to become president of Meridian House International in Washington, D.C., a large cultural and educational organization for international diplomacy. In 1986 he still filled that position.

Ambassador Jova is a member of the Mexican Academy of History, the Mexican Academy of International Law, and the Mexican Institute of History and General Studies. Among his many honors and awards are the Order of the Aztec Eagle from the Mexican government; Grand Cross, Order of Morazán from the Honduran government; and Grand Cross, Order of Isabel la Católica from the government of Spain. He has written a number of articles and lectured extensively on various subjects relating to Latin America and Hispanic contributions to the United States.

FURTHER READING: *The Biographical Register*, Washington, D.C.: The Department of State, 1974; *International Who's Who*, 43rd ed., 1979.

K

KASLOW, AUDREY A. ROJAS (1928?–   ), activist, parole commissioner. Audrey Anita Rojas was born in the small Arizona mining town of Miami, the fourth of five children of Cirilio and Isabel (Gutiérrez) Rojas. Her parents died when she was five, and she spent the next decade and a half moving about the Southwest, mostly staying with relatives. As a result she attended kindergarten and early grades in Arizona, the rest of elementary school in East Los Angeles, junior high in Santa Fe, and high school in Albuquerque. After high school she enrolled in the University of California at Los Angeles. Working her way through college, she earned her degree in clinical psychology and then went to work for the Los Angeles probation department. Throughout her long career in corrections she remained an activist, serving on numerous boards and committees and working with poverty groups.

By 1977 Audrey Kaslow had reached the position of administrator of the Los Angeles County Probation Department. In that year she was named by President Jimmy Carter as a commissioner on the U.S. Parole Commission in Washington, D.C.—the first person of Latino descent to serve on the commission. As commissioner she provided a Latino viewpoint and continued her aggressive stance, which at times led to conflict with the more conservative leadership and majority of the commission. Her valuable experience in the field has also led to appointment as advisor to international commissions. In November 1983 her term as commissioner expired, and she was looking forward to less bureaucratic and more rewarding and personal work in corrections.

FURTHER READING: Steve Padilla, "A Latino Voice on the Parole Commission," *Nuestro* 7:7 (September 1983).

L

LARRAZOLO, OCTAVIANO A. (1859–1930), politician, educator, lawyer. Octaviano Larrazolo was born 7 December 1859 in the small south Chihuahua town of Allende of a ranching family. When he was eleven, he moved to Tucson through family friendship with Jean Baptiste Salpointe, bishop of the Arizona diocese. Larrazolo, who planned to become a priest, spent his educationally formative years there, instructed personally by the bishop. In 1875 and 1876 he completed his formal education at St. Michael's College in Santa Fe where he first gave evidence of oratorical skills. At age eighteen he returned to Tucson to teach school and then the following year accepted a position as principal of the school at San Elizario, Texas, a short distance downstream from El Paso.

In the years 1878 to 1884 at San Elizario Larrazolo began to take an active interest in politics as a member of the Democratic party. As a result, at the end of that period he was appointed clerk of the U.S. District and Circuit courts at El Paso and was elected clerk of the 34th District Court at El Paso in 1886 and again in 1888. During his service as court clerk he had the opportunity to study for the law with one of the judges and in 1888 was admitted to the Texas bar at age twenty-nine. Following his two terms as court clerk he was elected to two terms as state attorney for the Western District of Texas. In 1895 Larrazolo moved to Las Vegas, New Mexico, apparently on the advice of a close friend, Félix Martínez,* the local Democratic political leader. Here he opened a law office and plunged into the political fray, helping to elect Harvey Ferguson the territorial delegate to the U.S. Congress in 1896. Four years later Larrazolo was the Democratic candidate for territorial delegate but was defeated. Again in 1906 and 1908 he lost closely contested elections to his Republican opponents, becoming increasingly convinced he was the object of ethnic discrimination within his party. His last political act as a Democrat was to support the 1910 New Mexico constitution, which he influenced but had no direct role in writing. More and more disgruntled with the Democratic party, in 1911 he resigned and joined the Republicans.

After his switch in allegiance Larrazolo fought strongly for complete political equality within the party structure, so much so that he was accused of introducing the race issue in elections. His support for Nuevo Mexicano candidates was so all-enveloping that in 1916 he helped elect the Democratic candidate for governor, his friend Ezequiel Cabeza de Baca.* Two years later Larrazolo himself was elected over his Democratic rival, Félix García. He proved an able executive, strongly supporting measures to help Nuevo Mexicanos, especially bilingual education. He was not renominated by the Republicans for another term, apparently because of his liberal viewpoints, particularly in the matter of a state income tax. After a short time in El Paso attending to some Mexican business affairs, he returned to his law practice in Las Vegas and continued to be active in Republican politics. During Republican President Warren G. Harding's presidency he was considered for appointment as governor of Puerto Rico, but was passed over. In 1924 he ran for justice of the New Mexico Supreme Court but lost in a general Democratic victory. Four years later he was nominated and elected to a short term in the U.S. Senate. Suffering from a serious liver ailment, he died at his Albuquerque home after one congressional session. During his nearly half-century in politics he used his gifted oratorical skills in both Spanish and English to work for equality for Nuevo Mexicanos.

FURTHER READING: Alfred C. Córdova and Charles B. Judah, *Octavanio Larrazolo, A Political Portrait*, Albuquerque: University of New Mexico, Department of Government, 1952; José A. Chacón, "Octaviano Larrazolo: New Mexico's Greatest Governor," *La Luz* 1:7 (November 1972); Lynn Perrigo, *Hispanos: Historic Leaders in New Mexico*, Santa Fe: Sunstone Press, 1985; Paul A. Walter, "Octaviano Ambrosio Larrazolo," *New Mexico Historical Review* 7:2 (April 1932).

LEON, NAPHTALI DE (1945–   ), writer, poet, activist. Naphtalí de León was born on the Texas border at Laredo on 9 May 1945 and grew up in the northwest Texas town of Lubbock. As a child he worked with his family in the harvest fields. He attended Texas Technological University during the rise of the Chicano Movement in the 1960s and became involved in its mystique. After his graduation with a B.A. in psychology, in 1968 he founded *La Voz*, a bicultural and bilingual weekly. Three years later he published a sociological study titled *Chicanos: Our Background and Our Pride*; it combined historical development with current events. In the same year, 1971, he also published *I Color My Garden* and two years later *I Will Catch the Sun*; these two children's books were both adopted by the California State Board of Education.

Naphtalí de León is the author of several other publications: *Chicano Poet* (1972), *5 Plays* (1972), *Coca Cola Dream* (1974), *Hey, Mr. President Man* (1975). In addition, he has written a number of articles for newspapers, journals, collected works, and anthologies. His poetry has appeared in the magazine *Caracol* and in *Festival de Flor y Canto*, edited by Alurista and others in 1976.

FURTHER READING: Sabino C. Garza, "Naphtalí De León," *La Luz* 6:12 (December 1977); Julio A. Martínez, *Chicano Scholars and Writers: A Bio-Bibliographical Directory*, Metuchen, N.J.: The Scarecrow Press, 1979.

LIMON, JOSE ARCADIO (1908–1972), concert dancer, choreographer. José Limón belongs to that generation of Mexican Americans whose families were uprooted by the great 1910 Mexican Revolution and fled to the security of the United States. He was born in January 1908 at Culiacán, capital of the west coast Mexican state of Sinaloa, of artistically inclined parents. When he was seven his father, a musician and orchestra director, brought the family into the United States, first to Arizona and finally to Los Angeles, California. There José grew up and attended the University of California at Los Angeles, aiming his education toward a career in painting. In 1928 he left Los Angeles to pursue this goal at the New York School of Design, but quickly discovered that his tastes, which favored an intense, mystical style, were at odds with a world that looked to the French modernist painters' movement for guidance.

Greatly upset, José Limón left art school, gave away his painting equipment, and for a time drifted aimlessly. Finally, persuaded by friends that dancing could be masculine and dignified, he took to modern dance with the same enthusiasm and dedication he had given earlier to painting. In 1928 he enrolled in dance classes at the Doris Humphrey-Charles Weidman Studio and soon proved an apt and intense pupil. By 1930 he was dancing on Broadway in the chorus of Norman Bel Geddes's *Lysistrata* and in the following year his first choreographed work was presented to the public. During the 1930s he danced in and choreographed several Broadway shows; by 1937 his choreographic talents were recognized by a fellowship at the Bennington School of Dance in Vermont. Here he decided to devote himself to concert dance and began to develop a number of compositions based on Mexican and Spanish themes. In 1939 he performed in his *Danzas Mexicanas* and during the following three years toured the West Coast, featuring some of his Latin works. As the tour progressed he was being described as one of the outstanding world dancers.

At the end of his tour World War II claimed its due; Limón entered the U.S. Army and served for two years. Upon leaving the army in 1945, he reorganized his dance company under the direction of Doris Humphrey, his mentor. By 1947 he was hitting his full stride, going from artistic success to artistic success. Although the critics' praise was lavish, his company was a financial failure, and Limón taught at numerous colleges and universities to support himself and his wife. In 1950, at the peak of his artistic powers, he turned down the Mexican government's offer of a permanent post as director of the National Academy of Dance, but did some important choreographic work in Mexico for several years. Limón's work in Mexico resulted in other important foreign engagements in South America, Central America, Europe, the Near East, and the Far East. Many of these tours were under the auspices of the U.S. State Department's cultural exchange program.

Limón's professional excellence and his charisma made these foreign tours outstanding successes and led, in part, to a 1957 *Dance Magazine* award and to the State Department's Capezio Award seven years later. Among numerous honors and awards, in 1960 he was given an honorary Doctor in Fine Arts degree by Wesleyan University and later was named artistic director of the short-lived American Dance Theatre. In 1969 Limón made his farewell appearance as a dancer, but he continued to choreograph new works for his company and continued to teach at the Juilliard School of Music in New York City almost up to his death from cancer in 1972. His modern dance company still survives.

Disdaining dance as merely an exhibition of technical prowess, José Limón viewed it as the highest dramatic expression of man's humanity. Among sixty-nine works he left as his legacy to modern dance, his best-known compositions are *Lament for Ignacio Sánchez Mejías*, *La Malinche*, *The Moor's Pavane*, and *Danza de la Muerte*.

FURTHER READING: *Current Biography Yearbook*, 1973 ed. "José Limón Dance Company," *Dance Magazine* 54 (May 1980); "José Limón Dance Company," *New York* 15 (20 December 1982); *Who Was Who in America*, vol. 5, 1969–1973.

LONGORIA, FELIX (?–d.1940s), soldier. Félix Longoria was killed during World War II on the Philippine Island of Luzon and buried there. After the war his body was returned in 1948 to his widow in the tiny town of Three Rivers about sixty miles south of San Antonio, Texas. A bitter and emotional dispute ensued over his reburial. The only mortuary in Three Rivers apparently did not want its chapel used for services for Longoria because he was a "Mexican," and the story made the front pages of newspapers all over the country. Public opinion in Texas was strongly opposed to this discrimination, and the (Texas) Good Neighbor Commission declared the mortician's alleged stand to be discriminatory. At the request of Dr. Héctor Pérez García,* freshman U.S. Senator Lyndon B. Johnson intervened, and Longoria was buried in Arlington National Cemetery. The incident was an important factor in Dr. García's founding the American G.I. Forum later that same year.

FURTHER READING: Tony Castro, *Chicano Power: The Emergence of Mexican America*, New York: Saturday Review Press, 1974.

LOPEZ, IGNACIO (1908–   ), editor, civic leader, crusader. Ignacio López was born in March 1908 at Guadalajara in the state of Jalisco, Mexico. Coming to the United States with his family as a young lad, he attended Pomona (California) High School, completed his first two years of college at Chaffey Junior College, and in 1931 received his B.A. from Pomona College. In 1932 he completed his master's degree at the University of California at Berkeley in Spanish and history and returned to southern California to edit and publish a crusading bilingual weekly newspaper, *El Espectador*. He continued in this activity until 1962.

During the years of World War II López worked for the Office of War Information in the Spanish department and in the immediate postwar years was active in the greater Los Angeles area establishing civic Unity Leagues, based on his wartime experience in organizing Liberty Leagues among East Coast minorities. Toward the end of the 1940s he worked with Fred Ross, Sr., of the

American Council on Race Relations in a continuing effort to obtain civil rights and political clout for Chicanos. During the 1950s he worked on a Ph.D. at the University of California, Los Angeles. Inevitably he himself became involved in politics; in 1964 he took active part in the Los Angeles District Attorney election and two years later directed the "Viva 'Pat' Brown" governorship campaign. He was also a leader in the Community Service Organization with Fred Ross and between 1964 and 1967 was a powerful voice for Chicanos as southern regional director of the Mexican American Political Association. He also worked for the Los Angeles Public Housing Authority and in 1968 joined the HUD (Housing and Urban Development) Southwest Area office.

FURTHER READING: Kaye Briegel, "Alianza Hispano-Americana and Some Mexican-American Civil Rights Cases in the 1950s," in *An Awakened Minority: The Mexican-American*, 2d ed., ed. Manuel Servín, Beverly Hills, Calif.: Glencoe Press, 1974; Arturo Palacios, ed., *Mexican-American Directory*, Washington, D.C.: Executive Systems Corp., 1969.

LOPEZ, LINO M. (1910–1978), civic leader, educator, social worker. Lino López was born in Mexico just at the outbreak of the Great Revolution to poor farmworker parents who soon moved to the greater security of the Texas side of the border. During his youthful Texas years he worked as a migrant in the fields to help support the family and to finance his early education. Later the family moved to Chicago where he worked his way through Loyola University, graduating with an A.B. in sociology. He later undertook postgraduate studies at the University of Tennessee in Nashville.

After graduation from Loyola and brief employment in a grocery Lino, seeing the midwestern Mexican American community's need for help to achieve social change, took a job with the Illinois Welfare Department. With the founding of the Catholic bishops' committee for the Spanish-speaking in 1945, he became deeply involved in its social welfare activities among Chicanos. An opportunity to work with delinquent Chicano youths in San Antonio took him to that Texas city as a juvenile court officer. In 1948 he went to Pueblo, Colorado, to assume a more positive leadership role as director of the Catholic Youth Center there.

In 1953 López moved to Denver where he served the Mexican American community for a decade both as a member of the mayor's Commission on Human Relations and as a consultant with the Denver public schools. In this new role he continued to urge Chicanos to join civic and ethnic organizations. He also helped organize the Latin American Research and Service Agency (LARASA), established a dozen chapters of the American G.I. Forum in the area, and took an important role in other Mexican American organizations.

At the invitation of local leaders, in 1963 Lino López moved to San Jose, California, a city with the largest Chicano population in the state except for Los Angeles, in order to establish the Mexican American Community Services Project (later Agency). During his years in San Jose he worked extensively with students, helping them organize Mexican American Youth Organization (MAYO) clubs in twenty-five Santa Clara Valley high schools. He also persuaded various government agencies to recruit more Chicanos and introduced bilingual programs in the schools.

Five years later Lino moved to Redlands University in southern California as an instructor and continued his work with young people. After a car accident there in which he was seriously injured, he suffered a stroke and left California in 1974 to return to Denver and semiretirement. Suffering from cancer and disoriented at times, he died tragically after wandering away from Colorado General Hospital in Denver during midwinter.

The recipient of numerous public service awards, including America's Legacy citation from the Anti-Defamation League, Lino López did his most valuable work with young people. He was a member of the national boards of the American G.I. Forum and the League of United Latin American Citizens (LULAC) and belonged to many other civic and educational organizations. He was posthumously awarded many honors.

FURTHER READING: Daniel Valdés, *Who's Who in Colorado*, Denver: Who's Who in Colorado, 1958.

LOPEZ, MICHAEL J. (1938–   ), ceramist. Born in Los Angeles on 19 October, 1938, López attended parochial schools there. Interested in drawing from childhood, he studied design and advertising art at Los Angeles City College over a period of four years in the late 1950s. He then received a scholarship to study sculpture at the California College of Arts and Crafts, Oakland, where he began to work in ceramics. In 1962 he received his B.F.A. and in the following year got his Master of Fine Arts and then went to the Chicago Art Institute, teaching ceramics there for the next two years. He returned to Oakland to teach ceramics at the California College of Arts and Crafts in 1965; after five years there he took a teaching position at Diablo Valley College in Pleasant Hill, California.

Influenced by Doña Rosa's black Oaxaca pottery and by the Spanish architectural style of Antonio Gaudí, López's experiments with a variety of techniques and finishes to his pottery have led to a successful career as an artist. He has exhibited widely all over the United States since the early 1960s. In 1963 he won the American Craftsmen Council Award of Merit, and in the same year won First Place in Ceramics at the Chicago Festival Art meeting. In 1971 he received the Association of San Francisco Potters' award.

FURTHER READING: Jacinto Quirarte, *Mexican American Artists*, Austin: University of Texas Press, 1973.

LOPEZ, NANCY (1957–   ), golfer. Born in Torrance, southern California, on 6 January 1957, Nancy López soon moved with her family to Roswell, New Mexico, where she grew up. As a second-grader she followed her parents around the golf course, and the next year when she was eight she began playing golf with a cut-down club. Within three years, she was beating her father, and by the time she was twelve she had won a state woman's tournament. At Goddard High School in Roswell she was number one on the previously all-boys golf team and led the team to the state championship. Her outstanding golfing skills brought her first a scholarship to the University of Tulsa and later a four-year $10,000 Colgate Golf Scholarship. After winning the intercollegiate golf title, Nancy withdrew from the university at the end of her sophomore year to turn professional.

In July 1977 Nancy López joined the Ladies Professional Golf Association (LPGA), and the following year she was the top prize money winner, breaking the previous LPGA record with earnings of $189,813. She also set a tournament record by taking the LPGA championship with a 72-hole total of 275 strokes. Her five consecutive tournament wins in 1978 earned her the LPGA Rookie of the Year, Player of the Year, and Female Athlete of the Year awards. During the 1979 season she played in twenty-two tournaments, won eight, placed within the top ten in eighteen, and earned $215,987, breaking the LPGA record she had set the year before. She was named Pro Golf Player of the Year.

In 1983 Nancy took maternity leave and came back in 1985 with five victories, including her second LPGA championship, $416,472 in tournament earnings, and Player of the Year award. Early in 1986 Nancy again took maternity leave and soon after the birth of her second daughter at midyear prepared to resume her professional career. On 8 February 1987 she qualified for the LPGA Hall of Fame by winning her thirty-fifth golf event, the $200,000 Sarasota Classic.

Possibly the outstanding woman golfer of all time, Nancy López has won 134 tournaments and earned more than one and a half million dollars. Noted on the golf course for her sunny disposition, she is usually followed by a large group of vociferous and admiring young supporters known as "Nancy's Navy."

FURTHER READING: Lamberto Armijo, "Women in Sports," *La Luz* 8:4 (November 1979); Mike Bartlett, "Nancy with the Laughing Face," *Golf Magazine* (June 1978); Ricardo Chavira, "Three to Cheer," *Nuestro* 1:5 (August 1977); *Current Biography*, 1978; Jerry Potter, "López Absence Sparks Rebirth on LPGA Tour," *USA Today* (31 March 1986).

LOPEZ, TRINI(DAD) (1937–   ), singer, entertainer. Trinidad López was born in the Dallas, Texas, "Little Mexico" district of poor parents who crossed the Rio Grande in 1927 without documentation in search of better economic conditions. The eldest son in a large family born to Trinidad López and his wife Petra from Guanajuato, Mexico, Trini early showed a love for music, which was encouraged by his parents. When he was eleven, his musically inclined father bought him a $12 guitar, taught him basic skills, and later got him music lessons. In high school he formed a small combo and soon found local favor with the band's blend of Tex-Mex folk rock. Within a few years he felt he had gone as far as he could in the country clubs, hotels, and night clubs of the Southwest, and he and the band went to Los Angeles. Taking a single, the only booking available, he quickly achieved enough popularity to be hired in leading Los Angeles night spots.

Early in 1963 Trini was signed up by Reprise Records, and his first album sold over a million copies while a single cut from it, "If I Had a Hammer," became an instant hit, reaching sales of over four million internationally and becoming the number one song in twenty-three countries. As a result Trini made his first foreign tour, to Europe, late that same year; it was a resounding success. Upon his return in 1964 he opened in New York in June with his own band. From New York he went on to Chicago, San Francisco, Reno, and Las Vegas and appeared on numerous television shows. In 1967 he made a second foreign tour, to South Africa and England; later he appeared on the concert stage in Australia, the Philippines, and Japan.

By 1970 Tini López had made fourteen albums, appeared in two movies, and made numerous television appearances. During the late 1960s and early 1970s he had also prudently invested his earnings in real estate, shopping centers, and music companies. In the 1970s and early 1980s Trini gave numerous benefits for charitable and educational institutions and continued to do international tours as well. With over twenty years in the entertainment business, he continues to record his songs, many of them old favorites with his fans. In 1980 he rerecorded "If I Had a Hammer" in a disco beat.

Considered by many to be the pioneer of Latin rock, Trini remains a rather shy, reserved person whose principal interest centers on his family and his philanthropies. Among the honors Trini has received are golden records for "If I Had a Hammer" and other songs and the Dallas Man of the Year award in 1967.

FURTHER READING: Harold Alford, *The Proud Peoples*, New York: David McKay, 1972; *Current Biography*, 1968; Clarke Newlon, *Famous Mexican Americans*, New York: Dodd, Mead & Company, 1972; Rose Mari Roybal, "Trini López," *La Luz* 4:8–9 (November–December 1985); "Trini López," *The Texican* (26 June 1983).

LOZANO, IGNACIO E., SR. (1887–1953), newspaper editor. Lozano was born of poor parents in Marín, Nuevo León, in northeastern Mexico and when he was twenty-one, moved to San Antonio, Texas. After working there in a bookstore and as journalist for five years, in 1913 he began publishing a Spanish-language weekly that he named *La Prensa*. Within a year *La Prensa* became a daily and Lozano added a bookstore. Following the trend of Mexican immigration to California, in 1926 Lozano began publishing a second Spanish-language paper in Los Angeles, *La Opinión*. It quickly became as successful as *La Prensa* and also had a bookstore adjunct. By 1930 *La Opinión* had a circulation of twenty-five thousand mostly in the Southwest, but it was also sold in Oregon and Kansas, recent centers of Mexican migration. Lozano aimed his two papers largely at Mexican immigrants rather than Mexican Americans. They were essentially Mexican newspapers published in the United States, and Lozano stressed news from Mexico. He took an active role in publishing both papers until early in 1953 when he became too ill to continue to work.

FURTHER READING: *"La Opinión" Nuestro* 8:8 (October 1984); Francine Medeiros, *"La Opinión*, A Mexican Exile Newspaper," *Aztlán* 11:1 (Spring 1980).

LOZANO, IGNACIO E., JR. (1927–   ), ambassador, publisher, editor. Lozano was born in January 1927 at San Antonio, Texas, to Ignacio E. Lozano, Sr.,* editor and publisher of *La Prensa* (San Antonio) and *La Opinión* (Los Angeles) and his wife Alicia Elizondo Lozano. He attended primary and secondary schools in that city. After graduating from Central Catholic High School in 1943, he entered Notre Dame University and graduated with a B.A. in journalism four years later. He then went to work as an assistant to his father and after six years of learning the newspaper business took over as publisher of *La Opinión*. In that capacity he has since maintained *La Opinión*'s outstanding position of influence among the Spanish-speaking of the Southwest.

Ignacio Lozano has been extremely active in civic affairs. In 1964 he was appointed as consultant to the Bureau of Educational and Cultural Affairs of the U.S. Department of State and three years later was named executive director of the Commission of the Californias. He has also served on the California advisory committee to the U.S. Commission on Civil Rights. From 1976 to 1977 he was U.S. ambassador to El Salvador, appointed by President Gerald Ford. As a prominent publisher and editor, Lozano has also taken notable roles in various journalism organizations: The Inter-American Press Association, California Newspaper Publishers Association, the Catholic Press Council of Southern California, and the Los Angeles Press Club. He is president of Lozano Enterprises and is on the board of directors of various other prominent businesses.

FURTHER READING: "Ignacio Lozano: Continuing a Tradition," *Caminos* 5:2 (February 1984); "Ignacio E. Lozano Jr. Named U.S. Ambassador to El Salvador," *La Luz* 5:9 (September 1976); "La Opinión," *Nuestro* 8:8 (October 1984); *Who's Who in America, 1978–1979*, 40th ed., 1978.

LUJAN, MANUEL, JR. (1928–   ), congressman. Manuel Luján was born in May 1928 to an important Nuevo Mexicano family, long involved in New Mexican politics and prominent in the insurance business. After grade and high school education in his home town of San Ildefonso northwest of Santa Fe on the Rio Grande, he attended the College of Santa Fe, graduating with a B.A. in 1950. For the next decade he devoted himself to the family insurance business. In 1964 he followed in the footsteps of his father, who had been mayor of Santa Fe and candidate for the governorship and Congress, by running for the state senate. Defeated in the elections by his Democratic opponent, he ran for the U.S. House of Representatives four years later and won. During the 1970s he easily won reelection over various candidates, two of them highly regarded Hispanos. In the 1980 election, however, he very nearly lost to a little-known former director of the state Democratic party. Helped by redistricting, he was reelected in the following elections and has served in the U.S. Congress longer than any other Republican in New Mexico's history. Despite triple bypass surgery in April 1986 he ran for a tenth term in November and won.

A member of the Congressional Hispanic Caucus, Manuel Luján has served on the House Committee on Interior and Insular Affairs and on the Committee on Science and Technology. He has been a long-time staunch supporter of nuclear energy development and is also concerned with the issue of nuclear waste disposal. As a fiscal conservative, he has been a strong advocate of private enterprise and usually has identified with pro-development policies on environmental issues. During the early 1970s he advocated opening more federal lands to mining, grazing, logging, and recreation; in the late 1970s he favored softening federal controls on strip mining. In 1981 he was briefly considered by the Reagan administration for the position of secretary of the interior, subsequently given to James Watt.

FURTHER READING: Alan Ehrenhalt, ed., *Politics in America*, Washington, D.C.: Congressional Quarterly, 1983; Ralph Nader Congress Project, *Manuel Luján, Jr. Republican Representative from New Mexico*, Washington, D.C.: Grossman Publishers, 1972; William J. Valdez, "Crossing Swords With the Liberals," *Hispanic Review of Business* (May 1986).

LUNA, SOLOMON (1858–1912), political leader, rancher, businessman. Member of a prominent and wealthy Nuevo Mexicano family, Solomón was born in October 1858 in the village of Los Lunas on the Rio Grande, named after his progenitors. After an early education by tutors he attended St. Michael's College in Santa Fe (today the College of Santa Fe) and later graduated from St. Louis University in Missouri. Returning to New Mexico, he joined his father in stockraising and agriculture on the large family land grant in Valencia County. A few years after marrying into the prominent Otero family he entered local Republican politics and was elected county clerk in 1885. Two years later he was elected sheriff, was subsequently reelected in 1892, and then became county treasurer, an office that he held for many years and that consolidated his position as the Republican boss of Valencia County and one of the party stalwarts in the state. In 1896 he was appointed to the highest New Mexico Republican office, Republican National Committeeman. When young Miguel Otero, II* became territorial governor in 1897, Luna quickly became one of his close advisors.

Actively interested in New Mexican statehood, Luna helped organize support for the movement and was elected to the 1910 constitutional convention. As a leading representative of Hispano Americans in that body, he endeavored to get included in New Mexico's constitution guarantees for the Spanish language and Nuevo Mexicano culture. His efforts, combined with those of others like Octaviano Larrazolo* led to inclusion of safeguard clauses in Article VII, Section 3, and Article XII, Sections 8, 9, and 10. These clauses, which dealt with rights of Mexican Americans, clearly specified that they could be amended only by a vote of three-fourths of voters in the entire state and two-thirds of the voters in each county. When the Republican 1911 convention met, Luna, the logical candidate for governor, declined that honor.

By the beginning of the new century Luna was one of the largest New Mexican landowners, the largest sheep raiser, and one of the wealthiest men in the territory. His extensive business interests also made him one of the most prominent men in New Mexican financial circles. He was president of the Albuquerque Bank of Commerce and later became vice-president of the First National Bank in the same city. He lived to see New Mexico enter the Union as the forty-seventh state in 1912.

FURTHER READING: Marion Dargan, "New Mexico's Fight for Statehood, 1895–1912," *New Mexico Historical Review* 14 (January 1939); Maurilio Vigil, *Los Patrones: Profiles of Hispanic Political Leaders in New Mexico History*, Washington, D.C.: University Press of America, 1980.

M

MADRID-BARELA, ARTURO (1939–   ), educator, administrator. Arturo Madrid was born 20 January 1939 in Albuquerque, New Mexico, where he received his early education. In 1960 he received his B.A. with honors from the University of New Mexico in that same city. Five years later he was awarded his M.A. and in 1969 his Ph.D. in Hispanic languages and literature by the University of California, Los Angeles. During the latter part of the 1960s he taught at Dartmouth College in New Hampshire, and from 1970 to 1973 he taught Spanish at the University of California, San Diego. He then went to University of Minnesota where he served as department chairman, associate dean for the Humanities and Fine Arts, and associate dean and executive officer of the College of Liberal Arts.

In 1974 Madrid also initiated a career in educational administration. Between 1974 and 1976 he was the national director of the Educational Testing Service graduate fellowships program for Mexican Americans, Native Americans, and Puerto Ricans. Returning to the University of Minnesota, he chaired the Department of Spanish and Portuguese from 1976 to 1978 and then was advanced to associate dean for the College of Liberal Arts, a post in which he served for two years. In 1980–1981 he became director of the Fund for the Improvement of Post-Secondary Education, U.S. Department of Education. In 1985 he was appointed president of the Tomás Rivera Center at Claremont Graduate School and University Center in southern California.

Arturo Madrid has been honored by appointment to numerous educational boards, commissions, and associations and has served as contributing editor to the Chicano journal *Aztlán*, *The New Scholar*, and other professional publications. He has authored several reports on aspects of minority education and has also written numerous journal articles on those topics and on the Mexican American experience and culture. In 1975 he founded the National Chicano Council on Higher Education.

FURTHER READING: "Latinos and Higher Education," *Nuestro* 6:10 (December 1982); Julio A. Martínez, *Chicano Scholars and Writers: A Bio-Bibliographical Directory*, Metuchen, N.J.: The Scarecrow Press, 1979.

MANZANARES, FRANCISCO A. (1843–1904), political leader, merchant. Francisco Manzanares was born in Abiquiu in Rio Arriba County, northwest New Mexico, on 25 January 1843 of middle-class parentage. After his early education by Spanish-speaking teachers he was sent to St. Louis University in 1863 and 1864. He became a clerk in a mercantile business in Kansas City and quickly rose to the position of partner. He then returned to New Mexico where he engaged in general merchandising at Las Vegas in 1866 and later in the wholesale grocery business throughout the state.

In 1882 the Democratic party nominated Manzanares as its candidate for territorial representative to the U.S. Congress, and he defeated the incumbent, Tranquilino Luna, but was initially denied his seat as the result of manipulation by the Santa Fe Ring. He decided not to run for reelection and returned from Washington at the end of his term to resume active direction of his mercantile business. His wholesale grocery business, Brown and Manzanares Company, had branches in Socorro and Las Vegas, New Mexico, and in Trinidad, Colorado. During the latter 1890s he was a member of the board of San Miguel County commissioners. He died in Las Vegas in September 1904.

MARQUEZ, LEO (1932–   ), general. Leo Márquez was born 27 January 1932 in the small New Mexican town of Peralta on the east bank of the Rio Grande just south of Albuquerque. He grew up and attended grade school there and in 1949 graduated from high school in nearby Belen. He then enrolled in New Mexico State University at Las Cruces, from which he graduated with a B.S. degree in zoology in 1954. Thirteen years later, while in the service, he earned an M.S. in business administration from George Washington University in Washington, D.C. He also completed Air Command and Staff College (1966–1967) and in the mid–1970s attended Carnegie-Mellon University's advanced management program for executives.

While at New Mexico State University Leo Márquez had enrolled in the Air Force Reserve Officers' Training Program (ROTC) and on graduation reported for active duty as a second lieutenant in the U.S. Air Force. After a year in pilot training he was sent to basic instructor school and then was transferred to Greenfield Air Force base in Mississippi as flight instructor. In September 1958 he was sent to take interceptor pilot training. Graduating late in the following spring, he was assigned to the 525th Fighter-Interceptor Squadron at Bitburg Air Base in West Germany. Early in 1962 he was reassigned to Chanute Air Force Base in Illinois to attend school for aircraft maintenance officers. After four years there he was sent to the Air Command and Staff College and, upon graduating with distinction in August 1967, was appointed maintenance control officer at Bien Hoa air base in Vietnam.

During the 1970s Leo Márquez filled several high-level positions in material management and in June 1979 was appointed deputy chief of staff for plans and programs at headquarters Air Force Logistics Command in Ohio. From mid–1981 to July 1983 he commanded Ogden Air Logistics Center in Utah and then was promoted to lieutenant general, deputy chief of staff for logistics and engineering, Headquarters U.S. Air Force, Washington, D.C.

General Márquez has been the recipient of numerous military awards and decorations including the Legion of Merit and the Distinguished Service Medal. In addition, he was named "distinguished alumnus" in 1978 by his alma mater, New Mexico State University.

FURTHER READING: "The Air Force's Hispanic General," *Nuestro* 5:9 (December 1981); *Rio Abajo Heritage*, Los Lunas: Valencia County Historical Society, circa 1981.

MARTINEZ, ANTONIO JOSE (1793–1867), priest, civic leader, politician, educator, landowner, publisher. Antonio José was born at Abiquiu in New Mexico's Rio Arriba country into the large and powerful Martínez family. He grew up in an atmosphere of leadership and power, and at age twelve moved northeast with the family to Taos. In 1812 he married, but his wife died shortly after giving birth to a daughter who did not survive to adulthood. Six years later the youthful widower left Taos to study for the priesthood at the seminary in Durango, Mexico. After a distinguished scholastic career he was ordained in February 1822 and early the next year returned to Nuevo México. Serving first as pastor in Tomé and then Abiquiu, in mid–1826 he was appointed pastor at Taos, where he was to serve the rest of his life.

Father Martínez used his position at Taos to make himself a leader of his people. Having great ambitions for himself and hopes for his people, he soon began a school in his Taos rectory and in 1833 instituted a preparatory college-seminary in which he trained most of the future Nuevo Mexicano leaders. Five years later he acquired the first printing press in the Southwest, which he used to print educational and religious materials, some of which he also authored. From the beginning of his Taos pastorate he took an active political role in the new Mexican republic and at the same time undertook a long and serious study of Spanish and Mexican civil law. During the Mexican period he served in the territorial legislature for five years and in 1833 was elected alternate deputy to the national congress in Mexico City. His exposition of Nuevo México's problems, sent to President Santa Anna a decade later, is notable for his well-thought-out suggestions for solutions.

In the years preceding the U.S.–Mexican War Father Martínez strongly opposed large land grants, especially to members of the local "American party," arguing that they violated both Spanish and Mexican law—and furthermore, the land belonged to the Indians. He was also the principal leader of the anti-U.S. faction in Nuevo México and warned both his religious and civil superiors that an American takeover was imminent. These views help to explain his strong anti-American stance at the beginning of U.S. occupation and his antagonism to individual powerful American leaders like Charles Bent. Differences between Martínez and the Americans were both cultural and personal.

At the United States takeover in 1846 Martínez seems to have felt that opposition to the conquest ought to be shown, but once he saw the fait accompli, he moved to get maximum benefits for his people from the new governmental system. He immediately began teaching his students English and civil law. In the anti-American Taos plot of 1846 his role is not clear. He was almost certainly aware of and sympathetic to the first aborted revolt, but there is no evidence to link him to the subsequent uprising in which Governor Charles Bent and others were massacred. In fact, he helped bring about the suppression of the rebels, and their court martial was held in his home. With the Treaty of Guadalupe Hidalgo in 1848 he became very active in governmental matters. He was one of the leading delegates to the statehood convention that year and was elected its president; he also headed a government problems convention the following year. For three terms he was elected to the territorial Legislative Council and in 1851 served as its president. During the 1850s he also was active in other aspects of New Mexican politics.

The quarrel between Father Martínez and his new bishop, Jean Baptiste Lamy, was another aspect of his ethnic leadership in American New Mexico. It began over the reintroduction of tithing, which Martínez had opposed in the 1830s, and escalated to a bitter personal quarrel between two hard-headed men who both were certain they were in the right. At no time did it center on faith or morals. In April 1856 Martínez resigned as pastor because of age (sixty-four) and infirmities. Lamy's appointment of an anti-Mexican Spaniard to replace him quickly led the New Mexican padre to act as a parish priest from his home chapel. After various admonitions from the bishop, Father Martínez was first suspended and finally officially excommunicated. Supported by most Nuevo Mexicanos, he continued to officiate as a priest, heading a schismatic church till his death.

In the late 1850s Martínez developed considerable interest in the growing issue of slavery. During the Civil War he was part of a group of prominent New Mexicans who assured the Lincoln government of their support. He also continued his interest in the education of Nuevo Mexicanos. On 28 July 1867 Father Martínez died peacefully, surrounded by family and friends, and was buried from his chapel by his friend and former student, Father Mariano de Jesús Lucero. He was an outstanding and controversial Nuevo Mexicano leader, a man who made great contributions to his people's political, cultural, and economic life.

FURTHER READING: Fray Angélico Chávez, *But Time and Chance: The Story of Padre Martínez of Taos, 1793–1867*, Santa Fe: Sunstone Press, 1981; E. K. Francis, "Padre Martínez: A New Mexican Myth," *New Mexico Historical Review* 31 (October 1956); Pedro Sánchez, *Memories of Antonio José Martínez*, Santa Fe: Rydal Press, 1978.

MARTINEZ, FELIX T., JR. (1857–1916), businessman, publisher, political leader. Félix Martínez was born 29 March 1857 in the village of Peñasco, just south of Taos, New Mexico, and received his early education in the parochial school at Mora, New Mexico. When the family moved to Colorado, he continued his education at Trinidad and later at Denver. At age fourteen he began clerking and after seven years' experience, when he became twenty-one, he and a partner started their own store in El Moro, Colorado. During the following years his mercantile activities included a sizable store in Las Vegas, which was as successful as his El Moro establishment. In 1886 he sold his mercantile interests and invested in real estate.

Meanwhile, Martínez had also become interested in newspaper publishing and politics. After an unsuccessful campaign for San Miguel County treasurer in 1884, he was elected two years later to the position of county assessor and at the end of his two-year term was elected to the territorial legislative assembly. At the end of that assembly term he bought *La Voz del Pueblo*, a leading weekly, as part of his political activity and moved it to Las Vegas, where it quickly became the voice of the New Mexican Democratic party. In the 1890 and 1892 elections he took a leading role in the territory in a populist third-party movement called El Partido del Pueblo Unido and was elected to the territorial council in 1892. In that same year he was head of the New Mexico delegation to the Democratic national convention. He served as clerk of the Fourth Judicial District court, New Mexico, from 1893 to 1897, and also edited and published the Las Vegas *Daily Optic*.

During this time Félix Martínez developed real estate and investment interests in El Paso, and in 1899 he moved to that city. Retaining his interest in *La Voz del Pueblo*, he now bought the *El Paso Daily News*, which he published for a decade. He then purchased a controlling interest in the Albuquerque *Tribune-Citizen*. At the same time he continued to be extremely active in numerous business enterprises, serving as executive or board member for various banks, real estate companies, and community projects. At the time of his death he was a member of the Dallas district Federal Reserve Board.

As a leading advocate of the very important Elephant Butte Dam and Irrigation Project on the lower Rio Grande, Martínez played an important role in securing the Mexican government's approval of the project. Partly as a result of this success he was appointed United States Commissioner General to South America and was sent on a number of goodwill missions by presidents William Howard Taft and Woodrow Wilson. At his death he was widely recognized as a pioneering entrepreneur, an important Texas businessman, and an international figure well known in many Latin American countries.

FURTHER READING: Maurilio Vigil, *Los Patrones: Profiles of Hispanic Political Leaders in New Mexico History*, Washington, D.C.: University Press of America, 1980.

MARTINEZ, OSCAR J. (1943–   ), historian, professor, administrator. Born 4 March 1943 in the small Chihuahua town of San Francisco del Oro, close to Hidalgo del Parral, Oscar Martínez grew up on the U.S.–Mexico border. He was one of six children of a *campesino* father and a former literacy-teaching mother, who encouraged him not only to get an education but also to excel academically. The family lived in Ciudad Juárez, and Oscar crossed the border daily to attend a parochial school in the Chicano barrio of South El Paso. Thus began a lifelong fascination for the border and its role as a phenomenon in both Mexican and American society. When he was fourteen, the family moved across the border to El Paso, and he attended and later graduated from El Paso High School. In 1966, after two years in the U.S. Army, he became a naturalized citizen.

Following his discharge from the army in that same year, Martínez attended East Los Angeles College and three years later earned his B.A. degree in Latin American Studies at California State University, Los Angeles. During these years he took leadership roles in the Chicano Movement, served as director, coordinator, and counselor in various community programs, and had his social concerns and historical interests further aroused. A fellowship from Stanford University led to an M.A. in Latin American studies there, and he then attended the University of California, Berkeley, in 1971 while teaching at Foothill Community College near Stanford. With the help of a Ford Foundation fellowship he returned to Los Angeles and completed his Ph.D. in history at the University of California in 1975. An opening at the University of Texas at El Paso took him back to the border as professor of history and director of the Institute of Oral History. In 1982 he was appointed director of the Center for Inter-American and Border Studies at the university.

One of the leading U.S. border historians, especially in the area of immigration, Oscar Martínez is best known for his monograph, *Border Boom Town; Ciudad Juárez Since 1848* (1978), winner of the 1978 Border Regional Library Book Award in the history category. Four years later a Spanish edition was published in Mexico. He is also the author of *Troublesome Border: U.S.–Mexico Borderlands Issues Through Time* (1987), and a short work, the *Chicanos of El Paso: An Assessment of Progress* (1980). In addition he has edited several books, the best known of which is probably *Fragments of the Mexican Revolution: Personal Accounts from the Border* (1983). He is the author of journal articles and chapters in books, most of them centering on the border and immigration, and has presented numerous papers at conferences and given a large number of invited lectures. He has also served extensively as a consultant for government agencies and for documentary films. Martínez has been very active serving in leadership roles in various organizations concerned with border problems. In 1981–1982 he was a visiting fellow at the Stanford Center for Advanced Study in the Behavioral Sciences.

MARTINEZ, VILMA SOCORRO (1944–   ), lawyer, civil rights leader. The eldest of five children of a San Antonio, Texas, carpenter, Vilma Martínez was born and grew up in that city. Resisting efforts to counsel her away from an academic career, she graduated from Jefferson High School in 1961, got a small scholarship at the University of Texas at Austin, and graduated as a political science major in 1964 in less than three years. Oppressed in Texas by discrimination against her both as a woman and a Mexican American, she went east on a scholarship to get her degree from Columbia University Law School in 1967. Upon graduation she took a position with the NAACP Legal Defense Fund as staff attorney and later worked for a major Wall Street law firm.

Associated with the Mexican American Legal Defense and Educational Fund (MALDEF) since its beginnings in 1968, Vilma Martínez took over leadership of the organization five years later and moved to California. As president of MALDEF, the leading Mexican American civil rights organization, she set her goals to broaden its funding base and to emphasize its activities in the areas of education, employment, and political access, thereby making it more self-sufficient and more effective. As general counsel for MALDEF she worked skillfully for Chicano rights and in 1974 won a case guaranteeing the right to bilingual education for non–English-speaking children in the public schools. As president she built a bridge between the barrio and the realms of wealth and conscience. In 1981 she stepped down as president of MALDEF. Currently she is an attorney in the firm Munger, Tolles & Rickershauser in Los Angeles.

Vilma Martínez has seen active service on more than a dozen important commissions, committees, boards, and panels. In 1976 California governor ''Jerry'' Brown appointed her a member of the University of California Board of Regents, and nine years later the regents elected her to chair of the board. She also served as a member of the Advisory Board on Ambassadorial Appointments for President Jimmy Carter. In 1983 she was elected to the board of directors of Anheuser-Busch, Inc. Among her honors is a Medal of Excellence from Columbia University, presented to her in 1978 as a major figure in civil rights.

FURTHER READING: Max Benavides, ''Vilma Martínez: Pulling No Punches,'' *Forum* (March 1982); Mario Evangelista, ''Advocate for La Raza,'' *Nuestro* 1:7 (October 1977); Al Carlos Hernández, ''Vilma Martínez, Una Chicana Ejemplar,'' *Nuestro* 5:6 (September 1981); Dean Johnson, ''Chair of the Board,'' *Nuestro* 4:7 (September 1985); Grace Lichtenstein, ''Chicana with a Backbone of Steel,'' *Quest* (February–March 1980).

MARTINEZ, XAVIER T. (1869–1943), painter. Xavier Timoteo Martínez y Orozco was born in Guadalajara, Jalisco, on 7 February 1869 of a comfortable middle-class Mexican family. From his bookshop-owner father he early learned to enjoy European literature, especially the romantic nineteenth-century poets. His early education in the Liceo de Varones, a private Guadalajara boys' school, gave evidence that he had some aptitude for sketching and painting and considerable apathy for more conventional areas of study. The death of his mother and his father's business difficulties led to Xavier's being put in the care of a prominent Guadalajara family, Alejandro Coney and his wife Rosalía, who gave direction to Xavier's further education.

In 1982 Martínez's foster father was appointed Mexican consul general in San Francisco, California, and Xavier soon followed him in hopes of pursuing formal art studies there. Señora de Coney supported his goals, and he soon enrolled in the Mark Hopkins Institute of Art, while still working at the consulate. He also studied under Arthur Matthews at the California School of Design. Although his artistic development was at first held back by his difficulties with English, he persisted and in 1897 graduated with the Avery Gold Medal for excellence in painting, sculpture, and anatomy.

The recipient of high praise in local art circles for his paintings, Martínez was appointed as assistant at the Mark Hopkins Institute, but his foster mother urged him to go to Paris for further study. As a result, in late 1897 he went there and soon became a popular figure among the many Latin Quarter students. Continuing his studies under the French symbolist, Eugène Carrière, as well as the American painter, James Whistler, he further developed his painting skills and in the next year sent some of his paintings to the Bohemian Club for an exhibition in San Francisco. His work received honorable mention in the Paris Exposition of 1900.

Martínez returned to San Francisco the following year, and his studio there quickly became a meeting place for artists, writers, and political radicals. Out of these meetings came the founding in the next year of the California Society of Artists to provide young painters greater opportunities to exhibit their works. In 1904 and 1905 Xavier returned to Mexico, spending several months making sketches and studies that later formed the bases of many paintings. His first extensive exhibition was held in San Francisco in the fall of 1905 and was so successful that he was invited to send it to one of the leading New York galleries.

Xavier Martínez's studio was destroyed in the great earthquake and fire of 1906, and he moved across the bay to stay at the Oakland home of his novelist friend, Herman Whitaker, whose daughter he married before the end of the following year. He built a small studio bungalow in the nearby Piedmont hills and painted dramatic landscapes based on local vistas. He also had various exhibitions of his works at San Francisco galleries and in 1908 began what was to be a lifetime teaching career at the California College of Arts and Crafts in the East Bay area.

During the years of World War I and following, in addition to his teaching, Martínez continued to paint and exhibit, his outstanding talent receiving nationwide recognition. However, in the 1920s commitment to his students limited his time and energies and reduced his artistic output. During the 1930s he continued to paint, and although his works were appreciated they no longer received the high acclaim of his earlier paintings. In 1942, too ill to continue teaching, he retired to Carmel where he died six months later at age seventy-three. The California legislature called an adjournment out of respect for his preeminent position among California artists. His best-known painting is probably "The Prayer of the Earth."

FURTHER READING: George W. Neubert, *Xavier Martínez (1869–1943)*, Oakland, Calif.: The Oakland Museum, 1974.

MEDELLIN, OCTAVIO (1907–   ), sculptor, art teacher. Octavio Medellín was born in Matehuala, state of San Luis Potosí, Mexico, just as the forces of the Mexican Revolution were breaking loose. His family was uprooted, drifted about, and finally settled in San Antonio, Texas, in 1920. There the teenager began his study of drawing and painting at the San Antonio School of Art. While continuing his studies in the school's evening program, he also began to teach himself sculpturing. In 1928 he enrolled in evening classes at the Chicago Art Institute, but his efforts the next year to enroll in the famous Academia de San Carlos (today the Escuela de Artes Plásticas at the national university) in Mexico were unsuccessful. As a result he traveled around rural Mexico, studying native and primitive crafts.

Returning to Texas in 1931, Medellín began his art career, soon concentrating on sculpture in wood and stone. With the help of Texas art benefactor Lucy Maverick, Medellín and a group of fellow artists soon founded the Villita Art Gallery in San Antonio. He taught sculpture at the gallery and at Witte Memorial Museum in San Antonio during the mid–1930s. In 1938 he did extensive research on Maya and Toltec art at the Yucatecan sites of Uxmal and Chichén Itzá.

Medellín has exhibited extensively in the United States since the 1930s in both one-man and group shows. From 1933 to 1942 he taught at North Texas State College (now University) at Denton and for two decades, from 1945 to 1966, trained art students at Southern Methodist University in nearby Dallas. He continued to teach at the Dallas Museum of Fine Arts. Since his resignation from the museum he has operated his own art school in Dallas.

Medellín's sculptures are strongly influenced by pre-Columbian Mexican Indian art and tend to be simple and monumental in style, with detail and texture subordinate. His best-known work perhaps is a large-scale sculpture titled "History of Mexico."

FURTHER READING: Jacinto Quirarte, *Mexican American Artists*, Austin: University of Texas Press, 1973.

MEDINA, HAROLD R. (1888–   ), jurist, author. The great American jurist Harold R. Medina was born in Brooklyn, New York, on 16 February 1888 of Yucatecan and Dutch American parents. His father, Joaquín, came to the United States at age twelve, a refugee from a bitter civil and race war in the Yucatán peninsula. Harold attended Public School 44 in Brooklyn, a preparatory school, and Princeton University where he proved himself both an outstanding athlete and scholar, graduating in 1909 with highest honors in French and the Edouard Ordonneau Prize. Offered a teaching position in French at Princeton, Medina chose instead to enroll in law school at Columbia University. He graduated in 1912 with a Bachelor of Laws after an outstanding scholastic career.

Having already passed the New York bar examination before graduation, Medina now began to practice law and in 1915 at the invitation of Dean Harlan Fiske Stone became a lecturer in law at Columbia, where he taught until 1947. In 1918 he formed his own law firm, at first specializing in appeals and winning a number of prominent cases. The best known of these was the Cramer treason case during World War II in which Anthony Cramer, a Brooklyn stoker, was accused of helping two Nazi spies who had landed from a submarine. Medina initially lost the case in the lower courts and then won it on appeal to the United States Supreme Court.

After World War II Judge Medina was appointed to the U.S. District Court in New York by President Harry Truman and eighteen months later was assigned to preside over the important and emotion-laden conspiracy trial of eleven top members of the National Committee of the American Communist party. During the nine-month trial, one of the longest in U.S. history, Medina's judicial forbearance and physical stamina both were severely tried as he became the object of insults, name-calling, and threats. However, he acquitted himself with courage, patience, and dignity. In 1951 Medina was promoted to the U.S. Circuit Court and seven years later "retired" to devote himself to sailing and to a concern very close to him—defense of the First Amendment to the U.S. Constitution. However, he has continued to serve as a senior judge on the U.S. Court of Appeals for the Second Circuit.

Judge Medina has written more than a dozen books on jurisprudence and the American juridical system, published between 1922 and 1959. Among them are *Cases on Federal Jurisdiction and Procedure* (1925), *Cases and Materials on Jurisdiction of Courts* (1931), *Digest of New York Statute Law* (1941), and *Judge Medina Speaks* (1954). His most recent book is *Anatomy of Freedom* (1959), which combines his personal judicial experiences and his concern for the First Amendment.

Judge Medina has been prominent on numerous committees and commissions whose goals were the improvement of laws and their administration. He is a trustee emeritus of both Princeton and Columbia universities and has received honorary degrees from twenty-five colleges and universities. A member of a large number of bar associations, he has been the recipient of a score of gold medals and distinguished service awards from a wide variety of organizations. On his ninetieth birthday the *Brooklyn Law Review* dedicated its sixth annual Second Circuit Review to him. On the same day he presided over an important appeals case in the Second Circuit court.

FURTHER READING: *American Bench: Judges of the Nation*, Minneapolis: Reginald Bishop Forster & Associates, 1979; *Brooklyn Law Review* 44 (1978); *Current Biography Yearbook*, 1949; *Who's Who in American Law*, 2d ed., 1979.

MENDEZ, MIGUEL M. (1930–   ), writer, teacher. Miguel Méndez was born in Bisbee, Arizona, on 15 June 1930, the eldest of six children in a Mexican immigrant family. That same year his father became unemployed, and the family moved to Sonora, Mexico, where Miguel grew up and got his early education. After six years of ejidal primary school he continued his education through intensive reading in various national literatures and by life experience. While still a teenager, he returned to the United States in 1946 and began to work as a field hand and construction laborer, and for the next quarter century earned his living by manual labor.

At eighteen, after three years in the United States, Méndez wrote his first novel, which he considered a training exercise. Two decades later Quinto Sol in Berkeley, California, published two short works by Méndez, then a bricklayer in Tucson, Arizona. Since then he has published a variety of works: novels, short stories, and poetry. When Pima Community College in Tucson was opened in 1970, he was hired as a teacher of Spanish, Chicano literature, and creative writing. He has also taught at various colleges and universities in the U.S. Southwest and in northern Mexico.

Among Méndez's best-known works are *Peregrinos de Aztlán* (1974), a novel about life on both sides of the Mexican–U.S. border, *Tata Casehua y otros cuentos* (1980), a collection of short stories, and *Los criaderos humanos (Épica de los desamparados) y Sahuaros*, a book of poems. His most recent work is a novel titled *El Sueño de Santa María de las Piedras* published in 1986 by the University of Guadalajara. His writing is characterized by a combination of dense, often baroque and poetic style with simple themes drawn in part from his life experiences.

FURTHER READING: Juan Bruce-Novoa, *Chicano Authors: Inquiry by Interview*, Austin: University of Texas Press, 1980; Julio A. Martínez, *Chicano Scholars and Writers: A Bio-Bibliographical Directory*, Metuchen, N.J.: The Scarecrow Press, 1979; Charles M. Tatum, *Chicano Literature*. Boston: Twayne Publishers, 1982.

MENDEZ, RAFAEL (1906–1981), musician. Born 26 March 1906 in Jiquilpán, Michoacán, just south of Lake Chapala in a musical family, Rafael Méndez learned to play the trumpet as a child. He may have played for General Francisco (Pancho) Villa; he certainly did play in the bullrings of Mexico and Spain. He is credited with popularizing the famous bullfight song, "La Virgen de Macarena." In 1926 he immigrated to the United States and after playing in the Detroit Fox Theatre orchestra, joined the Russ Morgan band. With Morgan he toured the country during the depression years, 1930 to 1937, and also perfected his musical skills.

In 1940 Méndez moved to Hollywood and shortly thereafter joined the Metro-Goldwyn-Mayer studio orchestra. He made solo appearances in several films and cut 154 records on the Decca label. During the 1940s and early 1950s he appeared on the Bing Crosby radio show and was a guest artist on several popular early television programs. During this same period he performed in many concerts across the U.S. and between 1954 and 1969 undertook several European concert tours. In 1964 he became the first trumpeter to play a solo performance at Carnegie Hall. He died at age seventy-five of a heart attack.

FURTHER READING: *ASCAP Biographical Dictionary of Composers*, 3d ed., 1966; "Rafael Méndez," *Variety* 304 (30 September 1981).

MENDOZA, LYDIA (1916–), singer, musician. Lydia Mendoza, "The Lark of the Border," was born in Houston, Texas, the second of seven children of a mechanic for Ferrocarriles Nacionales de México, who worked on both sides of the border. She grew up in Texas and in the Mexican border state of Nuevo León. Since her father saw little reason for educating girls, she had little formal schooling but was taught at home by her mother, the daughter of a schoolteacher.

Both parents were musically inclined, and Lydia absorbed musical education before she learned to read and write. By the time she was twelve she had mastered the guitar and mandolin and began studying the violin. About this time the family began to perform as a musical group, and soon her father quit his railroad job and took the family on the road. Calling themselves El Cuarteto Carta Blanca, they toured the Mexican barrios of the lower Rio Grande Valley and in 1928 made ten records in Spanish for OKeh Records at San Antonio. After the recording was completed, they followed the crops north, making a livelihood from their music and field work. After a brief stay in Michigan the family returned to Texas and by 1932 had settled in San Antonio. Here the Mendozas played bars, restaurants, and theaters, but especially the outdoor produce market in La Plaza de Zacate.

Here in San Antonio's plaza-market Lydia first sang solo and was "discovered" by a local Spanish-language radio announcer, who put her on his amateur contest. She won first prize. Her radio appearances led to a contract with Bluebird Record Company, for whom she recorded about 100 disks in the second half of the 1930s. During this same time the family made extensive tours of the Southwest. With the outbreak of World War II Lydia went into semiretirement, but the family group did some limited road tours until her mother's death in 1952.

By mid-century Lydia had become an almost legendary figure; many of her fans assumed that she was dead. In 1947 a California impresario persuaded her to reactivate her singing career and organized a series of tours. She appeared all over the Southwest, especially in California, and toured Mexico for six months in the early 1950s. She also made numerous records for Azteca, Falcon, Ideal, and Columbia of Mexico. She has recorded at least thirty-five long-playing albums alone.

In 1971 Lydia Mendoza's career entered a third stage when she made her first folk festival appearance in the Smithsonian Festival of American Folklife at the World's Fair in Montreal. Six years later she was a panelist and performer in the Ethnic Recordings in America Conference at the Library of Congress. She also gave concerts in the Americas, from Alaska in the north to Colombia in the south. Lydia Mendoza has also composed a few of the songs that she sings; she does not read music.

FURTHER READING: David Cavazos, "Entrevista con Lydia Mendoza," *Tejidos* 4:4 (Winter 1977); *Ethnic Recordings in America: A Neglected Heritage*, Washington, D.C.: Library of Congress, 1982; Carlos B. Gil, "Lydia Mendoza: Houstonian and First Lady of Mexican American Song," *The Houston Review* 3:2 (Summer 1981).

MESTER, JORGE (1935–   ), musician, conductor. Jorge Mester was born 10 April 1935 in Mexico City of musically inclined Hungarian immigrant parents. At an early age he began his musical education on the piano, but switched to the violin at age five. When he was eleven, his parents sent him to California to continue his study of the violin; as a result he grew up in both a Mexican and American cultural milieu. An introduction to Leonard Bernstein led to Mester's studying conducting at the Juilliard School of Music. In 1956 at age twenty-one he became the youngest professor of conducting at Juilliard, where he taught for twelve years. He also taught chamber music and opera, conducted the Juilliard Opera Theatre for six years, and directed composers' workshops and dance programs. In addition he was a noted violinist with the Beaux Arts String Quartet.

In 1967 Jorge Mester was appointed conductor and musical director of the Louisville Orchestra in Kentucky and soon made it one of the outstanding city orchestras in the country. He remained with the Louisville Orchestra until 1979, conducting approximately 200 first performances and recording seventy-two of them. In 1968 Mester became a United States citizen and also won the coveted Naumberg Award in that foundation's international competition for outstanding violinists. During his Louisville tenure he also served as conductor of the Kansas City Philharmonic from 1971 to 1975 and in 1970 he was named director of the annual Aspen (Colorado) Summer Music Festival. In the late 1970s he also did guest conducting in Europe, South America, Australia, and the Far East. In 1980 he returned to Juilliard to teach conducting and in the following year was invited to bring his Aspen Chamber Orchestra to the John F. Kennedy Center in Washington for four concerts. A noted guest opera conductor, in 1983 he conducted six performances for the New York City Opera and in the next year went to Germany to guest-conduct for the Stuttgart Opera. His reputation as a conductor has resulted in guest appearances with many outstanding orchestras, including those of Brussels, Boston, Cincinnati, Mexico City, Paris, Philadelphia, San Francisco, and Tokyo as well as the Royal Philharmonic and BBC Symphony in London. In April 1983 he was honored with a special award from the Organization of American States.

FURTHER READING: Mario Orozco, "Jorge Mester: Conductor," *Caminos* 4:11 (December 1984); Pilar Saavedra-Vela, "The Musical World of Jorge Mester," *Agenda* 8:5 (September/October 1978).

MICHEL-TRAPAGA, RENE DAVID (1942–   ), sculptor, painter. René Michel-Trapaga was born in Mexico and came to the United States in 1960 when he was eighteen years old. From 1960 to 1964 he served in the U.S. Air Force and then used the G.I. Bill plus scholarships and teaching assistantships to achieve a B.A. in fine arts at the University of Chicago and master's degrees in fine arts from the University of Indiana and Northern Illinois University at DeKalb. In the 1970s and early 1980s he taught fine arts at various institutions including the University of Chicago, the University of Florida, the Art Institute of Chicago, and Webster University in St. Louis, Missouri. Currently he lives in St. Louis, where he came originally to write and illustrate art books for a federally funded project. He also teaches at St. Louis Community College. His best-known work is a 16- by 70-foot kinetic sculpture titled "Susurro" (Whisper), which hangs in the St. Louis Convention Center.

FURTHER READING: "Talent is Not Enough," *Nuestro* 10:2 (March 1986).

MIRELES, JOVITA GONZALEZ (1904–), folklorist, writer, teacher. Jovita González was born 18 January 1904 in the small Rio Grande border town of Roma, Texas, where her ancestors had settled generations earlier. After receiving her education in Texas institutions of higher learning, she taught Spanish at St. Mary's Hall in San Antonio and later at Miller and Ray high schools in Corpus Christi.

A meeting with J. Frank Dobie in 1925 aroused in Jovita González an intense interest in folklore, and she began writing for publication in the Texas Folklore Society journal. One of the first Mexican Americans to write about Tejano culture in English, she made important and extensive contributions to southwest folklore. In 1936 she was elected president of the Texas Folklore Society, the first Tejana to hold that office. She and her husband, Edmundo Mireles, also became deeply involved in teaching Spanish in the primary grades, and in the 1940s they published a series of nine textbooks on the subject.

Between 1925 and 1980 she wrote sketches, short stories, and poems, many of which have been anthologized. She is perhaps best known for her essays, "With the Coming of the Barbwire, Came Hunger: Folk-Lore of the Texas-Mexican Vaquero" and "Among My People."

FURTHER READING: Alfredo Mirandé and Evangelina Enríquez, *La Chicana: The Mexican-American Woman*, Chicago: University of Chicago Press, 1979.

MOLINA, GLORIA (1948–), politician, activist, administrator. Gloria Molina was born in greater Los Angeles on 31 May 1948, the first of ten children born to Mexican parents who had immigrated to the United States a year earlier. She grew up and received her early education in the town of Pico Rivera and then attended East Los Angeles College. In 1967 an accident suffered by her father forced her to become the full-time provider for the family at the age of nineteen. Her job as a legal assistant did not prevent her from continuing her college education in evening classes and obtaining her A.B. degree from California State University, Los Angeles. In 1971 she became a job counselor at the East Los Angeles Community Union.

Taking a vigorous role in community affairs, Gloria Molina served on the board of United Way of Los Angeles and was active in the Latin American Law Enforcement Association. In 1973 she was the founding president of the Comisión Femenil de Los Angeles and served as national president of the organization from 1974 to 1976. Under her leadership the *comisión* helped develop social service programs for Chicanas in the Los Angeles area. She was also a founding member of Hispanic American Democrats, the National Association of Latino Elected and Appointed Officials (NALEO), and Centro de Niños.

In 1974 Gloria Molina became administrative assistant to California congressman Art Torres and three years later was selected by President Jimmy Carter as regional director of Intergovernmental and Congressional Affairs in the Department of Health and Human Services, Region 9. At the beginning of the 1980s she returned to California, where she became chief deputy to the speaker of the California State Assembly, Willie Brown. An active feminist, in November 1982 she won election to the California Assembly, the first Chicana to be elected to the California legislature; two years later she was easily reelected. Among awards recognizing her political stature are the 1984 *Ms. Magazine* Woman of the Year, MALDEF's Valerie Kantor Woman of Achievement Award, and 1983 *Caminos* magazine's Hispanic of the Year.

FURTHER READING: Katherine Díaz, "Hispanic of the Year: Gloria Molina," *Caminos* 4:1–2 (January–February 1983); Frank del Olmo, "Will Gloria Molina Lead Us Into Decade of the Hispanic?" *Los Angeles Times* (11 November 1982).

MONDRAGON, ROBERTO A. (1940–   ), politician. Roberto Mondragón was born in the tiny town of La Loma eighty-five miles east of Santa Fe, of a poor Nuevo Mexicano family and received his early education in a one-room schoolhouse. To help the family financially, he worked summers in west Texas cotton harvests from his eleventh to his sixteenth year. In 1958 he graduated from Albuquerque High School as senior class president and then studied electronics for two years, leading to a job in Albuquerque as a technician at Station KABC.

In the mid–1960s Mondragón began the first Spanish-language radio talk show in Albuquerque. Active in local politics since his late teens, he was elected to the lower house of the state legislature in 1966. He was reelected to the House of Representatives for a second term and was then elected lieutenant governor in 1970, the first full-time lieutenant governor of New Mexico, the first Mexican American lieutenant governor in the United States, and the youngest lieutenant governor in the country. In 1972 he took an active role at the Democratic national convention and then was named vice-chairman of the Democratic National Committee. Throughout the 1970s he remained prominent in national Democratic politics, serving as delegate to the national convention, and in 1980 was again elected lieutenant governor. In 1982 he ran for the U.S. House of Representatives but lost.

Mondragón has also taken an active part in private organizations and public agencies dealing with his chief concerns: civil rights, election reforms, equal opportunity, bilingual and bicultural education, and education generally. In 1971 he created the Mondragón Education and Scholarship Fund.

FURTHER READING: Jim Maldonado, "Lt. Governor of New Mexico," *La Luz* 1:8 (December 1972); Al Martínez, *Rising Voices: Profiles of Hispano-American Lives*, New York: The New American Library, 1974; Theodore E. B. Wood, *Chicanos y chicanas prominentes*, Menlo Park, Calif.: Educational Consortium of America, 1974.

MONTALBAN, RICARDO (1920–   ), actor. Ricardo Montalbán was born in Mexico City, the youngest of four children of Spanish immigrants Jenaro and Ricarda Montalbán. While he was still a small boy, the family moved north to

Torreón in the state of Coahuila, where his father operated a dry goods store and where Ricardo received his early education. In 1936 he joined his older brother Carlos in Los Angeles, attended Fairfax High School, and was soon smitten with the idea of becoming an actor like his brother. In 1940 Ricardo and Carlos left for New York, where the former got his big break that same year with a part in the Tallulah Bankhead play *Her Cardboard Lover*.

Montalbán's Broadway success enabled him to return in 1941 to Mexico, where he made over a dozen films in four years. His Mexican success in turn led to a ten-year Metro-Goldwyn-Mayer (MGM) contract. By the mid–1950s television had made serious inroads on the movies, and at the end of his MGM contract, during which he was given a series of indifferent roles, he was dropped. For the next decade he played in an occasional potboiler movie and had some television guest parts.

In the late 1960s Ricardo Montalbán had his ethnic consciousness raised by the Chicano Movement and as a result in 1969 founded a small organization of Latino actors called *Nosotros* (We) whose main goals were equal opportunity in motion picture and television employment for Hispanic Americans and improvement of the La Raza image in both media. After that, jobs became even more scarce in Hollywood, and he toured the United States, often doing one night stands in plays like *Don Juan in Hell*, *The King and I*, and *Accent on Youth*. His stage activity led to his selection to do a series of Chrysler Corporation's Cordoba television commercials, which in turn led to his successful role as Mr. Roarke in "Fantasy Island," a popular television series which ran for seven years in the late 1970s and early 1980s. Currently he has a prominent role in the television series "Dynasty: The Colbys." Meanwhile he had been awarded an Emmy in 1979 for his Indian chief portrayal in the miniseries *How the West Was Won* and had earlier received kudos for his stage acting.

FURTHER READING: Patricia Duarte, "Welcome to Ricardo's Reality," *Nosotros* 3:9 (October 1979); Ricardo Montalbán (with Bob Thomas), *Reflections: A Life in Two Worlds*, Garden City, N.Y.: Doubleday & Co., 1980; Clarke Newlon, *Famous Mexican Americans*, New York: Dodd, Mead & Co., 1972; "Ricardo Montalbán" (interview), *La Luz* 1:9 (January 1973).

MONTOYA, JOSE (1932–   ), painter, poet, art professor. José Montoya was born 28 May 1932 in rural New Mexico near Escoboza in the mountains northeast of Albuquerque. When he was six, the family moved to Albuquerque, and four years later went to California. After returning to New Mexico briefly, the family again moved back to California. José's early education was fragmented and sporadic as a result of the moves and migratory farm employment. Upon completing high school in 1951, he joined the Navy, serving in the Korean War, and after his service began his formal art education at San Diego City College in the latter 1950s. In 1959 he was awarded an art scholarship to the California College of Arts and Crafts in Oakland, where he graduated with a Bachelor of Fine Arts in 1962. He began teaching art at Wheatland (California) High School and at the same time completed a M.F.A. degree. Since 1971 he has taught art at Sacramento State University. He also has been largely responsible for a program of barrio art in Sacramento, in which the Mexican American experience is related to the universal human experience through the arts and crafts. His paintings have won prizes in art exhibitions in California and New Mexico and he has done numerous book cover and poster designs.

While he was studying art, Montoya also took a serious interest in writing, especially poetry, enrolling in classes in literature, creative writing and poetry. A meeting with Octavio Romano* led to his poetry being published in the journal *El Grito* in 1969 and subsequently in *El Espejo* (1972). In that latter year a book of his poems was published under the title *El Sol y Los de Abajo*. His poetry, according to Montoya, has been strongly influenced by the works of Walt Whitman.

FURTHER READING: Juan Bruce-Novoa, *Chicano Authors: Inquiry by Interview*, Austin: University of Texas Press, 1980; *Directory of American Poets*, 1975 ed.; Julio A. Martínez, *Chicano Scholars and Writers: A Bio-Bibliographical Directory*, Metuchen, N.J.: The Scarecrow Press, 1979.

MONTOYA, JOSEPH M. (1915–1978), senator, lawyer. Joseph Montoya was born 24 September 1915 at the small village of Peña Blanca in northwestern New Mexico, where his father served as Sandoval County sheriff and where he received his early education. His parents, Thomas and Frances Montoya, were descended from eighteenth-century Spanish immigrants to New Mexico. After graduating from Bernalillo (New Mexico) High School in 1931, he attended Regis College in Denver, Colorado, and in 1934 entered Georgetown University Law School in Washington, D.C.

In 1936, during his second year at Georgetown he was elected to the New Mexico House of Representatives from Sandoval County, the youngest representative in the states's history. Two years later he received his LL.B. degree and was reelected to the legislature; he also scored another first in the age category when he became Democratic majority floor leader. In 1940 with his election to the state senate, he became the youngest member of that body. Moving up the New Mexico political ladder, he served a total of twelve years in both houses, then served four terms as lieutenant governor in 1946, 1948, 1954, and 1956. Politically he was defeated only once, when he lost the Democratic congressional primary to Antonio M. Fernández in 1950. In 1957, at age forty-two, Montoya was elected to the first of four consecutive terms in the United States House of Representatives. During his first years in office he established a reputation as a hardworking legislator and loyal party man. He followed a moderate political course and was regularly returned to Congress with well over 60 percent of the vote. When Senator Dennis Chávez* died during Montoya's fourth term in the House, the latter won the election in 1964 to his unexpired term in the Senate as well as the next full six-year term. Six years later he was easily reelected. After the mid–1970s his popularity waned, and he was defeated for reelection in 1976 by a political newcomer, former scientist-astronaut Harrison Schmitt. Montoya's health rapidly declined after his defeat, and he died in June 1978 of complications arising from cancer surgery.

One of the most influential senators in Washington, Montoya served as a member of the Appropriations Committee, Pubic Works Committee, the Joint Committee on Atomic Energy, and the Air and Water Pollution Subcommittee. He represented the United States at numerous inter-American conferences. His liberal voting record in the Senate earned him high ratings from farm and labor organizations; he was an early opponent of American involvement in Vietnam. Particularly interested in consumer protection legislation and active in improving the lot of the nation's Spanish-speaking, he advocated measures to aid the poor, Indians, and elderly.

FURTHER READING: Al Martínez, *Rising Voices: Profiles of Hispano-American Lives*, New York: The American Library, 1974; Maurilio Vigil, *Los Patrones: Profiles of Hispanic Political Leaders in New Mexico History*, Washington, D.C.: University Press of America, 1980; Maurilio Vigil and Roy Luján, "Parallels in the Career [sic] of Two Hispanic U.S. Senators," *Journal of Ethnic Studies* 13:4 (Winter 1986).

MONTOYA, MALAQUIAS (1938–   ), artist, muralist, activist. Malaquías Montoya was born in Albuquerque, New Mexico, on 21 June 1938 and grew up there. In the late 1960s he attended the University of California at Berkeley where he graduated in 1970 with a bachelor's degree in art. Inevitably involved in the Chicano Movement at Berkeley, he was a contributor to *El Grito* even before his graduation. In addition he did the cover for *El Plan de Santa Barbara*, a declaration of Chicano educational aspirations, published in 1969. He was also a founding member of the Mexican-American-Liberation-Art-Front, and an active member of the Spanish-Speaking Unity Council, Centro Legal de la Raza, and La Raza Educators—all of Oakland, California.

Throughout the 1970s Montoya painted numerous cover posters and designs, many of them for activist causes such as the Olga Talamántez Defense League and the Trial of the San Quentin Six. During this period he participated in a large number of group exhibitions in northern and southern California and had one-man shows at a half-dozen northern California colleges and galleries. He also did artwork for Tri-continental Films and the North American Congress on Latin America in New York. Most recently, in 1986 he painted a mural for the Consejo de Recursos para la Atención de la Juventud (CREA) in Baja California Norte. He is the author of a number of critical art essays and currently teaches at the California College of Arts and Crafts in Oakland.

FURTHER READING: Julio A. Martínez, *Chicano Scholars and Writers: A Bio-Bibliographical Directory*, Metuchen, N.J.: The Scarecrow Press, 1979.

MONTOYA, NESTOR (1862–1923), politician, editor, businessman. Nestor Montoya was born 14 April 1862 in Albuquerque, New Mexico, son of Teodosio Montoya and Encarnación Cervantes de Montoya. He received his early education in the Albuquerque public schools and in 1881 was graduated from St. Michael's College at Santa Fe. Out of college, he went into the merchandising business and continued in that activity for many years. After early employment in the Santa Fe post office and later the U.S. Treasury office there, in 1889 he founded a weekly Spanish-language newspaper, *La Voz del Pueblo*, in the interest of New Mexico statehood. In 1900 he founded and began editing a second paper, *La Bandera Americana*; eight years later he was elected state press association president, a position he held for the rest of his life.

In addition to his journalistic and mercantile activity Montoya also entered political life. In 1892 he was elected to the lower house of the territorial legislature and was repeatedly reelected, serving until 1903, when he was speaker of the House. In the following year he was elected to the New Mexico upper house, the Territorial Council. When a New Mexico constitutional convention was authorized in 1910, Montoya was elected a delegate; in the convention he worked zealously for the protection of Hispanic rights. During the next decade he served in various appointive positions and in 1918 was elected Bernalillo County clerk. At the end of his term of office he won election as New Mexico's sole member of the U.S. House of Representatives and died before that term ended.

FURTHER READING: *History of New Mexico, Its Resources and People*, Los Angeles: Pacific States Publishing Co., 1907; Maurilio Vigil, *Los Patrones: Profiles of Hispanic Political Leaders in New Mexico History*, Washington, D.C.: University Press of America, 1980.

MORENO, LUISA (1907–   ), labor leader, organizer. Born in Guatemala and educated there, Luisa Moreno went to Mexico City as a newspaper correspondent and married there. In 1928 she and her husband immigrated to the United States, where she soon went to work in a New York garment factory.

Luisa Moreno began her labor career in New York City in the early 1930s as a member of the International Ladies' Garment Workers' Union and during the second half of that decade became a union organizer for the American Federation of Labor. In 1937 she joined the CIO and became an organizer and newspaper editor for the United Cannery, Agricultural, Packing and Allied Workers of America (UCAPAWA), an affiliate of the CIO. Traveling extensively in 1937, she helped organize workers in cotton, beets, canning, and pecan shelling from Texas to Colorado and Michigan. In 1938 she was involved in the San Antonio pecan shellers' strike and in that same year was a principal founder of El Congreso de los Pueblos de Habla Español, a broad-based progressive and sometimes radical organization aiming at fighting discrimination and poor working conditions.

During the early 1940s Luisa Moreno was active organizing UCAPAWA locals in California. She became vice-president of the Los Angeles Industrial Council in 1942 and also of the California CIO Executive Board as well as an international vice-president of UCAPAWA. In the next year she was an energetic member of the Sleepy Lagoon Defense Committee in Los Angeles. During the 1940s she remained deeply involved in labor organizing and in speaking out against the denial of civil rights to Mexican workers. Her activist and radical stance made her a natural target for McCarthyism in the early 1950s, and she was deported under the terms of the McCarran-Walter Immigration Act. She went to Mexico and from there to Cuba where she participated in the Castro revolution. Subsequently she returned to Mexico and settled in Guadalajara, state of Jalisco, where she currently lives. Although she has continued her interest in workers' problems and workers' organizations, she has not taken an active role, partly because of poor health.

FURTHER READING: Rodolfo Acuña, *Occupied America: A History of Chicanos*, New York: Harper & Row, 1981; Albert Camarillo, *Chicanos in California*, San Francisco: Boyd & Fraser Publishing Co., 1984; Alfredo Mirandé and Evangelina Enríquez, *La Chicana: The Mexican-American Woman*, Chicago: University of Chicago Press, 1979.

MORIN, RAUL R. (1913–1967), civic leader, author. Raúl Morín was born 26 July 1913 on a farm near the small town of Lockhart, Texas, and received his early education there and in nearby San Antonio. An early interest in art led him to the San Antonio Trade School and a commercial art education. After service in the Civilian Conservation Corps in Arizona during the mid–1930s he went to California where he eventually settled in Los Angeles. Here he attended the Frank Wiggins Trade School, did free-lance commercial art, and eventually opened the Olvera Sign Company.

World War II led to Morín's service as an infantryman in the Seventy-ninth Division of the Seventh Army until the Battle of the Bulge, when he was wounded. During his nearly two years in the hospital he took journalism and other classes and read extensively. After his discharge Morín returned to his sign-painting business, but with a much greater awareness of the discrimination Mexican Americans still suffered in the Los Angeles area. Asking himself what he in California might do to bring about improvement in race relations, he decided to write about Chicano service and valor in World War II. After long and difficult research he completed *Among the Valiant*, only to find publishers uninterested in it. Nearly ten years later, in 1963, it was published through the efforts of the Chicano veterans' organization, the American G.I. Forum.

During the 1950s and 1960s Morín was extremely active in Mexican American organizations, in Democratic politics, and in veteran and civic groups. In 1966 he ran for state senator in the Twenty-seventh District but lost. As a result of his constant concern for the welfare of La Raza, he was appointed to numerous boards and commissions—most importantly to the (Los Angeles) Mayor's Advisory Committee. By the time of his death in 1967 he had become widely recognized in California as one of the pioneers in working for greater dignity and equality for Mexican Americans. In the following year a veterans' memorial at Brooklyn and Lorena streets in East Los Angeles was officially dedicated as the Raúl R. Morín Memorial Square.

FURTHER READING: Raúl Morín, *Among the Valiant*, Alhambra, Calif.: Borden Publishing Co., 1963.

MORTON, CARLOS (1947–   ), dramatist, poet, journalist. Carlos Morton was born in Chicago on 15 October 1947. Son of a U.S. Army sergeant whose father had changed the family name from Pérez to Morton, he grew up in such places as the Panama Canal Zone, San Antonio, Chicago, San Francisco, and New York. In 1970 he entered the University of Texas at El Paso, where he majored in English and wrote and published poems and short stories. In 1973 his first play, *Desolation Car Lot*, was produced and in the next year he published in *El Grito* a play based on the fall of man, titled *El Jardín*. He completed his B.A. in 1975 and went on to the University of California at San Diego to study writing. He received his M.F.A. in 1978.

Morton's early attraction for the theater led to some work with Luis Valdez's Teatro Campesino and the San Francisco Mime Troupe. He has also served as an editor of the Latino magazines *La Luz*, *Nuestro*, and *Revista Chicano-Riqueña*. Morton's first book of poetry, *White Heroin Winter*, was published in 1971; however, he is best known for his plays. While a graduate student, he published *El Cuento de Pancho Diablo* (1976) and *Las Many Muertes de Richard Morales* (1977). Since then he has had several more publications, the most recent being in part a revision, *The Many Deaths of Danny Rosales and Other Plays*, in 1983. He continues to be active writing plays and teaches in the Drama Department at the University of Texas, Austin.

Morton's plays have been staged primarily at universities, including Harvard, and in Chicano communities. Generally in his works he emphasizes nonviolence, ethnic unity, and racial harmony. His message, at times disturbing to some people, is softened by the author's often outlandish slapstick humor. *El Jardín* and *The Many Deaths of Danny Rosales* are his best-known works.

FURTHER READING: Jorge A. Huerta, *Chicano Theater: Themes and Forms*, Ypsilanti, Mich.: Bilingual Press, 1982; Francisco Lomelí and Donaldo Urioste, *Chicano Perspectives in Literature*, Albuquerque: Pajarito Publications, 1976; Julio A. Martínez, *Chicano Scholars and Writers: A Bio-Bibliographical Directory*, Metuchen, N.J.: The Scarecrow Press, 1979; Carlos Morton, "Mexican Diary, 1954–1977," *Nuestro* 2:4 (April 1978).

MURIETA, JOAQUIN (also MURRIETA) (fl. 1850s), folk hero, bandit. The 1848 gold discovery in California created a mining society that had become plagued with lawlessness and banditry by the early 1850s. Some of these bandits were Californios and Sonorans who had been driven from the mines by vigilantes and ruffians.

As the result of mounting violence, in the spring of 1853 the California legislature created a temporary state ranger group with orders to capture bandits known as the five Joaquíns, who were identified as Joaquín Valenzuela, Joaquín Ocomorenia, Joaquín Carillo, Joaquín Botellier or Botilleras, and Joaquín Muriati or Murieta. Californios bitterly protested that this was a license to hunt Mexicans, since there was nothing to identify the five Joaquíns.

Nevertheless, the ranger force was organized under a Texan named Harry Love. Late in July Love's rangers, with only days left to their three-month mandate, encountered a small group of Mexicans. When the shooting ended the rangers had two corpses later identified as those of Joaquín and a wanted criminal known as three-fingered Jack García. The hand of García and head of Joaquín were placed in jars of alcohol. There was some doubt about these facile identifications and especially the later tacking of the name Murieta onto the head of Joaquín, but the head and hand became an instant success as touring curiosities. The head was finally destroyed in the San Francisco earthquake and fire of 1906.

In 1854 John Rollin Ridge, a writer, published *The Life and Adventures of Joaquín Murieta, the Celebrated California Bandit*, and the legend of Murieta was on its way. At least 90 percent fiction, his slim paperback used a Robin Hood motif and became an instant success. It was pirated both in the United States and abroad, dramatized, made into an epic poem and a biography, rewritten and embroidered on, and much later was Hollywood's basis for the Cisco Kid and Zorro. Toward the end of the nineteenth century the Murieta legend received some sanction by being included in the works of historians Hubert Howe Bancroft and Theodore Hittell.

Since then the Joaquín Murieta story has been kept alive by numerous reprintings and rewrites. Joaquín the historical figure has become lost, perhaps irrevocably, in the enormously expanded fame of Joaquín the legend.

FURTHER READING: Francis P. Farquar, *Joaquín Murieta, The Brigand Chief of California*, San Francisco, Calif.: Grabhorn Press, 1932; Joseph Henry Jackson, *Bad Company*, New York: Harcourt, Brace and Co., 1939; Frank Latta, *Joaquín Murieta and His Horse Gangs*, Santa Cruz, Calif.: Bear State Books, 1980; Remi Nadeau, *The Real Joaquín Murieta*, Corona del Mar, Calif.: Trans-Anglo Books, 1974; John Rollin Ridge, *The Life and Adventures of Joaquín Murieta, The Celebrated California Bandit*, Norman: University of Oklahoma Press, 1955 (new edition); Richard Rodríguez, "The Head of Joaquín Murrieta," *California* 10:7 (July 1985).

N ⎯⎯⎯⎯⎯⎯⎯⎯⎯⎯⎯⎯⎯⎯⎯⎯⎯⎯⎯⎯⎯⎯⎯⎯⎯⎯⎯⎯⎯⎯⎯⎯⎯⎯⎯⎯

NAVA, JULIAN (1927–   ), ambassador, historian, educator. Julian Nava was born 19 June 1927 in Los Angeles, California, the second son of eight children born to his immigrant parents, who had fled Mexico during her Great Revolution of 1910–1920. Growing up in the Mexican barrio of East Los Angeles, he attended public schools there, was an excellent student, and did migrant agricultural work with the family. He volunteered for naval service in World War II and became a combat aircrewman. Upon his discharge he worked in auto repair with his older brother and soon decided to use the G.I. Bill for a college education. An outstanding student and student body president at East Los Angeles Junior College, he went on to Pomona College to complete his A.B. in 1951 and then to Harvard University with two scholarships. Here he earned his M.A. and finally his doctorate in history in 1955. After a two-year teaching stint at the University of Puerto Rico Nava accepted a position at California State University at Northridge.

At Northridge Professor Nava soon became involved in the rising concern about Chicano problems, especially in education, and in 1967 he ran for the Los Angeles school board. He won an impressive victory and later was elected president of the board. At the end of his first four-year term he was reelected to the board—a feat he repeated in 1975. He also was a member of the board of the Plaza de la Raza and the Hispanic Urban Center and on the advisory committee of the Mexican American Legal Defense and Education Fund (MALDEF). In January 1980 he was named by President Jimmy Carter as ambassador to Mexico, where he served until early in the following year. With the advent of the Reagan administration he was replaced by Republican John Gavin* and returned to his teaching position at Northridge.

One of the pioneers in the history of Mexican Americans, Julian Nava has written a public school textbook, *Mexican Americans: Past, Present, and Future* (1969), and edited two books of readings: *The Mexican American in American History* (1973), and *Viva La Raza! Readings on Mexican Americans* (1973). In addition he is the author of several booklets and a number of journal articles.

He has served on numerous educational committees and boards and other professional bodies. In the early 1960s he was founding chairman of the Committee to Preserve the History of Los Angeles and the founding director of the Centro de Estudios Universitarios Colombo-Americano in Bogotá in 1965.

FURTHER READING: Harold J. Alford, *The Proud Peoples*, New York: David McKay Co., 1972; Al Martínez, *Rising Voices: Profiles of Hispano-American Lives*, New York: New American Library, 1974; Jess G. Nieto, "Julian Nava—Our Voice in Mexico," *Caminos* 1:7 (November 1980).

NAVARRO, JOSE ANTONIO (1795–1871), political leader, merchant, "Co-creator of Texas." Born in San Antonio, Texas, on 27 February 1795, Navarro was the son of Angel Navarro, a Spanish emigré who turned merchant on the Texas frontier. Despite the confused times of the Mexican movement for independence, his father managed to send him to school at Saltillo in Coahuila for a rudimentary education. After a few years in Saltillo he returned to San Antonio, where he went to work in one of the general stores until after his father's death. Because of the defeat of patriot forces of which the Navarro family were a part, in 1813 he was forced to flee across the border into Louisiana and remained there three years. Returning to San Antonio, he engaged in mercantile activity and became widely known in the town.

With Mexican independence achieved in 1821, the Navarros were on the winning side at last, and José Antonio was elected to the state legislature. In 1828 he was reelected a second term. During this time he met the Anglo *empresario* Stephen Austin with whom he formed a close lifelong friendship. Despite Navarro's effort to ease tensions between Tejano and Anglo Texan in the early 1830s, they continued to rise. As a strong federalist Navarro was one of three Tejanos who signed the Texan declaration of conditional independence from General Santa Anna's centralist government in Mexico City in 1835. He also helped write a constitution for the new country of Texas. After the fighting Navarro returned to rebuild his mercantile business and his ranches.

When Texas president Mirabeau B. Lamar planned the ill-fated Texas Santa Fe Expedition in 1841, Navarro agreed to be one of four commissioners to accompany the group to Santa Fe. The expedition ended in a fiasco, and Navarro, a former Mexican citizen and now a prisoner of the Mexicans, was initially condemned to death as a traitor. His sentence was later commuted to life imprisonment. When the other Texas prisoners were released, he was not and was sent to San Juan de Ulúa, reputedly the worst prison in Mexico. Only after President Santa Anna's overthrow in late 1844 did he manage to escape and return to Texas.

Upon his return Navarro barely had time to recoup his health when he was elected to the convention to write a state constitution, and following Texas annexation to the United States, he was elected to the state senate. Increasingly disturbed by the racial and ethnic intolerance of many Anglos, Navarro decided not to run for reelection when his senate term ended in 1849 and instead retired to private life and pursuit of his mercantile interests. Not even the divisive events leading up to the Civil War or that cataclysmic struggle drew him from his family and business. Although aloof from civic affairs, in the fall of 1869 he was nominated for the state senate but declined because of his poor health. He died of cancer two years later, a moderately well-to-do man.

In 1960 the governor of Texas declared that the birthday of this "co-creator of Texas" should be annually observed in the state.

FURTHER READING: Frederick Chabot, *With the Makers of San Antonio*, San Antonio, Texas: Artes Gráficas, 1937; Jacob de Córdova, *Texas, Her Resources and Her Public Men*, Waco: Texian Press, 1958; Joseph M. Dawson, *José Antonio Navarro: Co-Creator of Texas*, Waco: Baylor University Press, 1969; Thomas L. Miller, "José Antonio Navarro, 1795–1871," *Journal of Mexican American History* 2 (Spring 1972); R. M. Potter, "The Texas Revolution," *Magazine of American History* 2:10 (October 1978).

NERI, MANUEL (1930–   ), sculptor. Manuel Neri was born in the small California agricultural town of Sanger, near Fresno, of Mexican parents who had immigrated to the United States. He spent his childhood in the San Joaquin valley, where his parents worked as farm laborers. In 1944 the Neris moved to Oakland, California, where Manuel developed an interest in electronics in high school. Dropping out of school, he became an electrical technician for Western Union. In 1949 he entered San Francisco City College to work toward an engineering degree; however, he soon became interested in art through an elective ceramics class. He enrolled in the University of California, Berkeley, school of engineering and after a year left to attend the California College of Arts and Crafts in Oakland. In 1953 he went to study at the Bray Foundation in Helena, Montana, but was drafted into the service later that year.

On coming out of the service in 1955 Neri traveled to Mexico with ideas of studying art there. He was disappointed in Mexican art schools and returned to the San Francisco Bay Area, where he attended the California College of Arts and Crafts from 1955 to 1957 and the San Francisco Art Institute the following two years. In San Francisco he began to participate actively in the North Beach artist-musician-poet colony. At the same time he first exhibited his works. In 1959 he began to teach at the Art Institute and five years later joined the art faculty at the University of California, Davis, where he still teaches.

In the 1950s Neri's sculptures were life-sized human figures in plaster with paint added. Around 1960 his work evolved into a process of continuing change which literally left them in a state of perpetual uncompletedness. Influenced by a trip to Mexican and Peruvian Indian ruins, toward the end of the 1960s he did a number of works based on the pyramidal form. However, by the mid–1970s he had returned to the human figure and also began to explore the use of marble and bronze. In 1978 a two-year Guggenheim fellowship grant enabled him to do five bronze works. A visit to Carrara, Italy, two years earlier led to his working with marble, and he subsequently spent summer vacations working there. Neri's work has been exhibited in various galleries throughout the United

States. In 1977 there was a twenty-year retrospective of his works at the Oakland Museum.

FURTHER READING: Thomas Albright, "Manuel Neri's Survivors: Sculpture for the Age of Anxiety," *ARTnews* (January 1981); Jacinto Quirarte, *Mexican American Artists*, Austin: University of Texas Press, 1973.

NOGALES, LUIS (1943–   ), businessman, lawyer. Luis Nogales was born into a migrant farm worker family on 17 October 1943 in Calexico on the California border with Mexico. He grew up there, receiving his education in local schools and working beside his parents in San Joaquin valley harvests. From high school he entered San Diego State College (today University) in 1962 and graduated four years later with a degree in political science. His excellent scholastic record got him into Stanford University Law School where, as earlier, he combined an outstanding academic record with extracurricular distinction. At Stanford he was the first chairman of the Mexican American Student Confederation and served with distinction on university committees dealing with minorities. Even before he received his LL.B. in 1969, he was appointed minorities assistant to Stanford President Kenneth Pitzer. After three years as advisor to the president he left in 1972 to accept appointment as a White House Fellow for the Interior Department.

In 1973 Luis Nogales returned to California as legal counsel for Station KTLA in Los Angeles and from there rose by 1978 to executive vice-president and member of the Board of Directors of Los Angeles-based diversified media firm, Golden West Broadcasters. A disagreement with management led to his firing three years later, and he moved to the nationwide public relations and consulting firm of Fleishman-Hilliard as vice-president in charge of the Hispanic Division. In 1983 he joined United Press International (UPI) as executive vice-president and was soon appointed chairman of the company's executive committee. In August of the next year he was promoted to general manager as well because of UPI's financial problems. He was able to turn the company around and show a quarterly profit at the end of 1984, its first in twenty-two years. However, on 4 March 1985 Luis Nogales was fired by his hirers and on 5 March he was back in charge and his firers were out. In July he resigned from UPI.

Luis Nogales was national chairman of the Mexican American Legal Defense and Education Fund in 1983 and a member of the board of directors of Levi Strauss & Company, the Bank of California, Bancal Tristate Corporation, and the Inter-American Foundation. He also is currently a volunteer advisor to United Way of America.

FURTHER READING: Tom Díaz, "Man on Top of a Roller Coaster," *Hispanic Review of Business* (October 1984); "Faces Behind the Figures," *Forbes* (8 April 1985); "Luis Nogales Moves to UPI," *Caminos* 4:4 (July–August 1983).

NOVARRO, RAMON (1899–1968), actor. Born in the Mexican mining center of Durango on 6 February 1899, Ramón Novarro, the son of a dentist, was christened José Ramón Gil Samaniego (family name). When Ramón was

fourteen, the Samaniego family immigrated to the United States to escape the
Mexican Revolution, settling in Los Angeles. Because his father was ill and the
family desperately poor, Ramón went to work. Among his many jobs were small
acting and dancing parts in films and plays. His skill as a dancer came to the
attention of Hollywood director Rex Ingraham, who hired him to play a leading
role in the *Prisoner of Zenda* in 1923. Novarro was an instant success and quickly
starred in several successful films. Nevertheless, his career developed slowly,
since it came inopportunely at a time when Rudolph Valentino and John Gilbert
had established themselves as the leading Hollywood Latino male sex symbols.

In the late 1920s Novarro continued to be a reasonably successful box office
draw in films like *Ben Hur* (1926) and *The Student Prince* (1927). Valentino
died suddenly in 1926, and soon afterwards the lushly romantic films of the
mid–1920s also began to expire. On top of these changes came the talkies.
Novarro, who had a good singing voice, survived the change better than many
other stars and in 1932 costarred with Greta Garbo in *Mata Hari*. He followed
that with *The Son-Daughter* (1933) opposite Helen Hayes, and *The Cat and
Fiddle* (1934), probably his best film.

After 1934 a somewhat bitter Novarro largely abandoned Hollywood to make
concert and theater appearances, made a couple of films in Rome and in Mexico,
and did occasional character roles and some directing. He also spent much time
traveling, managing his real estate investments in the San Fernando valley north
of Los Angeles, and in Mexico, writing his autobiography, and painting. In
1960 his character role in Sofia Loren's *Heller in Pink Tights* received good
reviews. It was his last screen appearance. Eight years later he was brutally
beaten to death in his Hollywood Hills home and was quietly buried in Calvary
Cemetery, Los Angeles.

FURTHER READING: Elinor Hughes, *Famous Stars of Filmdom (Men)*, Boston: L. C.
Page, 1932; David Shipman, *The Great Movie Stars: The Golden Years*, New York: Hill
& Wang, 1979.

O

OBLEDO, MARIO GUERRA (1932–   ), lawyer, politician. Born in San Antonio, Texas, on 9 April 1932, Mario Obledo grew up in the Mexican barrio, eighth of twelve children of immigrant parents. When his father died, Mario joined his brothers and sisters doing odd jobs to support the family, though he was only five years old. He received his early education in public schools, and after graduating from San Antonio Technical High he entered the University of Texas at Austin. However, his college years were interrupted by four years in the U.S. Navy where he served as a radarman during the Korean conflict. Mustering out of the service, he returned to the University of Texas and earned a B.S. in pharmacology in 1957. While working as a pharmacist, he began the study of law, receiving his Bachelor of Law and Doctor of Jurisprudence degrees at St. Mary's University in San Antonio.

Upon completing his legal studies, Obledo was appointed Assistant Attorney General of Texas in 1965 and three years later became president and general counsel for the Mexican American Legal Defense and Education Fund (MALDEF), of which he was a cofounder. There followed two years as a member of the Harvard University law faculty. In 1975 he was appointed by Governor "Jerry" Brown as director of California's Department of Health and Welfare, where he served for the next six years. In 1981 he plunged into politics, running in the Democratic primary of the following year for the governorship of California on a platform of Latino issues. He came in third out of a dozen candidates. Legal counsel for the Coalition of Hispanic Organizations, he was elected earlier in 1983 to a two-year term as president of the League of United Latin American Citizens (LULAC). Currently he is an active partner in the Sacramento (California) law firm of Obledo, Alcalá and Cabral.

In addition to having been elected president of MALDEF and LULAC, Mario Obledo has been the recipient of numerous honors and recognition awards. Among them are the Hubert Humphrey Award and the Distinguished Urban Service Award from the Urban Coalition.

FURTHER READING: "We Will Change the Political Face of the U.S.," *U.S. News and World Report* 95 (22 August 1983).

OCHOA, ESTEBAN (1831–1888), merchant, freighter, civic leader. Born in Chihuahua on 17 March 1831, Esteban was the son of Jesús Ochoa of an important ranching and mining family which soon moved to the Nuevo México frontier. He grew up there in the freighting business and was educated and trained in Missouri as well. After learning English and completing his apprenticeship, he returned to New Mexico and began an active career as a freighter, merchant, and entrepreneur. By 1859 he was sufficiently prominent to be elected chairman of a Las Cruces committee seeking to create an Arizona Territory separate from New Mexico. In that same year he moved his headquarters to Tucson, making it the hub of his extensive business interests.

During the Civil War Ochoa temporarily abandoned Tucson rather than take an oath of allegiance to the Confederacy. Returned to Tucson, he soon set up a partnership with an Anglo freighter, creating Tully, Ochoa and Company. The partners benefited greatly from expanded mining activity and in the postwar period became the leading freighters in the Southwest border region and number one merchandisers in Tucson. In addition, the partners were also active in promoting mining, smelting, U.S. Army contracts, woolen mills, and sheep raising.

Ochoa's paramount role in the partnership made him a natural spokesman for the Spanish-speaking population of southern Arizona, and he was important as an intermediary between it and Anglo society. During the 1860s and 1870s he was elected to the territorial legislature and in 1875 became mayor of Tucson. More than any other person, except possibly the governor, he was responsible for the establishment of a public school system in the Arizona Territory. During the 1880s his fortunes declined considerably as the newly arrived railroads took over much of his earlier freighting business. He died in October 1888 a relatively poor man but highly respected for his honesty and integrity.

FURTHER READING: Frank C. Lockwood, *Pioneer Portraits*, Tucson: University of Arizona Press, 1968; Matt S. Meier, "Estaban Ochoa, Enterpriser," *Journal of the West* 25:1 (January 1986); Thomas E. Sheridan, "Peacock in the Parlor, Frontier Tucson's Mexican Elite," *Journal of Arizona History* 25 (Autumn 1984).

OLIVAREZ, GRACIELA (1928–   ), lawyer. Born 9 May 1928 in a small mining town near Phoenix, Arizona, and educated there, Graciela "Grace" Olivárez dropped out of high school at sixteen when the family moved to Phoenix. However, she did go to business school and then went to work. The first woman disc jockey in Phoenix, between 1952 and 1962 she was women's program director of Spanish-language radio station KIFN. During the 1960s civil rights movement she met the Reverend Theodore Hesburgh, president of Notre Dame University, who invited her to enter Notre Dame law school despite her lack of educational requirements.

In 1970 at age forty-two Olivárez became the first woman graduate of Notre Dame School of Law and then returned to the Southwest to teach law, to continue her role in the civil rights movement, and to work for various local and state government agencies. During 1972 she was appointed director of the University of New Mexico's Institute for Social Research and Development. Three years later she was named State Planning Officer for New Mexico. In 1977 she became the highest-ranking Hispana in the Carter administration when President Jimmy Carter named her director of the Community Services Administration in Washington. Early in 1980 she left the Community Services Administration to become senior consultant with United Way of America, a national service organization. Here she continues her work of helping the poor.

Graciela Olivárez received honorary doctorates from Amherst College in 1973, Michigan State University in 1975, and her own Notre Dame School of Law in 1978. In 1975 *Redbook* named her one of "44 Women Who Could Save America" in its April issue and earlier the League of Mexican-American Women named her Outstanding Woman of the Southwest. She has also been honored by appointments to numerous commissions, committees, and boards including Common Cause and the American Civil Liberties Union.

FURTHER READING: Al Martínez, *Rising Voices: Profiles of Hispano-American Lives*, New York: The New American Library, 1974; *News on Hispanic Affairs* 1:3 (March-April 1980), Washington, D.C.: Office of Hispanic Affairs; Larry Vélez, "Washington's Top Advocate for the Poor," *Nuestro* 3:5 (June-July 1979); *Who's Who in America, 1980–1981*, 41st ed., 1980.

OLMOS, EDWARD JAMES (1947–   ), actor, singer. Born 24 February 1947 in the heart of the East Los Angeles's Boyle Heights, Edward Olmos was the second of six children of parents who had emigrated from Mexico City at the end of World War II. When he was ten, the family moved out of the barrio into the suburban area of Montebello, where he graduated from high school in 1965. He then entered East Los Angeles City College to study sociology and criminology.

Meanwhile, in 1961 Olmos had started on a musical bent as a singer leading a teenage rock and roll group called Edward James and the Pacific Ocean. From the mid–1960s to the mid–1970s he worked as a nightclub entertainer on Hollywood's Sunset Strip at clubs like The Factory and Gazarri's. To perfect his acting skills, he worked extensively in small experimental theaters and acting workshops in the Los Angeles area, such as the Lee Strasberg Institute. During this time he also began a film career; in 1971 he had his first movie role in *Aloha Bobby and Rose*, and he played on television in episodes of "Hill St. Blues," "Kojak," "Cannon," "Hawaii Five-O," "Police Story," and "Starsky and Hutch." Among his Hollywood film credits are roles in *Virus*, *Hit-Man*, *Wolfen*, *Blade Runner*, and *Alambrista*; the last won a Gold Medal at the 1978 Cannes Film Festival.

In 1978 Olmos appeared in his first salaried stage role, as El Pachuco in Luis Valdez's *Zoot Suit* at the Mark Taper Forum's New Theater in Los Angeles. His interpretation was an immense success, earning him not only a Tony nomination but also a prestigious award for best performance from the Los Angeles Drama Critics Circle, a Theatre World award, a *Drama Loque* award, and a *Nosotros* Golden Eagle award. After *Zoot Suit*, the stage play, Olmos did the 1982 film version, which was not a great box office success. Since then he has starred in *The Ballad of Gregorio Cortez*, a film from Embassy Pictures and the television film *Seguín*. In 1983 he was recipient of the National Council of La Raza Rubén Salazar Award for Communication. More recently he received an Emmy Award for his performance as Inspector Castillo in the television series "Miami Vice."

For the past several years Edward Olmos has quietly been spending much of his free time in social and charity work. Among other activities he has been touring the United States speaking at prisons and juvenile detention centers with his message for the inmates: self-discipline, determination, and perseverance.

FURTHER READING: Katherine A. Díaz, "Edward James Olmos—You Ain't Seen Nothing Yet," *Caminos* 1:7 (November 1980); "Emmy Award Winner Inspires Young Chicanos," *The Forum*, October 1985; Jeff Meyers, "Keeping Close to the Street," *Los Angeles Times Magazine*, 22 June 1986.

ORD, ANGUSTIAS DE LA GUERRA (1815–1880), historian.

Born into a Californio presidial family at Santa Barbara, Angustias de la Guerra received a typically meager frontier education for young girls. At age fifteen she was married to Manuel Jimeno Casarín, who held various important government offices in the last years of Mexican rule in California. As a result of her marriage, she lived for twenty-five years in Monterey at the center of Californio politics.

Although her family had opposed American takeover in 1846, after her husband's death, Angustias married Dr. James L. Ord, a physician in United States Army service. Two years before her death she dictated to Thomas Savage (for historian Hubert H. Bancroft) her recollections of events in California from her early childhood until the United States takeover in 1846. In addition to their use for Bancroft's histories, these memoirs have been published as *Occurrences in Hispanic California*.

FURTHER READING: Angustias de la Guerra Ord, *Occurrences in Hispanic California*, Washington, D.C.: Academy of American Franciscan History, 1956.

ORENDAIN, ANTONIO (1931–), labor organizer.

Antonio Orendáin was born in the Mexican state of Jalisco, where he grew up in rural poverty. At the death of his parents when he was eighteen, Orendáin moved to Guadalajara, the capital of Jalisco, and in 1950 he moved north across the border into the United States. In Los Angeles he sought out César Chávez* and Fred Ross at the Community Services Organization. After twelve years of active service in the CSO he left that organization in 1962 with Chávez and others ultimately to establish the Farm Worker Association (today the United Farm Workers, UFW) and was elected as its first secretary-treasurer.

When the Delano Grape strike began in 1965 Orendáin became deeply involved and soon was sent by Chávez to Texas to lead the farm workers' movement there. In Texas Orendáin, who had some tactical disagreement with Chávez's leadership, took a more aggressive and emotional stance. Perhaps as a result, the Texas farm-labor movement developed very rapidly, but so did organized opposition to it. After a year in Texas he was replaced and returned to California, only to be sent back to Texas in 1969.

When César Chávez assigned Orendáin full-time to coordinating the UFW boycott programs in 1974, the split between the two men widened and in the following August Orendáin left the UFW to form the Texas Farm Workers Union. In 1977 and 1978 he led three dramatic marches by which he hoped to get collective bargaining and other rights for his union. Rivalry between the two agricultural unions continued and by the beginning of the 1980s the TFWU, while continuing as a symbol of the struggle for human rights in Texas, had not achieved any labor contracts.

FURTHER READING: Ignacio M. García, "The Many Battles of Antonio Orendain," *Nuestro* 3:11 (November 1979).

ORTEGA, KATHERINE D. (1934–   ), businesswoman, politician, treasurer of the United States. Born in rural south central New Mexico on 16 July 1934, the youngest of nine children, Katherine Ortega grew up and received her early education in Tularosa, New Mexico. From early years she leaned toward mathematics and accounting and in her senior high school year worked at the Otero County State Bank in nearby Alamogordo. After high school she worked in a bank for two years to earn money for college. At Eastern New Mexico State University at Portales she quickly caught up with her high school classmates and graduated with honors in 1957 in business and economics. Upon graduation she started an accounting firm at Alamogordo with one of her sisters and a decade later moved to Los Angeles, where she worked as a tax supervisor from 1969 to 1972. In the 1970s she became a vice-president of the Pan American National Bank in Los Angeles and then the first woman president of a California bank when she was named director and president of the Santa Ana State Bank in 1975.

For family reasons Ortega returned to New Mexico in 1978 as a consultant to Otero Savings and Loan Association of Alamogordo. Active in Republican political circles since her college days, she was appointed a member of the President's Advisory Committee on Small and Minority Business by the Reagan administration. In 1982 she was named to the five-man Copyright Royalty Tribunal and in September 1983 became the United States treasurer. In the following year she was selected to deliver the keynote address at the Republican National Convention that nominated Ronald Reagan for a second term.

Katherine Ortega was honored by her alma mater in 1977 with the Outstanding Alumni Award for the year. She also has been the recipient of the California

Businesswomen's Achievement Award and the Damas de Comercio Outstanding Woman of the Year Award.

FURTHER READING: Charlotte Saikowski, "GOP Keynoter Radiates Self-Help Ideal," *Christian Science Monitor* (17 August 1984).

ORTEGO Y GASCA, PHILIP D. (1926–   ), educator, poet, publisher. Phil Ortego was born 23 August 1926 in the Chicago suburb of Blue Island and grew up in Pittsburgh where his father was a steel worker. At the junior high school level he dropped out to go to work at a variety of jobs. During the latter part of World War II he served in the U.S. Marine Corps (1944–1947) and then used the G.I. Bill to enter the University of Pittsburgh. In 1953 he again interrupted his education, this time to serve nine years in the U.S. Air force. However, he did continue his studies and in 1959 received his A.B. in English and Spanish at Texas Western College (now University of Texas at El Paso). He resigned from the Air Force and in 1966 obtained his M.A. at the Univesity of Texas at El Paso (UTEP); five years later he earned his doctorate in English language and literature at the University of New Mexico.

During this time Ortego also taught at UTEP, where he was founding director of the Chicano Studies Program, and in 1971 he was a Fulbright lecturer in Argentina. After a period in the early 1970s as assistant to the president of Metropolitan State College in Denver he joined the Mexican American Graduate Studies department at San Jose State University in California. In 1981 Ortego's play *Madre del Sol*, a dramatization of the Mexican American experience, won wide acclaim both in the United States and Mexico. By 1983 he was named chairman of the Washington-based Hispanic Foundation, a research organization, and was appointed editor in chief of the *National Hispanic Reporter*.

Professor Ortego has been a very productive scholar. In addition to several books, he is the author or coauthor of more than 150 poems, essays, short stories, and reviews covering a wide variety of topics. In 1971 he was given the Most Honored Faculty award at UTEP and in the following year was the senior editor and literary director of the Hispanic magazine *La Luz*. By the end of the decade he also became associate publisher. In 1980 he was recipient of the Kathryn Stoner O'Connor Foundation Award.

FURTHER READING: *Directory of American Scholars*, 6th ed., 1974; Julio A. Martínez, *Chicano Scholars and Writers: A Bio-Bibliographical Directory*, Metuchen, N.J.: The Scarecrow Press, 1979; Theodore Wood, *Chicanos y Chicanas Prominentes*, Menlo Park, Calif.: Educational Consortium of America, 1974.

ORTIZ, FRANCIS V., JR. (1926–   ), ambassador. Frank Ortiz was born 14 March 1926 in Santa Fe, New Mexico, where he grew up and received his early education. Reaching age eighteen in 1944, he served till the end of World War II in the U.S. Army Air Force and was awarded the Air Medal. Upon separation from the service he entered Georgetown University and completed his B.S. degree in 1950. He then entered the U.S. Foreign Service and continued postgraduate studies at Georgetown, the University of Madrid, and the American University in Beirut. Between 1953 and 1958 he served in Ethiopia and in Mexico and then returned to Washington until 1961 when he was appointed special assistant to the U.S. ambassador to Mexico. In 1963 he was again returned to Washington to head the Spanish affairs section in the State Department. After a year (1966–1967) assignment to the National War College he was sent back to the field, serving three years each in the U.S. embassies in Peru and Uruguay.

In 1973 Ortiz was named country director in the State Department for Argentina, Uruguay, and Paraguay and subsequently deputy executive secretary. Four years later he was appointed ambassador to Barbados and Grenada and special representative to a number of former British possessions in the Caribbean. In 1979 he became U.S. ambassador to Guatemala, but was removed a year later in what was alleged to be a bitter quarrel over U.S. policy in Central America and Ortiz's support of the conservative military government of Guatemala.

Ambassador Ortiz, the highest-ranking Hispanic in the foreign service at the time of his dismissal, has been the recipient of a number of honors: an Honor Award and Superior Service Award from the Department of State and in 1964 the U.S. and Mexican presidential Chamizal Commemorative medals. He is Knight of Malta.

FURTHER READING: Nicolas Lemann, "How Realpolitik Undid One Diplomat," *Washington Post* (6 July 1980); *Who's Who in America, 1980–1981*, 41st ed., 1980; *Who's Who in Government, 1975–1976*, 2nd ed., 1975.

ORTIZ, RALPH (1934–   ), artist. Born 30 January 1934 in New York City, Ralph Ortiz grew up there, attending the High School of Art and Design, the Brooklyn Museum of Art School, and Pratt Institute. He has a B.S. degree and a Master of Fine Arts degree from Pratt and has received a doctorate in education at Columbia University. By his mid-twenties he began to exhibit his art in museums and galleries in the United States and England.

Ortiz has written extensively in explanation and defense of "destruction" art and has taught at New York University and at Columbia University Teachers College. In addition he has lectured extensively at universities, museums, and galleries and has appeared on television and radio. He is best known for his "Piano Destruction Concert" first presented on BBC television in 1966. He is also known for some earlier works that he links loosely with pre-Columbian Indian art. He was director and curator of the Museo del Barrio in New York City from 1969 to 1970 and a decade later was chairman of the board of Fondo del Sol in Washington, D.C. He is currently associate professor at the Mason Gross School of Arts, Rutgers University in New Jersey.

FURTHER READING: Jacinto Quirarte, *Mexican American Artists*, Austin: University of Texas Press, 1973; *Who's Who in American Art*, 16th ed., 1984.

ORTIZ, RAMON (1813–1896), priest, Mexican patriot. Born in Santa Fe, Ramón was the son of Antonio Ortiz and María Teresa Mier, descendants of early Nuevo Mexicano families. Vowed by his mother to the Church, he trained at the diocesan seminary in Durango, far to the south, and was ordained when he reached twenty-one. After serving in a small mining town, in 1837 he was appointed pastor at Paso del Norte (today Ciudad Juárez). During the tumultuous years of the early 1840s he befriended most of the Anglo traders who passed through Paso del Norte and in 1842 won many friends as a result of his help for the survivors of the Texas Santa Fe expedition. Nevertheless, in 1846 he actively promoted resistance to U.S. takeover and was arrested and held hostage by Col. Alexander Doniphan.

Father Ortiz was released when Doniphan's force captured Chihuahua. He returned to Paso del Norte, ran for the Mexican Chamber of Deputies, and was elected. He fought impassionedly in the chamber against acceptance of the Treaty of Guadalupe Hidalgo, but lost and was appointed to superintend the removal of those Nuevo Mexicanos who wished to move to Mexico after the treaty was ratified. In the often difficult post-treaty years he frequently found himself in the role of peacemaker as in the case of the Salt War of 1877 in which he gave a deposition on the Mexican claims. Increasingly suffering from poor health in the 1880s, he retired and in 1896 died of cancer.

FURTHER READING: Fidelia Miller Puckett, "Ramón Ortiz: Priest and Patriot," *New Mexico Historical Review* 25:4 (October 1950).

ORTIZ, SOLOMON P. (1937–   ), politician, law officer. Solomón Ortiz was born 3 June 1937 in Robstown, Texas, not far from Corpus Christi and attended Del Mar College in the latter city. Between 1960 and 1962 he served in the U.S. Army. In 1964 he was elected Nueces County constable and four years later became the first Mexican American to be elected county commissioner. In 1976 he became the first Mexican American sheriff of Nueces County, elected with a two-thirds majority.

When the 1980 census indicated Texas would get three additional seats in the House of Representatives, Ortiz ran as a law-and-order advocate in the newly created Twenty-seventh District and won with 64 percent of the votes cast. In Congress he serves on the Committee on Armed Services, the Committee on Merchant Marine and Fisheries, and the Select Committee on Narcotics Abuse and Control.

FURTHER READING: Alan Ehrenhalt, ed., *Politics in America*, Washington, D.C.: Congressional Quarterly, 1983.

OTERO, ANTONIO JOSE (1809–1870), merchant, judge. The son of Vicente Otero and Gertrudis Chaves, Otero was descended from two powerful old Nuevo Mexicano families. He was born 13 March 1809 in Valencia, south of Albuquerque and obtained part of his education at Father Antonio José Martínez's school in Taos. By the time of the American takeover in 1846 he had become firmly entrenched in the Santa Fe trade and was a member of the "American party." He readily accepted U.S. conquest and was named chief justice of the superior court by acting military governor Stephen Kearny. He took an active role as a member of the constitutional conventions of 1849 and 1850 at Santa Fe.

Judge Otero's district included the southern half of the present state of New Mexico and all of Arizona. A man of considerable influence among both Nuevo Mexicanos and Anglos, he had a reputation for honesty and intellectual ability. He died at his home in the small Rio Grande river town of Peralta, just south of Albuquerque.

FURTHER READING: Ralph Emerson Twitchell, *The History of the Military Occupation of the Territory of New Mexico . . .* , New York: Arno Press (reprint), 1976.

OTERO, MARIANO S. (1844–1904), merchant, congressman. Mariano was born in the tiny town of Peralta, about fifteen miles down the Rio Grande from Albuquerque on 29 August 1844 in the last years of the Mexican period. As a member of the powerful Otero clan, he attended local parochial and private schools and later studied at St. Louis University in Missouri. After college he was involved in cattle raising and mercantile pursuits and later became a banker. In the early 1870s he was probate judge of Bernalillo County. In 1874 he was nominated by the Democrats as their candidate for congressional delegate but turned down the offer. Four years later he was elected to the office as a Republican, but then declined renomination and returned to his business pursuits in New Mexico. Between 1884 and 1886 he was county commissioner but subsequently was twice defeated in candidacy for Congress. By the beginning of the 1890s he moved to Albuquerque, where he continued his banking activities. He died there in 1904 in his fifty-ninth year.

OTERO, MIGUEL A., SR. (1829–1882), businessman, political leader. Born in Valencia, Nuevo México, on 21 June 1829, Miguel Otero was a son of Vicente Otero, an important local leader during both the Spanish and Mexican eras. After his early education in Valencia, in 1841 he was sent to Missouri where he attended St. Louis University and six years later went to Pingree's College in New York. He later taught there and then began the study of law. In 1851 he returned to St. Louis where he continued his legal studies and was admitted to the bar.

Returning to New Mexico in 1852 to practice law in Albuquerque, Otero became private secretary to territorial governor William C. Lane and immediately plunged into politics, being elected in that same year to the legislature. Two years later he was appointed New Mexico attorney general. Because of his political experience and wide family connections (his older brother Antonio* was chief justice), Miguel was nominated by the Democratic party in 1855 for the office of territorial delegate to the United States Congress and won the election. Renominated in 1857 and 1859, he was reelected both times, serving a total of six years as New Mexico's representative to Congress.

In the U.S. Congress Otero worked hard to secure passage of the transcontinental railroad through New Mexico, thereby aligning himself and New Mexico with southern interests, which also favored a southern route. As a result of his leadership, in 1859 New Mexico legislated a slave code, and in the following year he supported Senator John H. Crittenden's compromise to avoid the Civil War by extending slavery in territories south of 36°30'—which would have included New Mexico. During this time he had a partial interest in the Santa Fe *Gazette* and a powerful voice in determining federal Indian policy in New Mexico. However, during Otero's third term the outbreak of the Civil War greatly reduced his political influence. He did not support the southern Confederacy, but he did favor a separate confederation of western states. At this time Otero declined nomination as minister to Spain by President Lincoln in favor of appointment as secretary of the territory of New Mexico. The Senate then failed to confirm him because of his political views.

During the Civil War Otero devoted himself to freighting and merchandising through his company, Whiting and Otero, to banking, and to his large ranching interests. At the end of the war he joined John Sellar to form Otero, Sellar & Company, commission merchants who followed the westward advancing railroads. In 1879 Otero, Sellar & Company established its permanent headquarters at Las Vegas, New Mexico. Meanwhile Otero had become extremely active in other business ventures in the Southwest and northern Mexico, particularly in lands, railroads, telephones, and banking. In 1870 he was part of a group that purchased the immense Maxwell land grant. During this time he also founded and was first president of the San Miguel National Bank and a director of the Maxwell Land Grant and Railroad Company and of the Atchison, Topeka, and Santa Fe Railroad. The first terminal of the Santa Fe in New Mexico was named Otero after him.

Despite failing health, in 1880 Otero was the Democratic candidate for territorial delegate to the United States Congress but was defeated. His poor health and a long-standing disagreement with John Sellar led to the dissolution of Otero, Sellar & Company early in the next year. Otero's health continued to deteriorate rapidly, and he died 30 May 1882 at age fifty-three.

FURTHER READING: *Biographical Directory of the American Congress, 1774–1971*, Washington, D.C.: U.S. Government Printing Office, 1971; William S. Speer, ed., *The Encyclopedia of the New West . . .* , Marshall, Tex.: The United States Bibliographical Publishing Co., 1881; Ralph Emerson Twitchell, *The Leading Facts of New Mexican History*, Cedar Rapids, Iowa: Torch Press, 1911–1917; Maurilio E. Vigil, *Los Patrones: Profiles of Hispanic Political Leaders in New Mexico History*, Washington, D.C.: University Press of America, 1980.

OTERO, MIGUEL A., JR. (1859–1944), governor, businessman, banker. Miguel Otero, Jr., was born in October 1859, the second of four children born to Miguel Otero, Sr. He received his early education in the dusty streets of frontier railroad towns where his father's mercantile company, Otero, Sellar & Company, did business. Young Otero was sent to St. Louis University, the U.S. Naval Academy, and Notre Dame University, but bouts of illness and some lack of enthusiasm for studies left him without a final degree. However, his experience as cashier, bookkeeper, and manager in his father's enterprises stood him in good stead after his father's death when he was twenty-two. From then on he took a leading role in the family business interests. In addition to being active in ranching, real estate, and mining, he naturally turned to politics, but as a Republican rather than a Democrat like his father.

In politics Otero moved from city treasurer (Las Vegas, 1883–1884) to probate court clerk (1886–1887) to county clerk (1889–1890), to district court clerk (1890–1893). Meanwhile he was a New Mexican delegate to the Republican National Convention of 1888 where he became acquainted with William McKinley. Six years later he was a candidate for the vice-presidential nomination. In 1898 McKinley, now president, named him territorial governor at age thirty-seven. As governor he was a vigorous leader and developed strong Nuevo Mexicano support and an effective political organization.

During his second term statehood became a heated issue. He strongly supported separate statehood for New Mexico and Arizona, calling a statehood convention in 1901. His opposition to President Theodore Roosevelt's National Forest policy caused much Republican resentment as his second term drew to an end, and Roosevelt decided not to reappoint him. Otero switched his allegiance to the Democratic party and stepped down from the governorship in January 1907.

After an extended trip to England and the Continent with Miguel III, Otero returned to New Mexican political life, being appointed territorial treasurer in 1909. The 1912 presidential election brought Democrat Woodrow Wilson to the White House and political preferment to Otero, who was appointed president of the New Mexico parole board and then United States marshal of the Panama Canal Zone. He continued active in Democratic politics in the 1920s, leading Canal Zone delegations to the national convention in 1920 and 1924. During World War II he died at age eighty-four.

Otero was author of three volumes of autobiographical reminiscences.

FURTHER READING: Howard Lamar, *The Reader's Encyclopedia of the American West*, New York: Thomas Y. Crowell, 1977; Miguel A. Otero II, *My Life on the Frontier, 1864–1882*, New York: Press of the Pioneers, 1935; *My Life on the Frontier, 1882–1897*, Albuquerque: University of New Mexico Press, 1939; and *My Nine Years as Governor of the Territory of New Mexico, 1897–1906*, Albuquerque: University of New Mexico Press, 1940; Ralph Emerson Twitchell, *Leading Facts of New Mexican History*, Cedar Rapids, Iowa: Torch Press, 1911–1917.

OTERO-WARREN, MARIA ADELINA EMELIA ("NINA") (1882–1965), educator, businesswoman. Nina Otero was born in 1882 at Los Lunas, New Mexico, the youngest of three children born to Eloisa (Luna) Otero and Manuel B. Otero. She attended private schools in New Mexico and the all-women's

Maryville College of the Sacred Heart in St. Louis, Missouri. In 1917 she accepted the New Mexico chair of a national suffragist organization called the Congressional Union and in the same year was appointed, and later elected, superintendent of schools in Santa Fe County, a position she held until 1929. During the 1930s she was one of five inspectors of the Indian Service, supervised adult education programs, and directed education in the Civilian Conservation Corps. In 1941 she was named to a position in Puerto Rico, directing an adult education program for the Works Progress Administration, and during World War II, having returned to mainland United States, she was Santa Fe director of the Office of Price Administration. During the postwar years she continued active in state Republican circles and served on a number of boards and commissions. In her later years she also operated Las Dos Realties and Insurance Agency in Santa Fe.

Nina Otero-Warren was perhaps the first Nuevo Mexicana to become professionally and politically prominent. In 1922 she was a nominee for the Republican candidacy for the U.S. House of Representatives. She was the author of *Old Spain in Our Southwest* (1936–1962), a recollection of her childhood in late nineteenth-century New Mexico and a valuable source for the social historian. In 1938 she was awarded an honorary doctorate in literature by Maryville College.

FURTHER READING: "Mrs. Otero-Warren Dies in Home Here," Santa Fe *New Mexican* (4 January 1965); Lynn Perrigo, *Hispanos: Historic Leaders in New Mexico*, Santa Fe: Sunstone Press, 1985.

P _____

PACHECO, ROMUALDO (1831–1899), governor, diplomat. Born at Santa Barbara on 31 October 1831, Romualdo Pacheco was a son of an aide to Mexican governor of California Manuel Victoria. His father having been killed in battle shortly after his birth, at age seven he was sent by his Scottish stepfather to Honolulu to be educated in an English missionary school. He returned to California and went to work on his stepfather's ships as a supercargo when he reached age fifteen. After the American takeover of California he left the sea to direct ranching operations on the large family estates. He early showed great interest in practical politics, and in the second half of the 1850s he was successively elected county judge and state senator. Having switched from the Democratic party to the Union party (and later the Republican party) at the outbreak of the Civil War, Pacheco was reelected to the senate and from 1863 to 1867 served as state treasurer. In 1871 he was elected lieutenant governor on the Republican ticket and advanced to governor in 1875 when the legislature sent Governor Newton Booth to the U.S. Senate. In the next election he failed to secure his party's nomination to either the governorship or the lieutenant governorship.

In the centennial year Pacheco was nominated and elected to the U.S. House of Representatives, and was reelected in 1879 and 1881. Not an aggressive congressman, he did serve on the committee on public expenditures and the committee on private land claims. During this time he was also a stock broker in San Francisco. In 1883 he was not a candidate for reelection and returned to his business interests in California, Mexico, and Texas. At the end of 1890 he was named minister plenipotentiary to Central America and served until Democrat Grover Cleveland took over the presidency in 1893. Pacheco returned to his San Francisco brokerage business and semiretirement; he died in Oakland, California, on 23 January 1899.

FURTHER READING: Peter T. Conmy, *Romualdo Pacheco, Distinguished Californian of the Mexican and American Periods*, San Francisco: Native Sons of the Golden West, 1957; Rockwell D. Hunt, *California Firsts*, San Francisco: Pearson Publishers,

1957; H. Brett Melendy and Benjamin Gilbert, *The Governors of California*, Georgetown, Calif.: The Talisman Press, 1965.

PALOMINO, CARLOS (1950–   ), boxer, actor. Born in the Mexican state of Sonora of a Mexican father and a Mexican American mother, Carlos Palomino came to the United States at age ten, after the family had waited two years in Tijuana to enter legally. The Palominos settled in Westminster, a suburb of Long Beach, California, where Carlos began his American education. After overcoming his language handicap, he did well in Orange County schools and at baseball. During his high school years he held two part-time jobs and on weekends played Mexican semi-pro ball. Upon completing high school, he was drafted during the Vietnam conflict into the U.S. Army where he quickly won a place on the Fort Hood, Texas, boxing team. He rose rapidly from Fourth Army Champion to All Army Champion and for his last two army years was All Services Runner-up at the World Military Games. He left the Army as World Military Champion, having won thirty-one of his thirty-four fights.

Returning to southern California, Carlos Palomino turned professional in 1972. After a string of thirty victories to a single loss, in June 1976 he won the World Welterweight title by defeating John Stracey of England. In the following two years he successfully defended his title against seven contenders. In mid–1979 he retired from fighting after he lost the world title in a decision bout and after it became evident there would be no rematch. He then embarked on a second career as a television color commentator, appeared in television commercials, and has played in films. Serious about his acting, he has taken lessons from several drama coaches. In addition to cohosting a Latino television variety show called "Bravísimo," he recently made two full-length movies as yet unreleased.

During the 1970s Palomino completed an undergraduate degree in recreational education at Long Beach State University, receiving his degree in December 1976. He also made numerous personal appearances before civic groups and high school students to encourage Chicano youths to complete their education. On the economic side, he wisely invested his ring earnings in real estate, principally apartment buildings, in the Los Angeles area. He is considered by many to be one of the great welterweight boxers of the twentieth century.

FURTHER READING: "Carlos Palomino Welterweight Champion of the World," *La Luz* 7:11 (November 1978); "The Champ," *Nuestro* 2:8 (August 1978); Pat Putnam, "Staying at the Top of His Class," *Sports Illustrated* 46:5 (31 January 1977); "Welterweight Now Into Acting," San Antonio *Express-News* (13 September 1981).

PALOMINO, ERNESTO RAMIREZ (1933–   ), sculptor, painter, filmmaker, teacher. Ernie Palomino was born 21 December 1933 to Jesús and Elvira (Ramírez) Palomino in Fresno, a city in the northern half of California's great central valley. He grew up there in extreme poverty and attended Fresno public schools, where he was able to exchange his early art materials, a shingle and rusty nail, for crayons and paper. At Edison High School he found a teacher who encouraged his artistic ambitions. Upon graduation from high school he served two years in the Marine Corps. Out of the service, he continued his artistic work and took courses at Fresno City College (1956) and Fresno State College (now California State University, Fresno) in the following year. Through the efforts of a patron he was given a one-term working scholarship to the San Francisco Art Institute early in 1956 and in that same year had a one-man show at the Legion of Honor Museum in San Francisco. In the following two years he had one-man shows at the Crocker Art Museum in Sacramento and at Fresno State College.

In 1960 Palomino enrolled in San Francisco State College and five years later received his B.A. degree. For his M.A. thesis project he made a forty-five-minute animated film, *My Trip in a '52 Ford* (1966), using some of his "found objects" sculptures. From 1968 to 1969 he worked in Denver for the Migrant Council and then in the next year accepted a position as assistant professor in the La Raza Studies Department, Fresno State College, where he still teaches. He has also devoted part of his time to painting murals.

Ernesto Palomino was the recipient of grants from the National Endowment for the Arts in 1973 and 1974 and from the California Arts Council in 1976. In addition to the one-man shows mentioned earlier he has had a number of one-man and group shows, mostly in California. In the vanguard of artists basing their work on the Chicano experience, he has collaborated with Luis Valdez* of the Teatro Campesino and has in recent years used Chicano themes more heavily.

FURTHER READING: Ernie Palomino, *in black and white: evolution of an artist*, Fresno, Calif.: Academy Library Guild, 1956; Jacinto Quirarte, *Mexican American Artists*, Austin: University of Texas Press, 1973; *Who's Who in the West, 1980–1981*, 17th ed., 1980.

PAREDES, AMERICO (1915–   ), folklorist, teacher, writer, poet. Américo Paredes, dean of Mexican American scholars, was born 3 September 1915 in the Texas border town of Brownsville. Here he attended grade school and high school, and completed his A.A. degree at Brownsville Junior College in 1936. During his junior college years he became a staff writer for the Brownsville *Herald*; at the same time he began contributing poems to the weekly literary supplement of *La Prensa* in San Antonio. In 1937 his first poetry collection, *Cantos de adolescencia*, was published. During the second half of the 1930s he also developed into a skilled guitarist, singer, and musical composer and performed professionally for several years.

In 1940 Paredes took a position with Pan American Airways from which he went into the U.S. Army four years later. The Army sent him to the Far East as a correspondent for *Stars and Stripes*, and after World War II he covered the Japanese war crimes trials. Finding Japanese culture very attractive, he took his discharge in Tokyo, remaining as public relations man and writer for the American Red Cross. In 1950 he returned to Texas to fulfill a longtime dream of becoming a professor of English. At the University of Texas in Austin he finished two years of college in one, receiving his B.A. degree in English and philosophy *summa cum laude* in 1951, and went on to complete his M.A. and Ph.D. by 1956. While accomplishing this he taught full time at the University and after a two-year stint at what is today the University of Texas at El Paso he returned to his alma mater as professor of folklore and creative writing.

In 1958 Paredes saw the publication of his doctoral dissertation under the title, *With His Pistol in His Hand: A Border Ballad and Its Hero*, his most widely acclaimed work. A prolific scholar, he is the author of two additional major folkloric works: *Folktales of Mexico* (1970) and *A Texas Mexican Cancionero* (1976). During the 1960s and 1970s in addition to teaching, training his numerous graduate students, and developing a folklore archives at the University of Texas, he has published some fifty articles in major journals and in the U.T. Offprint Series. Many of his studies have been seminal in areas such as machismo, folk medicine, the *corrido*, and border views of the Anglo. In recent years he has been concerned with the study of the folklorization of historic events. In the late 1960s he supported the Chicano student movement and with Professor George I. Sánchez* founded and was first director of the University of Texas Mexican American Studies program.

Professor Paredes in the past half-century has been the recipient of various first-prize awards and a 1962 Guggenheim fellowship, and was editor of the *Journal of American Folklore*. In 1975 he was cited by the Texas House of Representatives for his folkloric contributions.

FURTHER READING: "Américo Paredes: A Man from the Border," *Revista Chicano-Riqueña* 8:3 (Fall 1980); José Limón, "With a Corrido in His Heart," *Nuestro* 3:7 (Fall Special 1979); Julio A. Martínez, *Chicano Scholars and Writers: A Bio-Bibliographical Directory*, Metuchen, N.J.: The Scarecrow Press, 1979.

PATRON, JUAN B. (1855–1884), political leader. Born in the south-central New Mexico town of Lincoln less than a decade after the area was taken over by the United States, Juan Patrón was the son of a local merchant, Isidro Patrón. Because he was an intelligent and studious lad, he came to the attention of Bishop Jean B. Lamy of Santa Fe, who first supervised his education in New Mexico and then sent him to Notre Dame University in Indiana. Returning to New Mexico, Juan took over his father's small store in 1873, when the latter was among four Mexicans killed by a group of rampaging Texans, and also became the volunteer Lincoln schoolmaster. Due to his education and high repute he was made probate court clerk in 1875 although not yet twenty-one. During the following year in a special election he was chosen to fill a vacancy in the territorial legislature. In 1877 he was reelected to the legislature and was chosen speaker of the house despite his youth. By the later 1870s he was the leader of Nuevo Mexicanos in Lincoln County.

Both Patrón's community role and his elective position created conflict with the two powerful Anglo factions led by Thomas B. Catron and John S. Chisum.

In 1875 he was shot in the back while trying to arrest two Anglos for killing two young Mexicans, and in 1878 he was an important figure in the Chisum faction during the so-called Lincoln County War. Threatened by Catron followers and increasingly concerned for the safety of his family and himself, Patrón left Lincoln in the fall of 1878 to open a general store in Puerto de Luna, New Mexico, with an uncle of his wife's. Late one evening in April 1884 he was gunned down by a stranger as he left the local saloon. His assailant was tried, but the jury could not reach a verdict; it is unclear whether his murder was a result of the feuding connected with the Lincoln County War.

FURTHER READING: Maurice G. Fulton, *History of the Lincoln County War*, Tucson: University of Arizona Press, 1968.

PEÑA, AMADO M., JR. (1943–), painter, illustrator. Born in Laredo, Texas, on 1 October 1943, Amado Peña attended grade and high school as well as Laredo Junior College there. From grade school on he showed a serious interest in drawing and painting. In 1965 he received his B.A. in art and sociology at Texas Arts and Industries University in Kingsville and went on to complete his M.A. in art and education six years later. During his graduate work in the late 1960s he became involved in and then deeply committed to the Chicano Movement of that period. After teaching art for six years in a Laredo high school, he moved to Crystal City in 1971 to become more intimately involved with the movement under José Angel Guitiérrez's* leadership. From 1973 to 1979 he taught art at Anderson High School in Austin; since then he has devoted himself full time to painting.

Since the end of the 1960s Peña's works have appeared in some two dozen group exhibits across the United States, and he has also had more than a dozen one-man shows. He has been the recipient of a number of awards and prizes; his serigraphs and watercolors hang in various public and private collections, including those of two ex-presidents of Mexico.

FURTHER READING: *Who's Who in American Art*, 16th ed., 1984; "Work of Southwest Artist Sings to Soul, Heart," *Nuestro* 5:7 (October 1981).

PEÑA, FEDERICO (1947–), politician. Born in Laredo, Texas, on 15 March 1947, Federico Peña was the third son of Gustavo and Lucía (Farías) Peña. While he was still a small child, his father, a cotton broker, moved the family to Brownsville, Texas, where young Federico grew up and attended parochial school and St. Joseph's Academy. After graduating from St. Joseph's with honors he entered the University of Texas at Austin in 1964 and earned both his undergraduate and law degrees there. Descended from a Tejano family that had been in Texas public life for two centuries, he held various elective positions in school; during his college years he took an active part in state politics for liberal candidates and also marched against the Vietnam conflict. After receiving his law degree in 1971, he worked for a year in an El Paso legal aid office.

In 1972 Peña moved to Denver, Colorado, where he worked as a staff lawyer for the Mexican American Legal Defense and Educational Fund (MALDEF) for two years. He then took a job as legal advisor to the Chicano Education Project, which had bilingual education as its main goal. In 1978 with one of his brothers he formed the law firm of Peña and Peña and also decided the time was right to run for public office. He won election to the state legislature without much difficulty. Two years later he was easily reelected and then persuaded his fellow Democrats to choose him House Minority Speaker. By 1981, with only three years of legislative experience, he was considered one of the top legislators in Colorado.

A year later, in December Peña decided to run for mayor of Denver. Supported in his campaign by Governor Toney Anaya* of New Mexico and Mayor Henry Cisneros* of San Antonio, but running a nonethnic campaign, in June Peña won with 51 percent of the vote against a machine that had been in power for over fourteen years. At thirty-six Peña became the first Latino mayor of a U.S. city that is not heavily Latino. Early in 1987, after a very successful four years in office, Peña widely perceived as a potential national leader, decided to run for a second term.

FURTHER READING: "Hispanic Power Arrives at the Ballot Box," *Business Week* 2797 (4 July 1983); Chip Martínez, "Federico Peña, Denver's First Hispanic Mayor," *Nuestro* 7:6 (August 1983); *Who's Who in American Politics*, 7th ed., 1979.

PERALES, ALONSO S. (1899–1960), lawyer, civil rights activist. Alonso Perales was born at the end of the nineteenth century in the small town of Alice, county seat of Jim Wells County and forty miles west of Corpus Christi, Texas. Son of Nicolás and Susana (Sandoval) Perales, he faced poverty and economic struggle from his earliest years. After high school he served in the U.S. armed forces during World War I and apparently at the same time (c. 1917) began to discuss with other Tejanos the idea of founding an organization to promote the welfare and champion the civil right of Mexican Americans. Out of these discussions came the Order of Sons of America in 1921, the League of Latin American Citizens in 1927, and finally in 1929 the melding of these groups into the League of United Latin American Citizens (LULAC). Perales appears to have played a leading role in the development of the latter two organizations, being the founder of the first. He had, meanwhile, realized a youthful dream, earning his degree in the study of law and had begun to practice.

In the late 1920s and throughout the 1930s Alonso Perales was called on to serve the United States in the field of diplomacy. In all he served on thirteen missions to Mexico, the West Indies, Central America, and South America. At the beginning of the 1930s his first book, *El Mexicano Americano y la política del sur de Texas* (1931) came out; it briefly described thirty-five years of Tejano-Anglo relations. As a result of it he became an advisor to President Franklin D. Roosevelt on Mexican American concerns. His two-volume work describing the Mexican American struggle for civil rights, *En defensa de mi raza*, was published in 1936 and 1937. Four years later he was the chief force behind the introduction of Racial Equality Bill no. 909 in the Texas legislature; it was defeated. During this time Perales also was writing a column titled "Arquitectos de Nuestros Proprios Destinos" in the newspaper *La Verdad* of San Antonio, where he resided. At the end of World War II his other important work, *Are We Good Neighbors?*, came out (1948); it was a collection of testimony that we were not.

In 1952 Alonso Perales reached the culmination of his career. In March he was awarded by the government of Spain the rank of commander in The Spanish Order of Civil Merit for his long struggle for social equality and civil rights of Spanish-speaking peoples. He died on 9 May 1960 and was buried in San Antonio; six months later he was reinterred in Alice as was his wish.

FURTHER READING: Adela Sloss-Vento, *Alonso S. Perales: His Struggle for the Rights of Mexican-Americans*, San Antonio: Artes Gráficas, 1977.

PEREA, FRANCISCO (1830–1913), politician, businessman. Born in the small Nuevo México town of Los Padillas near Albuquerque to Juan and Josefa (Chávez) Perea, Francisco was descended from two important families. Having completed his early education in Los Padillas and in Santa Fe, he was sent to study with the Jesuits at St. Louis University from 1843 to 1845. After the American takeover in New Mexico he studied at the Bank Street Academy in New York City between 1847 and 1849. In the following year he returned to New Mexico to engage in the Santa Fe trade and in stock raising. He sent at least two large flocks of sheep to California to sell to the meat-hungry miners. His family and commercial prominence both helped him in 1858 to be elected to the territorial upper house, the Council. After the Civil War he was twice reelected to the Council.

An active supporter of the North during the Civil War, Perea recruited volunteers for Perea's Battalion, of which he was named lieutenant colonel. He fought against the Navajos and took part in the decisive defeat of the Confederate invaders of New Mexico at Glorieta Pass in 1862. Later in that year he was elected New Mexican delegate to the U.S. Congress, but was defeated in his bid for reelection two years later. As a result he returned to New Mexico, where he devoted himself to his various business activities. At the beginning of the 1880s he moved north from Bernalillo County to the town of Jemez Springs, where he became owner of the springs and operated a resort hotel. After serving as postmaster of Jemez Springs from 1894 to 1905, he moved to Albuquerque where he remained until his death seven years later.

FURTHER READING: Maurice G. Fulton, *New Mexico's Own Chronicle*, Dallas: B. Upshaw & Co., 1937; Ralph Emerson Twitchell, *The Leading Facts of New Mexican History*, Cedar Rapids, Iowa: The Torch Press, 1911–1917; Maurilio E. Vigil, *Los Patrones: Profiles of Hispanic Political Leaders in New Mexico History*, Washington, D.C.: University Press of America, 1980.

PEREA, PEDRO (1852–1906), politician, businessman. Pedro Perea was born 22 April 1852 in the central New Mexican town of Bernalillo in Sandoval County. After his early education there he was sent to St. Michael's College in Santa Fe and to Georgetown University in Washington, D.C., and in 1871 graduated from St. Louis University. Like many sons of prominent Nuevo Mexicano families of the era, he returned to New Mexico to engage in stock raising and business. From 1890 to 1894 he was president of the First National Bank of Santa Fe. Between 1889 and 1897 he served three terms on the Council, New Mexico's territorial upper house. In 1898 he was elected New Mexican delegate to the U.S. Congress, but did not stand for renomination two years later. He returned to his New Mexican banking and other business interests. Shortly before his death in January 1906 he was appointed territorial Insurance Commissioner. He died and was buried at Bernalillo.

FURTHER READING: *Biographical Directory of the American Congress, 1774–1971*, Washington, D.C.: U.S. Government Printing Office, 1971.

PICO, ANDRES (1810–1876), politician, soldier, governor. Andrés Pico, brother of Pío Pico,* was born in San Diego in the first year of the Mexican revolution for independence, one of three sons in a prominent early Californio family. By 1836 he was customs receiver at San Diego and active in California politics, being particularly concerned about the sectional struggle between northern and southern California. He was then and later in favor of dividing California into two sections and took a direct part in the sometimes military strife between the factions.

Andrés Pico's military career began with his appointment as a lieutenant in the San Diego militia in the late 1830s. During the mid–1840s he rose to captain and was given a commission to inventory the recently secularized missions. When the American forces invaded California in 1846, he rose from captain to commandant after military commander José Castro withdrew to Baja California. His notable military achievement was his victory at San Pascual; at Cahuenga a month later in January 1847 he surrendered to John Charles Fremont.

During the American period Pico remained a very influential Californio leader in the south; after operating a gold-mining enterprise in 1848–1849, he served in the assembly in 1851 and at the beginning of the 1860s was elected state senator. Having earlier been appointed a brigadier general in the state militia, he was offered command of a battalion of Californio cavalry at the beginning of the Civil War, but he declined because of poor health. In 1864 he actively worked in southern California for Lincoln's reelection on the Union ticket. In the post–Civil War period he was an ardent railroad booster and also promoted a plan to build a road between Los Angeles and the nearby settlements in the San Fernando Valley.

The last twenty years of Pico's life were filled with his land concerns. He owned two large ranches, to which he received U.S. patents in 1872 and 1875; he lived in the former San Fernando mission where he cared for acres of olives, grapes, and fruit trees. He is said to have distilled local petroleum into lamp oil. He died in February of the centennial year.

FURTHER READING: Pío Pico, *Don Pío Pico's Historical Narrative*, Glendale, Calif.: Arthur H. Clark Co., 1973; Leonard Pitt, *The Decline of the Californios*, Berkeley: University of California Press, 1966.

PICO, PIO DE JESUS (1801–1894), governor, political leader, landowner. Born at Mission San Gabriel (Los Angeles) on 5 May 1801, Pío Pico grew up there and in San Diego, where he seems to have received a limited formal education. Belonging to an important early Californio family and related by marriage to the equally influential Carrillo family, he was active both in business and local politics by his mid-twenties. Before he reached his thirtieth birthday he obtained his first land grant and continued to add to his holdings even after the American takeover. He eventually became one of the largest landowners in California but then lost all in his old age. From the mid–1820s on he occupied various positions in local and provincial government and in early 1832, with the overthrow of the new governor from Mexico City, he was briefly acting governor because of his position as head of the provincial legislature. When the missions were secularized during the 1830s, he was appointed administrator of ex-mission San Luis Rey by the governor but continued to be the center of opposition in the south to Mexican centralist government and to northern California domination.

Following the ouster of Mexican governor Manuel Micheltorena in 1845 Pío Pico again assumed the governorship with headquarters in Los Angeles, but compromised with northern leaders by appointing José Castro as military commander with headquarters at Monterey. During this period his governorship was confirmed by the Mexican government in April 1846, and he issued numerous land grants and sold mission lands and property, as he had a legal right to do. As governor when the Americans invaded, Pico organized resistance, but as the military situation became hopeless, he announced that fact and fled south into Baja California and then to Sonora.

After the Treaty of Guadalupe Hidalgo in 1848 Pío Pico returned to California and settled down to the routine of a southern rancher. Unlike his brother Andrés,* Pío Pico took no part in statewide politics in the American period, but was elected to the Los Angeles City Council in 1853 and was also county tax assessor. He participated indirectly in the suppression of banditry in the mid–1850s. When the Civil War broke out, at the request of the Union Army Pío Pico clearly defined his loyalty by firmly asserting his support of Abraham Lincoln. During the post–Civil War era the ex-governor, in his early seventies, built and operated Pico House, the largest hotel in Los Angeles. During the 1870s and 1880s he lost much of his extensive landholdings, mostly as the result of borrowing against them and being unable to repay.

In the decade of the 1880s Pío Pico dictated his reminiscences to the southern California historian Henry D. Barrows. He also gave testimony to one of historian Hubert Howe Bancroft's aides, Thomas Savage. At the beginning of the 1890s Pío Pico lost his last remaining piece of land in the case *Pico v. Cohn* and went to live with his godchild and friend of more than sixty years, John J. Warner. On 11 September 1894 at the advanced age of ninety-three, Pío Pico died, penniless.

FURTHER READING: Henry D. Barrows, "Pío Pico," *Annual Publication of the Historical Society of Southern California*, Los Angeles, 1894; Pío Pico, *Don Pío Pico's Historical Narrative*, Glendale, Calif.: Arthur H. Clark Co., 1973.

PLUNKETT, JAMES (1947–   ), football player. Of Mexican and German-Irish ancestry, Jim Plunkett was born in San Jose, California, on 5 December 1947, the only son and youngest child of blind parents. While still in grade school, he began helping the family's extremely limited finances by selling newspapers; later he worked in a gas station. As a fifth grader he discovered a natural talent for sports and by his junior high years excelled in baseball, basketball, wrestling, and track. In high school his football ability resulted in championship teams; in his senior year the team was named All-League Team, and Jim was selected to play on the North Shrine All-Star team in 1965.

With numerous football scholarships to choose from, Jim Plunkett decided to attend nearby Stanford University. At Stanford he majored in political science, maintained a B average, and set new records on the football field. He was named All-Pacific Coast in his sophomore year and All-American as a junior. In his senior year he led the Stanford team to victory in the Rose Bowl, and won for himself the Heisman Memorial Trophy, an annual award to the best college football player in the United States. During his university years and after, Plunkett spent much of his spare time giving career and life counseling to young Chicanos.

Upon completing his Stanford studies in 1971, Plunkett was drafted by the New England Patriots club. Although he threw nineteen touchdown passes his first year and was named "Rookie of the Year" by United Press International, in succeeding years he gradually became frustrated by coaching staff problems and repeated injuries requiring surgery. After a disastrous 3–11 season in 1975 he was traded to the San Francisco 49ers at his request. Although pleased to be close to his widowed mother, Plunkett found his job situation even worse than in Boston and came close to quitting football. In 1978 he joined the Oakland (now Los Angeles) Raiders as a free agent. After two years spent largely on the bench, in 1980 he came back and led the Raiders to the 1981 Super Bowl and to victory there. He was named NFL Comeback Player of the Year in 1980 and Most Valuable Player in the 1981 Super Bowl. After that successful season he again suffered an injury and lost his starting position. In 1984 he again quarterbacked the Raiders to a Super Bowl win. As the 1986 football season began, he was again in the Raider lineup, but injuries kept him on the sidelines during most games.

FURTHER READING: José Andrés Chacón, "Jim Plunkett, $200,000 Quarterback," *La Luz* 1:5 (September 1972); *Current Biography*, February 1982; Frank del Olmo, "The Born Again Quarterback," *Nuestro* 5:2 (March 1981); Jim Plunkett and Dace Newhouse,

The Jim Plunkett Story, New York: Dell Publishing Co., 1982; Paul Zimmerman, "A Runaway for the Raiders," *Sports Illustrated* 60:4 (30 January 1984).

PONCE DE LEON, MICHAEL (1922–   ), teacher, artist. Born in Miami, Florida, on 4 July 1922, Michael Ponce de León received his early education in Mexico City, where he grew up. Along with an early interest in architecture, which he studied at the national university, he also began to draw. While he served in the U.S. Air Force during World War II from 1943 to 1946, he began to publish cartoons in such magazines as *The New Yorker*, *Collier's*, and *The Saturday Evening Post*. Between 1948 and 1954 his cartoon series *Impulses* was syndicated in the United States and Europe. Meanwhile he studied art at various schools in the United States, Mexico, and Europe.

Between 1959 and 1966 Ponce de León taught printmaking at Hunter College in New York City and later at New York University, Pratt Institute, and at several schools of art in California. In 1972 he accepted a position at Columbia University, and from 1976 to 1977 he taught at New York University. His prints have gone through many editions from 1960 to the present, and beginning in 1970 his collages, collage intaglios, and lithograph intaglios were exhibited in London, Paris, and Venice as well as in all the leading U.S. museums. Under U.S. State Department cultural exchange auspices he was sent to Yugoslavia, India, Pakistan, Spain, and Venezuela between 1965 and 1982. In 1964 he was commissioned by the Post Office Department to design a U.S. stamp honoring the fine arts. He has been the recipient of more than sixty-five prestigious medals, awards, and grants; his works are represented in permanent collections all over the world. In addition, he has found time to write contributions to more than a dozen books on his area of specialization, printmaking.

FURTHER READING: Diane Cochrane, "Michael Ponce de León," *American Artist* 38 (August and October 1974); Jacinto Quirarte, *Mexican American Artists*, Austin: University of Texas Press, 1973; *Who's Who in American Art*, 16th ed., 1984.

PORTILLO TRAMBLEY, ESTELA (1936–   ), writer, dramatist. Estela Portillo was born 16 January 1936 in El Paso, Texas; she was raised by grandparents until she was twelve, at which time she returned to live with her parents. After grade and high school in El Paso she entered Texas Western College (now University of Texas at El Paso) from which she graduated with an A.B. in English in 1956. Between 1956 and 1978 she completed the requirements for her M.A., which she received in the latter year. Meanwhile she taught English in high school, was a drama instructor at El Paso Community College, ran a radio talk show over station KIZZ, and wrote and directed a cultural program on television station KROD. Her television experience rekindled her interest in serious writing and her resolve to make that her career. Largely in pursuit of that goal she switched from classroom teaching to a special services position in the El Paso public school system.

In 1971 Estela Portillo had her first play, *Day of the Swallows*, published, and in the following year she received the Quinto Sol Award for literature. The award opened doors; she was appointed editor of the September 1973 issue of *El Grito*, devoted solely to Chicana writers. Her *Impressions of a Chicana*, a collection of poems, was published in 1974, and in the following year her important short story collection, *Rain of Scorpions*, came out. Her play, *Sun Image*, saw publication in 1979, and two years later she was given a Writer Recognition Award by the Texas Commission of Arts. In September 1983 Western Public Radio Workshop produced her radio drama *The Burning*. In the following January her play *Puente Negro*, which had been published in *Sor Juana and Other Plays* (1983), won the Women's Plays competition at St. Edward's University, Austin. A year later her play *Blacklight* won second place in the New York Shakespeare Festival's Hispanic American playwrights' competition. Her most recent work is *Trini*, a novel.

In her writings Portillo shows great concern for the complete liberation and full equality of women, but she avoids any strictly social message, believing such an approach is limiting in literature. Nevertheless, she is seen by some as a feminist writer.

FURTHER READING: Juan Bruce-Novoa, *Chicano Authors: Inquiry by Interview*, Austin: University of Texas Press, 1980; Julio A. Martínez and Francisco A. Lomelí, *Chicano Literature: A Reference Guide*, Westport, Conn.: Greenwood Press, 1985; Charles M. Tatum, *Chicano Literature*, Boston: Twayne Publishers, 1982.

Q

QUINN, ANTHONY (RUDOLPH OAXACA) (1916–), actor, painter, writer, musician, sculptor. Anthony Quinn was born 21 April 1916 in the middle of the Mexican Revolution in Chihuahua of a Mexican mother and an Irish-Mexican revolutionary father. Before his first birthday he was taken across the border into El Paso by his mother. In 1920 the Quinn family moved to Los Angeles, where his father, Francisco, worked in a movie studio. When his father was killed in an accident five years later, Anthony began working at odd jobs to help support the family, while continuing his education in East Los Angeles public schools. He later dropped out of high school during the depression days of the 1930s but continued his self-education.

When he was fourteen, his mother's remarriage relieved Quinn of further family financial responsibility just as the Great Depression arrived. During those difficult years he worked at a wide variety of jobs including custodian, boxer, electrician's helper, ditch digger, and migrant farm laborer. Acting had long interested Quinn, and for a while he worked in the WPA's Federal Theater Project. After an operation to correct a speech defect he also acted in local theater groups and was picked by Mae West to play the lead in a 1936 Los Angeles stage production of *Clean Beds*.

That same year Quinn had a bit part in a movie and then won a role as an Indian in Cecil B. DeMille's *The Plainsman*. His considerable success as an actor led to a decade of Hollywood acting jobs as an Indian, swarthy villain, and Latin lover. He accepted all of these—usually supporting—roles and gave them the best that he was capable of. He also continued to improve his acting by working with local theater groups and in summer stock. In 1947 he became a U.S. citizen and made his Broadway debut, which was a disaster, but then he starred as Stanley Kowalski in *A Streetcar Named Desire* for two years.

During the 1950s Anthony Quinn divided his time between Hollywood and Italy, making *Viva Zapata!*, *The River's Edge*, *La Strada*, *Lust for Life*, and *Attila the Hun*. Following these films in the 1960s he did some of his most highly praised acting in *The Guns of Navarone*, *Lawrence of Arabia*, *Shoes of the Fisherman*, *Requiem for a Heavyweight*, and *Zorba the Greek*. Twice Quinn has won an Oscar for his work, first for his role in *Viva Zapata!* in 1952, and again in 1956 for his portrayal of Paul Gaugin in *Lust for Life*. In the 1970s Quinn's most notable film was perhaps *The Children of Sánchez*; his acting in other 1970s films seemed to many critics merely a reprise of *Zorba*.

By 1980 Anthony Quinn had appeared in over 200 films. Between 1983 and 1986 he toured the United States in a musical version of *Zorba*. In addition to his American success on the stage and worldwide acclaim in films, he has found time to paint, write, sculpt, and produce films. Since 1982 he has had three very successful one-man exhibitions of his paintings and sculpture. He has a personal library of over 5,000 volumes and owns a valuable collection of canvases by modern painters. A figure of herculean proportions, both artistically and physically, Anthony Quinn has always been very conscious of his Mexican cultural heritage.

FURTHER READING: *Current Biography*, December 1957; Julio A. Martínez and Francisco A. Lomelí, eds., *Chicano Literature, A Reference Guide*, Westport, Conn.: Greenwood Press, 1985; Anthony Quinn, *The Original Sin: A Self-Portrait*, Boston: Little, Brown & Co., 1972; Luis Reyes, "East L.A.'s Very Own Anthony Quinn," *Caminos* 4:7 (July–August 1983).

QUIRARTE, JACINTO (1931–   ), historian, educator. Born in the small central Arizona mining town of Jerome on 17 August 1931, Jacinto Quirarte grew up and received his early education there. After service in the U.S. Air Force he entered San Francisco State College (now University), graduating with a B.A. in 1954 and receiving his M.A. there four years later. He then accepted a position teaching art and art history at the Colegio Americano in Mexico City; from 1962 to 1964 he taught art history and was dean of men at the University of the Américas (Mexico). Meanwhile he was also an assistant to the leading Mexican archeologist, Alberto Ruz Lhuillier, and completed his doctorate in 1964 at the Universidad Nacional Autónoma de México.

After a two-year stint at the Centro Venezolano Americano in Caracas Quirarte returned in 1966 to the United States where he accepted a position as art historian at the University of Texas, Austin, after a year at Yale. In 1972 he transferred to the University of Texas, San Antonio as dean of the arts college and director of the Research Center for the Arts. At San Antonio he organized the new departments of art and music and developed a graduate art program.

Jacinto Quirarte is a leading authority on Mexican American art and on pre-Columbian art. Author of several works in these two fields, he is best known for his survey *Mexican American Artists* (1973).

FURTHER READING: Judith Hancock de Sandoval, "The Workaholic," *Nuestro* 2:10 (October 1978); *Who's Who in American Art*, 16th ed., 1984.

R

RAMIREZ, BLANDINA CARDENAS (1944–   ), public administrator. Born in the Texas bordertown of Del Rio on 25 October 1944, Blandina Cárdenas grew up and received her early education there. From 1961 to 1962 she attended Texas Women's University at Denton and later entered the University of Texas at Austin, graduating with an A.B. in journalism in 1967. After starting graduate studies at St. Mary's University in San Antonio, she then completed her doctorate in education at the University of Massachusetts in 1974.

During the second half of the 1970s Blandina held a wide variety of political appointments. From 1974 to 1975 she was a Rockefeller fellow on Senator Walter Mondale's staff, and for the next two years was director of the Center for Management of Innovation in Multicultural Education. During the same three years she was also a member of the Texas Advisory Committee to the U.S. Commission on Civil Rights. From 1977 to 1979 she held several high positions in the Department of Health, Education and Welfare, administering six large programs including Head Start. She also served on the board of directors of the Mexican American Legal Defense and Education Fund (MALDEF).

In 1980 Blandina Ramírez was appointed by President Jimmy Carter to a three-year term on the federal Civil Rights Commission. In October 1983, in an unprecedented move, President Ronald Reagan fired her and two other commissioners, apparently because of their vocal opposition to his bland civil rights policies, and made three replacement appointments. The courts failed to uphold the president, and Congress passed a bill to reauthorize the commission on a somewhat different basis. Then in December Congress appointed two members for three-year terms on the new commission. One of them was Dr. Blandina Cárdenas Ramírez.

FURTHER READING: "MALDEF Fights for Rights Commission," *MALDEF* 12:2 (Fall/Winter 1983).

RAMIREZ, FRANCISCO P. (1830s–1890?), journalist. Born in Mexican California, Francisco Ramírez grew up in the ferment of the United States takeover and the excitement of the gold rush period. His early journalistic apprenticeship was as a printer's devil and compositor for *La Estrella*, the Spanish-language page of the Los Angeles *Star*. Irritated by the *Star*'s anti-Mexican bias, he quit his job and in mid–1855 began to publish, edit, and print a one-sheet weekly, *El Clamor Público*, the first Spanish-language newspaper in Los Angeles. Dedicating his paper to law and order and to moral and material progress, he championed the civil rights of Mexicans and blacks. Clearly supported with Republican funds, he lectured his fellow Californios on their political rights and duties as Americans and the need to avoid voting a straight Democratic ticket.

From 1855 to 1859 Ramírez articulated in Spanish, English, and French the views of most Californios and defended them against the racism of the day. In 1859 he ran for assemblyman in Los Angeles and was decisively defeated. Apparently unable to get further support for his paper, on 31 December 1859 he published his last issue. He then crossed into Sonora, Mexico, where he got a job as state printer from 1860 to 1862. In 1864 he was back in the United States, being named postmaster of Los Angeles in October; the following year he was appointed an official state translator. During 1872 he was briefly editor of a new Los Angeles Spanish-language weekly, *La Crónica*, and a few years later appeared as counsel for a Mrs. Eulalia Pérez Guillén, who claimed to be 130 years old and wanted to retain the legal right to exhibit herself as a California curiosity at the Philadelphia Centennial Exposition. He then fades from history.

FURTHER READING: Harris Newmark, *Sixty Years in Southern California, 1853–1913* . . . , Boston: Houghton Mifflin Co., 1930; Leonard Pitt, *The Decline of the Californios*, Berkeley: University of California Press, 1970.

RAMIREZ, HENRY (1929–   ), educator, administrator, politician. Henry Ramírez was born 4 May 1929, one of eleven children in an immigrant Mexican family. Growing up in the Pomona (California) barrio, he became a migrant agricultural worker when the family went migrant after his father lost his railroad job because of an injury. Despite some juvenile years as a "pachuco" urban gang member, in 1952 he received his A.B. from St. John's College in Camarillo, California, and then began to study for the priesthood. After several years of study he left the seminary and taught foreign languages in the Whittier, California, school district where he also developed a "New Horizons" program to keep barrio students from dropping out of school. He later completed an M.A. at Loyola University in Los Angeles.

In 1968 Henry Ramírez went to Washington, D.C., to assume the post as director of the Mexican American Studies Division for the U.S. Commission on Civil Rights. Three years later, before the 1972 elections, he was chosen to fill the vacant position of chairman of the cabinet Council on Opportunities for Spanish-Speaking People. In Washington, Ramírez worked to secure appointment of other qualified Mexican Americans to positions of influence and power in the federal government and spoke out in the community for greater involvement of Hispanics in society and politics. In 1975 the council's mandate from Congress expired, and he returned to private life. He is currently a business consultant in Washington, D.C.

FURTHER READING: Al Martínez, *Rising Voices: Profiles for Hispano-American Lives*, New York: New American Library, 1974; Theodore Wood, *Chicanos y chicanas prominentes*, Menlo Park, Calif.: Educational Consortium of America, 1974.

RAMIREZ, JOEL TITO (1923–   ), painter, illustrator. Joel Ramírez was born 3 June 1923 in Albuquerque, New Mexico, and grew up there. After high school he served in the Air Transport Command of the U.S. Air Force in the China-Burma-India theater from 1942 to 1946. Although largely self-taught as a painter, he did undertake study at the University of New Mexico in 1949 and again in 1960. He also has had some private tutoring. The owner of Ramírez Art and Signs in Albuquerque, he also teaches oil painting.

In 1947 Ramírez had his first showing, "War with Japan," which came out of his wartime experience. Since then he has had exhibits in New York, Washington, D.C., South America, China, India, and his native New Mexico. His paintings, most of which are New Mexican village landscapes, are held in a number of private collections throughout the United States. He has won several awards in New Mexico showings.

FURTHER READING: Jacinto Quirarte, *Mexican American Artists*, Austin: University of Texas Press, 1973; *Who's Who in American Art*, 16th ed., 1984.

RAMIREZ, RICARDO, C.S.B. (1936–   ), bishop. Ricardo was the second of two sons born to Natividad and María (Espinosa) Ramírez on 12 September 1936 in Bay City, Texas. He grew up there, attending the local public elementary school and in 1955 graduated from Bay City High School. He then entered the University of St. Thomas in nearby Houston, where he completed his B.A. four years later. Having decided on a vocation to the priesthood, he entered St. Basil's Seminary in Toronto, Canada, in 1963 and two years later studied at the Seminario Conciliar in Mexico City. He received ordination in December 1966 and the next year began an M.A. program at the University of Detroit, receiving his degree in 1968. For the next five years he worked in Mexico, first as chaplain of university students and then with the Catequesis Familiar (Family Catechesis) program. In 1973–1974 he took further studies at the East Asian Pastoral Institute in Manila. He returned to Mexico briefly and was sent in 1976 to San Antonio, Texas, as executive vice-president of the important Mexican American Cultural Center founded by Bishop Patricio Flores.* Here he taught cultural anthropology courses and also taught at Our Lady of the Lake University in San Antonio during the same time.

After five years at the Center, during which he wrote *Fiesta, Worship and Family* (1981), Ricardo Ramírez was named auxiliary bishop of San Antonio and in December 1981 was consecrated by Archbishop Patricio Flores of San Antonio. Less than a year later he was named the first Ordinary Bishop of the newly created Diocese of Las Cruces, New Mexico. With a deep interest and expertise in the Mexican American family, he has been advisor to the U.S. Bishops Committee on Hispanic Affairs and the U.S. Bishops Committee on Liturgy since 1981. He is a board member of the National Catholic Council for Interracial Justice and the National Institute for Hispanic Liturgy. He is an active member of the Committee of Religious for Hispanic Ministry and serves as administrative secretary and coordinator of Hispanic American Input for the Comisión de Estudios de Historia de la Iglesia en Latinoamérica (CEHILA). Long active in civic and cultural affairs, he is a member of various other committees and boards and has been an invited speaker at various universities in the Southwest.

FURTHER READING: *American Catholic Who's Who, 1980–1981*, vol. 23, 1979; Mark Day, "Bishop: 'Why have we had to wait so long for Hispanic leaders?' " *National Catholic Reporter* 19 (24 December 1982); *Who's Who in America, 1984–1985*, 43rd ed., 1984.

RAMIREZ, SARA ESTELA (1881–1910), poet, feminist, teacher, revolutionary, political organizer. Sara Ramírez was born in the small Mexican village of Progreso, Coahuila, in 1881. Her mother died when she was quite young, and she kept house for her father and a younger sister. Her early education took place in Monterrey, across the state border in Nuevo León, and she later studied at the Ateneo Fuentes, a Saltillo teachers' institution. Upon graduation at age seventeen, she crossed the border in 1898 to teach Spanish to Tejano children at the Semanario of Laredo. Within months of her arrival in Laredo she began publishing poems and poetic essays she had written. Much of her poetry was romantic, but some was also political in content as she became active in liberal Mexican politics. During her dozen years in Texas her works appeared in the Laredo newspapers *El Demócrata Fronterizo* and *La Crónica*. In 1901 she founded a literary journal, *La Corregidora*, and later *Aurora* in which her writings were published.

Part of a network of organizers who acted as links between Texas Mexicans and those south of the Rio Grande, Sara Ramírez strongly supported in her writings the Partido Liberal Mexicano and the ideas of its leader, Ricardo Flores Magón. She was an official representative of Flores Magón and worked closely with other feminist revolutionary organizers in Texas. She also urged workers to organize in mutualist societies and women to take active roles, and demanded that feminist issues be included in the revolutionary struggle. Although she split ideologically with Ricardo Flores Magón in the last few years of her life, she continued to declare herself his friend and urged Mexicans to forget petty personal differences and work together.

Plagued by years of illness, she died on 21 August 1910 at age twenty-nine and was eulogized at the time as *"la mujer mexicana más ilustrada de Texas."* She was a principal precursor of Chicana feminism, an early activist in union organizing, a staunch defender of La Raza, and an outstanding poet.

FURTHER READING: Inés Hernández Tovar, "Sara Estela Ramírez: The Early Twentieth Century Texas-Mexican Poet," Ph.D. diss., University of Houston, 1984; Emilio Zamora, "Sara Estrela Ramírez: Una Rosa Roja en el Movimiento," in *Mexican Women in the United States: Struggles Past and Present*, ed. Magdalena Mora and Adelaida R. Del Castillo, Los Angeles: University of California, Chicano Studies Research Center, 1980.

RAMIREZ, TEODORO (1791–1871), businessman. Teodoro Ramírez was born 1 November 1791 in the village of San Ignacio, Sonora, of an old Arizona-Sonora family, his grandfather having served at the Tubac presidio. Because of his godfather, a Franciscan priest who had come to the area in the 1770s, Teodoro received a superior education for the time. At age twenty-one he was in Tucson assisting the priest in keeping church records and managing properties allowed the Franciscan by papal dispensation. When the old priest died in 1820, Teodoro was designated as his heir. His marriage in the following year to a young woman of an elite family added to his economic position, and he soon opened a general store in Tucson, serving both civilian and military needs. Because of his wealth and position he was able to supply the military with provisions for its campaigns against the Apaches in the 1830s and early 1840s and to wait for his money.

With the American takeover in the late 1840s and the California gold rush in the first half of the 1850s Teodoro, as Tucson's leading businessman, continued to prosper. He also acted on various occasions as intermediary between the white settlers and local Indian groups like the Pimas and Papagos. In the mid–1850s he moved his family to Santa Cruz (Sonora), where he was elected justice of the peace. He seems also to have maintained his home in Tucson, where in the summer of 1856 he signed a petition for territorial status for Arizona. Having reached sixty-five, he resigned from his Santa Cruz position in January 1857 and died fourteen years later. His obituary in the *Tucson Citizen* on 8 July 1871 described him as a "man of scholarly accomplishments" who had lived in Tucson most of his life.

FURTHER READING: James Officer and Henry Dobyns, "Teodoro Ramírez, Early Citizen of Tucson," *Journal of Arizona History* 25:3 (Autumn 1984).

RECHY, JOHN FRANCISCO (1934–   ), novelist, essayist, playwright. Born in El Paso of Mexican-Scottish descent, John Rechy grew up in poverty and received his early education in El Paso. As a child he wanted very much to write and to act and was briefly a professional child actor. Encouraged by some of his teachers, he wrote his first novel before graduating from high school. After completing his secondary education, he attended Texas Western College (today University of Texas at El Paso) on a scholarship and received his B.A. in English literature in 1956. When his undergraduate college studies were completed, he served in the U.S. armed forces in Germany, where he continued to write. After his army experience he traveled extensively in American cities with large gay populations.

One of John Rechy's first published works was an essay titled "El Paso del Norte" in *Evergreen Review* (1958), a sketch of some aspects of Chicano life that he later stressed in his novels. In 1963 he published his first novel, *City of Night*, which became a huge best-seller and immediately established him as an outstanding American novelist. It is still considered his best work by many. Since then he has published six more novels: *Numbers* (1967), *This Day's Death* (1969), *Vampires* (1971), *The Fourth Angel* (1972), *The Sexual Outlaw* (1977), and *Rushes* (1979). All seven of his novels center on homosexual life in America's large cities and are, by the author's statement, to some extent autobiographical. They also often reflect his Chicano background.

John Rechy's numerous essays and articles have been published in the *Evergreen Review*, *London Magazine*, *The Nation*, and other journals. He is also author of two plays, one based on *Rushes* and the other on *City of Night*, and a contributor to a number of anthologies. In 1961 he was awarded the Longview Foundation Fiction Prize for a short story which later became a chapter in *City of Night*. He has done translations from Spanish for *Evergreen Review* and *The Texas Quarterly*. During the early 1980s he conducted writers' seminars at Occidental College, University of California at Los Angeles, University of Southern California, and Columbia University.

FURTHER READING: Roger Austen, "An Interview with John Rechy," *San Francisco Review of Books* 3:3–4 (Summer 1977); *Contemporary Authors*, New Revision Series, vol. 6, Detroit: Gale Research Co., 1982; Julio A. Martínez and Francisco A. Lomelí, eds., *Chicano Literature: A Reference Guide*, Westport, Conn.: Greenwood Press, 1985; Charles M. Tatum, *Chicano Literature*, Boston: Twayne Publishers, 1982.

REDONDO, JOSE MARIA (1830–1878), businessman, politician. José Redondo was born in the north Mexican town of Altar, Sonora, where his family owned several large land grants. Immediately following the Gadsden Purchase he tried to establish a ranch near Yuma (Arizona) in 1854 with his brother Jesús, bringing large numbers of cattle north from the family's Sonora holdings. Discouraged by Indian depredations, José went to Calaveras County, California, with his father and worked there both at mining and commerce for several years. In 1859 José and Jesús returned to Arizona in time to participate in the 1862 La Paz gold rush. Later they were among the discoverers of the Pichaco gold placers and successfully established a ranch of over 1,000 acres near Yuma. Here José partially damned the Colorado River and built twenty-seven miles of irrigation canals, enabling him to raise two grain crops a year. His principal crops were wheat, barley, alfalfa, hay, and sugar cane. By the mid–1870s he had become a prominent merchant, liquor dealer, and real estate trader, and had contracts to supply the U.S. Army with large amounts of fodder.

José Redondo's army contracts were undoubtedly due in part to his political position. He was elected to the territorial legislature in 1864 but did not serve because his citizenship paperwork was incomplete. However, between 1873 and

1878 he served three terms in the legislature; he was a county supervisor for seven years, a member of the Yuma City Council, and in 1878 mayor of Yuma.

One of the wealthiest men in southern Arizona, Redondo had the kind of resources that enabled him to make successful investments in merchandising, mining, and agriculture. He was the first to settle in the Yuma area, the first to raise wheat there, and the first to establish a grist mill there. His obituary in the *Daily Arizona Sentinel* on 22 June 1878 credited him with principal responsibility for agricultural and mineral development in Yuma County.

FURTHER READING: Marcy G. Goldstein, "Americanization and Mexicanization: The Mexican Elite and Anglo-American in the Gadsden Purchase Lands, 1853–1880," Ph.D. diss., Case Western Reserve University, 1977; Jay J. Wagoner, *Arizona Territory, 1863–1912: A Political History*, Tucson: University of Arizona Press, 1970.

REQUEÑA, MANUEL (1802?–1876), merchant, politician. Born and raised in the Yucatán peninsula, Manuel Requeña left there for Mexico's west-coast port of Mazatlán in the early 1830s as a result of his commercial activities. In 1834 he moved to Los Angeles, where he quickly became an important business and political figure.

Avoiding conflict with the invading U.S. forces during the United States–Mexican War, Requeña was elected to the Los Angeles City Council in 1850 and was reelected to four more terms, serving most of the time as president. In 1852 he was also elected to the first county board of supervisors. Losing his 1855 bid for a sixth term on the council, he was reelected in the following year and was again elected president. When the Los Angeles mayor resigned, Requeña became mayor until an election was held eleven days later. He thus was briefly the only Mexican American to serve as mayor of Los Angeles during the American period.

In the mid–1850s Manuel Requeña switched his political loyalty from the Democratic to the Republican party and later was a founder of the Los Angeles Lincoln-Johnson Club. During a time of rising tensions over the slavery issue, in a town that was heavily southern Democratic, he failed to win a seat on the City Council again until toward the end of the Civil War in 1864. In 1867 he was elected to an eighth term. During the 1850s and 1860s he continued his business activities; as a substantial land owner he raised oranges and grapes in the Los Angeles area. He also pursued an active civic role, serving on the three-man school commission and taking an interest in bringing the Sisters of Charity to Los Angeles to found an orphanage.

FURTHER READING: Melvin G. Halli and Peter d'A. Jones, eds., *Biographical Dictionary of American Mayors, 1820–1980*, Westport, Conn.: Greenwood Press, 1981; Leonard Pitt, *The Decline of the Californios*, Berkeley: University of California Press, 1970.

REYNOSO, CRUZ (1931–), judge, lawyer. Cruz Reynoso was born 2 May 1931 of farm worker parents in the small town of Brea, California, on the northern edge of Orange County. Here he grew up and received his primary and secondary education. After earning his Associate of Arts degree from nearby Fullerton Junior College, in 1951 he entered Pomona College from which he received his A.B. two years later. From 1953 to 1955 he served in the U.S. Army as a special agent in the Counter Intelligence Corps. Discharged from the Army, he studied law at the University of California, Berkeley and was awarded his LL.B. in 1958. In the following year he began the private practice of law in El Centro (California) close to the Mexican border.

During the mid–1960s Reynoso acted as assistant chief of the Division of Fair Employment Practices in the California Department of Industrial Relations. From 1967 to 1968 he went to Washington, D.C., as associate general counsel to the Equal Employment Opportunities Commission, returning in 1968 to become first deputy director and then director of the California Rural Legal Assistance (CRLA). In 1972 he accepted a position at the University of New Mexico School of Law where he taught constitutional law until he was appointed associate justice of the Appellate Court in Sacramento in 1976. Six years later he was appointed to the California Supreme Court by Governor "Jerry" Brown, the first Latino on the court. However, during the 1986 election he failed to win reconfirmation from the voters after an orchestrated campaign against the chief justice, himself, and a third justice for their liberal viewpoints. At the beginning of 1987 he entered private practice with the firm of O'Donnell & Gordon in Los Angeles.

Cruz Reynoso has been honored by appointment to four presidential commissions, including the Select Commission on Immigration and Refugee Policy (1979–1981) and was appointed delegate to the U.N. Commission on Human Rights (1980). In 1981 he was given an honorary Doctor of Laws degree by Santa Clara University (California). He was a Ford Foundation fellow in 1958–1959 and received the Loren Miller Legal Services award from the California state bar association two decades later. In addition he has served on numerous committees, boards, and state commissions.

FURTHER READING: "Cruz Reynoso, A Distinguished Career," *Caminos* 5:2 (February 1984); *Who's Who in America 1984–1985*, 43rd ed., 1984.

RIVERA, TOMAS (1935–1984), writer, teacher, administrator. Born in Crystal City, Texas, in 1935, Tomás Rivera came from an immigrant family that annually followed the migrant labor stream that led north from Texas to various agricultural areas of the Midwest. His earliest education was acquired in Spanish-instruction barrio schools, and in 1954 he graduated from Crystal City High School. An English major in college, Rivera earned an A.A. from Southwest Texas Junior College at Uvalde and by 1964 a Bachelor of Science and a master's degree in educational administration at Southwest Texas State University in San Marcos. In 1969 he received his Ph.D. in Romance languages and literature from the University of Oklahoma.

Beginning his academic career in 1957 by teaching English and Spanish in a Texas secondary school, Dr. Rivera subsequently held various teaching and administrative positions. By 1965 he was chairman and instructor in the Department of Foreign Languages at Southwest Texas Junior College. Then he moved to Sam Houston State University as associate professor of Spanish, as director of the Division of Foreign Languages, Literature, and Linguistics, and associate dean of the College of Multidisciplinary Studies. Later he was vice president for administration at the University of Texas, San Antonio. In 1978 he became executive vice president at the University of Texas, El Paso, and a year later was appointed chancellor of the University of California at Riverside, the youngest and first minority chancellor in University of California history.

While he rose rapidly on the academic and administrative ladders in education, Tomás Rivera also developed a successful literary career. He began writing at an early age and over the years honed his literary skills until he made himself a leading Chicano author. Novelist, literary critic, and poet, he has had numerous works published in journals and anthologies. His novel, *Y no se lo tragó la tierra/And the Earth Did Not Part* (1971) won the Quinto Sol National Chicano Literary Award for 1969–1970. This work, one of the first of the current generation of Chicano novels, is still considered one of the best novels in the field. Before his death from a heart attack in 1984 Rivera received a Distinguished Alumnus award from Southwest Texas State University and a Pacesetters Award from the Inland Area Urban League. He served on numerous boards, councils, and associations.

FURTHER READING: Juan Bruce-Novoa, *Chicano Authors: Inquiry by Interview*, Austin: University of Texas Press, 1980; "Riverside Chancellor Tomás Rivera Called an Inspiration to Chicanos," *The Chronicle of Higher Education* (15 February 1984); "Tomás Rivera, 1935–1984," *Caminos* 5:6 (June 1984).

RODRIGUEZ, ARMANDO M. (1921–), educator, administrator. Armando Rodríguez was born 30 September 1921 in the town of Gómez Palacios, an agricultural and transportation center near Torreón in the state of Durango, Mexico. The thirteenth of fourteen children born to Andrés and Petra Rodríguez, he was ten years old when the family migrated to the United States, settling in San Diego. Armando grew up in the San Diego barrio where he attended the local public grammar and high schools.

A naturalized United States citizen, he entered the army late in 1942 and served in the Signal Corps until the end of the war. After World War II he used the G.I. Bill to go to college and in 1949 graduated from San Diego State College (now University) with a B.A. degree. Upon graduation he obtained a teaching position at Memorial Junior High School in San Diego and at the same time worked on a master's degree. He received his M.A. from San Diego State in 1951 and later did further graduate work at the University of California, Los Angeles.

In 1954 Armando moved from classroom teaching to take a job as guidance consultant in the San Diego city schools. Four years later he was named vice-principal at Gompers Junior High School, San Diego, and in 1965 was advanced to principal of Wright Brothers High School. In that same year he became the first Chicano consultant to the California State Department of Education and in the following year headed the department's Bureau of Intergroup Relations.

From the California State Department of Education Armando Rodríguez moved in 1967 to the United States Office of Education in Washington as director of what soon became the Office for Spanish-Speaking American Affairs. In late 1970 he was named Regents' Lecturer at the University of California, Riverside, and three years later he assumed new duties as president of East Los Angeles College, having been selected from more than 100 candidates for the position. After five years as a college president he was appointed by President Jimmy Carter to the Equal Employment Opportunity Commission but was not reappointed by President Reagan in 1983 when his term ended.

Dr. Armando Rodríguez has been active in many organizations related to education. He is a member of the World Affairs Council; College Entrance Examination Board; American Ethnic Studies Program; National Institute of Education, Commission on Compensatory Education, HEW; and other agencies. He has also been active in the National Education Task Force de la Raza; the National Urban Coalition; the Board of Trustees, Redlands University; Maravilla Housing Project; Hispanic Urban Center; Board of Trustees, Raza Association of Spanish Surnamed Americans; Commission on the Future of Higher Education, and others. An early advocate of bilingual and bicultural education, he is the author of a dozen important journal articles on the topic and has made numerous major speeches in its support. In October 1972 he was given the San Diego Region Honor Roll Award by the Board of the National Conference of Christians and Jews and later that year he received the Department of Health, Education and Welfare Secretary's Award for Outstanding Performance. He also is recipient of an honorary doctorate from John F. Kennedy College in Nebraska.

FURTHER READING: *Leaders in Education*, 5th ed., 1974; Armando Rodríguez, "Decade of the Hispanic American," *La Luz* 8:7 (August–September 1980); *Who's Who in Government, 1972–1973*, 1st ed., 1972.

RODRIGUEZ, CHIPITA (?–1863), civil rights figure. Chipita (possibly a diminutive for Josefa) Rodríguez, one of only three women in Texas history to be given the death penalty, was arrested in August 1863 in connection with the murder of a man whose body was found near her cabin northwest of Corpus Christi. The dead man is sometimes identified as an Anglo horse trader named John Savage. Despite the absence of any but very circumstantial evidence against her, Chipita was indicted along with one Juan Silvera when the grand jury met in October. After a two-day trial Chipita was convicted of first-degree murder, and Silvera was given a five-year sentence for second-degree murder. In spite of the meager evidence and the jury's recommendation for mercy, judge Benjamin Neal sentenced her to be hanged. There was some sympathy for Chipita among the local Irish settlers and a feeling that an injustice was being done. On Friday, 13 November 1863, she was hanged in the county seat of San Patricio.

FURTHER READING: Vernon Smylie, *A Noose for Chipita*, Corpus Christi: Texas News Syndicate Press, 1970.

RODRIGUEZ, PETER (1926–   ), painter, museum director. Peter Rodríguez was born in Stockton in California's great central valley of Mexican parents, Guadalupe (García) and Jesús Rodríguez, who had immigrated to the United States. While he was still a baby, the family moved northeast to the small foothill town of Jackson where his father found work as a gold miner. When he was ten, the family moved back to Stockton. Soon after he entered grade school he became fascinated by drawing; later in high school he began to work seriously toward becoming an artist.

In 1939, at age thirteen, Rodríguez exhibited in New York City and in the next year exhibited at San Francisco's World's Fair. Primarily self-taught as an artist, he studied at Stockton Community College and three decades later pursued museum management at the University of California in Berkeley. Just out of his teen years, he discovered abstract art—which was to dominate his subsequent work. In the decade between 1950 and 1960 he had seven one-man shows, one of them in Guadalajara, Mexico, and exhibited in thirteen group exhibitions, one of them in Mexico City.

In 1968 Rodríguez visited Mexico for the first time and was so enraptured by the people, the architecture, and the art that he stayed six months to start a collection of his Mexican works. Upon his return to the United States the next year, he located in San Francisco, California and soon began thinking of establishing an art museum. Through Luis Valdez* he became acquainted with a group of young Chicano artists, and they founded the Galería de la Raza in 1970. A disagreement in the concept of the gallery between the older Rodríguez and his younger colleagues ultimately led to his leaving the group and founding the Mexican Museum in San Francisco in 1973. After ten years as executive director of the museum, guiding it through its formative years, in September 1984 he stepped down. He still participates in the museum's operation as consultant to its board of directors. Most recently, late in 1986, he designed and installed the Nelson A. Rockefeller Collection of Mexican Folkart, a gift to the museum.

FURTHER READING: "Peter Rodríguez," *La Luz* 4:4–5 (July–August 1975); Jacinto Quirarte, *Mexican American Artists*, Austin: University of Texas Press, 1973.

RODRIGUEZ, PLACIDO, C.M.F. (1940–   ), bishop. Eleventh of fourteen children of Eutimio and María (Rosiles) Rodríguez, Plácido was born in the central Mexican city of Celaya in the state of Guanajuato on 11 October 1940. His father was a master cabinet maker and a strong supporter of the church during the Mexican church-state difficulties of the 1920s—an attitude he passed on to his children. In 1953 the parents moved to Chicago with their six minor children, and Plácido completed his primary education there two years later. Inclined toward a religious vocation, he went into the Claretian minor seminary and continued the process of learning the English language and American culture. He entered the Claretian novitiate in Los Angeles in 1959 and began his college education at the Calabazas (California) college seminary. In 1964 he received both his A.B. and his U.S. naturalization papers. After four more years of theological study at Catholic University in Washington, D.C., he was ordained to the priesthood in May 1968 at Lemont, Illinois.

After ordination Fr. Rodríguez was named assistant at Our Lady of Guadalupe parish in Chicago, where he also enrolled in a graduate program at Loyola University. During 1971 he completed his work for an M.A. in urban studies. Four years later an appointment as Claretian vocation director led to extensive U.S. travel, especially east of the Mississippi. In 1981 he was named pastor of Our Lady of Fátima church in Perth Amboy, New Jersey, and also was appointed diocesan director of Hispanic ministry. Two years later he was appointed auxiliary bishop of Chicago by Pope John Paul II.

RODRIGUEZ, RICHARD (1944–   ), writer, journalist. Born 31 July 1944 in San Francisco, California, a few years after his middle-class parents immigrated there from Mexico, Richard Rodríguez moved to Sacramento when he was three years old. He grew up in the state capital, living in an Anglo neighborhood, attending Catholic parochial grade and high schools, and learning to speak English in school. An outstanding student, he went from Bishop Armstrong High School in Sacramento to Palo Alto, where he earned his B.A. in English at Stanford University in 1967. After receiving an M.A. in philosophy at Columbia University two years later he entered the doctoral program in English at the University of California, Berkeley. Altogether he spent four years there, plus one year at the Warburg Institute in London on a Fulbright fellowship. Becoming increasingly concerned about his lost ethnicity and his alienation, he completed his dissertation on English Renaissance literature but did not submit it for his degree.

Meanwhile Rodríguez turned down several university teaching positions, did some free-lance writing, and started to write his intellectual autobiography. In 1981 he began to devote himself full-time to writing for a wide variety of magazines and newspapers, and in the following year his autobiography was published with the title *Hunger of Memory*. His critical view of bilingual education and affirmative action in this work made him an instant figure of controversy, and his clear and graceful writing style widened the market for his literary output. *Hunger of Memory* won him a gold medal for nonfiction from the Commonwealth Club (California), and in 1982 he won the Christopher prize for autobiography and the Anisfield-Wolf award for civil rights from the Cleveland Foundation. That same year he went on a national speaking tour for the English-Speaking Union. In 1984 he was the Perlman lecturer at the University of Chicago and has been a featured speaker at a number of colleges and universities.

Richard Rodríguez's writings have appeared regularly in such journals as *American Scholar* and the *New Republic* and in such newspapers as the *Wall Street Journal*, *Los Angeles Times*, and the *Washington Post*. He is currently at work on a book about the memory of Mexico in California and on another about Latin America.

FURTHER READING: Michael Christopher, "A Hispanic Horatio Alger," *U.S. Catholic* 47:8 (August 1982); *Contemporary Authors*, vol. 110, 1984; "Richard Rodríguez," *Publishers Weekly* (26 March 1982).

ROLAND, GILBERT (1905–   ), actor. Gilbert Roland was born in Ciudad Juárez, Chihuahua, Mexico, in 1905, the third son of Francisco and Consuelo Alonso, Spanish immigrants who owned a bullring there. Christened Luis Antonio, he spent his first six years in that border town. When Pancho Villa and his men attacked Juárez in 1911, the family, like many others, crossed the Rio Grande border into El Paso, Texas, for safety. Here young Luis Alonso went to school, learned to speak English, and began to study bullfighting with his *matador* father.

In El Paso Alonso also saw his first motion picture and soon developed a passion for the silver screen. At age thirteen, with $2.60 in his pockets, he hopped a freight train to California to become a movie star. His determination paid off, and soon he was working as an extra. After years of bit parts, in 1925 he was selected for a principal part in *Plastic Age*, with Clara Bow. However, after that part the nineteen-year old actor was assigned no immediate further roles. Subsequent acting jobs brought Alonso to the attention of Norma Talmadge, who picked him in 1927 to star opposite her in *Camille* for United Artists.

His work at United Artists quickly made Alonso part of a Hollywood era along with John Barrymore, Douglas Fairbanks, Mary Pickford, Dolores Del Río, Gloria Swanson, and others. For the screen he adopted the name Gilbert Roland, made by combining the names of two movie favorites, John Gilbert and the serial queen, Ruth Roland. When talking pictures came, his career suffered a temporary setback because of his accent. However, he accepted what film parts came his way and by 1933 he was back in lead roles in *We Were Strangers* and *The Bullfighter and the Lady*. From there he went on to one of the longest careers in show business with some sixty films (including *The Bad and the Beautiful*, *Cheyenne Autumn*, *My Six Convicts*, *Beneath the 12 Mile Reef*, *Juárez*, six Cisco Kid films), and even more numerous television appearances in such shows as "Bonanza," "Gunsmoke," and "Playhouse 90." His long acting career was interrupted only once, when, having become a U.S. citizen in 1942, he served in World War II with U.S. Army Air Corps Intelligence.

In addition to acting, Gilbert Roland has also been interested in writing, having authored an autobiographical novel, *Wine of Yesterday*, and numerous short stories, three of which won prizes in nationwide contests. His other important interests are tennis, at which he excels; bullfighting, whose leading practitioners have been his friends; and history, especially of the Mexican Revolution of 1910.

Not an active member of any Mexican American organizations, Roland spoke out against discrimination long before the Chicano Movement began in the 1960s and has continued to work for the betterment of La Raza. Although completely professional, he has been known to threaten to walk off a set rather than portray a Mexican character stereotypically or unrealistically. In 1969 he was awarded commendations by both the California legislature and the City of Los Angeles for his faithful portrayals of Mexicans and his promotion of better U.S.–Mexican relations.

FURTHER READING: "Gilbert Roland," *Hollywood Close-up* 2:26 (16 July 1959); Al Martínez, *Rising Voices: Profiles of Hispano-American Lives*, New York: New American Library, 1974; *Who's Who in America, 1980–1981*, 41st ed., 1980.

ROMANO-V., OCTAVIO I. (1932–   ), professor, editor. Born in Mexico City in the depths of the Great Depression, Octavio Romano came to the United States at an early age. Having earned his B.A. and M.A. from the University of New Mexico at Albuquerque, he received his doctorate in anthropology from the University of California at Berkeley in 1962. After several years of social anthropological research in New Mexico and Texas, he turned to literature with an activist bent. In 1967 he was one of the founders of Quinto Sol Publications in Berkeley.

As director of Quinto Sol and editor of its excellent journal *El Grito*, Octavio Romano was one of the earliest proponents and supporters of Chicano literature. In the pages of *El Grito* he published poetry, essays, and short stories (some his own) that explicated the Mexican American reality and introduced Chicano writers to the U.S. literary scene. In 1969 with Herminio Ríos he edited and published *El Espejo-The Mirror*, an anthology of Chicano writing, which quickly went through five printings. Four years later he published *Voices: Readings From El Grito . . . 1967–1971*, and in 1976 he began editing *Grito del Sol*, a sort of successor to *El Grito*, which ceased publication when Quinto Sol went out of business in 1974. *Grito del Sol* is published by Tonatiuh International, Inc., founded and directed by Octavio Romano.

In addition to his sociological essays like "Goodbye Revolution—Hello Slum" and short stories like "A Rosary for Doña Marina" and "The Veil," Octavio Romano also writes poetry. Best known perhaps for his editing and his activism in the late 1960s and early 1970s, he is also the author of "Don Pedrito Jaramillo: The Emergence of a Mexican-American Folk Saint," his doctoral thesis at Berkeley. He has served on various educational committees and commissions. For the past two decades he has taught behavioral sciences in the School of Public Health, University of California at Berkeley.

FURTHER READING: Julio A. Martínez, *Chicano Scholars and Writers: A Bio-Bibliographical Directory*, Metuchen, N.J.: The Scarecrow Press, 1979; Charles M. Tatum, *Chicano Literature*, Boston: Twayne Publishers, 1982.

ROMERO, EUGENIO (1837–1920), freighter, businessman, politician. Eugenio Romero, son of Miguel and Josefa (Delgado) Romero, was born 15 November 1837 at Santa Fe, Nuevo México, and was privately educated there. A member of an important Las Vegas mercantile family, he began working on the old Santa Fe Trail while still a teenager, frequently making the round trip to Missouri. He continued to work as a freighter until the coming of the railroad to New Mexico in the late 1870s. With the end of the Santa Fe trade he switched his investments to general merchandizing and lumber, and developed extensive cattle and sheep holdings. He had lumber yards and stores in Santa Fe and in four towns in Guadalupe and Torrance counties. As a result he was able to contract with the U.S. government to deliver supplies and with the Atchison, Topeka, and Santa Fe Railroad to supply ties.

In the late 1850s Eugenio Romero was one of the founders of the Republican party in New Mexico and remained a dominant political leader in San Miguel County and therefore important in state politics. He held numerous positions in city, county, and state government and in the Republican party for over half a century between 1865 and 1918. He played an active role in New Mexico's 1910 constitutional convention, where he helped lead a successful fight for the inclusion of guarantees to Nuevo Mexicanos. During the 1870s he was a staunch supporter of Archbishop Jean Baptiste Lamy, and in the following decade he founded and partly financed the Las Vegas volunteer fire department. At the beginning of the 1890s he was a prominent leader in opposing the belligerent confrontation tactics of the secret vigilante group called the White Caps (Las Gorras Blancas). Its members reciprocated by cutting his fences and burning his property. Eugenio Romero's life spanned the Mexican and American eras to the end of World War I. He died at eighty-three on 30 September 1920.

FURTHER READING: George Anderson, ed., *History of New Mexico, Its Resources and People*, 2 vols., New York: Pacific States Publishing Co., 1915; Maurilio Vigil, *Los Patrones: Profiles of Hispanic Leaders in New Mexico History*, Washington, D.C.: University Press of America, 1980.

RONSTADT, LINDA (1946–   ), singer. Born in Tucson on 30 July 1946 to Gilbert and Ruthmary Ronstadt, Linda Ronstadt is of Mexican and German ancestry. She was brought up in a musical household and attended local parochial and high schools. Her earliest public performance was with a Tucson folk group organized by her older sister and brother; and in 1964, at eighteen, she left the University of Arizona after only a few months there to seek a musical career in Los Angeles.

In Los Angeles Linda with some musician friends formed a soft-rock group called Linda and the Stone Poneys, which toured in the late 1960s opening concerts for big-name rock singers. Between 1966 and 1968 the group also made three albums for Capitol Records. With the breakup of the Stone Poneys and with encouragement from Capitol Records, Linda went solo in 1969 and in the next year had a hit single, "Long, Long Time." When she switched from

Capitol to the country-rock Asylum label in 1973, her singing career took off. Under the direction of Peter Asher, who later became her manager and has produced nearly all of her subsequent albums, in the next year she had a platinum (sale of over 1 million copies) album, "Heart Like a Wheel," which also had three gold singles. By 1977 she had five platinum albums and had reached the status of female superstar of rock. In that same year she sang at President Jimmy Carter's inaugural concert in January and in February was awarded her second Grammy.

In the late 1970s and early 1980s Linda Ronstadt continued to mature as a singer, continued to make successful albums, and continued to tour the country in concert appearances. In 1983 her broadening musical interest led her to do albums of prerock ballads with arranger Nelson Riddle. "What's New" soon achieved platinum status despite its radical change from mainstream rock, and "Lush Life" and "For Sentimental Reasons," which followed, were equally successful. Her shift away from rock has been emphasized by her appearance, both on Broadway and on film, in "The Pirates of Penzance" in 1980 and again in 1984 in Puccini's *La Boheme*, both highly successful. To her earlier pop style—a mix of rock, folk, and country-western—she now has added ballads and operetta. She is featured in Luis Valdez's *Corridos*, which will air as a special on PBS in the fall of 1987.

FURTHER READING: *Current Biography Yearbook*, 1978; Dennis Hunt, "For Linda What's New Is What's Old," *San Francisco Chronicle, Datebook* (2 October 1983); "A Pop Star Goes Puccini," *Newsweek* (10 December 1984); "Ronstadt: The Gamble Pays Off Big," *Family Weekly* (8 January 1984); *Who's Who in America, 1980–1981*, 41st ed., 1980.

ROSALDO, RENATO IGNACIO (1912–   ), professor, educator. Born 16 April 1912 in Minatitlán, state of Veracruz, Mexico, Renato Rosaldo was the son of Ignacio and Emilia (Hernández) Rosaldo. In 1930 the family came to the United States and Renato finished his junior and senior years of high school in Chicago. Two years later he earned his A.A. degree from the J. S. Morton Junior College in Cicero, Illinois, and then completed his A.B. at the University of Illinois. In 1937 he received his M.A. and five years later earned his Ph.D. in Spanish; both graduate degrees are also from the University of Illinois. Meanwhile, he was employed by the university as a teaching assistant (1936–1942) and as an instructor in Spanish (1942–1945). In 1945 he moved from Chicago to the University of Wisconsin, where he remained until 1955. From 1955 until his retirement he taught at the University of Arizona. For many years he directed the University of Arizona's summer school at Guadalajara, Mexico. He also was visiting professor at a number of American universities.

In 1966 Renato Rosaldo coauthored *Six Faces of Mexico*; he was the editor of *Flores de Baria Poesía* (1952) and coeditor of *Chicano: The Evolution of a People* (1973). His main activity as a Spanish language specialist has been in writing articles and he has authored and coauthored numerous essays on literature,

Latino culture, and the teaching of Spanish. He has also taken a leadership role in a number of academic associations, among them the Modern Language Association, Instituto Internacional de Literatura Ibero-Americana, Philological Association of the West Coast, and the American Association of Teachers of Spanish and Portuguese. As a result of his expertise in the area of Hispano culture, he has been appointed to a number of commissions and has been cited for his contributions.

FURTHER READING: Julio A. Martínez, *Chicano Scholars and Writers: A Bio-Bibliographical Directory*, Metuchen, N.J.: The Scarecrow Press, 1979; *Who's Who in America, 1982–1983*, 42nd ed., 1982.

ROYBAL, EDWARD R. (1916–   ), politician. Edward R. Roybal was born 10 February 1916 in Albuquerque, New Mexico, into a middle-class Mexican American family. When he was four, the family moved to the Boyle Heights area of Los Angeles, California, and here he began his education in the city's public schools. He graduated from Roosevelt High School in 1934 during the depths of the depression and after graduation entered the Civilian Conservation Corps. Later he continued his education in business administration at the University of California and at Southwestern University in Los Angeles.

Interested in health problems, Roybal obtained a position as public health educator with the California Tuberculosis Association in the late 1930s. His work was interrupted by World War II and his service in the armed forces during 1944 and 1945. After his discharge he returned to health work, becoming a director for health education in the Los Angeles County Tuberculosis and Health Association.

In the post–World War II era a number of concerned Mexican Americans formed a group to elect one of La Raza to the Los Angeles City Council. Their candidate in 1947 was Edward Roybal, but his bid for the council seat was not successful. Instead of giving up, the group decided to intensify its efforts and with the help of Fred Ross created the Community Service Organization, a grass-roots community movement. In the 1949 elections the CSO held voter registration and get-out-the-vote drives in East Los Angeles, and Edward Roybal was elected to the City Council, the first Mexican American on that board since 1881. In 1954 he was unsuccessful in a bid for lieutenant governor and four years later lost his race for the Los Angeles Board of Supervisors. However, he was repeatedly reelected to the City Council, twice without opposition, serving a total of thirteen years. During this time, he served on many important committees and in 1961 acted as president pro tempore of the council. He devoted his main concern and efforts to developing community health and child care programs. Elected to the U.S. Congress in November 1962, Roybal has been reelected in every election since then; since 1964 he has always received more than two-thirds of the votes cast. In the House he continued his work for social and economic reforms.

During his two and a half decades in the nation's Congress Roybal has served on a number of very important committees, among them the Interior and Insular Affairs Committee, the Post Office and Civil Service Committee, the Committee on Foreign Affairs, and the Veterans Affairs Committee. In 1971 he became a member of the all-important House Appropriations Committee and at present sits on three subcommittees of this key committee. In his years on the committee he has pursued a carefully focused and generally modest role; he has been an outspoken advocate of federal help for bilingual education programs. Most recently he was appointed to the Select Committee on Aging and in 1980 persuaded the House to restore $15 million it had cut from senior citizens' programs.

In his Washington work Congressman Roybal has been concerned for problems of La Raza. In 1967 he introduced and won approval for the first federal bilingual education act. The following year he introduced a successful bill to create a cabinet-level Committee on Opportunities for Spanish-Speaking People. In 1982 as chairman of the Hispanic Caucus, he led the opposition to the Simpson-Mazzoli immigration bill, against which he has continued to speak out. Throughout a third of a century in public service he has consistently advocated greater citizen participation in party politics and in federal and local government.

Among Edward Roybal's achievements are honorary Doctor of Law degrees from Pacific States University (Los Angeles) and Claremont Graduate School. In 1973 he was honored by Yale University, which appointed him a Visiting Chubb fellow. Three years later he was given the Excellence in Public Service Award by the American Academy of Pediatrics, and in the early 1980s he received the Joshua Award for his support of better Jewish-Hispanic relations. He is an active member of the National Association of Latino Elected Officials (NALEO) as well as the Hispanic Congressional Caucus. He is also a vice-chairman in the Democratic National Committee and a member of the Democratic Advisory Council of Elected officials.

FURTHER READING: Harold Alford, *The Proud Peoples*, New York: David McKay Co., 1972; Katherine A. Diaz, "Congressman Edward Roybal: Los Angeles Before the 1960s," *Caminos* 4:7 (July–August 1983); Alan Ehrenhalt, ed., *Politics in America*, Washington, D.C.: Congressional Quarterly, 1983.

RUIZ, RAMON EDUARDO (1921–   ), historian, educator. Ramón Eduardo Ruiz was born 9 September 1921 at Pacific Beach just north of San Diego, California, of Mexican parents who were refugees of the Great Revolution. He grew up there and received his early education in parochial schools. After high school he began university studies, but they were interrupted by service in the U.S. Army Air Force during World War II (1943–1946). A year out of the Air Force he finished his B.A. at San Diego State College (now University) and then in the next year earned his M.A. at Claremont Graduate School in the Los Angeles area. In 1954 he completed his doctorate in history at the University of California, Berkeley. After short-term teaching positions at the University of

Oregon and Southern Methodist University he taught at Smith College in Massachusetts from 1958 to 1969. Since 1969 he has taught at the University of California at San Diego, where he has also held administrative positions. He has been a visiting professor at a number of colleges and universities in Mexico and the United States.

A specialist in Mexican history with emphasis on the Great Revolution, Ramón Eduardo Ruiz has written nearly half a dozen books on that topic and one on the Cuban revolution of Fidel Castro. A number of these books have been translated into Spanish and published, most in Mexico. Because of reader interest in the topic, he is perhaps most widely known for *Cuba: The Making of a Revolution* (1968), which was selected as one of the top twenty-one history books of 1968 and was later published in Italian as well as in Spanish. He is also the author of two juvenile histories and has edited several works in Latin American and Mexican history. In addition, he has written a score and a half of articles published in collected works and in scholarly journals.

Ramón Eduardo Ruiz has served as associate editor of *Sociology of Education Review* and as contributing editor of *Aztlán*. He has been active in various professional associations and has acted as consultant to the Ford Foundation and the National Endowment for the Humanities and he is currently working on a history of Mexico—a personal interpretation.

FURTHER READING: Julio A. Martínez, *Chicano Scholars and Writers: A Bio-Bibliographical Directory*, Metuchen, N.J.: The Scarecrow Press, 1979; *Who's Who in America, 1984–1985*, 43rd ed., 1984.

S

ST. VRAIN, CERAN (1802–1870), trader, fur trapper. Ceran St. Vrain was born near St. Louis, Missouri, just two years after the area had been retroceded to France by Spain. While he grew up there, the western fur trade boomed, and as a youth he clerked for one of the larger trading companies. In 1824 he became active in the Santa Fe trade and in less than a decade he had formed Bent, St. Vrain and Company to take advantage of that trade's rapid expansion. He soon moved to Taos where he became a Mexican citizen in 1831; during Manuel Armijo's* governorship he received large land grants from the Mexican government. He became one of the leaders of the pro-American party in northern Nuevo México during the first half of the 1840s. When the second Taos rebellion occurred in early January 1847, he raised a volunteer company to assist in suppressing it, and during the U.S. Civil War he helped recruit and organize the First Regiment of New Mexico Volunteers of which he was briefly colonel.

After the United States takeover of New Mexico St. Vrain continued his land activities and was also an investor in railroads, milling, publishing, and banking. Inevitably he was deeply involved in politics, being a proponent of territorial status rather than statehood for New Mexico. Although he was much interested in public office and was even nominated for lieutenant governor, he was never elected. In 1870 he died in Mora, a small town southeast of Taos.

FURTHER READING: William A. Keleher, *Turmoil in New Mexico, 1846–1868*, Santa Fe, N.M.: Rydall Press, 1952; Howard Lamar, *The Far Southwest, 1846–1912: A Territorial History*, New York: W. W. Norton & Co., 1970.

SALAZAR, EULOGIO (?–1968), law officer. Salazar was a long-time Rio Arriba County jailer who put up resistance in the Tierra Amarilla, New Mexico, courthouse raid of Reies López Tijerina's* Alianza Federal de Pueblos Libres followers in June 1967. In court he later testified that he had been wounded by Tijerina himself in the fray. On 3 January 1968 his battered corpse was found in his car. There was never any evidence to tie Aliancistas to his murder, and the case remains unsolved despite considerable effort by the district attorney to clear it up.

FURTHER READING: Patricia Bell Blawis, *Tijerina and the Land Grants*, New York: International Publishers, 1971; Peter Nabokov, *Tijerina and the Courthouse Raid*, Berkeley, Calif.: The Ramparts Press, 1969.

SALAZAR, RUBEN (1928–1970), journalist. Rubén Salazar was born 3 March 1928 to Salvador and Luz (Chávez) Salazar in Ciudad Juárez, Chihuahua, Mexico. When he was one year old, the family crossed the Rio Grande and settled in El Paso, Texas, where he went to school and grew up. After two years in the U.S. Army and the attaining of citizenship, he completed his formal education with a B.A. from the University of Texas, El Paso, in 1954. Meanwhile his strong interest in journalism had led to a reporter's job on the El Paso *Herald-Post*. After two years that gave evidence of deep interest and great ability in investigative reporting he moved to the *Press-Democrat* in Santa Rosa, California, and then in 1957 to the much larger and more prestigious *San Francisco News*. Having served his seven-year apprenticeship, he joined the *Los Angeles Times* in 1959.

After six years in the *Times* city room, during which he won awards for a 1963 series on the Los Angeles Spanish-speaking community, Salazar was assigned to cover the fighting in Vietnam. In 1966 he was transferred to Mexico City where he was appointed bureau chief. When he returned to Los Angeles three years later, he was selected for a special assignment. With the rise of Chicano awareness and militancy the *Times* editorial staff decided early in 1970 to create a special column to explain Mexican American life and culture to the Los Angeles community. Rubén Salazar, a Mexican American, a political moderate, and an outstanding journalist, was asked to undertake the task. To add to his qualifications he had just been hired as news director of Spanish-language television station KMEX. Salazar gave his weekly column his best, regularly turning out hard-hitting essays that exposed inequities, prejudice, and racism, and detailed Mexican Americans' serious grievances. Inevitably there was a reaction and pressure was exerted to tone down, if not muzzle Salazar.

Toward the end of August 1970 Mexican Americans from all over the United States gathered in East Los Angeles to march in protest against the war in Vietnam, and Rubén Salazar went to Laguna Park to cover the story for the *Times* and KMEX. Trouble in a nearby liquor store quickly led to a massive confrontation between marchers and police and to rioting and looting that eventually covered twenty-eight blocks. Late in the afternoon Salazar and two KMEX coworkers entered the Silver Dollar Cafe. Shortly afterwards police fired a number of pointed, high-velocity tear gas projectiles through the door. One of them pierced Salazar's head, killing him instantly.

Rubén Salazar's funeral was a muted testimony to Chicano struggles for social and economic equality. Later a park in East Los Angeles was renamed after him, and he received the highest Raza accolade—a *corrido* in his honor. On the tenth anniversary of his death his widow dedicated the Rubén Salazar Library in Santa Rosa, California.

FURTHER READING: "Death in the Barrio," *Newsweek* (14 September 1970); David F. Gómez, "Killing of Rubén Salazar: Nothing has Changed in the Barrio," *Christian Century* 88 (13 January 1971); Al Martínez, *Rising Voices: Profiles of Hispano-American Lives*, New York: New American Library, 1974; Sally Salazar, "Rubén Salazar: The Man not the Myth," *The Press Democrat*, Santa Rosa, Calif. (29 August 1980). Steve Weingarten, "The Life and Curious Death of Rubén Salazar," *Reader* (Los Angeles) 3:44 (26 August 1981).

SALINAS, LUIS OMAR (1937–   ), poet, teacher. Luis Omar Salinas was born 27 June 1937 in the small Texas village of Robstown near Corpus Christi to Rosendo and Olivia (Treviño) Salinas. When he was three, the family returned to Mexico for a time. His mother died the following year, and Luis was adopted by an uncle. He began his early education at St. Anthony's school in Robstown and later completed high school in Bakersfield, California, to which his stepfather had moved. After graduation from Bakersfield High School in the mid–1950s he attended several California colleges for three years while supporting himself with a variety of part-time jobs. Since the late 1960s he has lived in the Fresno area and been a part of the Chicano literary and activist movements centered in California State University, Fresno. From 1969 to 1970 he was editor of *Backwash*, a University literary magazine.

Salinas first published his poetry in the mid–1960s and had his first collection of poems, *Crazy Gypsy*, published in 1971. During the 1970s he was extremely productive, with his poems appearing in numerous anthologies, collections, journals, and newspapers. In 1973 he coedited a collection of poetry under the title *From the Barrio: A Chicano Anthology*, and two years later he was published in *Entrance: 4 Chicano Poets; Leonard Adamé, Luis Omar Salinas, Gary Soto, Ernesto Trejo*. More recently he has published three short volumes of his poems: *I Go Dreaming Serenades* (1979), *Afternoon of the Unreal* (1980), and *Prelude to Darkness* (1981). His latest (as yet unpublished) work is titled *Darkness Under the Trees: Walking Behind the Spanish*. Salinas is best known for two of his earlier poems, "Aztec Angel" and "Quixotic Expectations." His work is described as combining a powerful realism with a dreamlike and equally powerful surrealistic quality.

FURTHER READING: Wolfgang Binder, ed., "Partial Autobiographies: Interviews with Twenty Chicano Poets," *Erlanger Studien*, Band 65/I (1985), Erlangen, Germany: Verlag Palm & Enke Erlangen; Julio A. Martínez, ed., *Chicano Scholars and Writers: A Bio-Bibliographical Directory*, Metuchen, N.J.: The Scarecrow Press, 1979; Julio A. Martínez and Francisco A. Lomelí, *Chicano Literature: A Reference Guide*, Westport, Conn.: Greenwood Press, 1985.

SALINAS, PORFIRIO (1912–1973), painter. Born in 1912 southeast of Austin near Bastrop, county seat of Bastrop County, Texas, Porfirio Salinas was the third of seven children in a rural Tejano family. Growing up in San Antonio, he had only three years of formal schooling but from a very early age showed considerable artistic ability. Completely self-taught as an artist, he was hired by Robert Woods, a well-known landscape painter, to fill in bluebonnets in his rustic scenes. As his painting skills increased, Porfirio developed an eye for typical southwestern vistas and specialized in landscapes of his native state, especially "bluebonnet scenes." He also painted matadors, bulls, and bullfight scenes as a hobby. Although he painted to sell and therefore to please people, he created a style described as heightened realism, notable for the honesty and vividness with which it depicts Texas landscapes. As a result he became one of Texas's most popular artists.

During the 1960s Salinas's works gained national exposure, and he was known as President Lyndon B. Johnson's favorite painter. He was commissioned by Lady Bird Johnson to paint some of the president's best-loved scenes along the Pedernales River. At one time five of his paintings hung in the White House. He died April 18, 1973.

FURTHER READING: Ruth Goddard, *Porfirio Salinas*, Austin: Rock House Press, 1975; John H. Jenkins, "Porfirio Salinas," *Southwestern Art* 1 (1967); Jacinto Quirarte, *Mexican American Artists*, Austin: University of Texas Press, 1973.

SAMANIEGO, MARIANO G. (1844–1907), politician, businessman, rancher. Mariano Samaniego was born in northern Sonora into a wealthy mercantile family just before the U.S.–Mexican War. At the beginning of the 1850s he moved with his widowed mother to Mesilla, Arizona, where the family owned a general store. As a result of the Gadsden Purchase he became a citizen of the United States in 1854, and eight years later he graduated from St. Louis University. Returning to Arizona, he settled in Tucson where he used his education, his frontier skills, and his family connections to make himself a leading politician and businessman.

Beginning in the 1860s Samaniego achieved his early success in merchandizing and freighting; he was also a leader in the ongoing Arizona struggle against Apache depredations. With his friend Yjinio Aguirre he hauled supplies for civilians and also for army posts in Arizona, New Mexico, and western Texas. He was a mail route contractor. By the time the railroad arrived in Tucson in 1880 he had diversified his financial interests, investing extensively in ranching property and in urban real estate around Tucson. In 1881 he sold his freighting interests to devote himself to ranching but then operated several stage lines in southern Arizona. He was also involved in water and irrigation companies and in mining. He appears to have been sufficiently flexible and adaptable to the changing conditions in the Southwest to remain a leading businessman and public official.

Between the end of the 1860s and the end of the century Mariano Samaniego held more public offices than any other Arizona Hispano. In the 1868 election he ran for territorial assessor and then became an advisor to Governor Anson P.K. Safford (1869–1877). In 1877 he was elected to the Ninth Arizona

SAMORA, JULIAN

207

legislative assembly and between 1880 and 1895 was reelected three times. During the 1880s and 1890s he was repeatedly elected to the Pima county board of supervisors and also served as the first county assessor. In addition he had three terms on the Tucson city council.

One of very few Arizona university graduates of the day, Mariano Samaniego was a strong advocate of public education at both lower and university levels. With the founding of the state university, he became a member of the first board of regents in 1886, and for a while was acting treasurer. He took an active role in the Arizona Pioneers Historical Society, serving many years in leadership positions. He also was a founder and president of the Alianza Hispano-Americana, which encouraged acculturation while defending Mexican American civil rights and cultural identity.

FURTHER READING: Marcy Goldstein, "Americanization and Mexicanization: The Mexican Elite and Anglo-American in Gadsden Purchase Lands, 1853–1880," Ph.D. diss., Case Western Reserve University, 1977; Thomas E. Sheridan, "Peacock in the Parlor: Frontier Tucson's Mexican Elite," *Journal of Arizona History* 25 (Autumn 1984).

SAMORA, JULIAN (1920–), sociologist, educator. Julian Samora was born 1 March 1920 in the small town of Pagosa Springs in southwestern Colorado, where he attended grade and high schools. Receipt of a Frederick G. Bonfils Foundation grant enabled him to enter Adams State College of Colorado, where he received his B.A. degree in 1942. He taught in a Colorado high school for one year and then was able to continue work for an advanced degree as the result of being selected for three scholarships. In 1947 he received his M.S. in sociology from Colorado State University at Fort Collins and meanwhile had begun teaching at Adams State (1944–1955). Having completed his M.S., he enrolled in the Ph.D. program at Washington University in St. Louis, where he earned his doctorate in sociology and anthropology in 1953—the first Mexican American in the field. His thesis was on minority leadership in a bicultural community. After two short-term teaching positions, in 1959 he accepted an associate professorship in sociology at Notre Dame University, where he has taught since. He has also been a visiting professor at a number of outstanding universities including the Universidad Nacional de Colombia. In the spring of 1985 he retired from Notre Dame.

From the beginning of his academic career Julian Samora has been deeply interested in research and has presented the results of his interest in nearly thirty journal articles and in several seminal books. Among his most important publications are *La Raza: Forgotten Americans* (1966), *Mexican-Americans in a Midwest Metropolis* (1967), *Los Mojados: The Wetback Story* (1971), and *Gunpowder Justice: A Reassessment of the Texas Rangers* (1979). He is currently working on a historical account of four families living in the Southwest from the sixteenth century to the present.

As a result of his experience and expertise, Dr. Samora has been invited to serve on many important boards and commissions, both governmental and private. Among the more salient are the U.S. Commission on Civil Rights, the National Institute of Mental Health, and the President's Commission on Rural Poverty. He has also served as an editor for *International Migration Review*, *Nuestro*, and other journals. At Notre Dame he directed the Mexico Border Studies Project, sponsored by the Ford Foundation. He has been the recipient of numerous prestigious grants and awards over the past forty years.

FURTHER READING: Julio A. Martínez, *Chicano Scholars and Writers: A Bio-Bibliographical Directory*, Metuchen, N.J.: The Scarecrow Press, 1979; Arturo Palacios, ed., *Mexican American Directory*, 1969–1970 ed., Washington, D.C.: Executive Systems Corps., 1969; *Who's Who in America, 1982–1983*, 42nd ed., 1982.

SANCHEZ, ANTONIO R., SR. (1916–   ), entrepreneur, banker. Antonio Sánchez, youngest son of a poor Tejano ranch family, was born in Webb County, Texas, just as the United States became involved in World War I. In less than robust health from infancy, he took up boxing as a youth to improve his lung capacity. During his sophomore year he quit high school in the middle of the Great Depression to help support the family. Soon he had a family of his own to support; this he did by becoming an aggressive salesman of business machines. He also became a general factotum for a Laredo political machine called the Independent Party which helped his business machines company and led to some local political jobs. During the early 1960s he went to work for Coastal States Producing Company, scouting oil and gas leases.

With his ambition and contacts Sánchez expanded this beginning into a leasing and brokerage firm that served many large oil companies. In 1966 he was a cofounder of the International Bank of Commerce in Laredo, in which he ultimately came to have a controlling interest. His heavy investment in petroleum leases began to pay off in the early 1970s with the 1973 oil crisis and in the next year the new Sánchez-O'Brien Petroleum Group drilled its first well. By 1977 Sánchez not only was financially able to greatly expand Sánchez-O'Brien but also had added two banks, a construction company, an industrial park, a horse farm, and various real estate properties to his holdings. By 1984 Sánchez and his son Antonio, Jr., had organized Bankshares, a multimillion dollar holding company, which controls three border banks. The Sánchez financial empire also includes automobile agencies, a savings and loan company, a Laredo daily newspaper, and real estate.

FURTHER READING: Diana R. Fuentes, "A Texas Dream Becomes a Multimillion Dollar Enterprise," *Nuestro* 8:8 (October 1984); Reed Wolcott, "The Latino Petro-Baron," *Nuestro* 1:4 (July 1977).

SANCHEZ, GEORGE ISIDORE (1906–1972), educator. Born in the small town of Barela, New Mexico, on 4 October 1906 of parents whose families had been among the early Mexican settlers, George I. Sánchez grew up in Jerome, Arizona. His father worked there in the copper pits of the then booming mining town, and George received his early education there. The mining boom collapsed with the end of World War I, and in the depression of the early 1920s he contributed to the family support by playing coronet at fiestas, dances, and weddings. While still a teenager, he also had a short boxing career as Kid Féliz.

After attending high schools in Arizona and New Mexico George Sánchez entered the University of New Mexico and at the same time began teaching at the tiny settlement of Irrisarri, fifty miles east of Albuquerque. During the second half of the 1920s he served in the Bernalillo County schools as a principal and supervisor. After completing his B.A. in Spanish and education, he received a scholarship enabling him to go to the University of Texas at Austin, where he received his M.S. in educational psychology and Spanish in 1931. With scholarship assistance he went from Texas to Berkeley and by 1934 was awarded his doctorate in educational administration by the University of California.

With a doctorate in hand George Sánchez became a research associate for the Julius Rosenwald Fund of Chicago, surveying rural schools in the Southwest and in Mexico. In 1937 he went to Venezuela as director of the government's Instituto Pedagógico Nacional and returned to teach at the University of New Mexico from 1938 to 1940. He then moved to the University of Texas at Austin where he remained as professor of Latin American education until his death. For the next two decades he lectured, consulted, and directed numerous workshops, institutes, and programs on bilingual and bicultural education, minority education, and Latin American education. In the World War II years he worked for the Office of Coordinator of Inter-American Affairs in Washington.

During the last thirty-five years of his life George I. Sánchez was clearly established as one of the foremost experts on the educational and social needs of Spanish-speaking groups in the United States. He also became an authority and specialist in the broader field of Latin American education. His pioneering philosophy and methods form the heart of most bilingual-bicultural programs today. His ideas and programs were detailed in over 100 journal articles and reports. He is best known for his seminal work, *The Forgotten People: A Study of New Mexicans* (1940), partially the result of a 1938 research grant from the Carnegie Foundation. He also wrote many other books including *Mexico, Revolution by Education* (1938), *The Development of Higher Education in Mexico* (1944), *The People: A Study of the Navajos* (1948), *The Development of Education in Venezuela* (1963), and *Mexico* (1965).

Dr. George I. Sánchez was an outstanding scholar who lived a versatile and productive life on several levels. He was active in the League of United Latin American Citizens (president, 1941–1942) and was a spokesman against discrimination and social as well as educational segregation. Between 1945 and his death in 1972 he was president of the Southwest Council on Education of Spanish-Speaking People, and in 1960 he served as a member of President John F. Kennedy's Citizens Committee on a New Frontier Policy in the Americas. He truly deserves the title of most distinguished Mexican American scholar of our time.

FURTHER READING: Harold J. Alford, *The Proud Peoples*, New York: David McKay Co., 1972; Daniel J. Gómez, ''Jorge Isidro Sánchez y Sánchez (1904–1972)—

A Man for All Seasons,'' *Journal of Mexican-American Studies* 1:3–4 (Spring–Summer 1971); Américo Paredes, ed., *Humanidad: Essays in Honor of George I. Sánchez*, Los Angeles: University of California, Chicano Studies Center, 1977.

SANCHEZ, PHILLIP VICTOR (1929–   ), administrator, ambassador, businessman. Phillip Sánchez was born 28 July 1929 in Pinedale, a small town north of Fresno, California, of parents who had emigrated from Mexico in the 1920s. One of seven children, he grew up in the great central valley working the harvests with the rest of the family when his father abandoned his wife and children. After each year's picking season he attended school at Pinedale—a positive experience, which led him to Coalinga Junior College and to Fresno State College (today University). He received his A.B. at the latter in 1953, graduating as "outstanding male graduate." Out of college, he got a job as an administrative analyst in the Fresno County government. In 1962 at age thirty-two he was asked by the Board of Supervisors to take the job of county manager; he accepted, becoming the youngest county executive in the state. A member of three college boards and also active in Mexican American community affairs, he was named Fresno's Outstanding Man of the Year (1959), and five years later was listed as one of California's five outstanding young men. In 1966 he received the Medal of Merit from the state of California.

Phil Sánchez's skill as an administrator came to the attention of Washington, and in 1971 he was appointed assistant director and then director of the Office of Economic Opportunity (O.E.O.) by President Richard M. Nixon. Before leaving for Washington, he received his master's degree in political science at Fresno State. The skill with which he managed the O.E.O., its 4,200 employees, and its billion-dollar budget led Nixon to appoint him as ambassador to Honduras two years later. Again a job well done led to promotion, and in June 1976 President Gerald Ford named him ambassador to Colombia, a position he held until replaced in the following year by the incoming Democratic administration.

Sánchez then returned to Fresno, California, did some consulting work, and then helped found the Woodside Consulting Group, of which he is president. Just before the Ronald Reagan administration took over, he turned down an offered cabinet position as secretary of Housing and Urban Development because of possible conflict of interests. At the end of April 1987 he was appointed publisher of the New York-based chain of Spanish language dailies *Noticias del Mundo*, with which he was earlier associated. In addition to the *Noticias del Mundo* and the Woodside jobs, he serves on several corporate boards, is active in the U.S. Army Reserve, and speaks widely at conferences for Causa U.S.A. and Causa International. In 1985 ambassador Sánchez was named Man of the Year by the American Association of State Colleges and Universities.

FURTHER READING: Diane Alverio, "No Thank You, Mr. President," *Nuestro* 5:3 (April 1981); "Embajador Phillip V. Sánchez: The Simpático Ambassador," *La Luz* 6:6 (June 1977); Al Martínez, *Rising Voices: Profiles of Hispano-American Lives*, New York:

New American Library, 1974; U.S. Department of State, *Biographic Register* (July 1974); *Who's Who in American Politics, 1981–1982*, 8th ed., 1981.

SANCHEZ, RICARDO (1941–   ), poet. Born in El Paso, Texas, on 29 March 1941 to poor Nuevo Mexicano parents who had migrated there a year earlier, Ricardo Sánchez grew up in the grim realities of the Mexican *barrio del diablo*. While still in grade school, he began to write poetry but received little or no encouragement from the educational system. As a result of this negative reinforcement and a rebellious nature he dropped out of high school and enlisted in the U.S. Army. In the armed services his feeling of being on the outside continued, but he did complete the work necessary for a general equivalency diploma.

Out of the army and devastated by a string of family deaths, Ricardo entered upon a series of felonies that landed him in California's Soledad prison. In 1963 he was paroled, soon married, and worked at a series of jobs. Two years later, despairing of his inability to finance the birth of his first child, he again wound up in prison for armed robbery and parole breaking. Released on a second parole in 1969, he soon found living in El Paso increasingly difficult because of his pent-up anger and resentment at society.

With the aid of a Frederick Douglass Fellowship in journalism Ricardo Sánchez spent 1969–1970 in Richmond at Virginia Commonwealth University and then went to the University of Massachusetts as instructor and research assistant. During the next two or three years he became increasingly aware that his lack of proper credentials was professionally limiting and soon secured a Ford Foundation fellowship to work on his doctorate. A year and a half later, in December 1974, he received his Ph.D. in American Studies from Union Graduate School in Yellow Springs, Ohio. Since then he has taught at El Paso Community College, University of Wisconsin, University of Alaska, and the University of Utah.

A prolific writer since his army days, Ricardo Sánchez has published a half dozen books, and his poems have appeared in numerous journals. His works have been republished in two dozen anthologies; but this represents only the tip of the iceberg of his writings. He is perhaps best known for his first book, *Canto y grito mi liberación* (1971) which blares out his passion, resentment, and anger. Since then he has published *Hechizo-spells* (1976), *Mihuas Blues y gritos norteños* (1979), *Brown Bear Honey Madness: Alaskan Cruising Poems* (1982), *Amsterdam cantos & poemas pistos* (1982). He has given readings and lectures at more than fifty universities and colleges.

Ricardo Sánchez has been active in a wide variety of Chicano publications, member of the board of Mictla Publications, editor of *Quetzal*, editor at large of *La Luz*, and others. He has been equally active in the Chicano community. He founded Project H.E.L.P. in New Mexico and taught at a number of prisons. He has repeatedly protested loudly against oppression of Mexican Americans. Much of his poetry as well as his prose has a sociopolitical message. Early in

1979 he was featured on the cover of *Tiempo*, a Mexican news weekly, in connection with a lengthy article on Chicano literature.

FURTHER READING: Juan Bruce-Novoa, *Chicano Authors: Inquiry by Interview*, Austin: University of Texas Press, 1980; Julio A. Martínez and Francisco Lomelí, eds., *Chicano Literature: A Reference Guide*, Westport, Conn.: Greenwood Press, 1985; Charles Tatum, *Chicano Literature*, Boston: Twayne Publishers, 1982.

SANCHEZ, ROBERT FORTUNE (1934–   ), archbishop, teacher. Robert Sánchez was born in Socorro, a small town on the west side of the Rio Grande in south central New Mexico, one of three sons born to Julio and Priscilla (Fortune) Sánchez. Encouraged by his lawyer father, a strong believer in the value of education, he attended grade school and the first two years of high school in Socorro. His father then sent him to St. Mary's Boys High School in Phoenix, Arizona, and in 1950 he began his studies for the priesthood at the seminary in Santa Fe. From there he went to Rome to study at the North American College. In 1959 he was ordained in Rome and received his degree from the Gregorian University in the following year.

Father Sánchez then returned to teach philosophy and ethics at St. Pius High School in Albuquerque. During the 1960s he was also pastor of two New Mexican parishes and found time to earn a certificate in counseling at the University of New Mexico and to study canon law for a year at Catholic University in Washington, D.C. In 1972 and 1973 he was elected by his fellow priests to two representative positions, one in the Archdiocesan Priests Senate and the other in the National Federation of Priests Councils. In the following year Pope Paul VI appointed him archbishop of Santa Fe.

Tenth archbishop of the Santa Fe diocese, Robert Fortune Sánchez was the first Mexican American to be raised to the archbishopric, one of the youngest archbishops in the past several centuries, and the highest-ranking America-born Latino in Catholic church history. A voice of the new church, he stresses a closeness to his flock—Mexican American, Anglo, and Indian. At his request, his consecration to archbishop was held in the University of New Mexico's sports arena, so that a maximum number could attend. In office he has continued his policy of being of service to his people; he has doubled the number of Mexican Americans in his archdiocese attracted to the priesthood. He celebrated the first trilingual mass in U.S. history: in English, Spanish, and Tewa.

FURTHER READING: *American Catholic Who's Who, 1980–1981*, vol. 23, 1980; Stan Steiner, "Archbishop of All the People," *Nuestro* 1:1 (April 1977).

SANDOVAL, MOISES (1930–   ), journalist, editor. Moisés Sandoval was born 29 March 1930 to Amada (Perea) and Eusebio Sandoval in the tiny New Mexican town of Sapello east of Santa Fe. The oldest of ten children, he grew up and received his early education in the public school in nearby Rociada. When he reached high school age, his parents, determined to give their children the advantages of an education, gave up their farm and moved to a town with a high school—Brighton, Colorado, just north of Denver. After high school Moisés enrolled in Marquette University in Milwaukee and received his B.S. in 1955. A decade later he earned a certificate in international reporting from Columbia University in New York. Meanwhile he went to work for the *Albuquerque Tribune* as a reporter and also acted as a stringer for *Newsweek*. In 1964 he became senior editor of *Maryknoll Magazine*, and six years later he was promoted to managing editor.

Moisés Sandoval has taken an active role in journalist organizations; he is a member of the board of directors of the Catholic Press Association; member of the writing committee, Call to Action; chairman of the journalism awards committee of the Catholic Press Association (1975–1977); and member of the Inter-American Press Association. He is coauthor of *Reluctant Dawn: historia del padre A. J. Martínez,* cura de Taos* (1976). Among the honors he has received are 1962 National Headliners Club award for outstanding public service (investigative reporting for the *Albuquerque Tribune*); 1963–1964 Ford Foundation fellowship in international reporting; and 1976 Alicia Patterson Foundation award for travel and research.

FURTHER READING: *American Catholic Who's Who, 1980–1981*, vol. 23, 1979. "Man on the Move," *La Luz* 6:3 (March 1977).

SANDOVAL, SECUNDINO (1933–   ), designer, artist. Born 4 June 1933 in the small town of Buena Vista northeast of Santa Fe, New Mexico, Secundino Sandoval showed an aptitude for art from his kindergarten days. When he transferred to school at Los Alamos after 1943, he continued his interest in art and after high school studied painting at Santa Fe and Albuquerque with several prominent local artists. He later attended the University of New Mexico and then completed his A.B. at Adams State College in Alamosa, Colorado, in 1958.

After two years as a technical illustrator for the U.S. Army Sandoval went to work as a draftsman and designer for the Los Alamos Scientific Laboratory. His avocation as a painter in oils, acrylics, and watercolors led to a number of successful exhibitions and then to painting full time. Sandoval's paintings, usually of New Mexican vistas, are held in many private collections throughout the United States. He paints with realism and a spontaneous naturalism that captures the mood of the moment. His paintings have been shown in many galleries and art fairs and have won him numerous awards.

FURTHER READING: "Hispanic American Artist," *La Luz* 7:9 (September 1978).

SCHECHTER, HOPE MENDOZA (1921–), labor leader, business-woman. Hope Mendoza was born in the Arizona copper-mining town of Miami, but her family moved to Los Angeles, California, the next year. Here she attended grade and high schools. In 1938 she dropped out of school to go to work in the garment industry and during World War II worked in defense factories. After the war she returned to the garment industry as an organizer for the International Ladies Garment Workers Union (ILGWU) and later became its business agent as well. She continued in these capacities until the mid–1950s. In 1948 she was a founding member of the Community Service Organization (CSO) in Los Angeles and for the next seven years was active on its executive board and in various committees. During this time she also served on committees of the state Democratic party and the Central Labor Council and began taking college classes.

In 1955 Hope Mendoza's marriage to Harvey Schechter marked a change in her life. She resigned from the ILGWU, completed her high school education and was graduated, and from 1957 to 1959 attended stenotype school leading to her certification as a shorthand reporter and to a career as a free-lance reporter. In 1961 she established Schechter Deposition Service, which she ultimately merged with another firm in 1973. During this period she was a member of the board of directors of the Council of Mexican-American Affairs and the Mexican-American Youth Opportunities Foundation, and was appointed by President Lyndon Johnson to the National Advisory Council for the Peace Corps. She also continued her active role in politics, serving as delegate to two Democratic national conventions and as president of the Democratic Women's Forum.

Concerned with the needs of fellow Mexican Americans in the Los Angeles area, Hope Mendoza Schechter's life has revolved around diverse but related groups—cultural, social, and political—and encompassed the Mexican American community, the labor movement, and the Democratic party.

FURTHER READING: "Hope Mendoza Schechter," an interview in the University of California, Berkeley Oral History Project, The Bancroft Library, 1978.

SEGUIN, JUAN NEPOMUCENO (1806–1890), political leader, soldier. Born 27 October 1806 into a prominent and influential family of French origins in San Antonio, Texas, Juan Seguín was the son of civic-minded and politically active Erasmo Seguín. Young Juan attended school in San Antonio and quickly followed in his father's footsteps, being elected alcalde at eighteen. His father was an elected representative to both the provincial and national Congress, where he acted as friend and supporter of the Anglo settlers in Texas. Juan shared his father's attitudes toward and close association with the Anglo settlers.

When President Antonio López de Santa Anna began his efforts to create a centralized Mexican government in the mid–1830s, Juan Seguín, who was then the local *jefe político*, led the opposition in San Antonio; and when the Texans revolted for federalism and eventually for separation from Mexico, his loyalties were clear. Appointed a captain in the Texas cavalry, he headed the small contingent of Tejanos at the Alamo, but was sent through the Mexican lines to get help just before Santa Anna's final attack. He continued to serve in the rest of the fighting and was promoted to lieutenant colonel.

At the end of the revolt in 1836 Juan Seguín was put in command of the devastated town of San Antonio, a job made more difficult not only by continuing Mexican attempts to reconquer the city but also by recently arrived Anglo adventurers, many of whom routinely abused Tejanos. In 1838 he was elected to the Texas senate; when he stepped down from that position two years later, he was elected mayor of San Antonio. In this position his firm defense of fellow Tejanos before the continuing onslaught of disorderly Anglo elements earned him much enmity. He was unjustly accused of betraying the ill-fated Texas Santa Fe Expedition of 1841 and of being friendly to invading Mexican forces. In April 1842 Seguín finally bowed to Anglo pressures and resigned.

Fearing for his family and himself in the tense atmosphere, Juan Seguín moved across the Rio Grande into Mexico. At Nuevo Laredo he was arrested by Mexican authorities. Fearing for his life and his family, he was constrained to accept army service as an alternative to being sent to Santa Anna in Mexico City. In 1846–1847 he served on the Mexican side during the U.S.–Mexican War. After the Treaty of Guadalupe Hidalgo he requested permission to return to his native Texas. Permission was granted, and he went to live quietly on his father's rancho. However, suspicion, envy, hatred, and personal attack plagued the second half of his life, making him a foreigner in his native land. After two decades of unobtrusive residence in the United States, in 1867 he again crossed the Rio Grande. At age eighty-four he died in Nuevo Laredo and was buried there.

FURTHER READING: Frederick C. Chabot, *With the Makers of San Antonio*, San Antonio: Artes Gráficas, 1937; Milton Lindheim, *The Republic of the Rio Grande: Texans in Mexico, 1839–1840*, Waco, Tex.: W. M. Morrison, 1964; Juan N. Seguín, *Personal Memoirs of John N. Seguín, From the Year 1834 to . . . 1842*, San Antonio: Ledger Book & Job Office, 1858.

SERVIN, MANUEL P. (1920–   ), historian, professor, editor. Manuel Servín was born 8 August 1920 at El Paso, Texas, and grew up there and in Calexico, California. After graduating from Calexico Union High School in 1939, he entered the seminary to study for the priesthood but dropped out in the mid–1940s. From 1945 to 1947 he served in the U.S. Air Force. Upon his return to civilian life he entered Loyola University in Los Angeles, where he completed his A.B. in 1949. From Loyola he went to Boston College, earning a master's degree in social work two years later. He subsequently returned to California, taught at the high school level from 1953 to 1958, and completed his M.A. (1954) and his Ph.D. (1959)—both in Latin American history at the University of Southern California.

Professor Servín began teaching at El Camino College in Torrence, a southern suburb of Los Angeles, in 1958 and three years later left to teach at the University of Southern California. Here he became one of the first professors in the country to train graduate students in the field of Mexican American history. At the beginning of the 1970s he moved to Arizona State University, Tempe, where he was professor of southwestern and Mexican history and coordinator of the American Studies Program. He continued to train graduate students in Mexican American history until his poor health forced him into semiretirement.

Manuel Servín's first publication was an annotated translation titled *The Apostolic Life of Fernando Consag, Explorer of Lower California* (1968), followed in the next year by *Southern California and its University: The History of U.S.C.*, which he coauthored. In 1970 he published one of the very early collections of historical essays on the Mexican American experience with the title *The Mexican-Americans: An Awakening Minority*. It was widely used in Chicano studies courses. Servín revised and updated this text in 1974 under the title *An Awakened Minority: The Mexican-Americans*. In addition, he wrote a number of articles that appeared in historical journals, mostly on the topic of anti-Mexican bias and discrimination, which he saw as beginning with the Spaniards. He was the long-time editor of the *California Historical Society Quarterly* and very active in several historical associations.

FURTHER READING: Julio A. Martínez, *Chicano Scholars and Writers: A Bio-Bibliographic Directory*, Metuchen, N.J.: The Scarecrow Press, 1979; *The National Directory of Chicano Faculty and Research*, Los Angeles: Aztlán Publications, Chicano Studies Center, UCLA, 1974.

SOTO, GARY (1952–   ), poet, teacher. Gary Soto was born in Fresno, California, on 12 April 1952 and grew up in the barrio there and in the fields of the surrounding agricultural area. After attending local grade and high schools, he entered California State University, Fresno, and in 1974 graduated *magna cum laude*. He went on to the University of California at Irvine where he received his M.F.A. in creative writing two years later and where he was selected Graduate Student of the Year in Humanities. After a sojourn in Mexico City, a brief return to Fresno, and a year as writer-in-residence at San Diego State University he joined the Chicano studies department faculty at the University of California, Berkeley, in 1977. He is currently chairman of the department.

While Soto was still in graduate school at Irvine, his poetry began to be accepted and published by various outstanding literary journals. In 1975 he won the first of a long series of prestigious awards, the Academy of American Poets Prize, and after that *The Nation* Award. Then in the next year he received the United States Award of the International Poetry Forum and during 1977 he was awarded the Bess Hokin Prize by *Poetry* and his poetry was selected by *Nuestro* magazine. In 1978 he was nominated for a Pulitzer Prize and the National Book Award as a result of his second collection of poems, *The Tale of Sunlight*.

His books *The Elements of San Joaquin* (1976), *The Tale of Sunlight* (1978), *Father is a Pillow Tied to a Broom* (1980), and *Where Sparrows Work Hard* (1981) faithfully reflect his experiences in agricultural and factory work. He has also been published in *Entrance: 4 Chicano Poets* in 1975 by Greenfield Review Press. He has given readings of his poems at many universities and poetry centers throughout the country. His poems, which generalize the Mexican American experience, are characterized by sharply defined images and by carefully precise, accurate, and spartan use of language.

FURTHER READING: Julio A. Martínez and Francisco A. Lomelí, eds., *Chicano Literature: A Reference Guide*, Westport, Conn.: Greenwood Press, 1985; "Poetry: $2,000 United States Award to Gary Soto," *La Luz* 6:2 (February 1977); Charles M. Tatum, *Chicano Literature*, Boston: Twayne Publishers, 1982.

T

TELLES, RAYMOND L., JR. (1915–   ), diplomat, business and political leader, soldier. Raymond Telles was born 5 September 1915 in El Paso, Texas, to Ramón and Angela (López) Telles. He grew up in El Paso, attending grade school and graduating from Cathedral High School there. He then entered and graduated from International Business College and later attended Texas Western College (today University of Texas, El Paso). In 1934 he began seven years of public service as a cost accountant and administrator in the Department of Justice. During World War II Telles enlisted in the Air Force in February 1942 and served until April 1947, principally as chief of lend-lease to Latin American countries. During the Korean conflict he returned to active duty as executive director of the 67th Tactical and Reconnaissance Group from May 1951 to September 1952. He attained the rank of lieutenant colonel.

Meanwhile, in 1948 Telles was elected El Paso County clerk and was reelected for the next three terms, 1951–1957. In 1957 he was elected mayor of El Paso and two years later was reelected without opposition. In 1961 Telles was nominated by President John F. Kennedy as ambassador to Costa Rica, a position he held for six years, during which he was influential in bringing that country into the Central American Common Market. At the end of this tour of duty he was appointed by President Lyndon B. Johnson to chair the United States section of the joint United States–Mexico Commission for Border Development and Friendship. At the end of four years he returned to private business briefly as a consultant. In 1971 President Richard Nixon appointed him to the Equal Employment Opportunity Commission, where he continued his public service for five more years—when he again returned to the private sector.

Telles served as military aide to presidents Truman, Eisenhower, and Kennedy as well as to a number of visiting Latin American dignitaries. From the U.S. government he has received the Bronze Star and was also decorated by Mexico, Brazil, Peru, and Nicaragua. He also has been the recipient of numerous civic awards.

FURTHER READING: Al Martínez, *Rising Voices*, New York: New American Library, 1974; *Who's Who in America, 1978–1979*, 40th ed., 1978.

TENAYUCA (BROOKS), EMMA (1916–   ), labor leader. Emma Tenayuca was born in San Antonio, Texas, and grew up in the Mexican barrio there. As a youngster she attended political rallies with her father; later her grandfather, with whom she lived, introduced her to socialist thought. She was a serious and inquisitive student who spent hours in the library and who had begun to question American society and institutions by the time she entered high school at the end of the 1920s. Her reading of Charles Darwin, Tom Paine, and later Karl Marx led her from Catholicism to a more radical materialist position. While in Brackenridge High School, she helped organize a march of the unemployed on Austin in February 1931 under the auspices of the Communist-sponsored Trade Union Unity League. Later she became a self-avowed Communist.

Upon completing high school in 1934, she went to work as an elevator operator and began to help organize San Antonio Mexican American workers into a militant labor union, the Workers Alliance. Frequently arrested but seldom kept in jail, even overnight, she emerged from each experience more determined to speak out for civil rights and social justice. After she led a 1937 sit-in of unemployed Mexican Americans at city hall to protest relief policies, she became a special object of police vigilance.

In the fall of 1937 Emma Tenayuca married Homer Brooks, a Houston organizer for the Communist party; however, she remained in San Antonio. Because of her position in the Chicano community and in the Workers Alliance, early in the following year she became one of the principal leaders in the San Antonio pecan shellers' strike.

Emma and the Workers Alliance dominated the strike initially; however, Donald Henderson, president of the United Cannery, Agricultural, Packing and Allied Workers of America, soon took the leadership away from her in a purge of local Communists. The workers responded by electing her honorary strike leader, and she continued to support the strike in a more restrained fashion. In 1939 she made plans for a Communist rally in the municipal auditorium. The meeting was broken up by a mob and the Workers Alliance's influence never recovered from the incident. Nor did Emma Tenayuca; she subsequently gave up her role of political activist.

FURTHER READING: Julia Kirk Blackwelder, *Women in the Depression*, College Station: Texas A & M University Press, 1984; Roberto Calderón and Emilio Zamora, "Manuela Solis Sager and Emma Tenayuca: A Tribute," in *Chicana Voices*, Austin: Center for Mexican American Studies, University of Texas, 1986; Carlos Larralde, *Mexican American Movements and Leaders*, Los Alamitos, Calif.: Hwong Publishing Co., 1976.

TIJERINA, FELIX (1915?–   ), businessman. Félix Tijerina was born in the small Texas town of Sugar Land about thirty miles west of Houston to agricultural worker parents who had emigrated from Mexico. The death of his father when

Félix was nine put him into the cotton fields for the next four years with his mother and four sisters to support the family and ended his formal education. When he was thirteen, he left home and went to work in a Houston restaurant. Finding his inability to speak English held him back, he enrolled in a night school course and then studied on his own. With great determination to succeed, he saved his money and then borrowed additional funds to start his own restaurant. By 1961 he had four restaurants in Houston and nearby Beaumont.

Meanwhile, Félix Tijerina was also active in community affairs, serving on a number of local boards. In 1956, as president of the local League of United Latin American Citizens (LULAC) group, he tried in vain to persuade the State Board of Education to initiate a preschool program to teach English to Spanish-speaking students. He then started, at his own expense, the first of what came to be known as the Little Schools of the Four Hundred (basic vocabulary words). With the help of financing from businessmen and LULAC the program had been expanded to ten schools by 1961 when its success led the State Education Department to take it over and greatly expand it.

FURTHER READING: Harold J. Alford, *The Proud Peoples: The Heritage and Culture of Spanish-Speaking Peoples in the United States*, New York: David McKay Co., 1972.

TIJERINA, REIES LOPEZ (1926–   ), leader, activist. Born 21 September 1926 near Falls City southeast of San Antonio, Texas, into a large and poor Tejano sharecropper family, Reies Tijerina grew up in the Great Depression years doing stoop labor in the fields. When the Tijerinas went migrant, the family followed the crops to Michigan, Colorado, and Wyoming and in winter scraped together a living in San Antonio. Altogether Reies's meager education was pieced together in about twenty rural schoolhouses.

Greatly influenced in his preschool years by his mother's religiosity, Tijerina later became a serious student of the Bible and joined the Assembly of God church. At eighteen he entered its Bible Institute at Ysleta, Texas. Here he was seen as a sincere, intense, but not always orthodox student who stood out because of his inspirational fire. After three years of Bible studies he left the school, married, and hit the evangelical circuit along the border. For the next decade he was an itinerant preacher. By 1950 the Church of God had revoked his ministerial credentials, but he continued his preaching, now as a nondenominational minister. In 1955 he established a short-lived (because of local hostility and harassment) cooperative settlement of seventeen Mexican American families in Arizona near Eloy, called Valle de la Paz (Valley of Peace).

During the late 1950s Tijerina began to develop an interest in southwestern Spanish and Mexican land grants and gradually became convinced that all the problems of Mexican Americans could be traced back to loss of their lands. In 1958 and 1959 he spent time in Mexico studying the history of land grants and trying to interest the Mexican government in the issue. By 1960 he had moved from Arizona with his followers to Albuquerque, where he quietly began to develop his land grant movement. For the next few years he continued to study and research land grant history, and in February 1963, with his five brothers and a few dozen followers, he created the Alianza Federal de Mercedes (Federal Alliance of Grants), with the goal of returning pueblo common lands to the heirs of original grantees.

Quiet no longer, Reies Tijerina then began an evangelistic stumping of northwestern New Mexico to win converts to his land grant views. He also solicited political recognition and support. By mid–1966 he claimed twenty thousand followers and led a group of them on a sixty-mile march from Albuquerque to the capitol at Santa Fe, where they made their demands on Governor Jack Campbell. In October he also headed an occupation of part of Kit Carson National Forest, which he declared to be the Republic of Rio Chama. This act led to his arraignment on federal charges; violence, arson, and vandalism against Anglos mounted. Fearing arrest, Tijerina stepped down as head of the Alianza and dissolved it in mid–1967, but then reorganized it immediately as the Alianza Federal de Pueblos Libres (Federal Alliance of Free Towns).

On 5 June 1967 the arrest of Alianza members led to a dramatic confrontation at the Tierra Amarilla courthouse when an attempt was made to make a citizen's arrest of the district attorney, Alfonso Sánchez. In the melee a policeman and a jailer were wounded. After a massive manhunt Tijerina was arrested and charged with numerous offenses in connection with the raid. Already under indictment for his part in the 1966 Kit Carson National Forest incident, he was found guilty (of assault) in November in the state courts, but appealed his conviction.

Reies Tijerina now branched out from New Mexico in his activities. His attendance at the National Conference for New Politics in Chicago was followed in mid–1968 by a leading role in the Poor People's March on Washington, D.C., and then by his candidacy for governor of New Mexico. He was disqualified as a candidate because of his felony conviction.

In mid-December 1968 Tijerina's trial on federal charges stemming from the courthouse raid ended in acquittal; however, the following February his earlier conviction was upheld (and again appealed). During June 1969 he had a confrontation with Forest Service officers that led to a three-year federal prison sentence. That fall the U.S. Supreme Court rejected his earlier appeal, and in October Tijerina began serving his federal sentence. His trial on state charges stemming from the courthouse raid was now held and in January 1970 resulted in his receiving two state prison terms of one-to-five and two-to-ten years, to run concurrently. On 27 July 1971 Tijerina was released from prison on five-year parole with the condition that he hold no office in the Alianza, a condition he accepted.

At the El Paso Raza Unida convention in September 1972 Reies Tijerina acted as a moderating influence and two months later took a similar restrained stance at a national Chicano Congress on Land and Cultural Reform, which he organized. When his five-year parole ended, Tijerina resumed presidency of the

Alianza. However, Tijerina, no longer a confrontational leader after the mid–1970s, called for brotherhood and devoted much of his time to an attempt to interest the presidents of Mexico in the New Mexican land grant issue on the basis of the Guadalupe Hidalgo Treaty of 1848. Two presidents have listened to his presentations, but no action was followed.

In the mid–1980s, Tijerina turned away from his brotherhood theme and began blaming the Jews for Mexican Americans' problems. At a 6 June 1987 twentieth anniversary celebration of the Tierra Amarilla incident, he accused Jews of being responsible for the loss of Spanish and Mexican land grants and for contemporary discrimination against Hispanos. His audience numbered fewer than 100 persons.

Although Tijerina's plans include some cultural separatism, his dominant theme has always been the recovery for Nuevo Mexicanos of land grants, especially communal grants, lost since 1848. Most Chicano leaders have given at best qualified endorsement of Tijerina and his ideas, but until the mid–1970s he received strong support from older rural Nuevo Mexicanos and young Chicano activists.

FURTHER READING: Patricia B. Blawis, *Tijerina and the Land Grants: Mexican Americans in Struggle for Their Heritage*, New York: International Publishers Co., 1971; Mary Frei, "Coyote Gathering Marks Rio Arriba Courthouse Raid," *Albuquerque Journal* (7 June 1987); Richard Gardner, *Grito, Reies Tijerina and the New Mexico Land Grant War of 1967*, Indianapolis: Bobbs-Merrill Co., 1970; Charles Garrett II, "El Tigre Revisited," *Nuestro* 1:5 (August 1977); John C. Hammerback et al., *A War of Words: Chicano Protest in the 1960s and 1970s*, Westport, Conn.: Greenwood Press, 1985; Miguel Montoya, "Reies López Tijerina: The Man He Created," *La Luz* 1:6 (October 1972) and 1:7 (November 1972); Peter Nabokov, *Tijerina and the Courthouse Raid*, Albuquerque: University of New Mexico Press, 1969; Reies López Tijerina, *Mi lucha por la tierra*, México: Fondo de Cultura Ecónomica, 1978.

TORRES, ESTEBAN E. (1930–   ), ambassador, labor leader, organizer. Esteban Torres was born 27 January 1930 in Miami, Arizona, where his Mexico-born father was employed as a copper miner. When his father was deported in 1936 for union organizing activities, the family moved to East Los Angeles, where young Torres began his education. After graduating from Garfield High School in 1949, he entered the U.S. Army and served in the Corps of Engineers during the Korean conflict. Discharged in 1954, he took a job as an assembly-line welder with the Chrysler Corporation where his union activities ultimately led to his election as chief steward of Local 230 of the United Auto Workers (UAW) seven years later. At the same time he attended evening classes at East Los Angeles College and later at California State University at Los Angeles, receiving his B.A. in education in 1963. For the following two years he served as UAW International Representative, and from 1965 to 1968 he was the union's Inter-American Representative in Washington, D.C., obtaining experience as an organizer in Central and South America.

In 1968 President Walter Reuther of the UAW sent Torres back to Los Angeles to develop a community action program. Out of this came TELACU, The East

Los Angeles Community Union, which grew under Torres's leadership into one of the largest antipoverty agencies in the U.S. He also became politically active. In the elections of 1974 he narrowly lost his bid for Democratic nomination to the U.S. House of Representatives; however, he did return to Washington that year as assistant director of the UAW's International Affairs Department. From this position, which involved foreign policy and liaison with European and Third World countries, he was selected by President Jimmy Carter in 1977 as the U.S. Permanent Representative to UNESCO with ambassadorial rank. At UNESCO he served as vice-president to the 1978 twentieth General Conference and then chaired the Geneva Group, a UNESCO budgetary watchdog organization. In the spring of 1979 President Carter appointed Torres as his special assistant for programs and policies concerning Mexican Americans.

With the advent of the Reagan administration Torres returned to private life, using his graduate studies in economics (University of Maryland, 1965) and in international labor (American University, 1966) to establish a foreign trade firm named International Enterprise and Development Corporation in 1981. In the following year Torres won election to the U.S. House of Representatives and in November 1984 was reelected. In Congress he is a member of the Committee on Small Business and the Committee on Banking, Finance and Urban Affairs and has been active in Latin American and ecological concerns. He is a member of various boards and commissions.

FURTHER READING: Alan Ehrenhalt, ed., *Politics in America*, Washington, D.C.: Congressional Quarterly, 1983; Julio Morán, "Esteban Torres: Our Hot Line to the President," *Nuestro* 4:1 (March 1980).

TREVIÑO, LEE ("BUCK") (1939–   ), golfer. Born 1 December 1939 on the outskirts of Dallas, Texas, Lee Treviño grew up in that city, raised by his mother Juanita and her Mexican-immigrant father. The Treviños lived in a house without utilities but on the edge of a golf course where Lee early developed an interest in the game. By age six he had his own cut-down club and his own two-hole "course." On completing the seventh grade Lee dropped out of school at fourteen to help with family finances by getting work full time helping the greenskeeper. Three years later he enlisted in the U.S. Marines, where he served two two-year hitches.

While playing for the Marine Corps, Treviño first began to take golf seriously, and on his discharge in 1961 obtained a job as a golf pro in a small Dallas club. Four years later he began to compete on the tournament circuit. After an uncertain start he found his stride and in 1967 burst on the national scene by leading all the qualifiers for the U.S. Open. The next year he won the U.S. Open and earned a total of over $125,000 in prize money. By 1971 he was earning nearly a quarter of a million dollars and in that year had the distinction of being the first golfer to win the U.S., Canadian, and British opens in the same year. As a result *Sports Illustrated* designated him 1971 Sportsman of the Year, and

Associated Press named him Male Athlete of the Year. The next year he again won the British Open.

After winning the Mexico Open Tourney in 1976, Lee Treviño was operated on for a herniated disc. His back problem inevitably affected his golf game, but he was soon back in the tournaments, playing in the money. He was inducted into the Texas Golf Hall of Fame in 1978, into the American Golf Hall of Fame in the following year, and into the World Golf Hall of Fame in 1981. Three years later at age forty-five he won the coveted PGA championship, his sixth major title. In October 1985 Treviño, who had become a golf commentator for NBC television, announced his retirement from professional golf. While he waits to qualify for the Senior Tour, he is busy conducting Learn with Lee clinics.

Often a joking, wise-cracking extrovert on the links, Lee Treviño is also a quiet generous philanthropist in private life. He has given a part of his more than $3 million winnings to local charities and also played numerous free exhibition rounds for the benefit of national charities like March of Dimes, children's hospitals, and Multiple Sclerosis. Often he has organized impromptu hot dog and pop parties for crowds of children at tournaments. Treviño's affability and liberality, as well as his golfing skills, helped create a large following of youths and adults affectionately called "Lee's Fleas."

FURTHER READING: *Current Biography*, 1971; Al Martínez, *Rising Voices: Profiles of Hispano-American Lives*, New York: New American Library, 1974.

U

ULIBARRI, SABINE R. (1919–   ), educator, author, poet. Sabine Ulibarrí was born 21 September 1919 in Tierra Amarilla, a tiny town on the Rio Chama in extreme north central New Mexico. He was the eldest of six children in a family that dates back to Spanish colonial days. His father died when he was very young, and he grew up in a cattle- and sheep-raising rural environment, learning the skills of a vaquero. He attended local schools, graduating from Tierra Amarilla High School in 1937 and going on to the University of New Mexico (UNM) for two years. At age nineteen he began teaching in Rio Arriba County schools and continued until 1942, when he entered the U.S. Army Air Force. After three years of service as a gunner in the European Theater he was mustered out with the Distinguished Flying Cross and other decorations.

Returning to New Mexico Ulibarrí completed his A.B. in Spanish in 1947 with the help of the G.I. Bill and two years later received his M.A., also from the University of New Mexico. He then entered the University of California at Los Angeles where for the next nine years he taught and worked to complete his doctoral studies. He also continued to do some teaching at the University of New Mexico. With Ph.D. in hand he returned to New Mexico to teach full time in the Department of Modern and Classical Languages, of which he became long-time chairman. During 1963 and 1964 he directed a National Defense Education Act (NDEA) language institute in Quito, Ecuador, and four years later returned to organize the University of New Mexico's Andean Center there and to direct it for a year. By invitation from the U.S. Embassy in Mexico City he did a lecture tour of Mexico in 1971; he has also lectured in Spain, South America, Central America, and the United States.

Primarily a short story writer, Sabine Ulibarrí is unusual among Mexican American authors in that almost all of his writing has been in Spanish. His first book of short stories, *Tierra Amarilla: Cuentos de Nuevo México*, was based on his childhood experiences and was published in 1964 in Quito; seven years later an English translation was published by the UNM Press. Two books of poetry, *Amor y Ecuador* and *Al cielo se sube a pie*, were published in Madrid in 1966; much of his other poetic work has remained unpublished. Ulibarrí is probably best known for his second collection of short stories based on childhood memories and titled *Mi Abuela Fumaba Puros: Y Otros Cuentos de Tierra Amarilla; My Grandmother Smoked Cigars: And Other Tales of Tierra Amarilla*, a bilingual edition published by Quinto Sol Publications in 1977. He has also written textbooks, scholarly works, and philosophical essays. In addition to his military decorations Ulibarrí has been honored in Ecuador by being named Distinguished Citizen of Quito (1964) and in the U.S. by being elected president of the American Association of Teachers of Spanish and Portuguese (1969).

FURTHER READING: Harold J. Alford, *The Proud Peoples*, New York: David McKay Co., 1972; Julio A. Martínez and Francisco A. Lomelí, eds., *Chicano Literature: A Reference Guide*, Westport, Conn.: Greenwood Press, 1985; Charles Tatum, *Chicano Literature*, Boston: Twayne Publishers, 1982.

UNZUETA, MANUEL (1949–   ), artist, muralist. Manuel Unzueta was born in Mexico and grew up in the border city of Juárez across from El Paso, Texas. Living in a bicultural environment, from childhood on he showed an interest in art and music and was playing in a local band at age eleven. Three years later he came to Santa Barbara, California, where, after undergoing some cultural trauma, he devoted himself in high school to music and the arts. By the time of his graduation toward the end of the 1960s he was part of a hard rock band and had also become deeply involved in the Chicano Movement. In 1970 he entered Santa Barbara City College and then was awarded a summer scholarship to study art in Europe. The experience had great impact on the young artist, and on his return his painting interests switched from landscapes to social themes. Manuel traveled to Mexico the following year and for the first time became directly impressed by the works of the great Mexican muralists.

Upon his return from Mexico Manuel Unzueta undertook to paint a mural in the Santa Barbara Chicano Community Center—the first of four he did in the next three years. Since 1970 he has painted more than twenty murals in California, the Southwest, and Mexico and has come to be considered one of the top muralists in America. In 1970 Unzueta, whose artistic production has been enormous, had his first one-man show in Los Angeles. Since then he has exhibited in various California centers, in New York, El Paso, and Mexico. In 1975 he earned his master's degree in Mexican/Chicano Art at the University of California Santa Barbara (UCSB), where he teaches. He also teaches at Santa Barbara City College and is a cultural facilitator for the college's Educational Opportunities program. Unzueta was given the Distinguished Achievement in the Arts award by the UCSB alumni association in 1982 and in the following year was nominated "An Outstanding Young Man in America" by the National Junior Chambers of Commerce.

FURTHER READING: William Lewis, "Mexico & U.S. Influence Muralist's Work," *Nuestro* 8:10 (December 1984).

URISTA, ALBERTO. See ALURISTA.

URREA, TERESA (1873–1906), mystic, *curandera*. Teresa Urrea was born 15 October 1873 on Rancho Santana north of Ocoroni in the state of Sinaloa, Mexico, the illegitimate daughter of Tomás Urrea and an Indian mother, Cayetana Chávez. When she was seven, the entire Santana ranch personnel moved to Cabora, apparently for political reasons. She was raised by her mother and an aunt in nearby Aquihuiquichi, and about 1888 she moved to her father's home at Cabora when her mother left the area. Here she learned the use of herbs in caring for the sick and in 1889 experienced some sort of trauma which left her in a catatonic state for a time. After three months of recovery she began to experience trances and believed she had been charged by the Virgin Mary to cure people. By 1891 a stream of devotees were coming to Cabora as her fame as a *curandera* as well as reports of miracles spread. She soon had a large following, especially among the Yaqui and Mayo Indians—which aroused both government and church concerns.

A series of revolts by Mayo and Yaqui groups who called themselves Teresistas caused the Mexican government of Porfirio Díaz to exile Teresa Urrea in mid-1892. She arrived in Nogales, Arizona, in July and immediately began ministering to the sick and the poor. She lived with her father first at Nogales and then at El Paso, but kidnap threats and continued harassment from the Mexican government forced the family to move away from the border to Clifton, Arizona.

Already famed in Mexico as the "santa de Cabora" because of her cures, Teresa quickly became the center of a southwestern cult whose members believed she had preternatural power to cure both physical and mental illnesses. In 1900 she was persuaded to become part of a medical company through which her skills would be made available to people all over the United States. Four years later, disillusioned with the commercialism of the organizers of the company, Teresa dissolved her contract and went back to Clifton to live. During this time she also seems to have undergone a personality change; however, she continued to minister to the needs of the sick and distressed. On 11 January 1906 she died of pulmonary tuberculosis.

FURTHER READING: Mario Gill, "Teresa Urrea," *Historia Mexicana* 6 (April–June 1957); William C. Holden, *Teresita*, Owings Mills, Md.: Stemmer House, 1978; Frank B. Putnam, "Teresa Urrea, 'the Saint of Cabora,' " *Southern California Quarterly* 45 (September 1963); Richard Rodríguez and Gloria C. Rodríguez, "Teresa Urrea: Her Life as it Affected the Mexican–U.S. Frontier," *El Grito: Journal of Contemporary Mexican American Thought* 5 (Summer 1972).

V

VALDES, DANIEL T. (1918–), publisher, professor. Daniel Valdés was born 14 May 1918 in south central Colorado at Alamosa, the county seat of Alamosa County, and grew up there. After his graduation from Alamosa High School he entered Adams State College (at Alamosa) and received his A.B. at the beginning of World War II. During the war years he worked as an economist for the National War Labor Board. In the immediate postwar era, from 1947 to 1949, he was attaché at several U.S. embassies in Latin America. For the next five years he was employed by the Presidential Fact Finding Board, Railways & Airlines. In 1954 he was appointed executive director of the Colorado Welfare Conference, a position he left six years later to enter a doctoral program in sociology at University of Colorado (Boulder). He received his Ph.D. in 1964.

In 1963 Daniel Valdés began his teaching career at Metropolitan State College (now University) in Denver and by the early 1970s was professor of sociology and chairman of the Division of Behavioral Sciences. In 1972 he was the principal founder of the important Hispanic journal, *La Luz*, which he edited and published until his resignation in 1979. He was also editor of *Who's Who in Colorado* (1958) and the author of *A Political History of New Mexico* (1960, revised edition in 1971). He coauthored *Ethnic Labels in Majority—Minority Relations* (1974) and two years later coedited *Who's Who Among Hispanic Americans, 1976 Bicentennial Edition*. Valdés has been active in educational, political, and professional organizations. Among his honors are the Distinguished Service Award from the Anti-Defamation League of B'nai B'rith and the Distinguished Service Medal from the League of United Latin American Citizens.

FURTHER READING: Julio A. Martínez, *Chicano Scholars and Writers: A Bio-Bibliographical Directory*, Metuchen, N.J.: The Scarecrow Press, 1979; Theodore Wood, *Chicanos y Chicanas Prominentes*, Menlo Park, Calif.: Educational Consortium of America, 1974.

VALDEZ, ABERLARDO LOPEZ (1942–), lawyer, ambassador, engineer. Abelardo Valdez was born during World War II in Floresville, Texas, a small town southeast of San Antonio. He received his early education in various towns on the migrant agriculture circuit until he was fourteen, when his father became a sharecropper near Floresville, so that Abelardo could complete his four years of high school in one place. After graduating with honors from the Floresville high school, he attended Texas A & M University, partly on an American G.I. Forum academic scholarship, and received his B.S. in civil engineering and his military commission there in 1965. Upon graduation he served in the U.S. Army for two years, most of that time as military aide to President Lyndon B. Johnson. Subsequently he studied law at Baylor Law School and the Hague Academy of International Law, receiving his J.D. from Baylor in 1970. That same year he entered Harvard Law School on a MALDEF fellowship in international law and in 1974 he was awarded his LL.M. During this period he acted successively as attorney for three government agencies and finally became a partner in a Washington, D.C., law firm which he helped organize.

In April 1977 Valdez left private practice to accept appointment in the Agency for International Development as chief officer for economic assistance programs in Latin America and the Caribbean. Twice named special ambassador to represent the United States at Latin American presidential inaugurations, he was appointed by President Jimmy Carter two years later as chief of protocol for the White House with ambassadorial rank. With the advent of the Reagan administration he returned to private practice, becoming a partner in the large firm of Finley, Kumble, Wagner, Heine, Underberg, Manley & Casey, in Washington, D.C. He has been admitted to the practice of law in Texas, in Washington, D.C., and before the U.S. Supreme Court.

Ambassador Valdez is the author of a dozen articles dealing with various aspects of international law, mostly concerning Latin American economic and agrarian issues. He has been a visiting professor at Harvard University, Texas A & M University, and Trinity University in San Antonio and in 1986 was a visiting Woodrow Wilson fellow at Santa Clara University in California. In addition he serves on numerous professional and civic boards, councils, associations, and committees. In 1984 he was decorated by the government of Spain with the prestigious Order of Isabel la Católica.

FURTHER READING: "Carter Names Hispanics to Navy, Protocol Posts," *National IMAGE Inc. Newsletter* 1:1 (Fall 1979).

VALDEZ, LUIS M. (1940–   ), dramatist, political activist. Luis Valdez was born in Delano, California, on 26 June 1940, second eldest in a family of ten children of a migrant farm worker family. Because the family followed the various California harvests, he attended schools throughout the great central valley and graduated from James Lick High School in San Jose, where the family had finally settled out of the harvest circuit. He then entered San Jose State College (today University) in 1960 on a scholarship, majoring in mathematics and English. Here his long-time interest in drama was nurtured, and he wrote his first full-length play, *The Shrunken Head of Pancho Villa*, which the Drama Department at San Jose State produced in 1963.

After graduating in 1964 with a B.A. in English, Luis Valdez further developed his theatrical skills by working with the San Francisco Mime Troupe for several months and in October 1965 joined César Chávez* in Delano, where he created El Teatro Campesino, the farm workers' theater. Without scripts, props, or stage he used the theater to educate both the Delano grape strikers and the general public. After two years with the farm workers' union and a national fund raising tour, in 1967 Valdez broadened his focus by setting up an independent cultural center in Del Rey, California. In 1969 he again moved the Teatro (and cultural center) to Fresno, exposing its message to a greater number of people, Chicano and Anglo.

In Fresno Luis Valdez produced a film entitled *I am Joaquín*, which won several awards, published a new work, *Actos*, and created a national organization of Chicano theater groups throughout the Southwest called Tenaz. During this time he also taught at Fresno State College, helped to shape the newly created La Raza Studies program there from 1968 to 1970. He taught at the University of California at Berkeley and at U.C. Santa Cruz from 1971 to 1974.

In 1969 Luis Valdez took his theater to the Theatre des Nations, an international festival at Nancy in northeastern France, and two years later he traveled to the Philippines as one of three United States representatives to the first Third World Theater Conference. In the same year the Teatro made its final move—to San Juan Bautista, California, a mission town ninety miles south of San Francisco. Here at El Centro Campesino Cultural Valdez turned the organization into a professional production company, playing New York City and touring Europe and Mexico. In 1978 Valdez wrote and produced *Zoot Suit*, based on the Los Angeles Sleepy Lagoon case of 1942. The play won both popular acceptance and critical acclaim, becoming the first work written and produced by a Mexican American to play Broadway. A subsequent film version was less successful at the box office but enabled Valdez to buy a warehouse-theater in San Juan Bautista. During 1984–1985 Valdez wrote a new play *I Don't Have to Show You No Stinking Badges*, following hard on his *Corridos*, which was a California road show success the year before. *Corridos* will be shown as a special on PBS in the fall 1987, featuring Linda Ronstadt.* He is also scheduled to direct a film, *Viejo Gringo*, for which he wrote the script based on a novel about Ambrose Bierce by the prominent Mexican writer Carlos Fuentes.

Luis Valdez has been the recipient of a number of honors. His company has toured Europe six times and won three Los Angeles Drama Critics' Circle awards as well as an Emmy. In 1983 President Reagan's Committee on Arts and Humanities honored him along with James Michener, and in the following year he was selected to be a Regents' lecturer in theater at the University of California, Irvine. He also serves on various national advisory boards.

FURTHER READING: Robert Hurwitt, ''The Evolutionary/Revolutionary Luis Valdez,'' *Image* (5 January 1986); Sergio Muñoz, ''Encuentro con Luis Valdez,'' Sunday

Supplement to *La Opinión*, Los Angeles (13 December 1981); Elizabeth Venant, "Valdez—A Life in the River of Humanity," Los Angeles *Times Calendar* (2 February 1986).

VALDEZ, PHIL (1946–1967), military hero. Filiberto Valdez, son of Mr. and Mrs. Carlos Valdez, grew up in the Rio Grande river towns of Dixon and Española in northern New Mexico. At nineteen he enlisted in the U.S. Navy and trained as a hospital corpsman for the Vietnam conflict. On 29 January 1967 he was killed near Danang. In a helicopter airlift he repeatedly exposed himself to enemy fire in order to rescue two wounded U.S. Marines. Credited with saving their lives, Valdez was posthumously awarded the Navy Cross, the second-highest U.S. naval decoration. On 27 July 1974 the United States Navy named a 4,200-ton anti-submarine destroyer escort (later designated a frigate) the U.S.S. *Valdez* in honor of Petty Officer Filiberto Valdez.

FURTHER READING: "Dean M. Martínez Serves on the USS Valdez," *La Luz* 4:5 (September–October 1975); "Hispanic War Hero Honored," *Hoy* 3:7 (August 1974).

VALLEJO, MARIANO GUADALUPE (1808–1890), civil, political, and military leader, rancher. Born 7 July 1808 into the upper-class Californio family of Ignacio and María Antonia (Lugo) Vallejo at Monterey, the capital of Alta California, Mariano Vallejo grew up during the sometimes exciting years of the Mexican revolution for independence. As a youngster his interest in the world outside of California was awakened by the privateering raid of the French-Argentine raider Hypolite Bouchard in 1818 and by his clerking in the store of English trader William Hartnell. His practical training in the trades and skills so necessary on the frontier was accompanied by formal education, first with the local schoolmaster and later under the personal supervision of Governor Pablo Vicente Solá. At fifteen he became a cadet at the Monterey presidio; by the time he reached twenty-one he commanded a force that put down an Indian rebellion at Misión San José and two years later he was named *comandante* of the San Francisco presidio.

Meanwhile, in 1827 Vallejo was elected to the territorial legislature and seven years later was named a delegate to the congress in Mexico City but did not serve. In the Mexican period (1821–1848) he quickly became the outstanding northern Californio leader and in 1833 was appointed military commander of the entire northern part of the territory by Governor José Figueroa. He was also named administrator of missions San Francisco Solano and San Rafael Arcángel during secularization. He was instructed to forestall the Russians coming down the coast from Alaska, which led to his founding settlements at Santa Rosa, Petaluma, and Sonoma. In his various capacities he acquired several sizable land grants.

During the 1830s and early 1840s Mariano Vallejo trod cautiously in the shifting sands of Mexican California politics and gradually split with his nephew, Governor Juan Bautista Alvarado. While warning the Mexican government of imminent foreign threat, more and more he came to the conclusion that an American takeover would be best for California. Despite his friendly feelings for Americans, when the Bear Flag Revolt broke out in 1846, Vallejo was seized and jailed at Sutter's Fort for two months. Under American rule he was named to the legislative council and later was appointed by Colonel Stephen Kearny as Indian agent in the north. In September 1849 he was one of eight Californios who shared in the writing of the state's first constitution and then was elected to the first state senate.

In the early 1850s Vallejo was one of the first Californios to file for validation of his land grants. His joy at confirmation in 1855 was short-lived when squatters and speculators appealed this favorable decision all the way to the U.S. Supreme Court, which invalidated his title to the large Soscol land grant. The expenses involved in defense of his property caused the family fortunes to slump severely as did his failed efforts to have the state capital located at Vallejo. When he died on 18 January 1890, he owned only 280 acres of his once immense holdings.

Highly respected, Mariano Vallejo devoted his twilight years to writing a history of his native state; to improving the quality of the fruits, especially grapes, that he grew on his rancho; to promoting his idea of a California–Mexico City railroad, to fulfilling civic duties; and to enjoying his children, grandchildren, and friends.

FURTHER READING: Rockwell D. Hunt, *California's Stately Hall of Fame*, Caldwell, Idaho: Caxton Publishers, 1950; Myrtle M. McKittick, *Vallejo, Son of California*, Portland: Binford & Mort, 1944; Leonard Pitt, *The Decline of the Californios*, Berkeley: University of California Press, 1970.

VASQUEZ, RICHARD (1928–   ), author, journalist. Richard Vásquez was born into a family of ten children on 11 June 1928 in Southgate, a southeastern suburb of Los Angeles. He grew up in the greater Los Angeles area, mostly in Pasadena, and upon completion of high school joined the U.S. Navy in the last months of World War II. After musterirng out of the navy, over the years he developed a small but successful construction company. At the end of the 1950s he began to write a newspaper column; this led to a job as reporter, first for the *Santa Monica Independent* and in 1960 for the *San Gabriel Valley Daily Tribune*. During the 1965–1970 period he worked at various jobs and in the latter year was hired by the *Los Angeles Times* as a feature writer and correspondent more or less replacing Rubén Salazar.* He also taught a course in literary creativity at the local junior college.

During this time Vásquez wrote two novels: *Chicano*, published in 1970, and *The Giant Killer*, which came out in 1978. Four years later a third novel, *Another Land*, was published. In addition to these three works he has also written hundreds of journalistic articles, many of them literary reviews, but many others of sufficient merit to be reprinted in collections and professional journals.

Vásquez's best-known work is his first novel about immigrant family experience in the United States, *Chicano*. Although it has been criticized by some as stereotyping and failing to present the cultural complexity of Chicanos, other critics have called it the second Mexican American novel, after José Antonio Villarreal's* *Pocho*. Some have pointed out its value as a historical and sociological document on the process of Mexican acculturation in the United States.

Among his notable achievements Richard Vásquez received the Sigma Delta Chi Award in 1963 for the best newspaper story of the year as the result of investigative reporting on municipal corruption.

FURTHER READING: Rafael F. Grajeda, "José Antonio Villarreal and Richard Vásquez: The Novelist Against Himself," in Francisco Jiménez, ed., *The Identification and Analysis of Chicano Literature*, New York: Bilingual Press/Editorial Bilingüe, 1979; Julio A. Martínez and Francisco A. Lomelí, eds. *Chicano Literature: A Reference Guide*, Westport, Conn.: Greenwood Press, 1985; Charles Tatum, *Chicano Literature*, Boston: Twayne Publishers, 1982.

VASQUEZ, TIBURCIO (1835–1875), bandit, activist. Tiburcio Vásquez was born into a respected Californio family in Monterey on 11 August 1835. One of six children, he received at least an elementary education and became fluent in both English and Spanish.

Tiburcio Vásquez had his first brush with the law in 1852 when a fight broke out at a dance he was attending in Monterey and an Anglo constable was killed. Tiburcio fled into the nearby mountains to avoid capture and lynching—the fate of one companion who was caught. Forced into a life outside the law, he soon became a notorious bandit to Anglos. On the other hand he was seen by many poorer Californios as an avenger of their treatment by Anglo society, and they often supplied him with information, shelter, and support.

Arrested in Los Angeles County in 1857 for horse stealing, Vásquez was sentenced to five years in San Quentin prison; however, during a prison break two years later he escaped. After a few months he was recaptured and returned to serve his full sentence. Upon release from prison he seems to have worked as a professional gambler at the California mercury mining center of New Almadén for a while; but in 1867, after several accusations, he was arrested on cattle rustling charges and served three more years in San Quentin. Out of prison, he organized a small band and began a series of daring payroll holdups and stage robberies. In mid–1873 the governor of California offered a reward for Vásquez's capture, $2,000 dead or $3,000 alive. Despite a massive manhunt by local lawmen and citizens' posses, he eluded capture.

Tiburcio Vásquez's downfall came about not because of the reward, but because of his amorous attentions to the wife of one of his men, Abdón Leiva. The latter informed the Los Angeles County sheriff of the gang's various hideouts, and in May 1874 Vásquez was finally captured near La Brea. After recovering from wounds received during his capture, he was transferred to San Jose and his trial was set for January 1875. In jail Vásquez, a handsome man, continued the role of bandit-hero. He had many visitors, mostly women, posed for photographs, and talked to newsmen, justifying his life of crime as a defense of Mexican American rights against Anglo injustice.

Vásquez's trial, which began on 5 January, lasted only four days and the jury was out only two hours. Both Abdón Leiva and his wife, whom Vásquez had subsequently abandoned, testified against him. He was found guilty of murder, and Governor Romualdo Pacheco and the state Supreme Court refused to intervene in the case despite many pleas. On March 19 Vásquez was hanged at the San Jose courthouse and buried the next day at nearby Santa Clara Catholic Cemetery.

FURTHER READING: Robert Greenwood, *The California Outlaw: Tiburcio Vásquez*, New York: Arno Press, 1960; Ernest May, "Tiburcio Vásquez," *Historical Society of Southern California Quarterly* 29 (1947); Eugene T. Sawyer, *The Life and Career of Tibercio Vásquez*, Oakland, Calif.: Biobooks, 1944; Ben C. Truman, *Life, Adventures and Capture of Tiburcio Vásquez, the Great California Bandit and Murderer*, Los Angeles: Los Angeles Star Office, 1874.

VELASCO, CARLOS I. (1837–1914), journalist, ethnic leader, lawyer. Carlos Velasco was born on 30 June 1837 into a prominent and well-to-do family of Hermosillo, capital of the Mexican state of Sonora. He grew up in this northern frontier town and upon completion of his early education studied for law and set up private practice. A promising young lawyer, he was appointed superior court judge of the Altar district in northern Sonora in 1857 and two years later was elected to the state legislature. As a result of his support of the Liberal Sonoran leader, Ignacio Pesqueira, he was forced to cross the northern border into Arizona in 1865 when the former was defeated by the French-Conservative allied forces.

Although his fellow exiles returned during the following year, Valasco remained in Arizona and moved to Tucson, where he worked as a clerk in a general store. When the political situation in Mexico turned more favorable and more stable at the beginning of the 1870s, Velasco returned to Sonora with his family. He quickly resumed his political career, serving in the state legislature and in 1874 becoming a member of the Mexican border commission. He also wrote for pro-Pesqueira newspapers in Guaymas, where the family lived. In 1877 the Pesqueira dynasty was overthrown, and he again became a political refugee in Tucson, Arizona.

After a brief return to merchandizing he now turned to journalism and in September 1878 his four-page Spanish-language weekly, *El Fronterizo*, appeared. In *El Fronterizo*, which was to become a daily in the early 1890s and was to survive until his death, he espoused the economic and social improvement of the Spanish-speaking on both sides of the border. As time went on he came to feel that this objective could be achieved by a Positivist society with its twin goals of order and progress. A molder of public opinion, especially among the Mexican population, he militantly defended the Spanish-speaking from Anglo prejudice and mistreatment when Anglo-Mexican relations worsened in the

1880s. He also encouraged greater political participation by Mexican Americans—all of this in *El Fronterizo* and *El Hijo de El Fronterizo* in Phoenix.

In January 1894 Velasco led some forty prominent *Tucsonenses* in founding the Alianza Hispano-Americana and was elected the first president. Velasco saw the society as a defense against Anglo discrimination as well as a mutualist organization. In both goals it seems to have been successful. Anglo hostility decreased measurably by the end of the century, while the Alianza expanded to a sizable regional organization. At the beginning of the 1900s Velasco's support of President Porfirio Díaz and his law and order caused him to fall out with a majority of the *aliancistas*. He became active in the 1907 Sociedad Mutualista Porfirio Díaz and five years later organized a Tucson newspaper also called *El Hijo de El Fronterizo*, to defend the exiled dictator. When Velasco died on 6 October 1914, he was serving as president of the Sociedad Mutualista Porfirio Díaz. Despite his latter-day estrangement from the majority political feeling among Mexican Americans along the border, Carlos Velasco was a leading voice in the Southwest for more than a quarter of a century.

FURTHER READING: Manuel G. Gonzales, "Carlos I. Velasco," *Journal of Arizona History* 25 (Autumn 1984); James Officer and Adela A. Stewart, *Arizona's Hispanic Perspective*, Tucson: Arizona Academy, 1981; Tomás Serrano Cabo, *Crónicas Alianza Hispano Americana*, Las Cruces, N.M.: La Estrella y Las Cruces Citizen, 1929; Charles L. Sonnichsen, *Tucson: The Life and Times of an American City*, Norman: University of Oklahoma Press, 1982.

VIGIL, DONACIANO (1802–1877), political leader, soldier. Born 6 September 1802 at Santa Fe into a family that had lived on the Nuevo Mexicano frontier since the end of the 1600s, Donaciano Vigil's youth was spent in that provincial capital. Although formal education was lacking on Mexico's northern frontier, Donaciano and his three siblings were tutored by their father, Juan Cristobal, a minor public official who came from a family that appreciated the advantages of education. Throughout his life Donaciano constantly expanded his knowledge by voracious reading and was considered one of the best educated persons in New Mexico during his lifetime.

In 1823 Vigil initiated his military career by joining the Santa Fe presidial company and later gained some renown by participating in numerous campaigns against predatory Indians. Supported by Governor Manuel Armijo,* he began his political career in 1838 with election to the Nuevo México legislature and was appointed the governor's civil-military secretary in the following year. In 1846 when war between Mexico and the United States appeared imminent, Vigil directed much of the Nuevo Mexicano preparation. With Armijo's last-minute withdrawal south of Chihuahua, Vigil and the other military leaders decided not to resist the advancing American forces. General Stephen Kearny and his army took over Santa Fe in August 1846 and set up an American government with Vigil, who enjoyed wide Hispanic and American support, as territorial secretary.

When Governor Charles Bent was assassinated in the Taos revolt of January 1847, Donaciano Vigil became acting governor and in December was formally appointed civil governor. As a result of the territorial convention of 1848 he stepped down from the governorship and was reappointed territorial secretary. After New Mexico became an official territory by the Compromise of 1850, he continued to serve in both the legislative assembly (1852) and the territorial council (1857, 1858, 1862, 1863). In the mid–1850s Vigil acquired a claim to two ranches on the Pecos River and in 1855 moved his family there from Santa Fe. Although he was a Democrat politically in the early 1850s, he then eschewed partisan politics and was noted during the Civil War as a staunch, uncompromising Union supporter. In his late 1860s his last governmental position was that of San Miguel County school director. Vigil died at the home of his son Epifanio in Santa Fe at age seventy-five, respected by Anglos and Hispanos alike, and was buried with highest honors.

With his abiding faith in an educated and democratic electorate, Donaciano Vigil provided moderate and wise leadership that helped accomplish New Mexico's transition from Mexican to United States territory with minimal difficulties.

FURTHER READING: Stanley Francis Crocchiola, *Giant in Lilliput: The Story of Donaciano Vigil*, Pampa, Tex.: Pampa Print Shop, 1963; G. Emlen Hall, "Giant Before the Surveyor-General: The Land Career of Donaciano Vigil," *Journal of the West* 19:3 (July 1980); W. G. Ritch, "Governor Donaciano Vigil," Santa Fe *Weekly New Mexican* (28 August 1877); David J. Weber, ed., *Arms, Indians, and the Mismanagement of New Mexico: Donaciano Vigil, 1846*, El Paso: The University of Texas, Texas Western Press, 1986.

VIGIL, RALPH H. (1932–   ), professor. Born in the southern Colorado county of Las Animas on 6 September 1932, Ralph Vigil grew up and received his early education there. Upon graduation from Trinidad High School during the Korean conflict he entered the U.S. Air Force, serving from 1951 to 1955. Out of the service, he entered Pacific Lutheran University in Tacoma, Washington, and graduated *cum laude* in 1958. After his A.B. Vigil continued his graduate history studies at the University of New Mexico, taking time out from 1962 to 1964 to work for the U.S. Treasury Department. He received his M.A. in 1964 and his Ph.D. five years later.

Ralph Vigil's first full-time teaching position was at Washburn University in Topeka, Kansas, 1965 to 1969. Then after a two-year teaching stint at Fresno State College (now University) in California and a one-year appointment at the University of Texas at El Paso, he went to the University of Nebraska-Lincoln as associate professor of history and director of the Institute for Ethnic Studies. He currently is associate professor of history at this institution.

Ralph Vigil has been extremely active in writing articles, mostly on the Southwest and Borderlands, published in the *New Mexico Historical Review*, *The Americas*, and other journals. He is also the author of essays appearing in the *Encyclopedia of Latin America* (1974) and *Encyclopedia of Southern History* (1979). He was an associate editor of and wrote three chapters in the *Borderlands Sourcebook: A Guide to the Literature on Northern Mexico and the American Southwest* (1983). He has presented papers and acted as chairman, moderator, and commentator at numerous professional conferences. His book, *Alonzo de Zorita, Royal Judge and Christian Humanists, 1512–1585*, is scheduled for publication by the University of Oklahoma Press in late fall 1987.

Ralph Vigil has received a number of commendations for his historical writing and for his contributions to La Raza. From 1967 to 1968 he was a Fulbright scholar to Spain, and in the following year the American G.I. Forum of Nebraska awarded him a Certificate of Merit for his services to the Latino community.

FURTHER READING: Félix D. Almaraz, Jr., and M. O. Almaraz, *Reading Exercises on Mexican Americans*, Elizabethtown, Pa.: Continental Press, 1977.

VILLALPANDO, CATALINA V. (1940–   ), public official, business-woman. Born 1 April 1940 in the small Texas town of San Marcos, midway between San Antonio and Austin, Cathi Villalpando is the eldest of six children in the close-knit family of Agustín and Guadalupe Villapando. Although her Mexico-born father, a hardware store clerk, completed only the sixth grade, he encouraged his children to seek the benefits of education. Cathi's early education was in the local parochial school, and she then continued on at the San Marcos High School. After graduating from high school, she worked in a jewelry store and later did secretarial work at Southwest Texas State College in San Marcos while continuing her education. Although she does not have a degree, she has taken course work at five colleges and universities including Southern Methodist.

While studying at Austin College of Business Cathi Villalpando accepted part-time work at local Republican headquarters and as a result of this experience in 1969 switched her allegiance from the Democratic to the Republican party, in which she became a dedicated worker. In that same year she became an assistant to the regional director of the Community Services Administration, the beginning of a variety of rewarding federal positions involving minorities and small businesses. In 1979 she went private, organizing V.P. Promotions, a firm with a federal contract to provide assistance to minority-owned savings and loan associations. At the same time she became a vice president of Mid-South Oil Company of Dallas.

During the 1980 elections, Villalpando jumped into the political fire statewide, first in the George Bush for President campaign and then for the Reagan-Bush ticket. With the Republican victory this effort led to short-term Washington employment in 1980–1981 during the Reagan inauguration and transition. She then returned to Texas and the business world, becoming a senior vice-president of Communications International, based in Atlanta. In 1983, at the recommendation of Texas senator John Tower, she was appointed as special assistant to President Ronald Reagan, responsible for Hispanic affairs in the

Public Liaison office. This important communications position she continues to hold.

Cathi Villalpando has been the recipient of special achievement awards from several U.S. government agencies and has been honored by appointment to various committees and boards including the U.S. commission on Civil Rights and by election to civic offices such as vice-president of the Republican National Hispanic Assembly of Texas.

FURTHER READING: Stephen Goode, "Cathi Villalpando, Special Assistant to the President," *Nuestro* 9:1 (January–February 1985); *The Washington Times* (15 September 1983).

VILLANUEVA, DANIEL (1937–   ), football player, businessman. Born in a two-room adobe house at Tucumcari in eastern New Mexico, Danny Villanueva was ninth of eleven children born to Pilar and Primitivo Villanueva, migrant missionary workers. While he was small, the family moved, first to Arizona and then to the Imperial Valley in southern California. Here he worked the harvest circuit and attended public grade and high schools, where he showed great interest in sports. He attended Reedley (Junior) College in California and graduated from New Mexico State University in Las Cruces, majoring in English, editing the school newspaper, working part time on the local newspaper, and playing football.

After college he turned professional and from 1960 to 1964 was a field goal kicker for the Los Angeles Rams. Traded to the Dallas Cowboys in the following football season, he punted for them for three seasons and then retired from professional football to accept a job as news director of Spanish-language station KMEX-TV in Los Angeles. In 1969 he was promoted to station manager and two years later became general manager and vice-president. As director of the station's community relations he became deeply involved in problems of the barrio for which he often acted as spokesman. By 1972 he had organized a Spanish-language television network called Spanish International Network-West (SIN-West) of which he was also vice-president and general manager. As president of KMEX, Villanueva continued his policy of social involvement; in 1984 he raised $240,000 for the victims of a disastrous gas explosion in Mexico City and in the following year led in organizing a telethon which raised $5 million for Mexico City earthquake victims.

Because of his social commitment Danny Villanueva is a member of a dozen boards and committees. He has served on the California State Recreational Commission and the State Park and Recreation Commission and is deeply involved in speaking schedules for scholarship fund raising and barrio youth programs. In 1984 he volunteered to be boxing commissioner for the Los Angeles summer olympics, taking leave of absence from KMEX-TV to do so. As a result of his varied community involvement he has received numerous awards.

FURTHER READING: Gary Libman, "He Gets His Kicks Serving Latino Community," *Los Angeles Times* (29 September 1985); Pauline Márquez, "Doing What Comes

Naturally,'' *Caminos* 5:7 (July–August 1984); Al Martínez, *Rising Voices: Profiles of Hispano-American Lives*, New York: New American Library, 1974.

VILLANUEVA, TINO (1941–   ), poet, short story writer, critic. Born 11 December 1941 in the small Texas town of San Marcos halfway between San Antonio and Austin, Tino Villanueva is the only child of Mexican immigrant parents, Leonor (Ríos) and Lino Villanueva. During the post–World War II years they traveled the migrant harvest circuit from central Texas, and Tino grew up having both the urban experience of selling newspapers and the agricultural harvesting experience. In high school he was interested mainly in sports and upon graduation in 1960 went to work in a furniture factory. Drafted into the U.S. Army, he spent the years from 1964 to 1966 in the Panama Canal Zone. Upon being mustered out of the service, he entered Southwest Texas State University at San Marcos and earned his B.A. in 1969. Two years later, after a summer at the University of Salamanca in Spain, he received his M.A. in Romance languages from the State University of New York at Buffalo and then initiated a Ph.D. program at Boston University while teaching Spanish at Wellesley College.

Tino Villanueva began writing poetry in the mid–1960s, greatly influenced by Dylan Thomas. In 1972 he published a collection of his poems with the title *Hay Otra Voz Poems*. It met with a warm reception from readers, fellow poets, and the critics. His next publication was *Chicanos: Antología histórica y literaria*, published in 1980 by Fondo de Cultura Económica, Mexico City; a shortened version was published five years later by Cultura Sep in Mexico. In 1984 he published *Shaking Off the Dark*, a book of poems. He has also been a contributor to a number of literary collections, including *We Are Chicanos: An Anthology of Mexican-American Literature* (1974). His poems have been published in a wide variety of literary journals. Villanueva is an editor of *Imagine*, an international Chicano poetry journal published in Boston. He is considered one of the finest contemporary Chicano poets.

FURTHER READING: Wolfgang Binder, ed., "Partial Autobiographies: Interviews with Twenty Chicano Poets," *Erlanger Studien*, Band 65/I (1985), Erlangen, Germany: Verlag Palm & Enke Erlangen; Juan Bruce-Novoa, *Chicano Authors: Inquiry by Interview*, Austin: University of Texas Press, 1980; *Contemporary Authors*, vols. 45–48, 1974.

VILLARREAL, CARLOS CASTAÑEDA (1924–   ), engineer, administrator, businessman. Carlos Villarreal was born 9 November 1924 in Brownsville, Texas, and was raised there by two unmarried aunts after the death of his mother. From the time he was in the fourth grade, he worked to help family finances. After high school he attended Texas A & M University until entering the armed services during the latter part of World War II. While in the army he won an appointment to Annapolis and graduated from the U.S. Naval Academy in 1948 with a B.S., followed by a M.S. from the Naval Postgraduate School two years later. During the next six years he commanded several ships, and participated actively in the Korean conflict.

In 1956 Villarreal resigned his navy commission and entered the world of business, working for the first ten years for General Electric Company as a manager in its marine and industrial operations. He then joined the Marquardt Corporation as vice-president in charge of marketing and administration. When Richard Nixon entered the presidency in 1969, Villarreal was appointed head of the Urban Mass Transit Administration, a post he held for the next four years. He then became a member of the U.S. Postal Rate Commission and was its vice-chairman from 1975–1979. After ten years of public service he took over the Washington operations of Wilbur Smith and Associates, an engineering design and construction company. He soon added membership on its board of directors to his vice-presidential duties and in 1984 was named senior vice-president.

Carlos Villarreal has published articles in a number of professional journals and also lectured on his field of specialization. He has been the recipient of various awards and honors, including knighthood in the Military Hospitaller Order of St. John of Jerusalem.

FURTHER READING: Al Martínez, *Rizing Voices: Profiles of Hispano-American Lives*, New York: New American Library, 1974; *Who's Who in America, 1984–1985*, 43rd ed., 1984.

VILLARREAL, JOSE ANTONIO (1924–   ), novelist, teacher. José Villarreal was born 30 July 1924 in Los Angeles, California, where his parents, José and Felícitaz (Ramírez) Villarreal, had come two years earlier after emigrating from Zacatecas, Mexico. His early years were spent with the family following the California harvests. In 1930 the Villarreals settled in the Bay area at Santa Clara, California, where José, who up to this point had lived totally within a Mexican *campesino* culture, entered the first grade and began to learn English. By the third grade he began to write short stories and poems and soon knew that he wanted to be a novelist when he grew up. Just as he finished high school, the United States entered World War II, and he joined the navy in late 1942, serving over three years in the Pacific. After his discharge he entered the University of California at Berkeley where he earned his B.A. in English in 1950. Subsequently he did graduate studies at Berkeley and at the University of California, Los Angeles.

During the 1950s Villarreal worked and traveled throughout the United States, began to write his first novel, came back to college, married, and returned to the Bay area where he went to work for the Stanford Research Institute as an editor and translator. He spent 1960 to 1968 as senior technical editor for Lockheed Aircraft Corporation, followed by three years as a supervisor for technical publications at Ball Brothers Research Corporation in Boulder, Colorado. From that job it was only a short step to teaching English at the University of Colorado, the University of Texas at El Paso, and Santa Clara

University. Meanwhile he put in more time in Mexico free-lancing and writing his novels, short stories, and articles.

In the mid–1970s Villarreal decided to give up his U.S. citizenship and returned to Mexico, where he taught at the Universidad Nacional Autónoma de México, the University of the Americas, and the Preparatoria Americana (in Mexico City). He also has continued to teach at various U.S. institutions, most recently (1985–1986) at California State University, Los Angeles. A confessed idealist and romantic, Villarreal is the author of short stories, poems, and essays but is best known for two novels: *Pocho* and *The Fifth Horseman*. *Pocho* was first published by Doubleday in 1959, long before the Chicano literary renaissance of the 1970s. It is of particular historical significance, since it was the first Chicano novel to be published in the United States by a major American publishing company. Partly autobiographical, *Pocho* is based on Villarreal's youth in the Santa Clara valley in the late 1930s. In 1974 *The Fifth Horseman*, Villarreal's second novel, was also published by Doubleday. This historical novel, a broad epic set in the 1910 Mexican Revolution, ends at the point where *Pocho* begins. The third novel of the trilogy, *Clemente Chacón*, published in 1984, fits in between *The Fifth Horseman* and *Pocho* and has as its theme the price of the immigrant's success in the United States.

FURTHER READING: Juan Bruce-Novoa, *Chicano Authors: Inquiry by Interview*, Austin: University of Texas Press, 1980; Julio A. Martínez and Francisco A. Lomelí, eds., *Chicano Literature: A Reference Guide*, Westport, Conn.: Greenwood Press, 1985.

X _____

XIMENES, VICENTE TREVIÑO (1919–   ), public official, economist, educator. Vicente Ximenes was born in Floresville, Texas, where he grew up working as a farmhand, clerking in a grocery, and attending local public schools. After graduation from Floresville High School he took a job as company clerk in the Civilian Conservation Corps. He then taught elementary school for a year before entering the armed services in 1941. During World War II Ximenes flew some fifty missions as a bombardier with the United States Air Force, earning the Distinguished Flying Cross and the Air Medal.

After his discharge with the rank of major and with seven years of service Ximenes returned to college and received his B.A. and M.A. from the University of New Mexico in 1950 and 1951 respectively. During this time he also was active in establishing a branch of the American G.I. Forum in New Mexico. He was then appointed professor and research economist at the University of New Mexico.

Having worked ten years in academia, in 1961 Vicente Ximenes accepted a State Department position in the Agency for International Development (A.I.D.) at Quito, Ecuador. After four years there (1961 to 1964) he returned to the United States to work in the Office of Economic Opportunity and then was sent to Panama for A.I.D. Early in 1967 President Lyndon Johnson named Ximenes to head the newly created Inter-Agency Committee on Mexican American Affairs, and in mid-year he was appointed to the U.S. Equal Employment Opportunity Commission (E.E.O.C.) for a four-year term. After his E.E.O.C. service he became vice-president of field operations for the National Urban Coalition, and in 1977 he was coordinator of the G.I. Forum national convention. Currently he lives in retirement in Albuquerque, New Mexico.

In addition to his military awards, Vicente Ximenes was national chairman of the American G.I. Forum from 1957 to 1958 and two years later was the recipient of the Forum's national leadership award. That same year he also received the United Nations human rights award.

FURTHER READING: Harold J. Alford, *The Proud Peoples*, New York: David McKay Co., 1972; "Vicente T. Ximenes—Educator, Economist," *La Luz* 6:8 (August 1977).

Y

YZAGUIRRE, RAUL (1939–   ), civil rights leader. Born 22 July 1939 at San Juan in Hidalgo County, south Texas, Raúl Yzaguirre was the first of five children born to Eva (Morín) and Rubén Yzaguirre. The Yzaguirre family was typical of the Texas–Mexico border region, having relatives and strong ties on both sides of the border. Raúl's early years were spent in Brownsville, Texas, but when he was six, he went to live with his maternal grandparents, so that he could attend the San Juan schools. At thirteen he ran away to Corpus Christi to go to work on a deep-sea fishing vessel; here he became acquainted with Dr. Héctor García,* upon whose advice he returned to San Juan and to high school. At Pharr-San Juan-Alamo High School he was an excellent student and concerned himself with improving educational conditions and opportunities for Chicano students. While in high school, he also began to organize youth chapters of Dr. García's American G.I. Forum, ultimately instituting more than twenty.

After graduation from high school in 1958 Yzaguirre entered the Air Force with the hope of becoming a pilot; however, he was assigned to the Medical Corps where he spent four years, mostly at Andrews Air Force Base near Washington, D.C. While still in the service, he began to take classes at the University of Maryland; upon mustering out, he continued his college education at George Washington University while working as a chief technologist in a Washington medical laboratory. In 1967 he graduated with a B.S. in business administration and took a position in the Migrant Division of the Office of Economic Opportunity (O.E.O.), where he was program analyst and member of the advisory committee for the director of Mexican Affairs. Meanwhile in 1964 he had led a group of Washington-based Chicano activists in founding an umbrella Chicano organization called the National Organization for Mexican American Services.

In 1969 Raúl Yzaguirre, seeing a need, left the O.E.O. to found and direct the first Chicano research and consulting organization, Interstate Research Associates; four years later he became vice-president of another consulting firm, the Washington-based Center for Community Change (CCC). During that same year he made a brief return to south Texas, working for CCC, but in 1974 was persuaded to take over the heavy responsibilities of directing the National Council of La Raza (NCLR). As a result of a long-time concern about the need for coalition organizations, in 1975 he used the NCLR to organize the Forum of National Hispanic Organizations which included Puerto Rican and Cuban groups under its umbrella. Three years later he was cofounder and cochairman of the National Committee on the Concerns of Hispanics and Blacks. Since 1974 Yzaguirre has led the expansion of the NCLR from ten employees and a dozen affiliated organizations to the nation's largest Hispanic federation with a $5 million budget and more than 100 affiliates.

Clearly one of the foremost contemporary Chicano leaders, outstanding in his organizational skills, in 1979 Yzaguirre was the first Latino to receive the Rockefeller Public Service Award.

FURTHER READING: "Interview with Raúl Yzaguirre," *La Luz* 1:11 (March 1973); Douglas Martínez, "Yzaguirre at the Helm," *Américas* 32:6–7 (June–July 1980); "The Movement's Organization Man," *Nuestro* 6:2 (March 1982).

Z _____

ZAPATA, CARMEN (1927–), actress, director, community activist. Of Mexican and Argentine parentage, Carmen Zapata was born and grew up in New York City. Accustomed to speaking Spanish at home, she was thrust into an English-only society in school with traumatic results. Later, after the trauma subsided, she felt driven to speak English as correctly and fluently as possible—ultimately leading to a career on the stage. After study at Actors Studio and with Uta Hagen, she got her first job in the chorus of *Oklahoma*, from which she later graduated to a lead when *Oklahoma* went on the road. Back on Broadway she took over one of the principal roles in *Stop the World. I Want to Get Off*. Between plays she did a singing and comedy act in East Side night clubs under the name Marge Cameron. Then she was selected in 1966 as one of the principals in Duke Ellington's *Pousse-Cafe*, which closed after two weeks on Broadway.

With the disaster of *Pousse-Cafe* Carmen Zapata decided to try her luck in Hollywood. Here she found her Latino background led to stereotyping and to a very limited number of roles, but she had better luck in television, playing in various popular series. Her frustration with Hollywood limitations on her acting repertoire and her discovery of a Spanish-language audience led her to found her own theater company in 1973. By the mid–1970s the company had gone bilingual, doing a play in Spanish one night and in English the next. Zapata remains the director of the Bilingual Foundation of the Arts, which provides drama for the large Los Angeles Latino audience. Meanwhile she became widely known as Doña Luz in the Public Broadcasting System's bilingual show, ''Villa Alegre.''

Zapata is active in a number of Chicano organizations and has taught drama at East Los Angeles College. In 1981 she was one of ten area women honored by the Los Angeles YWCA with Silver Achievement Awards for outstanding accomplishments and leadership. The recipient of numerous acting and other awards and honors including three Emmy nominations and the El Angel award, she is perhaps the most visible Chicana in the theatrical profession today.

FURTHER READING: David Ragua, *Who's Who in Hollywood, 1900–1976*, New Rochelle, N.Y.: Arlington House, 1976; Stacey Peck, "Home Q&A: Carmen Zapata," *Los Angeles Times* (28 October 1979).

ZAVALA, ADINA EMILIA DE (1861–1955), civic leader, historian, folklorist. Adina de Zavala, granddaughter of Lorenzo de Zavala, was born at De Zavala's Point near Houston, Texas, at the beginning of the Civil War and grew up in a pro-Southern family in Galveston and San Antonio. After a parochial school education she graduated from Sam Houston State College (today University) at Huntsville and then taught school in Dallas County and at San Antonio.

Due to family background Adina de Zavala during her twenties became deeply interested in the preservation of historical sites and about 1890 organized a women's group, associated with the Daughters of the Republic of Texas, for this purpose. Her most important achievement was preventing the razing of part of the Alamo in the early 1900s. In 1912 she founded the Texas Historical and Landmarks Association and soon thereafter became a charter member of the Texas State Historical Association. She also belonged to the United Daughters of the Confederacy, the Folk-Lore Society, Museum Society, and numerous other civic and patriotic groups.

Because of her deep historical interests, in 1923 Adina de Zavala was appointed by the governor to the Texas Historical Board, and in the mid–1930s she served on the Texas Centennial Committee. The president of the Texas Historical and Landmarks Association, she also founded a number of libraries and historico-patriotic societies. Until her death she remained active in numerous Texas historical and civic organizations. She was the author of a number of historical works including *History and Legends of the Alamo* (1917).

FURTHER READING: L. Robert Ables, "The Second Battle for the Alamo," *Southwestern Historical Quarterly* 70 (1966–1967).

ZAVALA, LORENZO DE (1788–1836), political leader, physician. Born in Mérida, the capital of Yucatán, on 3 October 1788, Lorenzo de Zavala grew up and was educated there. Even in his early teen years he was an ardent liberal and as the result of an excellent education in preparation for the priesthood was able to become a leading political figure while still in his mid-twenties. First he was appointed secretary to the Mérida city council (1811–1814) and then was elected a delegate to the Spanish parliament. However, he was intercepted on his way to Madrid and was jailed in San Juan de Ulúa by the reactionary Ferdinand VII for nearly three years. Upon his release in 1817 he practiced medicine in Mérida to support himself and his family. In 1820 he was elected secretary of the Yucatecan assembly and then became representative to the Spanish parliament again. A member of the Mexican Constituent Congress of 1823 and later of the first Senate, he was also governor of the state of México (1827–1829) and briefly national minister of finance.

In March 1829 Zavala became one of the few Mexicans to receive an *empresario* grant to settle 500 families in the province of Texas but did not personally pursue the matter. There followed three years of political self-exile in the United States and Europe. He then returned to Mexico, became a principal federalist leader, was elected to the Mexican national congress, and was reelected governor of the state of México. In the fall of 1833 he was appointed minister to France. Concerned about President Santa Anna's moves toward centralism, Zavala resigned from this position and returned to Texas in 1835 to take a leading role in the Texas movement for federal separatism. In the fall he was elected to the Consultation (a Texas assembly) and then to the independence convention. He signed the declaration of Texas independence and then helped write the Texas constitution. When an interim Texas government was organized in March 1836 he was unanimously elected vice-president of the new republic, an office from which he resigned in October because of ill health. He died a month later. He was the author of several books on early Mexican political history including *Ensayo histórico de las revoluciones de México, desde 1808 hasta 1830* (1831).

FURTHER READING: *Diccionario Porrúa de Historia, Biografía y Geografía de México*, 2d ed., México, D.F.: Editorial Porrúa, 1965; R. M. Potter, "The Texas Revolution: Distinguished Mexicans Who Took Part . . . ," *Magazine of American History* 2:10 (October 1878).

APPENDIX A _____

List of Biographees by Field of Professional Activity

This appendix lists the biographees by professional activity under the following categories:

Administration, Education
Administration, Government
Business
Civic Leadership
Diplomatic Service
Education, Scholarship
Education, Teaching
Engineering
Finance
Fine Arts
Journalism
Labor
Law
Literature, Poetry
Literature, Prose
Medicine
Military
Performing Arts
Politics and Government
Publishing
Religion
Science
Social Activism

Social Sciences
Sports

Administration, Education

Angel, Frank, Jr.
Aragón, John A.
Arciniega, Tomás A.
Atencio, Alonso Cristóbal
Burciaga, Cecilia Preciado de
Cavazos, Lauro F., Jr.
Gonzales, Eugene
Madrid-Barela, Arturo
Otero-Warren, María Adelina
Rivera, Tomás
Rodríguez, Armando M.

Administration, Government

Alvarado, Juan Bautista
Alvarez, Everett, Jr.
Anaya, Toney
Apodaca, Jerry
Armijo, Manuel
Bañuelos, Romana Acosta

Cabeza de Baca, Fernando E.

Canales, Antonio

Castillo, Leonel J.

Castro, Raúl H.

Chaves, José Francisco

Chávez, Linda

Coronel, Antonio Franco

García, Ernest E.

Hernández, Benigno Cárdenas

Hidalgo (Kunhardt), Edward

Kaslow, Audrey A. Rojas

Olivárez, Graciela

Ortega, Katherine D.

Ramírez, Blandina Cárdenas

Ramírez, Henry

Reynoso, Cruz

Telles, Raymond L., Jr.

Torres, Esteban E.

Villalpando, Catalina V.

Ximenes, Vicente Treviño

Zavala, Lorenzo de

Business

Alvarez, Manuel

Apodaca, Jerry

Armijo, Manuel

Armijo, Salvador

Bañuelos, Romana Acosta

Barceló, María Gertrudis

Barela, Casimiro

Beaubien, Carlos

Benavides, Plácido

Benavides, Santos

Bravo, Francisco

Cabeza de Baca, Fernando E.

Candelaria, Nash

Chaves, Manuel Antonio

Chávez, Felipe

Coronel, Antonio Franco

Fernández, Benjamín

Gavin, John

Hernández, Benigno Cárdenas

Luna, Solomón

Manzanares, Francisco A.

Martínez, Félix T., Jr.

Navarro, José Antonio

Nogales, Luis

Ochoa, Esteban

Ortega, Katherine D.

Otero, Antonio José

Otero, Mariano S.

Otero, Miguel A., Sr.

Otero, Miguel A., Jr.

Perea, Francisco

Perea, Pedro

Ramírez, Teodoro

Redondo, José María

Requeña, Manuel

Romero, Eugenio

St. Vrain, Ceran

Samaniego, Mariano G.

Sánchez, Antonio R., Sr.

Sánchez, Phillip Victor

Schechter, Hope Mendoza

Tijerina, Félix

Vallejo, Mariano Guadalupe

Villalpando, Catalina V.

Villanueva, Daniel

Villarreal, Carlos Castañeda

Civic Leadership

Alurista

Benavides, Plácido

Bravo, Francisco

Buono, Antonio del

Cabeza de Baca, Fernando E.

Carbajal, José M. J.

Chávez, Dennis

Cisneros, Henry G.

Coronel, Antonio Franco

Gallegos, José Manuel

García, Héctor Pérez

Gonzales, Rodolfo ("Corky")

Hernández, María L.

Larrazolo, Octaviano A.

López, Ignacio

López, Lino M.

Martínez, Antonio José

Martínez, Vilma Socorro

Molina, Gloria

Nava, Julián

Navarro, José Antonio

Obledo, Mario Guerra

Ochoa, Esteban

Ortiz, Ramón

Perales, Alonso S.

Sánchez, Ricardo

Seguín, Juan Nepomuceno

Tijerina, Reies López

Velasco, Carlos I.

Yzaguirre, Raúl

Zavala, Adina Emilia de

Diplomatic Service

Castro, Raúl H.

Gavin, John

González, Raymond E.

Hernández, Benigno Carlos

Jaramillo, Marí-Luci

Jova, Joseph John

Lozano, Ignacio E., Jr.

Nava, Julián

Ortiz, Francis V., Jr.

Pacheco, Romualdo

Perales, Alonso S.

Sánchez, Phillip Victor

Telles, Raymond L., Jr.

Torres, Esteban E.

Valdez, Abelardo López

Education, Scholarship

Acuña, Rodolfo

Campa, Arthur León

Castañeda, Carlos E.

Chávez, (Fray) Angélico

Cortés, Carlos

Espinosa, Aurelio M.

Galarza, Ernesto

Gómez-Quiñones, Juan

Guzmán, Ralph C.

Paredes, Américo

Samora, Julián

Sánchez, George Isadore

Education, Teaching

Acosta, Robert J.

Acuña, Rodolfo

Alurista

Amador, Luis Valentine

Angel, Frank, Jr.

Aragón, John A.

Arciniega, Tomás A.

Arias, Ronald F.

Atencio, Alonso Cristóbal

Baca Zinn, Maxine

Barrio, Raymond

Camarillo, Albert M.

Campa, Arthur León
Carrillo, Eduardo
Castañeda, Carlos E.
Castro, Salvador B.
Cavazos, Lauro F., Jr.
Chávez, Joseph A.
Corona, Bert N.
Cortés, Carlos E.
Elizondo, Sergio D.
Espinosa, Aurelio M.
Galarza, Ernesto
García, Mario T.
Gilbert, Fabiola Cabeza de Baca
Gómez-Quiñones, Juan
Gutiérrez, José Angel
Guzmán, Ralph C.
Hinojosa-Smith, Rolando
Jaramillo, Marí-Luci
Jiménez, Francisco
López, Lino M.
Madrid-Barela, Arturo
Martínez, Oscar J.
Medellín, Octavio
Montoya, José
Nava, Julián
Ortego y Gasca, Philip D.
Palomino, Ernesto Ramírez
Paredes, Américo
Ponce de León, Michael
Quirarte, Jacinto
Romano-V., Octavio I.
Rosaldo, Renato Ignacio
Ruiz, Ramón Eduardo
Samora, Julián
Sánchez, George Isadore
Servín, Manuel P.
Soto, Gary
Ulibarrí, Sabine R.

Unzueta, Manuel
Vigil, Ralph H.
Villarreal, José Antonio

Engineering

Chacón, José Andrés
Villarreal, Carlos Castañeda

Finance

Bañuelos, Romana Acosta
Bravo, Francisco
Sánchez, Antonio R., Sr.

Fine Arts

Acosta, Manuel Gregorio
Arreguín, Alfredo Mendoza
Arriola, Gus(tavo) Montaño
Barela, Patrocinio
Barrio, Raymond
Burciaga, José Antonio
Carrillo, Eduardo
Casas, Melesio
Cervántez, Pedro
Chávez, Edward A.
Chávez, Joseph A.
Cisneros, José
García, Antonio
García, Rupert
Gómez, Glynn
González Amezcua, Consuelo
Jiménez, Luis A.
López, Michael J.
Martínez, Xavier T.
Medellín, Octavio
Michel-Trapaga, René David

Montoya, José
Montoya, Malaquías
Neri, Manuel
Ortiz, Ralph
Palomino, Ernesto Ramírez
Peña, Amado M., Jr.
Ponce de León, Michael
Ramírez, Joel Tito
Rodríguez, Peter
Salinas, Porfirio
Sandoval, Secundino
Unzueta, Manuel

Journalism

Arías, Ronald F.
Barrio, Raymond
Cabeza de Baca, Ezequiel
Garza, Catarino
Lozano, Ignacio E., Sr.
Montoya, Nestor
Morton, Carlos
Ramírez, Francisco P.
Ramírez, Sara Estela
Rodríguez, Richard
Salazar, Rubén
Sandoval, Moisés
Vásquez, Richard

Labor

Buono, Antonio del
Chávez, César Estrada
Corona, Bert N.
Corona, Juan V.
Galarza, Ernesto
González Parsons, Lucía
Huerta, Dolores Fernández

Moreno, Luisa
Orendaín, Antonio
Schechter, Hope Mendoza
Tenayuca (Brooks), Emma

Law

Acosta, Oscar Zeta
Avila, Joaquín G.
Castro, Raúl H.
Hernández, Benigno Carlos
Hidalgo (Kunhardt), Edward
Martínez, Vilma Socorro
Medina, Harold R.
Obledo, Mario Guerra
Olivárez, Graciela
Reynoso, Cruz
Valdez, Abelardo López

Literature, Poetry

Alurista
Burciaga, José Antonio
Cervantes, Lorna Dee
Delgado, Abelardo Barrientos
Elizondo, Sergio D.
Gómez-Quiñones, Juan
Gonzales, Rodolfo (''Corky'')
González Amezcua, Consuelo
Hinojosa-Smith, Rolando
Hoyos, Angela de
León, Naphtalí de
Montoya, José
Ramírez, Sara Estela
Salinas, Luis Omar
Sánchez, Ricardo
Soto, Gary

Ulibarrí, Sabine R.

Villanueva, Tino

Literature, Prose

Acosta, Oscar Zeta

Anaya, Rudolfo A.

Arias, Ronald F.

Barrio, Raymond

Burciaga, José Antonio

Candelaria, Nash

Delgado, Abelardo Barrientos

Hinojosa-Smith, Rolando

Jiménez, Francisco

Méndez, Miguel M.

Morton, Carlos

Portillo Trambley, Estela

Rechy, John Francisco

Rivera, Tomás

Ulibarrí, Sabine R.

Valdez, Luis M.

Vásquez, Richard

Villanueva, Tino

Villarreal, José Antonio

Medicine

Alvarez, Francisco Sánchez

Amador, Luis Valentine

Atencio, Alonso Cristóbal

Bravo, Francisco

Cavazos, Lauro F., Jr.

García, Héctor Pérez

Jaramillo, Pedro

Urrea, Teresa

Zavala, Lorenzo de

Military

Alvarez, Everett, Jr.

Archuleta, Diego

Benavides, Santos

Canales, Antonio

Carbajal, José M. J.

Cárdenas, Roberto L.

Chaves, Manuel Antonio

Longoria, Félix

Márquez, Leo

Valdez, Phil

Performing Arts

Alonzo, Juan A.

Báez, Joan

Carr, Vikki

Carrillo, Leo(poldo) A.

Carter, Lynda Córdoba

Escovedo, Peter

Gavin, John

González, Pedro J.

Guerrero, Eduardo (''Lalo'')

Limón, José Arcadio

López, Trini(dad)

Méndez, Rafael

Mendoza, Lydia

Mester, Jorge

Montalbán, Ricardo

Novarro, Ramón

Olmos, Edward James

Quinn, Anthony

Roland, Gilbert

Ronstadt, Linda

Valdez, Luis M.

Zapata, Carmen

Politics and Government

Alvarado, Juan Bautista

Alvarez, Manuel

Anaya, Toney

Apodaca, Jerry

Archuleta, Diego

Armijo, Salvador

Baca, Elfego

Baca-Barragán, Polly

Barela, Casimiro

Benavides, Santos

Cabeza de Baca, Ezequiel

Castro, Raúl H.

Chaves, José Francisco

Chávez, Dennis

Cisneros, Henry G.

Fernández, Benjamín

Gallegos, José Manuel

Garza, Eligio de la ("Kika")

González, Henry Barbosa

Gutiérrez, José Angel

Larrazolo, Octaviano A.

López, Ignacio

Luján, Manuel, Jr.

Luna, Solomón

Martínez, Félix T., Jr.

Molina, Gloria

Mondragón, Roberto A.

Montoya, Joseph M.

Montoya, Nestor

Ortiz, Solomón P.

Otero, Miguel A., Sr.

Otero, Miguel A., Jr.

Pacheco, Romualdo

Patrón, Juan B.

Peña, Federico

Pico, Andrés

Pico, Pío de Jesús

Redondo, José María

Requeña, Manuel

Roybal, Edward R.

Samaniego, Mariano G.

Vigil, Donaciano

Publishing

Barrio, Raymond

Cabeza de Baca, Ezequiel

Chacón, Felipe Maximiliano

Garza, Catarino

Lozano, Ignacio E., Sr.

Lozano, Ignacio E., Jr.

Martínez, Félix T., Jr.

Ortego y Gasca, Philip D.

Romano-V., Octavio I.

Valdés, Daniel T.

Velasco, Carlos I.

Religion

Alemany, José Sadoc

Chávez, (Fray) Angélico

Elizondo, Virgil P.

Flores, Patricio Fernández

Garriga, Mariano S.

Martínez, Antonio José

Ramírez, Ricardo, C.S.B.

Rodríguez, Plácido, C.M.F.

Sánchez, Robert Fortune

Science

Alvarez, Francisco Sánchez

Social Activism

Acosta, Oscar Zeta
Acuña, Rodolfo
Alurista
Avila, Joaquín G.
Báez, Joan
Buono, Antonio del
Castro, Salvador B.
Corona, Bert N.
Cortez Lira, Gregorio
Cortina, Juan Nepomuceno
Elizondo, Sergio D.
Elizondo, Virgil P.
Flores, Patricio Fernández
García, Héctor Pérez
Garza, Catarino
Gómez-Quiñones, Juan
Gonzales, Rodolfo ("Corky")
González, Pedro J.
González Parsons, Lucía
Gutiérrez, José Angel
León, Naphtalí de
Montoya, Malaquías

Moreno, Luisa
Ramírez, Sara Estela
Tijerina, Reies López
Valdez, Luis M.
Vásquez, Tiburcio

Social Sciences

Jaramillo, Cleofas Martínez
Mireles, Jovita González
Morín, Raúl R.
Ord, Angustias de la Guerra
Paredes, Américo

Sports

Chacón, Robert
Flores, Tom
Gonzales, Richard Alonzo ("Pancho")
Herrera, Efrén
López, Nancy
Palomino, Carlos
Plunkett, James
Treviño, Lee ("Buck")
Villanueva, Daniel

APPENDIX B

List of Biographees by State

Arizona

Castro, Raúl H.
Méndez, Miguel M.
Ochoa, Esteban
Quirarte, Jacinto
Ramírez, Teodoro
Redondo, José María
Ronstadt, Linda
Rosaldo, Renato Ignacio
Samaniego, Mariano G.
Urrea, Teresa
Velasco, Carlos I.

California

Acosta, Oscar Zeta
Acosta, Robert J.
Acuña, Rodolfo
Alemany, José Sadoc
Alonzo, Juan A.
Alurista
Alvarado, Juan Bautista
Alvarez, Everett, Jr.
Alvarez, Francisco Sánchez
Arciniega, Tomás A.

Arias, Ronald F.
Arriola, Gus(tavo) Montaño
Avila, Joaquín G.
Báez, Joan
Bañuelos, Romana Acosta
Barrio, Raymond
Bravo, Francisco
Buono, Antonio del
Burciaga, Cecilia Preciado de
Burciaga, José Antonio
Camarillo, Albert M.
Candelaria, Nash
Cárdenas, Roberto L.
Carr, Vikki
Carrillo, Eduardo
Carrillo, Leo(poldo) A.
Carter, Lynda Córdoba
Castro, Salvador B.
Cervantes, Lorna Dee
Chacón, Robert
Chávez, César Estrada
Corona, Bert N.
Corona, Juan V.
Coronel, Antonio Franco
Cortés, Carlos E.
Escovedo, Peter

Fernández, Benjamín

Flores, Tom

Galarza, Ernesto

García, Mario T.

García, Rupert

Gavin, John

Gómez-Quiñones, Juan

Gonzales, Eugene

Gonzales, Richard Alonzo ("Pancho")

González, Pedro J.

González, Raymond E.

Guerrero, Eduardo ("Lalo")

Guzmán, Ralph C.

Herrera, Efrén

Huerta, Dolores Fernández

Jiménez, Francisco

Kaslow, Audrey A. Rojas

Limón, José Arcadio

López, Ignacio

López, Michael J.

Lozano, Ignacio E., Sr.

Lozano, Ignacio E., Jr.

Martínez, Vilma Socorro

Martínez, Xavier T.

Méndez, Rafael

Mester, Jorge

Molina, Gloria

Montalbán, Ricardo

Montoya, José

Montoya, Malaquías

Moreno, Luisa

Morín, Raúl R.

Murrieta, Joaquín

Nava, Julián

Neri, Manuel

Nogales, Luis

Novarro, Ramón

Obledo, Mario Guerra

Olmos, Edward James

Ord, Angustias de la Guerra

Pacheco, Romualdo

Palomino, Carlos

Palomino, Ernesto Ramírez

Pico, Andrés

Pico, Pío de Jesús

Plunkett, James

Quinn, Anthony

Ramírez, Francisco P.

Rechy, John Francisco

Requeña, Manuel

Reynoso, Cruz

Rivera, Tomás

Rodríguez, Armando M.

Rodríguez, Peter

Rodríguez, Richard

Roland, Gilbert

Romano-V., Octavio I.

Roybal, Edward R.

Ruiz, Ramón Eduardo

Salazar, Rubén

Salinas, Luis Omar

Sánchez, Phillip Victor

Schechter, Hope Mendoza

Servín, Manuel P.

Soto, Gary

Torres, Esteban E.

Unzueta, Manuel

Valdez, Luis M.

Vallejo, Mariano Guadalupe

Vásquez, Richard

Vásquez, Tiburcio

Villanueva, Daniel

Villarreal, José Antonio

Zapata, Carmen

Colorado

Atencio, Alonso Cristóbal
Baca-Barragán, Polly
Barela, Casimiro
Espinosa, Aurelio M.
Gonzales, Rodolfo ("Corky")
López, Lino M.
Peña, Federico
Valdés, Daniel T.

New Mexico

Alvarez, Manuel
Amador, Luis Valentine
Anaya, Rudolfo A.
Anaya, Toney
Angel, Frank, Jr.
Apodaca, Jerry
Aragón, John A.
Archuleta, Diego
Armijo, Manuel
Armijo, Salvador
Baca, Elfego
Barceló, María Gertrudis
Barela, Patrocinio
Beaubien, Carlos
Cabeza de Baca, Ezequiel
Cabeza de Baca, Fernando E.
Campa, Arthur León
Cervántez, Pedro
Chacón, Felipe Maximiliano
Chacón, José Andrés
Chaves, José Francisco
Chaves, Manuel Antonio
Chávez, (Fray) Angélico
Chávez, Dennis
Chávez, Edward A.

Chávez, Felipe
Chávez, Joseph A.
Elizondo, Sergio D.
Gallegos, José Manuel
Gilbert, Fabiola Cabeza de Baca
Gómez, Glynn
Hernández, Benigno Cárdenas
Hernández, Benigno Carlos
Jaramillo, Cleofas Martínez
Jaramillo, Marí-Luci
Larrazolo, Octaviano A.
López, Nancy
Luján, Manuel, Jr.
Luna, Solomón
Manzanares, Francisco A.
Márquez, Leo
Martínez, Antonio José
Martínez, Félix T., Jr.
Mondragón, Roberto A.
Montoya, Joseph M.
Montoya, Nestor
Olivárez, Graciela
Ortega, Katherine D.
Ortiz, Ramón
Otero, Antonio José
Otero, Mariano, S.
Otero, Miguel A., Sr.
Otero, Miguel A., Jr.
Otero-Warren, María Adelina
Patrón, Juan B.
Perea, Francisco
Perea, Pedro
Ramírez, Joel Tito
Ramírez, Ricardo, C.S.B.
Romero, Eugenio
St. Vrain, Ceran
Salazar, Eulogio
Sánchez, George Isadore

Sánchez, Robert Fortune
Sandoval, Secundino
Tijerina, Reies López
Ulibarrí, Sabine R.
Valdez, Phil
Vigil, Donaciano
Ximenes, Vicente Treviño

New York

Hidalgo (Kunhardt), Edward
Jova, Joseph John
Medina, Harold R.
Ortiz, Ralph
Ponce de León, Michael
Sandoval, Moisés

Texas

Acosta, Manuel Gregorio
Benavides, Plácido
Benavides, Santos
Canales, Antonio
Carbajal, José M. J.
Casas, Melesio
Castañeda, Carlos E.
Castillo, Leonel J.
Cavazos, Lauro F., Jr.
Cisneros, Henry G.
Cisneros, José
Cortez Lira, Gregorio
Cortina, Juan Nepomuceno
Delgado, Abelardo Barrientos
Elizondo, Virgil P.
Flores, Patricio Fernández
García, Antonio
García, Héctor Pérez
Garriga, Mariano S.

Garza, Catarino
Garza, Eligio de la ("Kika")
González, Henry Barbosa
González Amezcua, Consuelo
Gutiérrez, José Angel
Hernández, María L.
Hinojosa-Smith, Rolando
Hoyos, Angela de
Jaramillo, Pedro
Jiménez, Luis A.
León, Naphtalí de
Longoria, Félix
López, Trini(dad)
Martínez, Oscar J.
Medellín, Octavio
Mendoza, Lydia
Mireles, Jovita González
Morton, Carlos
Navarro, José Antonio
Orendáin, Antonio
Ortiz, Solomón P.
Paredes, Américo
Peña, Amado J., Jr.
Perales, Alonso S.
Portillo Trambley, Estela
Ramírez, Blandina Cárdenas
Ramírez, Sara Estela
Rodríguez, Chipita
Salinas, Porfirio
Sánchez, Antonio R., Sr.
Sánchez, Ricardo
Seguín, Juan Nepomuceno
Telles, Raymond L., Jr.
Tenayuca (Brooks), Emma
Tijerina, Félix
Treviño, Lee ("Buck")
Valdez, Abelardo López
Villalpando, Catalina V.

Villanueva, Tino
Villarreal, Carlos Castañeda
Yzaguirre, Raúl
Zavala, Adina Emilia de
Zavala, Lorenzo de

Miscellaneous

Illinois

González Parsons, Lucía
Rodríguez, Plácido, C.M.F.

Indiana

Samora, Julián

Kansas

García, Ernest E.

Michigan

Baca Zinn, Maxine

Minnesota

Madrid-Barela, Arturo

Missouri

Michel-Trapaga, René David

Nebraska

Vigil, Ralph H.

Washington

Arreguín, Alfredo Mendoza

Washington, D.C.

Chávez, Linda
Ortego y Gasca, Philip D.
Ortiz, Francis V., Jr.
Ramírez, Henry

Index ─────────────────────────────────

Note: **bold** page numbers indicate main subject entries.

About the Author

MATT S. MEIER is the Patrick A. Donohoe Professor in the Department of History at Santa Clara University. His many books include *The Chicanos: A History of Mexican Americans*, *Bibliography for Chicano History*, *Dictionary of Mexican American History* (Greenwood Press, 1981), and *Bibliography of Mexican American History* (Greenwood Press, 1984). He has contributed articles to such publications as the *Journal of Mexican American History* and *Historia Mexicana*.